HONDA WORKSHOP MANUAL SINGLE CYLINDER

1971-1984 CB125
CB125S - CB125J - CD125S

1970-1976 CB100 - CL100
SL100 - SL125 - TL125

**A Floyd Clymer Publication
This edition published in 2022 by
www.VelocePress.com**

All rights reserved. This work may not be reproduced or transmitted in any form without the express written consent of the publisher.

INTRODUCTION

Welcome to the world of digital publishing ~ the book you now hold in your hand was printed using the latest state of the art digital technology. The advent of print-on-demand has forever changed the publishing process, never has information been so accessible and it is our hope that this book serves your informational needs for years to come. If this is your first exposure to digital publishing, we hope that you are pleased with the results. Many more titles of interest to the classic automobile and motorcycle enthusiast, collector and restorer are available via our website at www.VelocePress.com. We hope that you find this title as interesting as we do.

NOTE FROM THE PUBLISHER

The information presented is true and complete to the best of our knowledge. All recommendations are made without any guarantees on the part of the author or the publisher, who also disclaim all liability incurred with the use of this information.

TRADEMARKS

We recognize that some words, model names and designations, for example, mentioned herein are the property of the trademark holder. We use them for identification purposes only. This is not an official publication.

INFORMATION ON THE USE OF THIS PUBLICATION

This manual is an invaluable resource for those interested in performing their own maintenance. However, in today's information age we are constantly subject to changes in common practice, new technology, availability of improved materials and increased awareness of chemical toxicity. As such, it is advised that the user consult with an experienced professional prior to undertaking any procedure described herein. While every care has been taken to ensure correctness of information, it is obviously not possible to guarantee complete freedom from errors or omissions or to accept liability arising from such errors or omissions. Therefore, any individual that uses the information contained within, or elects to perform or participate in do-it-yourself repairs or modifications acknowledges that there is a risk factor involved and that the publisher or its associates cannot be held responsible for personal injury or property damage resulting from the use of the information or the outcome of such procedures.

WARNING!

One final word of advice, this publication is intended to be used as a reference guide, and when in doubt the reader should consult with a qualified technician.

CONTENTS

I. PROCEDURE OF PERFORMING THE WORK 1
    SPECIAL TOOLS 2

II. MAINTENANCE OPERATIONS 5
    1. Tappet adjustment 5
    2. Carburetor adjustment 5
    3. Breaker point and ignition timing adjustment 6
    4. Clutch adjustment 7
    5. Spark plug inspection 7
    6. Engine oil change 8
    7. Oil filter cleaning 8
    8. Cam chain adjustment 9
    9. Fuel system inspection 9
    10. Air cleaner element servicing 9
    11. Brake adjustment 10
    12. Drive chain adjustment 11
    13. Battery electrolyte inspection 11
    14. Front fork oil replacement 11
    15. Cylinder compression check 12

III. ENGINE 13
    1. Work which can be performed without removing the engine 14
    2. Engine removal and installation 14
    3. Cylinder, cylinder head and piston ... 15
    4. Valve removal 20
    5. Oil pump and oil filter 22
    6. Clutch 25
    7. Gearshift mechanism 27
    8. Cam chain tensioner and A.C. generator 29
    9. Crankshaft 30
    10. Transmission and primary kickstarter 32
    11. Carburetor 35

IV. CHASSIS 37
    1. Front brake and front wheel 37
    2. Rear brake and rear wheel 40
    3. Steering unit 43
    4. Front suspension 45
    5. Rear suspension 48
    6. Frame body 50

V. ELECTRICAL 53
    1. Generating system 53
    2. Charging system 54
    3. Ignition system 55
    4. Battery 56
    5. Auxiliary electrical equipment 58

VI. DISK BRAKE 61
    1. DISK 61
    2. Exploded view of disk type front wheel 61
    3. Exploded view of caliper 62
    4. Front disk brake and front wheel 63

TROUBLESHOOTING 71
PERIODIC MAINTENANCE 76
TECHNICAL DATA 77
WIRING DIAGRAMS 79

SUPPLEMENTS & ADDENDUMS
    '73 TL125 SUPPLEMENT 85
    '75 CB125S2 SUPPLEMENT 107
    '75 TL125K2 SUPPLEMENT 112
    '76 TL125 SUPPLEMENT 115
    '76 CB100K3/CB125J/CB125S SUPPLEMENT 119
    '78 CB125S ADDENDUM 136
    '79 CB125S ADDENDUM 139
    '80 CB125S ADDENDUM 177
    (USA and Canada only)
    '81 CB125S ADDENDUM 189
    '82 CB125S ADDENDUM 217
    '84 CB125S ADDENDUM 225

I. PROCEDURE OF PERFORMING THE WORK

1. When performing an overhaul, all the parts which have been disassembled should be separated in their respective groups so that they will not become mixed.
2. All packings, gaskets and cotter pins which have been removed should be replaced with new items when reassembling. Any snap rings which are deformed shoud also be replaced.
3. All engine parts should be cleaned after disassembly. Metal surfaces which are subject to friction must be coated with oil.
4. The work should be performed with special tools for better results.
5. All nuts and bolts are normally torqued starting from those of large diameter and from inside to outside symmetrically.
6. Refer to torque values shown in the following table.

UNIT: kg-m (ft-lb)

Engine		Frame	
Item	Torque values	Item	Torque values
Cylinder head	1.8~ 2.0 (11.5~14.5)	Front axle nut	4.0~ 5.0 (29.0~36.0)
Spark advance	0.8~ 1.2 (5.8~ 8.7)	Rear axle nut	4.0~ 5.0 (29.0~36.0)
Cam sprocket	0.8~ 1.2 (5.8~ 8.7)	Rear fork pivot bolt	3.0~ 4.0 (21.7~29.0)
Cylinder mount bolt, 6mm	1.2~ 1.8 (8.7~13.0)	Engine mounting bolt	2.0~ 2.5 (14.5~18.8)
Left crank case cover	0.8~ 1.2 (5.8~ 8.7)	Handle mounting bolt	0.9~ 1.1 (6.50~7.95)
A.C rotor	2.6~ 3.2 (18.8~23.2)	Steering stem nut	6.0~ 8.0 (43.3~57.8)
A.C generator mounting screw	0.8~ 1.2 (5.8~ 8.7)	Front cushion mounting bolt	4.0~ 5.0 (29.0~36.0)
Cam chain tensioner arm	0.8~ 1.2 (5.8~ 8.7)	Rear cushion mounting nut	3.0~ 4.0 (21.7~29.0)
Right crank case cover screw	0.8~ 1.2 (5.8~ 8.7)	Torque link mounting bolt	2.0~ 2.5 (14.5~18.0)
Oil filter cover screw	0.8~ 0.4 (2.2~ 2.9)	Top bridge lock nut	4.0~ 4.8 (29.0~34.7)
Oil filter (lock nut, 16mm)	4.0~ 5.0 (29.0~36.0)	Final driven sprocket	2.0~ 2.5 (14.5~18.0)
Oil pump gear cover bolt	0.4~ 0.6 (2.9~ 4.4)	Seat mounting bolt	2.0~ 2.5 (14.5~18.0)
Clutch mounting bolt	0.8~ 1.2 (5.6~ 8.7)	Caliper joint (6×25)	0.8~ 1.2 (5.8~ 8.7)
Gear shift drum stopper bolt	0.8~ 1.2 (5.6~ 8.7)	Caliper pin (nut, 8mm)	1.5~ 2.5 (10.9~18.0)
Gear shift drum cam bolt	0.8~ 1.2 (5.6~ 8.7)	Fender stay (right side) 6×12	0.8~ 1.2 (5.8~ 8.7)

Standard parts

Bolt hex. 6mm	0.8~1.2 kg/m (5.8~8.7)
Screw cross, 6mm	0.8~1.2 kg/m (5.8~8.7)
Nut, 6mm	0.8~1.2 kg/m (5.8~8.7)
Screw cross, 5mm	0.3~0.4 kg/m (2.2~2.9)

SPECIAL TOOLS

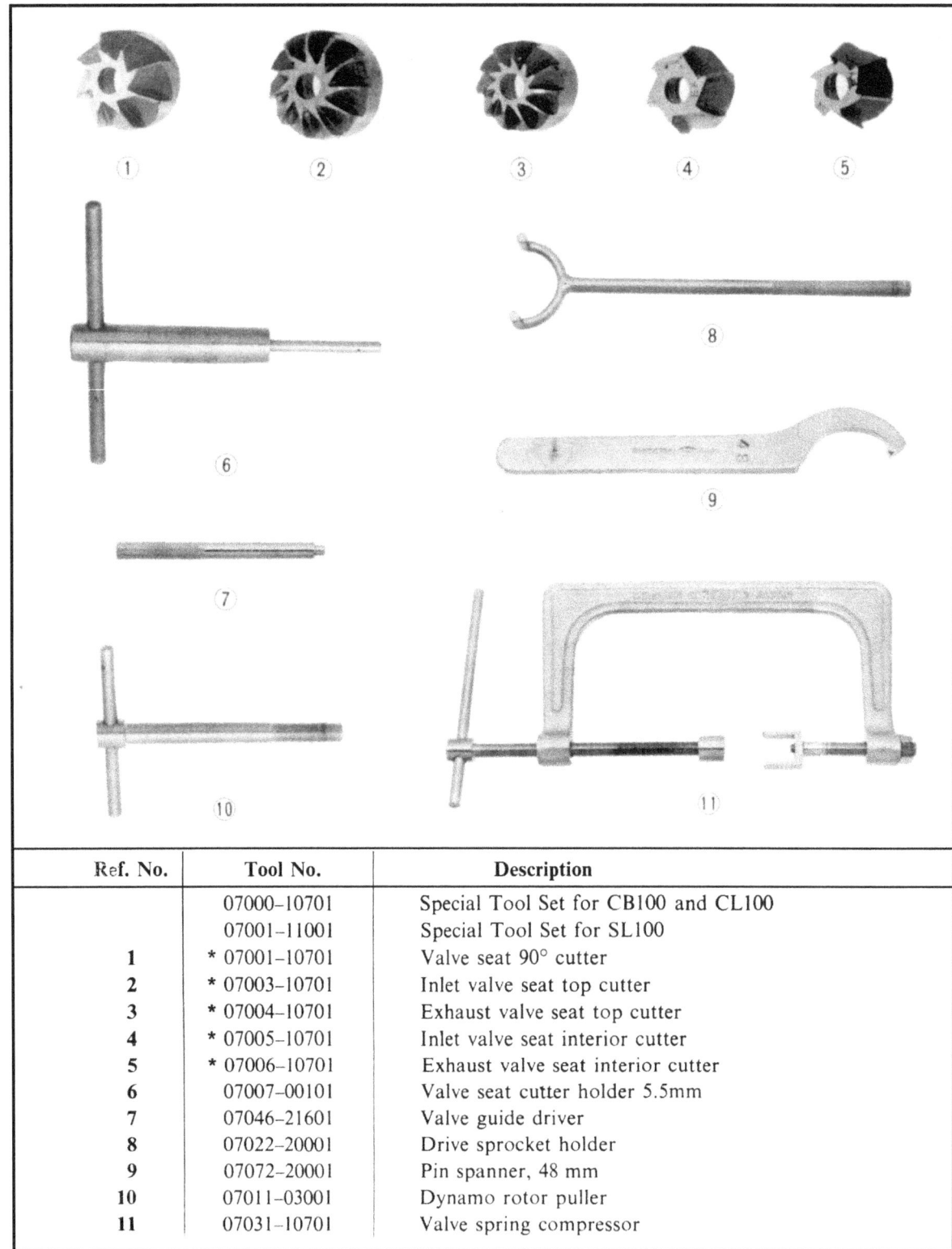

Ref. No.	Tool No.	Description
	07000–10701	Special Tool Set for CB100 and CL100
	07001–11001	Special Tool Set for SL100
1	* 07001–10701	Valve seat 90° cutter
2	* 07003–10701	Inlet valve seat top cutter
3	* 07004–10701	Exhaust valve seat top cutter
4	* 07005–10701	Inlet valve seat interior cutter
5	* 07006–10701	Exhaust valve seat interior cutter
6	07007–00101	Valve seat cutter holder 5.5mm
7	07046–21601	Valve guide driver
8	07022–20001	Drive sprocket holder
9	07072–20001	Pin spanner, 48 mm
10	07011–03001	Dynamo rotor puller
11	07031–10701	Valve spring compressor

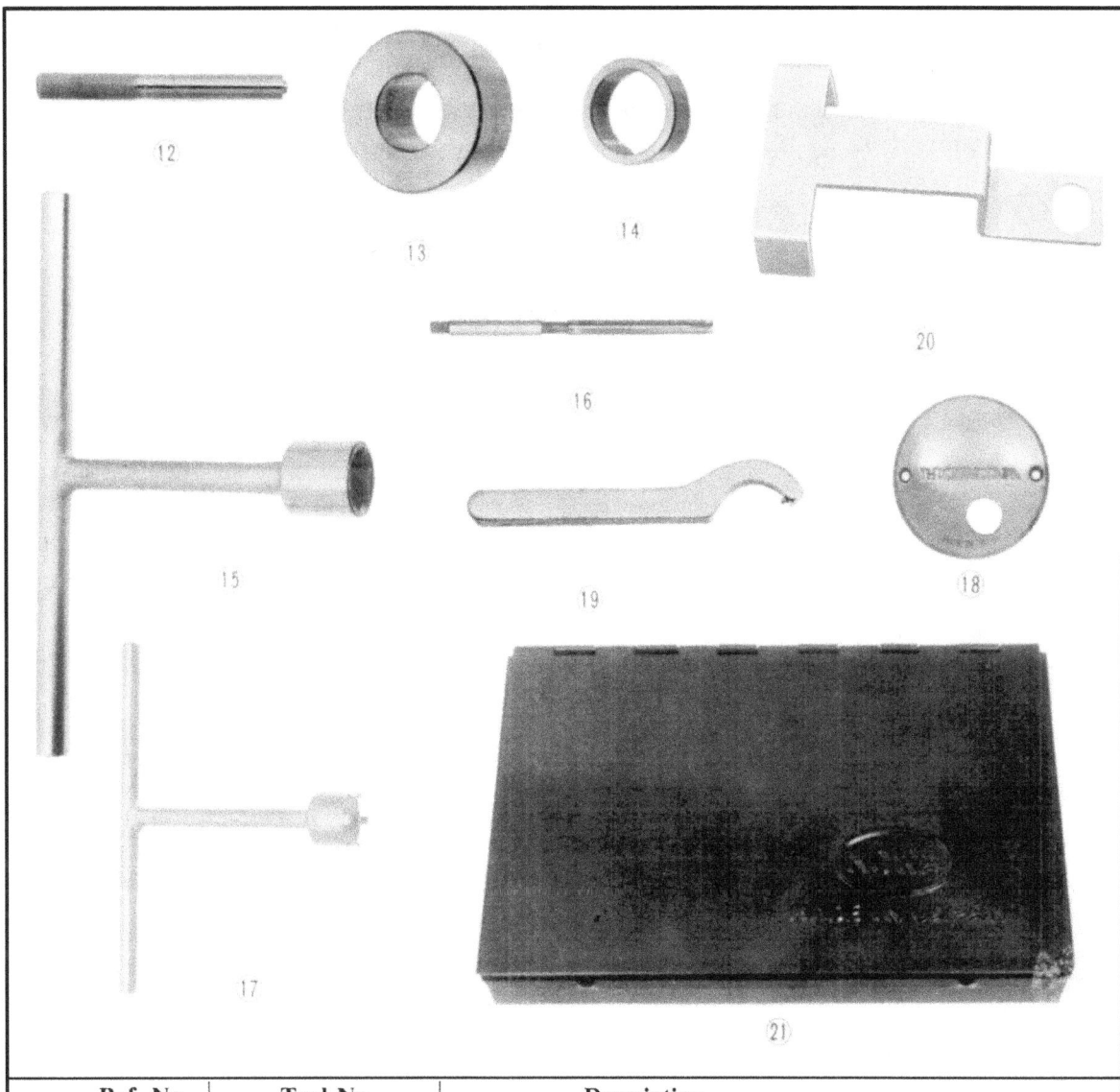

Ref. No.	Tool No.	Description
12	07047–04001	Valve guide remover
13	07054–02802	Front fork oil seal driving weight
14	* 07054–02803	Front fork oil seal driving guide (CB100, CL100)
15	07083–21601	Stem nut box wrench, 29 mm
16	07008–24001	Valve guide reamer
17	07086–28301	T-handle box wrench, 16 mm
18	* 07061–10701	Timing inspection cover
19	07071–25001	Main switch spanner
20	* 07024–10701	Clutch outer holder
21	07997–05101	Valve seat cutter case
	07790–29201	Tool case

SPECIAL TOOLS FOR CB125S, CD125S AND SL125

Tool No.	Description
07000-32401	Special Tool Set for CB125S, CD125S and SL125
07001-32401	Valve seat 90° cutter
07003-32401	Inlet valve seat top cutter
07004-32401	Exhaust valve seat top cutter
07005-32401	Inlet valve seat interior cutter
07006-32401	Exhaust valve seat interior cutter

II. MAINTENANCE OPERATIONS

1. TAPPET ADJUSTMENT

The inspection and adjustment must be performed while the engine is cold.

1) Unscrew the two 8mm seat mounting bolts and remove the seat.
2) Remove the fuel tank.
3) Unscrew and remove the tappet hole caps.
4) Remove the dynamo cover.
5) Turn the crankshaft so that the "T" (timing) mark aligns with index mark on the stator and the piston is in the compression stroke. The piston in the compression stroke can be determined by feeling rocker arms for clearance. (Fig. 1)
6) Check tappet clearances with a thickness gauge and if it is necessary to adjust, loosen the lock nut and adjust the tappet adjust screw. (Fig. 2)

Tappet clearances: Intake   0.05mm (0.002 in.)
                    Exhaust 0.05mm (0.002 in.)

When tightening the lock nut, exercise care so that the tappet clearance will not be disturbed. Recheck the tappet clearance.

Fig. 1 1 "T" aligning mark

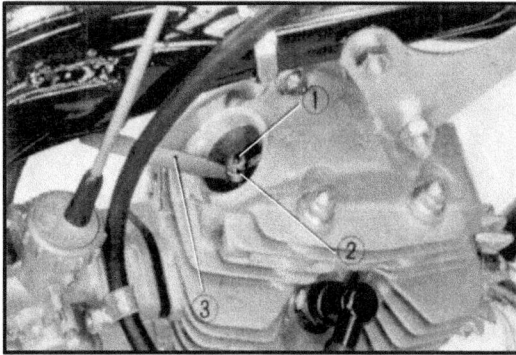

Fig. 2 Tappet adjustment
1 Lock nut 2 Tappet adjust screw 3 Thickness gauge

2. CARBURETOR ADJUSTMENT

Warm up the engine before setting the engine idle speed and make the idle adjustment with the pilot air screw and throttle stop screw. (Fig. 3)

1) Adjust the throttle stop screw to give idle speed of 1,200 rpm. Use a tachometer when it is available.
2) Turn the pilot air screw in and out to locate the position where engine rpm is highest. Turning the screw in will provide a rich fuel mixture, turning the screw out will give a lean fuel mixture.
3) If engine rpm has increased by the adjustment of air screw, the engine rpm should be set to the proper idle speed by using the throttle stop screw.
4) Turn the pilot air screw in or out within the range of 1/8 to 1/4 turn to obtain the optium idling condition.

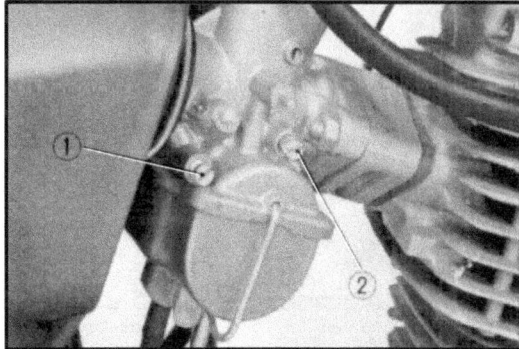

Fig. 3 Idling adjustment
1 Air screw 2 Throttle stop screw

Fig. 4　① Breaker arm slipper　② Cam

Fig. 5　① Breaker arm retaining screws　② Adjusting position

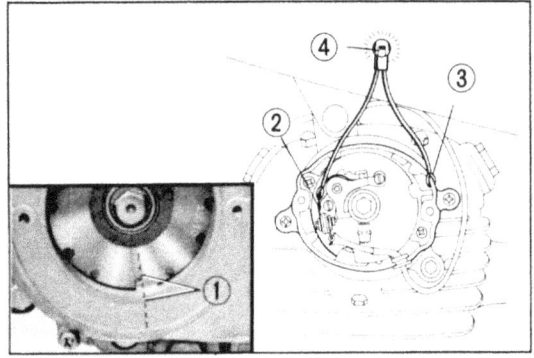

Fig. 6　① "F" aligning mark　② Breaker arm spring
　　　③ Ground to earth　④ Bulb

Fig. 7　① Base plate mounting screw　② Base plate

3. BREAKER POINT AND IGNITION TIMING ADJUSTMENT

Adjust breaker point gap, before performing the ignition timing adjustment.

A. Breaker point gap

1) Remove the point and dynamo covers. Turn the crankshaft with the pin spanner provided as a service tool until the breaker arm slipper is on the highest point of cam lobe. (Fig. 4)
2) Measure point gap using a thickness gauge. The gap should be **0.3–0.4 mm (0.012–0.016 in.)**.
3) If it is necessary to make adjustment, loosen the breaker arm retaining screws, insert a screwdriver in the adjusting screw slot, and pry to adjust to the above value. Retighten the screw securely after setting is made. (Fig. 5)
4) Check the ignition. When the point contact surfaces are pitted or dirty, grind contacts with a point file or oil stone to remove transfer or contamination. If the metal build-up on the point is greater than 0.5 mm (0.02 in.), it should be replaced.

B. Ignition timing adjustment

1) Disconnect the contact breaker cord (green cord) at the connector and connect a 12V–3W lamp across the line. (Fig. 6)
2) Set the combination switch to "ON" position.
3) Turn the rotor slowly until the lamp goes out and check the position of "F" mark on the rotor against the index mark on the L. crankcase. If they are in line, the ignition timing is correct. **(Fig. 6)**
4) If ignition timing is required for adjustment, loosen two base plate mounting screws and move the base plate. Turning the base plate clockwise will retard the timing and counter clockwise will advance it. Tighten the screw after adjustment is made. (Fig. 7)

C. Adjustment with timing light

1) Insert the plug or timing light cord into the jack of timing light.
2) Remove spark plug cap, and connect timing attachment between spark plug and cap.
3) Connect high tension voltage cord of timing light to timing attachment. Sot control knob on the meter to "TIMING", and then start the engine.
4) See if "F" mark aligns with timing mark by directing the beam of timing light to the timing mark. Timing mark should be positioned between the two matching lines adjacent to "F" mark, with the engine operating at **5,000~5,600 rpm**, for normal ignition timing when advanced angle is maximum.

NOTE:

The most accurate method is to use a stroboscopic type timing light

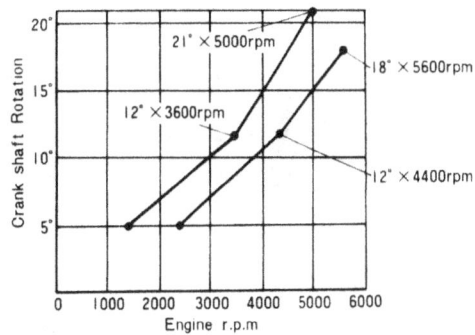

Fig 7-1

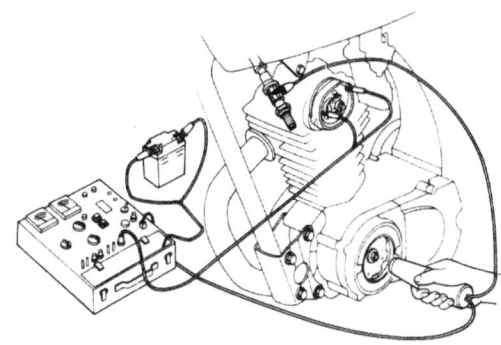

Fig 7-2

4. CLUTCH ADJUSTMENT

Check the clutch free play at the end of the clutch lever. The play should be **1-2 cm (3/8-3/4 in.)**. (Fig. 8) If it is not within this range, adjust it in accordance with the following procedure.

1) Loosen the clutch cable adjuster lock nut and turn the adjuster clockwise to make the cable free. Then loosen the lock nut of the clutch adjuster on the right crankcase cover. Turn the adjuster screw counter clockwise until a slight drag is felt and return it by 1/8 to 1/4 turn. Tighten the lock nut securely. (Fig. 9)
2) Turn the adjuster in the cable counter clockwise to adjust the lever end play. (Fig. 10)
3) Check for proper adjustment by starting the engine, applying clutch, and operating gear change. If the clutch does not disengage, the engine will stall or the motorcycle will tend to creep.

   If the clutch does not fully engage, the clutch will slip and the motorcycle will not accelerate in response to the acceleration of engine.

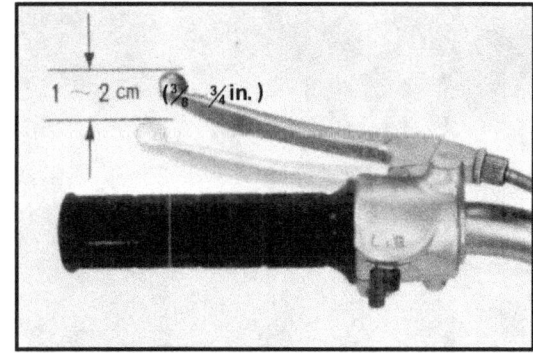

Fig. 8 Clutch lever play

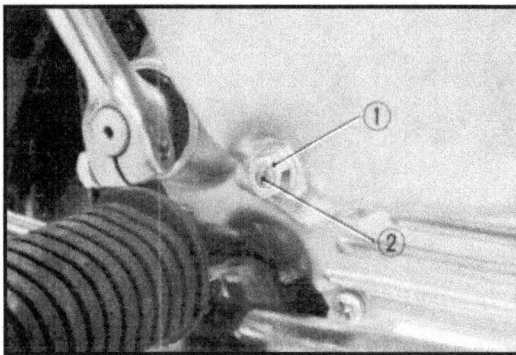

Fig. 9 Clutch adjustment
1. Lock nut 2. Adjuster screw

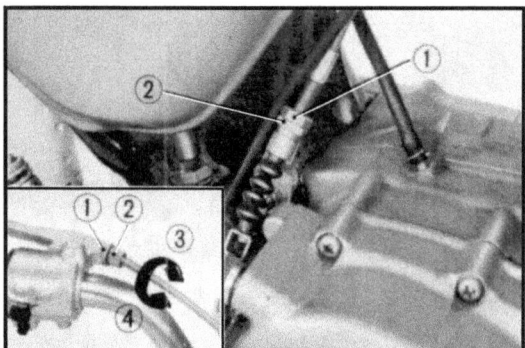

Fig. 10 ① Lock nut ② Adjuster ③ Increase ④ Decrease

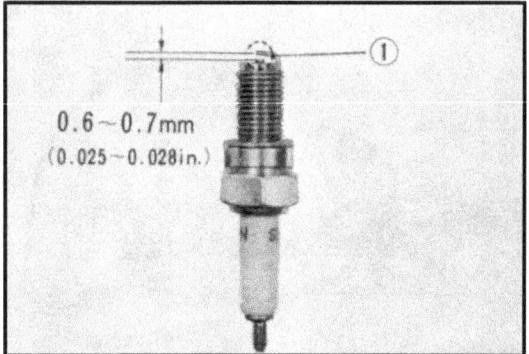

Fig. 11 ① Electrode

Fig. 12 ① Oil level gauge

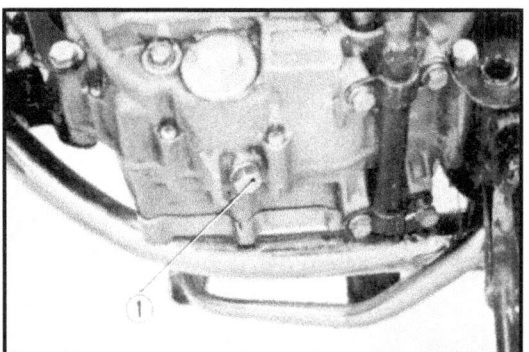

Fig. 13 ① Drain plug

5. SPARK PLUG INSPECTION

Remove the spark plug with a spark plug wrench and visually check conditions of electrodes and insulator.

The standard spark plugs equipped in the original engine are **D-8ES (NGK)** or **X24ES (Nihon denso)**.

1) If the plug is carboned up, sooty or has a hard deposit from the chemical fuel additivies, it should be cleaned with a spark plug cleaner or a wire brush.
2) Replace the plug if it insulator is cracked or chipped.
3) Check the gap between the electrodes with a thickness gauge and if necessary, adjust the ground electrode by bending. The standard clearance is **0.6 - 0.7 mm (0.025 - 0.028 in.)**. (Fig. 11)
4) Check the plug gasket before installation and replace if it is damaged.

6. ENGINE OIL CHANGE

The oil change is better performed while the engine is warm as this will expedite thorough draining of oil.

1) Remove the oil cap and remove the drain plug to drain oil. (Fig. 13)
2) When the oil is thoroughly drained, replace the drain plug.
   Fill with a brand name oil SAE 10W-30, in the quantity of 1 lit. (1.05 qt.). Check the level by placing the dip stick in its hole, but not screwing it in. In this position, the level should be within the upper and lower marks. (Fig. 12)

7. OIL FILTER CLEANING

1) Remove the muffler.
2) Remove the step bar.
3) Remove the right crankcase cover.
4) Remove the centrifugal oil filter cap and clean inside. (Fig. 14)

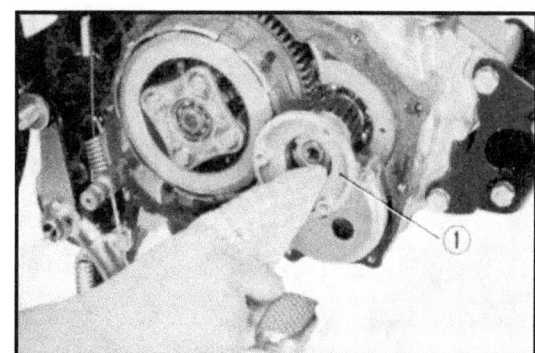

Fig. 14   ① Oil filter

Oil Pump Screen Cleaning

Whenever the right crankcase cover is removed, check the oil pump screen to see if dirt is trapped. If it is dirty, remove the screen by taking off the cap. Clean the screen by blowing compressed air through it. (Fig. 15)

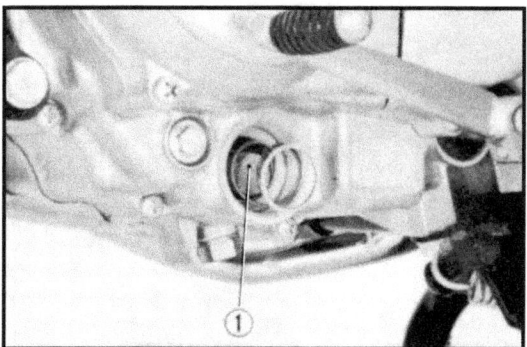

Fig. 15   ① Oil pump screen

8. CAM CHAIN ADJUSTMENT

Perform the adjustment with the adjuster screw. Loosen the lock nut and turn the adjuster screw counter clockwise to decrease the slack in the cam chain. The procedure for adjustment is, first loosen the screw and then tighten until it meets resistance. Tighten the lock nut after completing the adjustment. (Fig. 16)

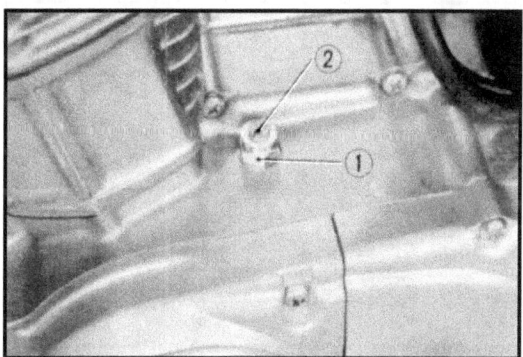

Fig. 16   ① Lock nut   ② Adjuster screw

9. FUEL SYSTEM INSPECTION

Inspect the fuel tank, fuel cock, carburetor and fuel piping system for any fuel leaks. If fuel is spilled at any time during the replacement of fuel system component, it should be cleaned up immediately as it is a fire hazard.

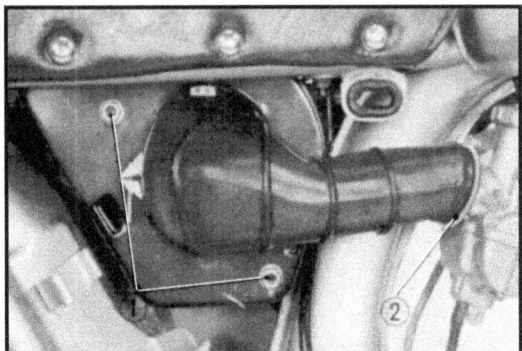

Fig. 17 1 Mounting nut   2 Air cleaner connecting clamp

Fig. 18 1 Air cleaner element

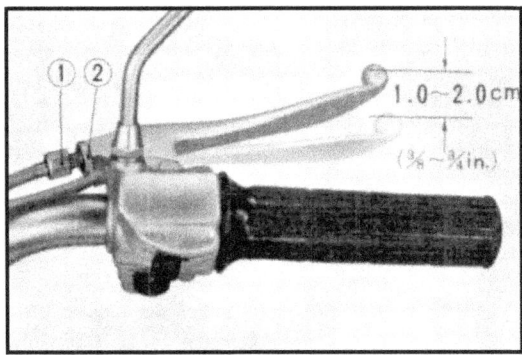

Fig. 19 Brake cable play adjustment
1 Adjuster nut   2 Lock nut

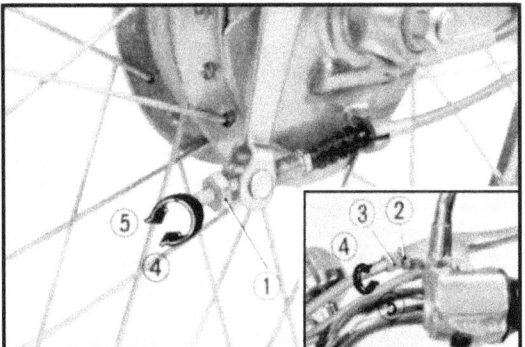

Fig. 20 1 Adjuster nut 2 Lock nut   **Fig. 20-A**
3 Adjuster nut 4 Decrease 5 Increase

10. AIR CLEANER ELEMENT SERVICING

1) Remove the right side cover.
2) Loosen air cleaner connecting clamp and the two mounting nuts to remove the air cleaner element. (Fig. 17)

3) Wash the element in solvent and then allow to dry. Apply a small quantity of oil on the element before installation. (Fig. 18)

Note:
Do not use gasoline to wash the filter element.

11. BRAKE ADJUSTMENT

(Front wheel)
Check the brake free play at the end of the brake lever. The play should be **1–2 cm (3/8–3/4 in.)**. (Fig. 19) If it is not within this range, adjust it in accordance with the following procedure.

1) Turn the adjuster nut clockwise to reduce play in the brake lever. (Fig. 19)

(Rear wheel)
2) Minor or fine adjustment can be made with adjuster nut on the brake lever. (Fig. 20-A)

Check the brake free play at the end of the brake pedal. The play should be **2–3 cm (3/4–1·1/8 in.)**. (Fig. 21) If it is not within this range, adjust it in accordance with the following procedure.
1) Turn the adjuster nut clockwise to reduce the amount of play in the brake pedal. (Fig. 20) and (Fig. 22)

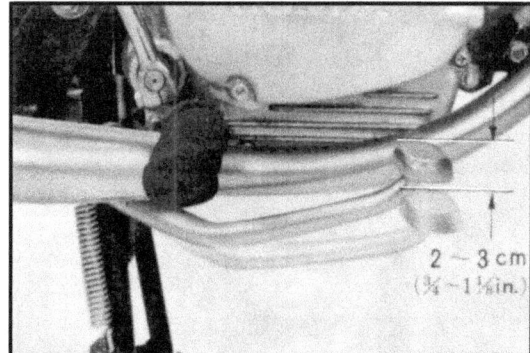

Fig. 21 Brake pedal play

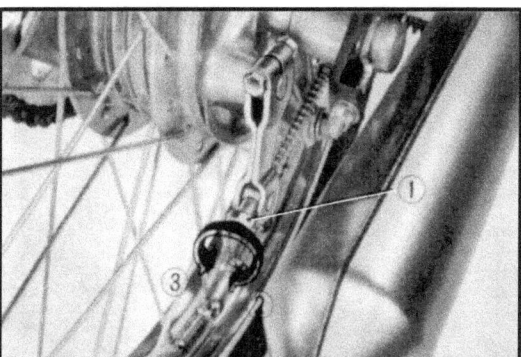

Fig. 22 ① Adjuster nut ② Decrease ③ Increase

12. DRIVE CHAIN ADJUSTMENT

Adjust the chain slack to **1–2 cm (3/8–3/4 in.)** with adjuster nuts after the axle nut is loosened. (Fig. 23)

Note:

Both right and left adjuster nuts should be turned equal amounts. This can be varified by the position of the adjuster indicator plate on both sides.

13. BATTERY ELECTROLYTE INSPECTION

Remove the left side cover and check the level of battery electrolyte to level indicator marks on battery case. (Fig. 24)
1) If the electroyte level is low, remove the battery to refill it.
2) Add distilled water to bring electrolyte level to upper level marked on the case.

Note:

Over filling will cause electroyte to overflow and result in corrosion around the battery compartment.

Fig. 23 ① Index mark and side scale ② Rear axle nut ③ Adjuster nut

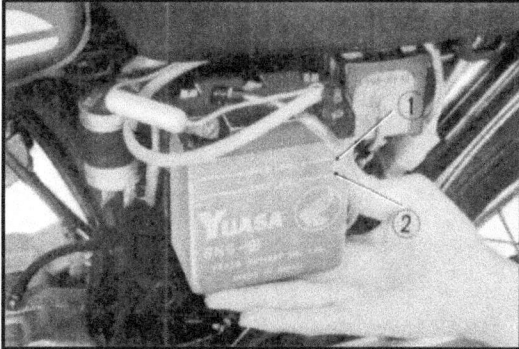

Fig. 24 ① Upper level ② Lower level

Fig. 25 ① Fork bolt

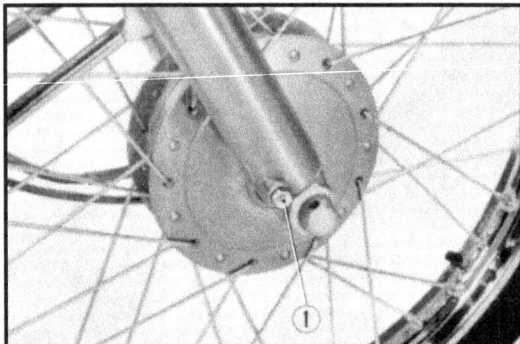

Fig. 26 ① Drain plug

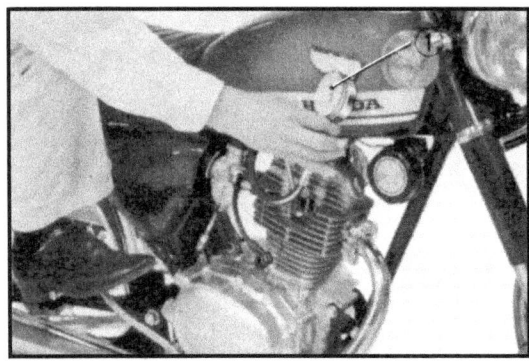

Fig. 27 ① Compression gauge

14. FRONT FORK OIL REPLACEMENT

1) Remove the fork bolts and remove the drain plug to drain oil. Actuate the fork for complete draining. (Fig. 25-26)
2) Flush out the interior using solvent.

Note:

Do not use gasoline for cleaning.

3) Reinstall the drain plug and tighten before refilling with new oil.(Fig. 26)

Recommended oil: SAE 10W-40

Capacity:

CB100, CB125S
CL100, CD125S   130–140cc (4.4–4.7 ozs)

SL100, SL125   180–190cc (6.1–7.2 ozs)

4) Replace the fork bolt.
   Torque to **4.0–5.0 kg-m (29.0–36.0 ft lbs)**.

15. CYLINDER COMPRESSION CHECK

Low compression and pressure leak will cause unstable engine rpm and loss of power. Compression is checked with a cylinder compression gauge by the following procedure. (Fig. 27)

1) Remove the spark plug.
2) Insert the rubber tip of compression gauge into the spark plug hole and operate the kick starter while holding the throttle grip fully open.

Note:

Perform the check after warming up the engine.

3) The normal compression pressure is **12 kg/cm^2 (170 psi)**.

   ① Low compression is due to one of the following causes:
   - Leaking valve.
   - Defective or sticking piston rings.
   - Blown cylinder head gasket.
   - Improper tappet adjustment.

   ② Unusually high compression pressure is due to excessive carbon deposits on the combustion chamber or on the piston head.

Engine must be disassembled for complete inspection or repair in these cases.

III. ENGINE

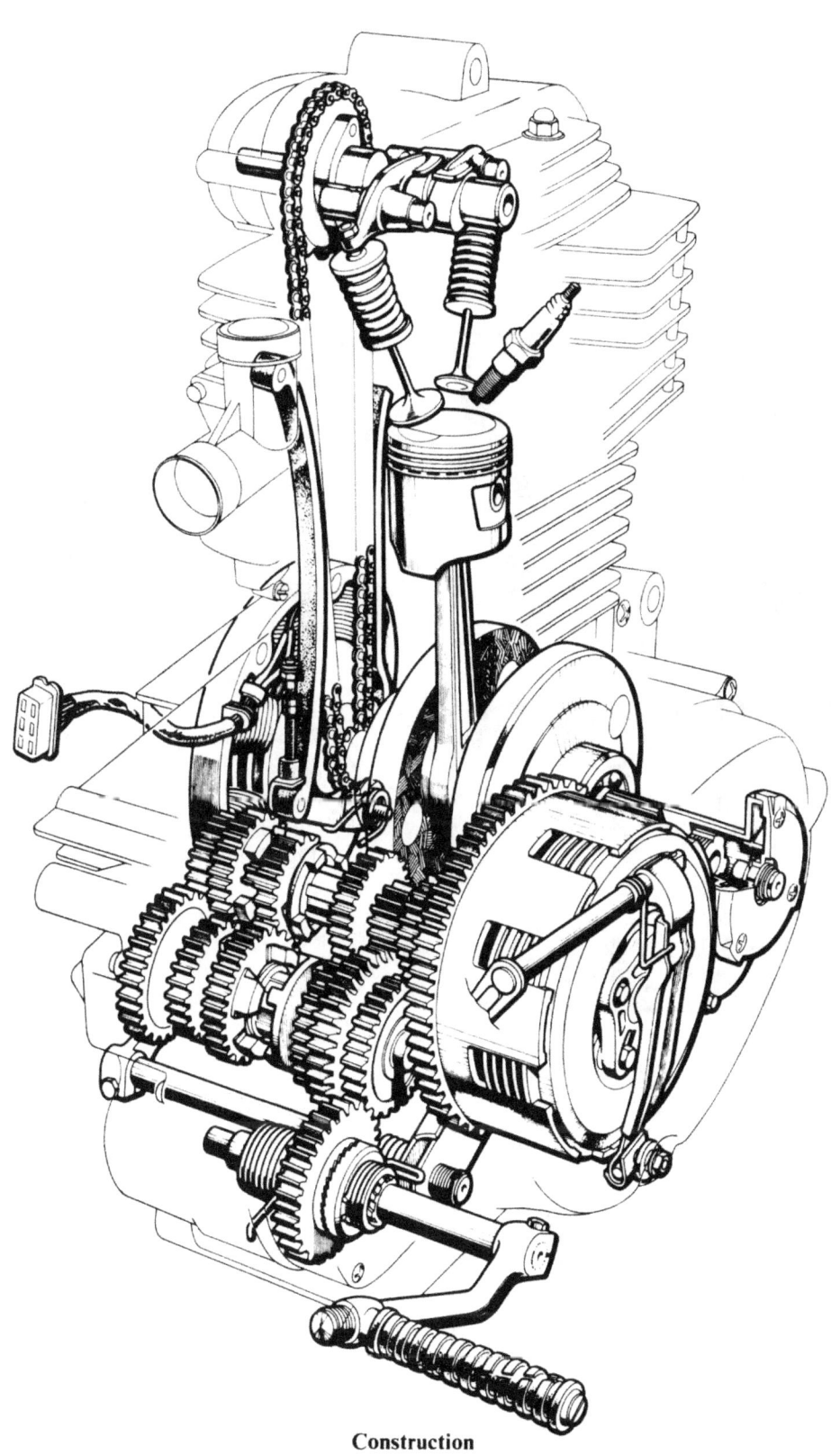

Construction

1. WORK WHICH CAN BE PERFORMED WITHOUT REMOVING THE ENGINE.

Work Item	Page
1) Oil pump, oil filter	22
2) Clutch	25
3) Gear shift mechanism	27

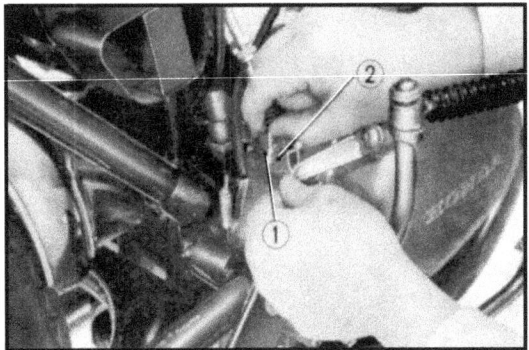

Fig. 28 1 Clutch cable 2 Clutch lever

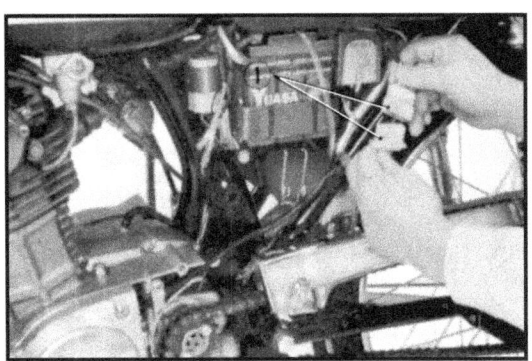

Fig. 29 1 Electrical coupler

Fig. 30 1 Engine hanger bolts

2. ENGINE REMOVAL AND REINSTALLATION

A. Engine Removal

1) Remove the exhaust pipe and muffler.
2) Remove four 8 mm step bar mounting bolts and remove the step bar.
3) Loosen the clutch cable lock nut, provide additional cable slack and then disconnect from the clutch lever. (Fig. 28)
4) Unscrew the two carburetor mounting bolts and separate the carburetor from the inlet pipe.
5) Remove the gear change pedal.
6) Remove the left rear crankcase cover.
7) Disconnect and remove the drive chain.
8) Disconnect the coupler from wire harness. (Fig. 29)

9) Remove nuts from the engine hanger bolts, raise engine toward the rear, and remove engine bolt while supporting the engine. (Fig. 30)

B. Engine Reinstallation

1) Reinstall engine in the reverse order of removal.
2) To simplify installation, use the "T" handle screwdriver to hang the engine temporarily followed by installing the support bolt.
3) Temporarily install the exhaust pipe joint and muffler and then perform the final torquing.
4) When connecting drive chain, make sure that the chain joint clip is properly installed. (Fig. 31)

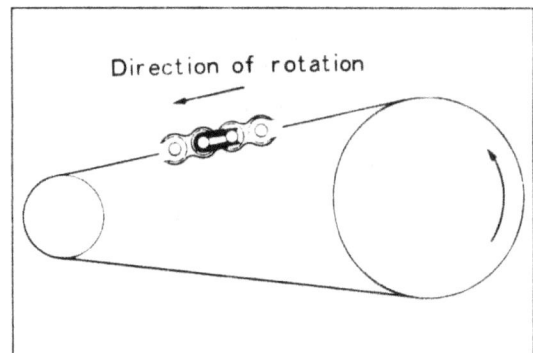

Fig. 31 Direction of rotation

3. CYLINDER, CYLINDER HEAD AND PISTON

A. Disassembly

1) Remove two 5mm screws and disassemble the point cover.
2) Loosen two 5mm mounting screws and remove the contact breaker. (Fig. 32)
3) Loosen the 6mm mounting bolt and remove the governor. (Fig. 32)
4) Loosen two 6mm screws and remove the point base. (Fig. 32)
5) Position the piston at top-dead-center, loosen the cam sprocket mounting bolts and remove the cam sprocket from the cam chain. (Fig. 33)

Note:
Do not loosen the cylinder head bolts.

6) Remove four 8mm cap nuts.
7) Align both the inlet and exhaust cams to the cutout on the cylinder head and then remove the camshaft from the cylinder. (Fig. 34)

Fig. 32 ① 5mm screws ② 6mm bolt ③ 6mm screws

Fig. 33 ① Cam chain ② 6mm bolts ③ Cam sprocket ④ "T" aligning mark ⑤ Cam shaft

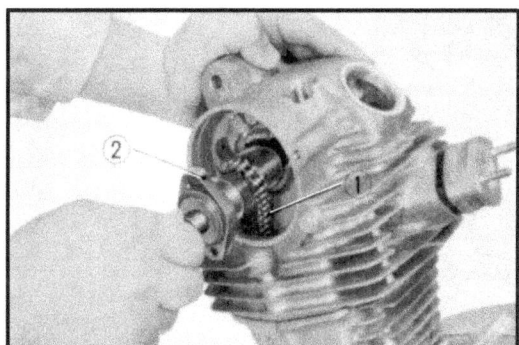

Fig. 34 **Camshaft removal**
① Cam chain ② Camshaft

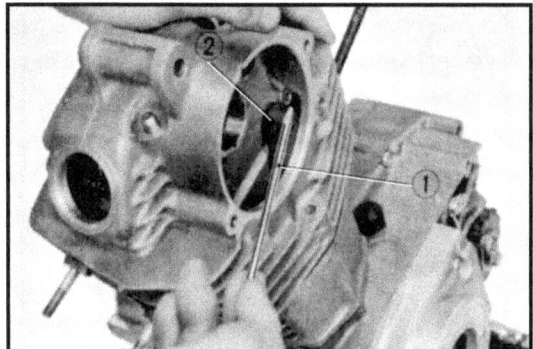

Fig. 35 1 Screwdriver 2 Cam chain tensioner

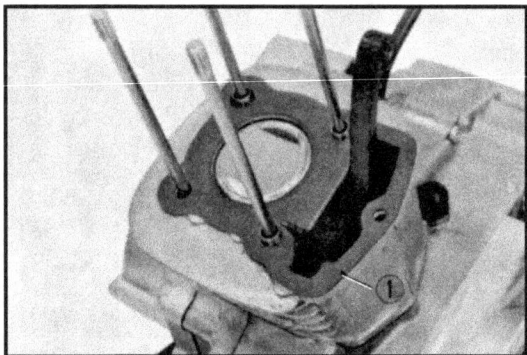

Fig. 36 Cylinder removal
1 Cylinder

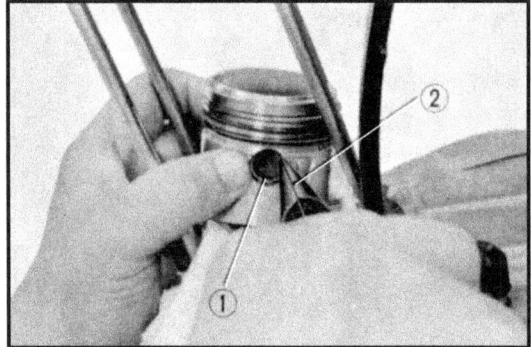

Fig. 37 Piston pin removal
1 Piston pin clip 2 Long nose pliers

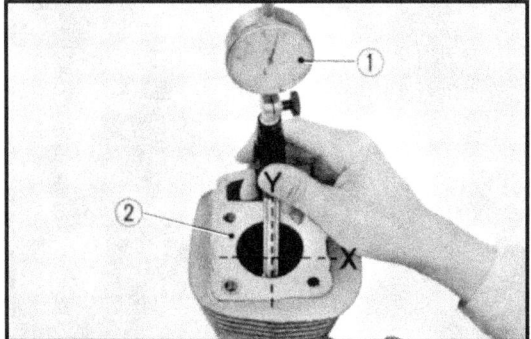

Fig. 38 Cylinder bore measurement
1 Cylinder gauge 2 Cylinder

8) Remove the tensioner stopper bolt and then remove the cam chain tensioner from the cylinder head. (Fig. 35)
9) Lift off the cylinder head.
10) Remove the cam chain guide.
11) Lift and remove the cylinder. (Fig. 36)

Note:
If cylinder head is frozen on the cylinder or if it is difficult to remove, tap the cylinder base with a wooden hammer to loosen. Exercise care not to strike the cylinder with a hard blow as the cooling fins may be damaged.

12) Remove piston pin clip and piston pin, and then separate the piston from the connecting rod. (Fig. 37)

Note:
When removing the piston pin clip, exercise care not to drop the clip into the crankcase.

13) Remove the piston rings.

B. Inspection

1) Inspect the condition of the cylinder bore. Measure diameter of the cylinder bore in both the X and Y directions and at the top, center and bottom of the cylinder. (Fig. 38)

Item		Standard value	Serviceable limit
Bore diameter	CB100 CL100 SL100	50.50–50.51mm (1.9881–1.9885 in)	50.6mm max. (1.992 in.)
	CB125S CD125S SL125	56.00–56.01mm (2.2047–2.2051 in)	56.1mm max. (2.2086 in.)

Camshaft OD

	Standard value	Service limit
Left side	19.937–19.927mm (0.7849–0.7845in)	19.88mm (0.7827in.)
Right side	29.930–29.917mm (1.1784–1.1779in)	29.87mm (1.1760in.)

Cylinder head ID

	Standerd value	Service limit
Left side	20.000–20.021mm (0.7874–0.7882in.)	20.079mm (0.7885in.)
Right side	30.000–30.021mm (1.1811–1.1819in.)	30.079mm (1.1822in.)

If the cylinder bore is less than 52.6 mm, rebore and hone the cylinder, and replace the piston with an oversize piston. The standard clearance between the piston and the cylinder should be **0.01–0.05mm (0.0004–0.0020 in.)** at the piston skirt. The oversize pistons are available in the oversize of 0.25, 0.50, 0.75 and 1.0mm (0.010, 0.020, 0.030 & 0.040 in.).

2) Piston diameter inspection
Measure the piston at the skirt. (Fig. 39)

Item	Standard value		Serviceable limit
Piston diameter	CB100 CL100 SL100	50.47–50.49mm (1.987–1.988 in.)	50.3mm (1.980 in.)
	CB125S CD125S SL125	55.97–55.99mm (2.2035–2.2043 in.)	55.80mm (2.1968 in.)

Replace if beyond the serviceable limit.

3) Measure the piston ring side clearance using a thickness gauge. Replace the piston ring or piston if beyond the serviceable limit.

Item	Standard value	Serviceable limit
Piston ring side clearance	0.025–0.030mm (0.0008–0.0011 in.)	0.7mm (0.0275 in.)

4) Piston ring gap
Insert the piston ring into the cylinder so that it is normal to the cylinder axis and then measure the ring gap using a thickness gauge. (Fig. 40)

Item	Standard value	Serviceable limit
Top and second rings	0.15–0.35mm (0.0059–0.0138 in.)	0.5mm max. (0.0197 in.)
Oil ring	0.15–0.04mm (0.0059–0.0158 in.)	0.5mm max. (0.0197 in.)

Replace if beyond the serviceable limit.

C. Reassembly

1) Assemble the piston ring on the piston.
Note:
The ring marking located adjacent to the ring gap should be toward the top. (Fig. 41)

When installing new piston rings, roll the rings around their respective piston ring grooves to make sure that the ring side clearances are adequate. Rings should roll smoothly.

2) Install the piston. (Fig. 42)
Note:
Install the piston so that the IN marking on the piston head is toward the rear.
Replace all piston pin clips with new items.

3) Space the piston ring gaps equally apart (120°) and then install the cylinder.
Note:
Do not forget to install the two dowel pins in the mounting base.

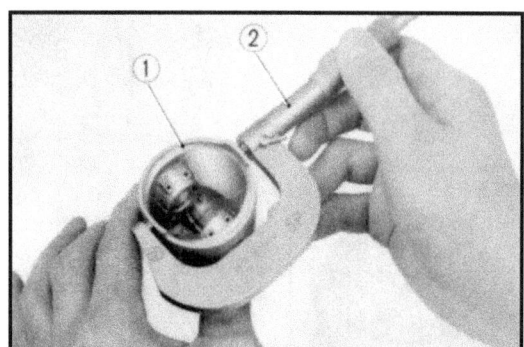

Fig. 39 Piston diameter measurement
① Piston ② Micrometer

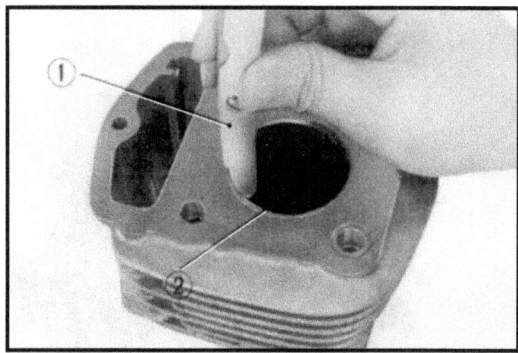

Fig. 40 Piston ring gap measurement
① Thickness gauge ② Piston ring

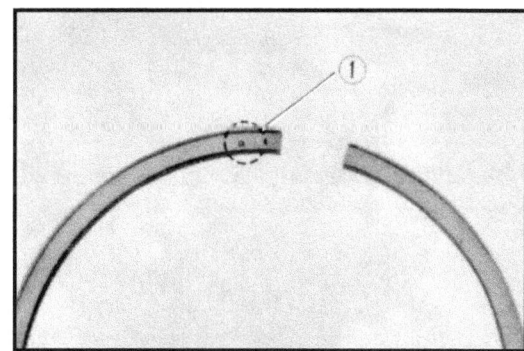

Fig. 41 ① Piston ring marking

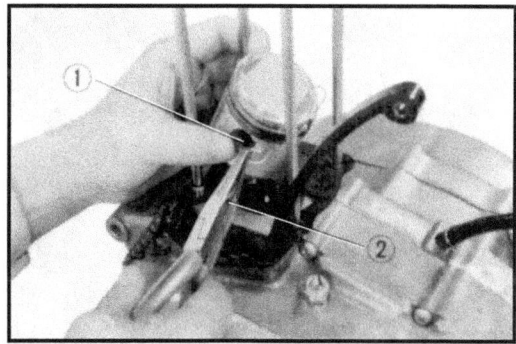

Fig. 42 Piston installation
① Piston pin clips ② Long nose pliers

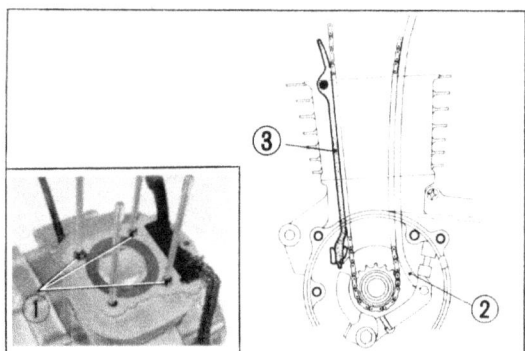

Fig. 43 ① Dowel pins ② Cam chain tensioner
③ Cam chain guide ④ o-ring

Fig. 44 ① Cam chain ② Screwdriver ③ 8mm cap nuts

Fig. 45 Camshaft installation
① Camshaft ② Cam lobe

Fig. 46 Valve timing procedure
① "T" mark ② Mounting holes ③ Cam sprocket
④ index mark

4) Reinstall the cam chain guide. (Fig.43)

5) Reinstall the three dowel pins and o-ring. (Fig. 43)

   Install the cam chain tensioner.

6) Install the cylinder head gasket.

7) Pull the cam chain up and install the cylinder head. Hold the chain up with a screwdriver. (Fig. 44)

8) Tighten the four 8 mm cap nuts and then 6 mm cylinder bolt.

   Torque: 8 mm cap nuts 1.8–2.0 kg-m
   (13–14 ft-lb)
   6 mm bolt   1.2–1.8 kg-m
   (9–13 ft-lb)

9) Back out the tappet adjusting screws.

10) Align the camshaft lobes with the cylinder head cutout and install the camshaft through the chain. (Fig. 45) Rotate the camshaft about 180 degrees to bring it to the top-dead-center position.

    NOTE:

    The sprocket mounting holes should be in line with the left crankcase index mark, (Fig. 46) and the advancer pin should be facing up.

11) Align the crankshaft "T" mark with the left crankcase index mark to put the crankshaft at TDC. (Fig. 46)

12) Install the cam sprocket, aligning the mounting holes.
    Place the cam chain onto the sprocket making sure the crankshaft is at TDC and the cam sprocket mounting holes are perpendicular to the crankshaft.

13) Install the cam sprocket bolts.

    Torque: 0.8–1.2 kg-m (6–9 ft-lb)

14) Install the cam chain tensioner upper bolt.

15) Reinstall the breaker point base assembly using the oil seal guide.

16) Reinstall the spark advancer. (Fig.47)

17) Reinstall the contact breaker point assembly.

18) Adjust the point gap and ignition timing. (Page 6)

19) Install the point cover.

20) Adjust the valve tappet clearances. (Page 5)

21) Install the valve adjustment caps.

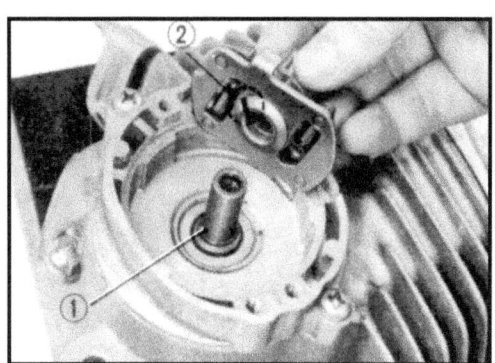

Fig. 47 Advance installation
1 Pin 2 Pin hole

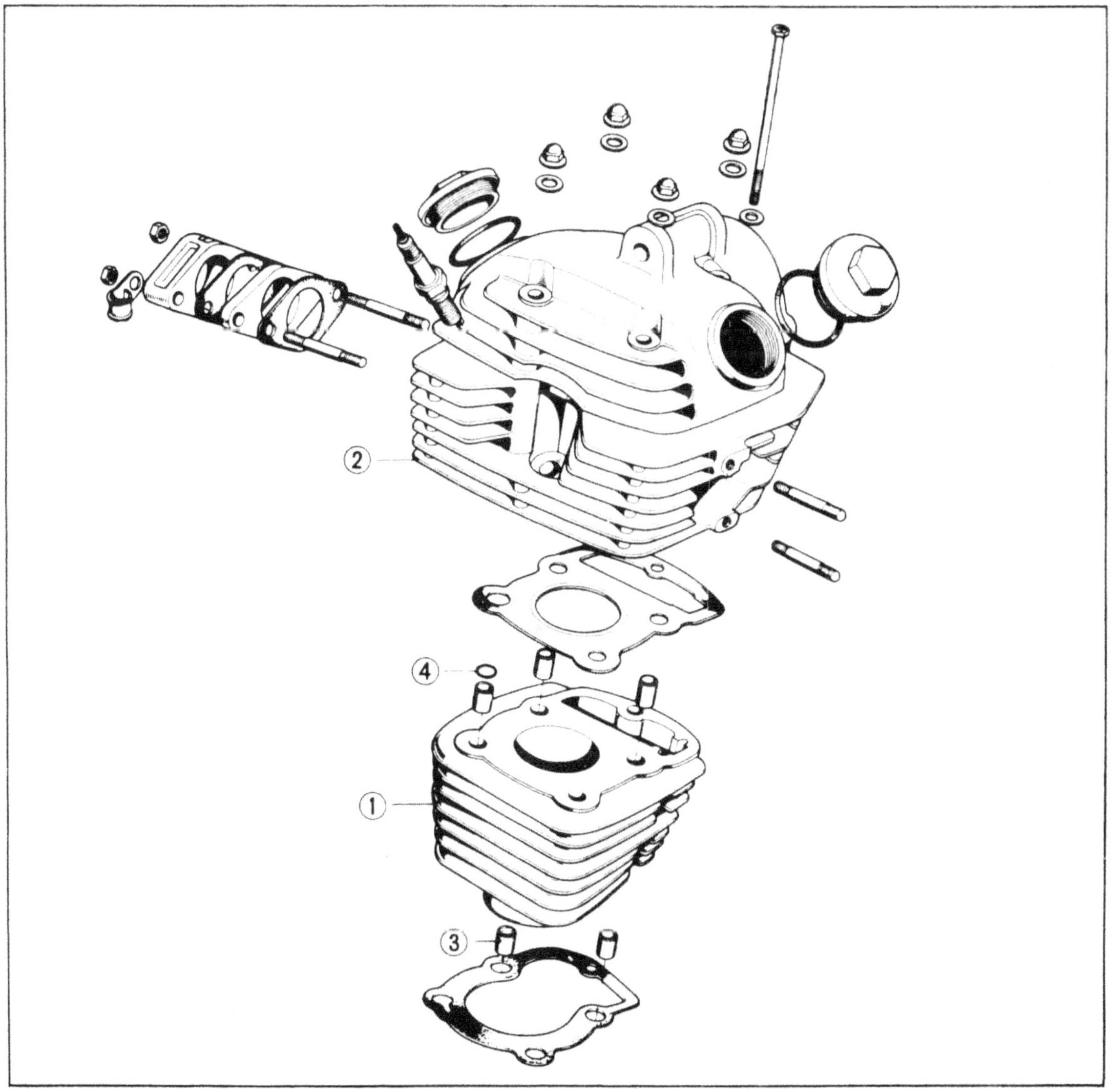

Fig. 48 1 Cylinder 2 Cylinder head 3 Dowel pins 4 O ring

4. VALVE REMOVAL

A. Disassembly

1) Remove the cylinder head in accordance with section 3. A.
2) Compress valve spring with a valve lifter and remove valve cotter and valve spring. The valve can then be removed. (Fig. 49)

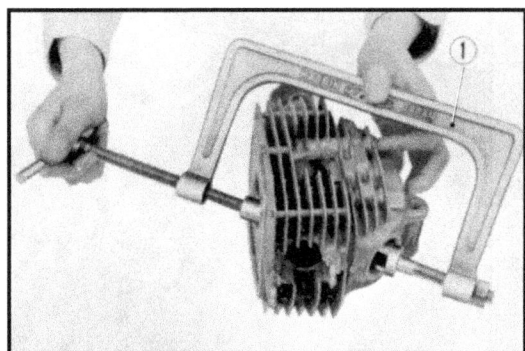

Fig. 49 Valve removal
① Valve spring compressor (Tool No. 07031-10701)

B. Inspection

1) Valve stem clearance is measured by raising the valve off its seat and measuring the amount of side play by applying the dial gauge against the valve stem.
   The play is measured along both the X and Y axes. (Fig. 50)
   Exhaust valve with a TIR of greater than 0.08 mm (0.0032 in.) or inlet valve with TIR greater than 0.1 mm (0.004 in.) should have either the valve or guide replaced.

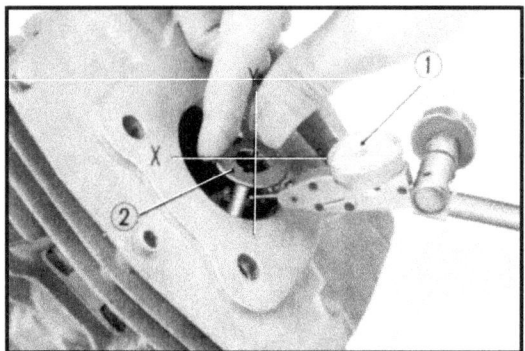

Fig. 50 Valve stem clearance measurement
① Dial gauge ② Valve

Item		Standard value	Serviceable limit
Valve stem diameter	IN	5.450–5.465mm (0.2145–0.2150 in.)	5.420mm min. (0.2130 in.)
	EX	5.430–5.445mm (0.2138–0.2146 in.)	5.400mm min.) (0.2126 in.)

2) Valve guide replacement
   Remove and reinstall valve guide using a valve guide driver (special tool No. 07046-21601). Use an oversize replacement valve guide. After replacing the valve guide, run a reamer through the valve guide to assure that the guide will be of standard diameter.
3) Valve face dimensional check
   Apply thin coating of red lead or bluing on the valve face, press valve against the valve seat and rotate. Remove and check to see if there is a uniform width impression of the valve face. (Fig. 51)

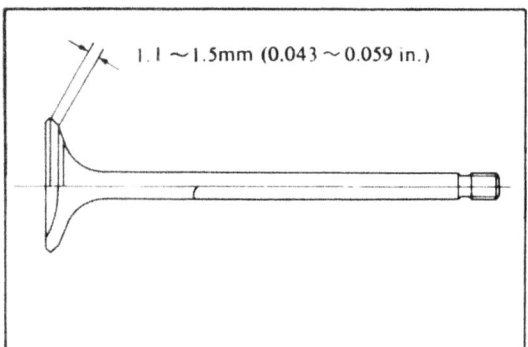

Fig. 51 Valve face

Item	Standard value	Serviceable limit
Valve seat width	0.7mm (0.028 in.)	1.5mm max. (0.059 in.)

If there is uneven contact, the valve seat should be cut by first using the valve seat interior cutter followed by the top cutter and then finished with the 90° seat cutter. (Fig. 52)

4) Valve lapping

Finally, lap the valve into the seat using a fine valve grinding compound. A uniform lap ring on the face of the valve indicates a good seating.

5) Valve spring

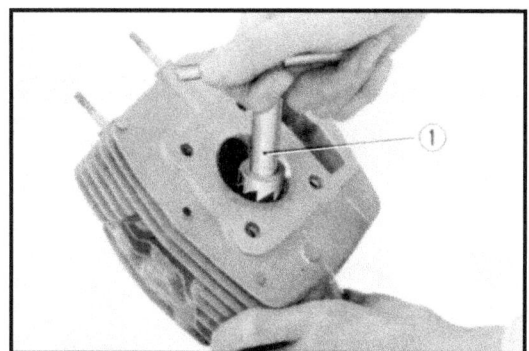

Fig. 52 Valve seat dressing
① Valve seat 90° cutter (Tool No. 07001-10701)

Item	Standard value		Serviceable limit
Free length	CB100 CL100 SL100	Outer	40.4mm (1.591 in.)	39.0mm (1.535 in. min.)
		Inner	35.7mm (1.406 in.)	34.5mm (1.358 in. min.)
	CB125S CD125S SL125	Outer	40.9mm (1.610 in.)	39.5mm (1.555 in. min.)
		Inner	33.5mm (1.318 in.)	32.0mm (1.259 in. min.)

C. Reassembly

1) Clean all parts with solvent or kerosene and perform the reassembly in the reverse order of diassembly.
2) Reassemble the cylinder head in accordance with paragraph 3.C.

Caution

Use the valve seat grinder (tool No 07782-0020000, A set) to correct the valve seat width and contact from the following serial number.

FNO.
CB100-1236861~
CB100-1231851~
CL100S-1300001~
SL100-1225981~

FNO.
CB125S-1030132~
CD125S-1008491~
SL125S-1131076~

Read carefully the instruction provided with the valve seat grinder.

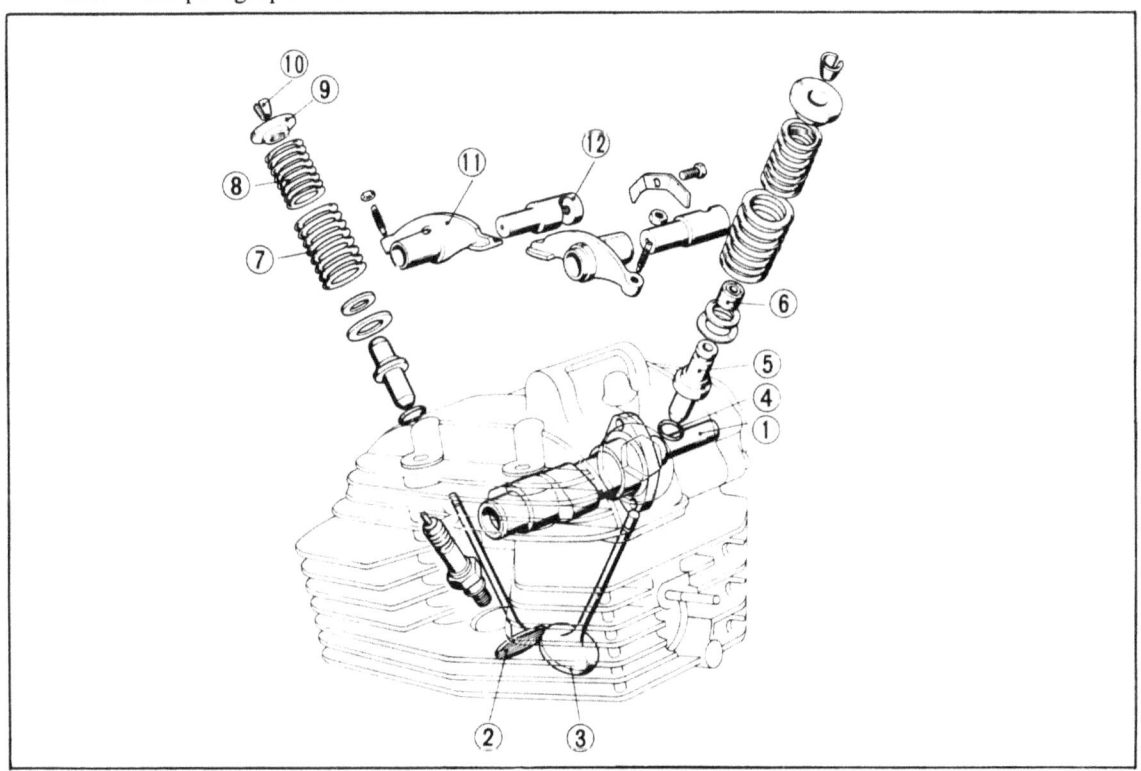

Fig. 53 ① Camshaft ② Inlet valve ③ Exhaust valve ④ O ring ⑤ Valve guide ⑥ Valve stem seal ⑦ Valve outer spring ⑧ Valve inner spring ⑨ Valve spring retainer ⑩ Valve cotter ⑪ Valve rocker arm ⑫ Valve rocker arm shaft

5. OIL PUMP AND OIL FILTER

The oil pump is a trochoid type driven from the primary drive gear through the oil pump drive gear and supplies oil to all the rotating components.

The oil filter is mounted directly on the crankshaft. The impurities in the oil, due to its heavier weight, are deposited along the rib of the oil filter cap by centrifugal force and only the purified oil is allowed to be supplied to the various components of the engine.

Discharge volume..2.4 l per min./10,000RPM

Lubricating system

The oil in the crankcase is picked up by the oil pump and pressure fed through the right crankcase where it is diverted into two routes. In one direction, it is routed through the passage in the right crankcase cover, oil filter and to the crankshaft. The other direction, the oil is routed through the passage in the cylinder head stud, to the cylinder head and then to the camshafts and rocker arms.

From the right crankcase, the oil is also supplied under pressure to the transmission.

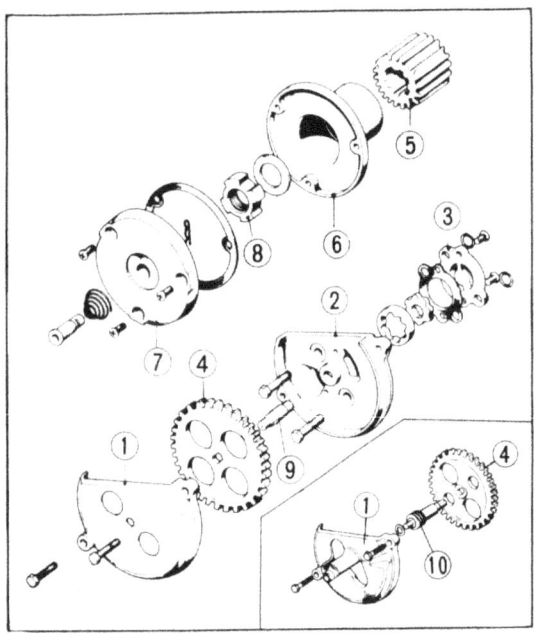

CB100, CL100, SL100 / CB125S, CD125S, SL125S

Fig. 54 ① Oil pump gear cover ② Oil pump body ③ Oil pump plate ④ Oil pump drive gear ⑤ Primary drive gear ⑥ Oil filter complete ⑦ Oil filter rotor cap ⑧ 18mm lock nut ⑨ Oil pump shaft ⑩ Pinion gear

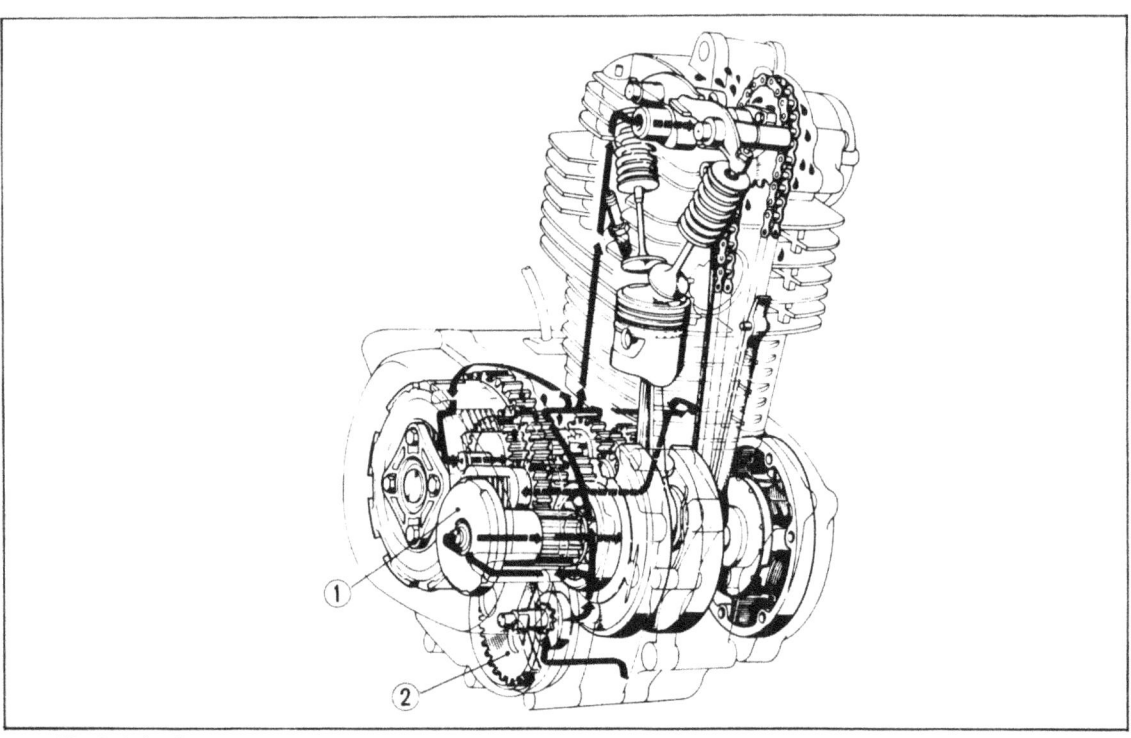

Fig. 55 Lubrication system
① Oil filter ② Oil pump

A. Disassembly

1) Remove the right crankcase cover.
2) Remove the oil filter rotor cover.
3) Unscrew the 6mm lock nut and remove the oil filter rotor. (Fig. 56)

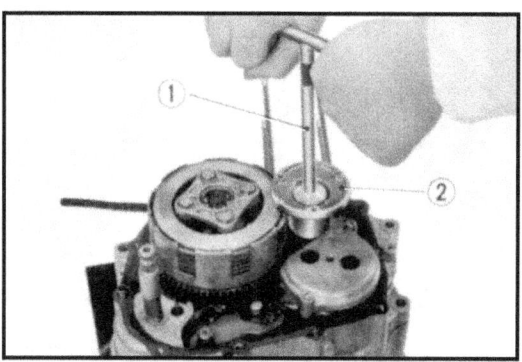

Fig. 56 **Lock nut removal**
1 16mm, T-handle box wrench (Tool No. 07086-28301)
2 Oil filter

4) Remove the oil pump gear cover.
5) **(CB125S, CD125S, SL125)**
   Remove the tachometer pinion gear.
6) Remove the oil pump drive gear. (Fig. 57)

Fig. 57 **Oil pump drive gear removal**
1 Oil pump drive gear 2 Shaft

7) Unscrew two 6mm oil pump body mounting bolts and then remove the pump body. (Fig. 58)

Fig. 58 **Oil pump body removal**
1 6mm bolts 2 Oil pump body

8) Pull out the oil pump shaft, loosen two 4mm pump outer rotor mounting screws and then remove the outer rotor. (Fig. 59)

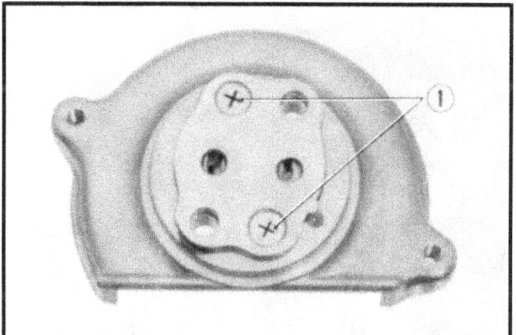

Fig. 59 **Oil pump disassembly**
1 4mm screws

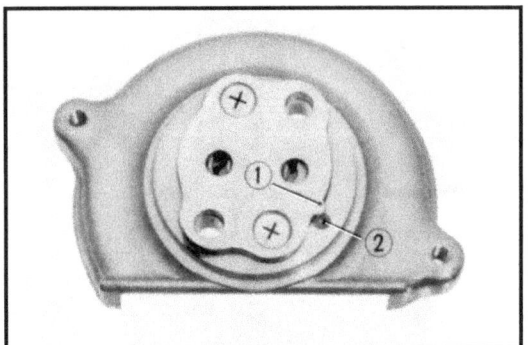

Fig. 60 1 Convex 2 Concave

Fig. 61 1 O ring

Fig. 62 1 Oil pump shaft

Fig. 63 **Lock nut tightening**
1 16mm lock nut

B. Reassembly

1) Perform the reassembly in the reverse order of disassembly. Align the concave part on the oil pump to the convex part on the oil pump plate and install (Fig. 60)

2) Reinstall the oil pump body.
   Note:
   Do not forget to assemble two 2.4 × 9.4 "O" rings. (Fig. 61)

3) Align oil pump shaft to the cutout on the inner rotor gear and then assemble. (Fig. 62)
   (CB125S, CD125S, SL125)
   Assemble the tachometer pinion gear.

4) Assemble the oil pump drive gears and install the pump gear cover with the 5mm mounting bolts.

5) Mount the oil filter rotor with the 16mm lock nut. (Fig. 63)
   Torque to **4.0–5.0 kg-m (29–36 ft-lbs)**.
   Note:
   Do not forget to install the lock washer.

6) Reinstall the right crankcase cover.

6. CLUTCH

The clutch is a multi-disc, wet type. The friction disc is bonded to a heat dissipating center plate.

The clutch consists of five cork molded disc plates, four clutch plates and four clutch springs which are all assembed within the clutch outer.

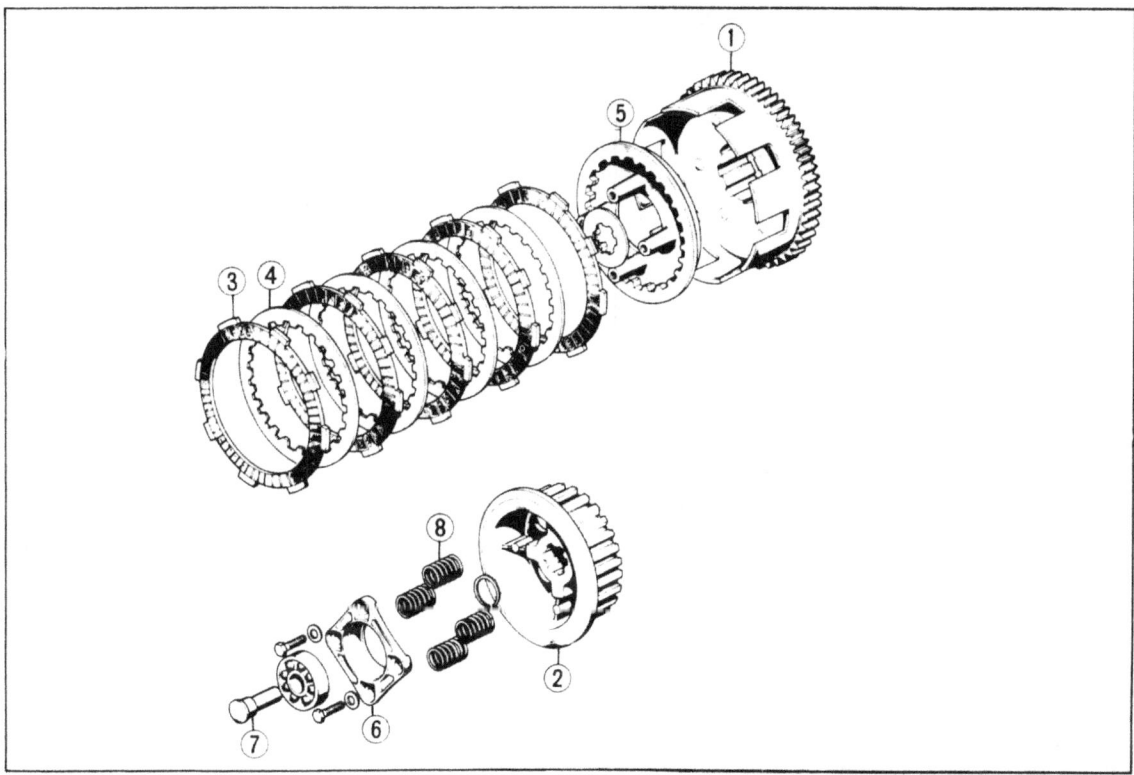

Fig. 64 ① Clutch outer complete ② Clutch center ③ Friction disc ④ Clutch plate ⑤ Clutch pressure plate ⑥ Clutch lifter plate ⑦ Clutch lifter guide pin ⑧ Clutch spring

A. Disassembly

1) Remove the right crankcase cover and the oil filter rotor in accordance with section 5.A.
2) Remove four 6mm bolts and remove the clutch lifter plate. (Fig. 65)

Fig. 65 Clutch removal
① 6 mm. bolts

Fig. 66 Clutch outer removal
1 Special pliers 2 20 mm set ring 3 Clutch center

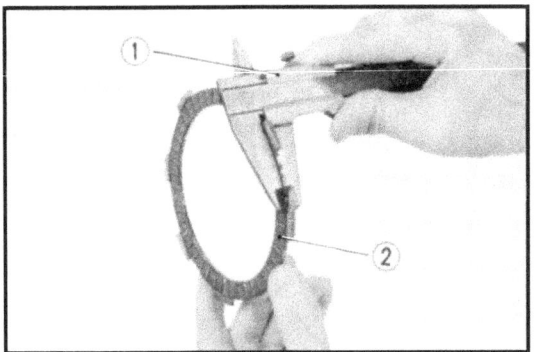

Fig. 67 1 Vernier caliper gauge 2 Clutch friction disc

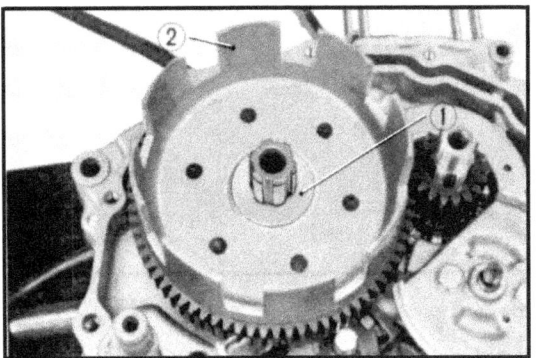

Fig. 68 Spline washer installation
1 20 mm spline washer 2 Clutch outer

Fig. 69 Clutch installation
1 Clutch center 2 Clutch friction disc 3 Splines

3) Unfasten the 20mm set ring and remove the clutch center together with the friction disc. (Fig. 66)
4) Remove the 20mm spline washer and then remove the clutch outer assembly.

B. Inspection

1) Clutch friction disc (Fig. 67)

Item	Standard value	Serviceable limit
Thickness	2.9mm (0.114 in.)	26mm (0.102 in.)

Replace the friction disc if beyond the serviceable limit.

2) Replace any worn or damaged clutch plates.

C. Reassembly

1) Install the clutch outer assembly and pressure plate. (Fig. 68)
2) Install the 20mm splined washer. (Fig. 68)

3) Assemble the friction discs and clutch plates alternately on the clutch center. Assemble the clutch plates after aligning the splines. (Fig. 69)

Note:
First, align the spline to the main shaft and then align the clutch outer spline while rotating the friction disc.

4) Install the 20mm set ring.
5) Assemble the clutch spring and install with the 6mm mounting bolts.
   Torque to **0.8–1.2kg-m (5.8–8.7 ft-lbs)**.

Note:

Do not forget to install the clutch lifter guide pin. (Fig. 70)

6) Assemble the oil filter rotor, and install the right crankcase cover in accordance with section 5.C.

Fig. 70 1 Clutch lifter guide pin

7. GEAR SHIFT MECHANISM

The gear shift mechanism consists of gear shift plate, gear shift drum, three gear shift forks, gear shift cam and the gear shift drum stopper bar. When the gear shift pedal is depressed, the gear shift cam drum rotates to perform the gear shifting. Also, a feature is incorporated into the system to prevent gear jumping during shifting.

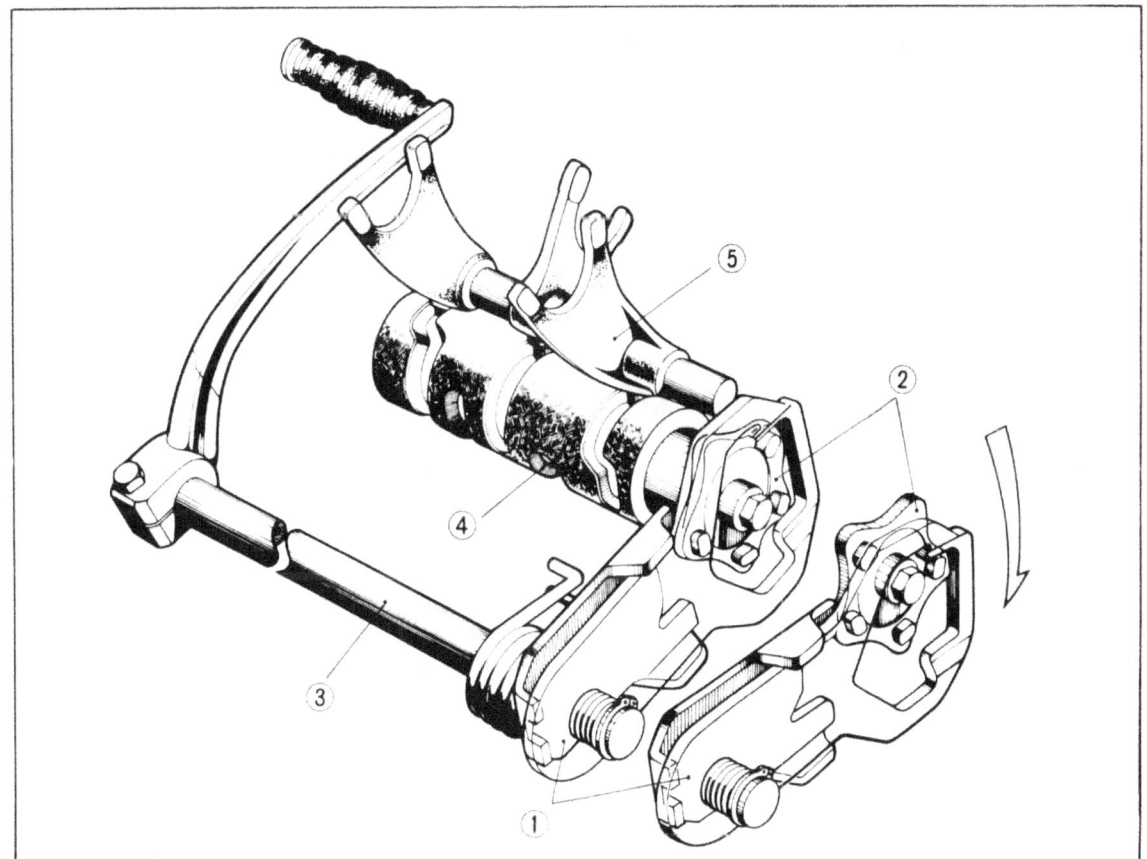

Fig. 71 1 Gear shift plate 2 Gear shift cam 3 Gear shift spindle 4 Gear shift drum 5 Gear shift fork

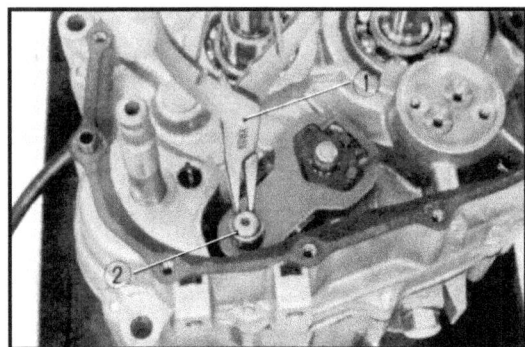

Fig. 72 Circlip removal
① Special pliers ② Circlip

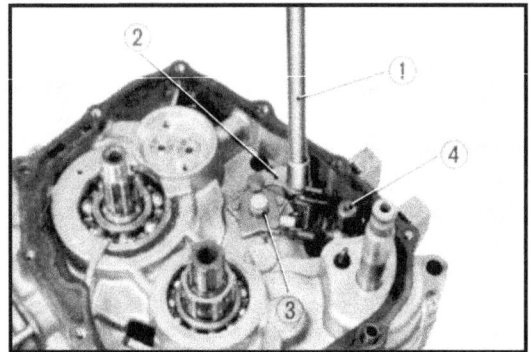

Fig. 73 ① 6 mm, T-handle box wrench ② Gear shift drum stopper ③ Gear shift cam ④ Gear shift spindle

Fig. 74 Pin alignment
① Cam pin ② Pin hole

Fig. 75 Spindle installation
① Boss ② Return spring

A. Disassembly

1) Remove the right crankcase cover and oil filter rotor in accordance with paragraph 5.A.
2) Remove the clutch in accordance with section 6.A.
3) By removing the circlip, the spring and gear shift plate can be disassembled. (Fig. 72)

4) Unscrew the 6mm gear shift drum stopper bolt and remove the drum stopper. (Fig. 73)
5) Unscrew the 6mm gear shift cam bolt and remove the shift cam. (Fig. 73)
6) Remove the gear shift pedal and then pull out the gear shift spindle. (Fig. 73)

B. Reassembly

1) Assemble the gear shift cam so that the cam pin is inserted into the hole in the drum. (Fig. 74)

2) Assemble the gear shift assembly. (Fig. 75)
Note:
Install gear shift return spring so that the end of the spring is hooked to the boss on the case.
3) Install the gear shift drum stopper.
4) Install gear shift plate, assemble the spring and set into the case with the circlip.
5) Install the clutch in accordance with section 6.C.
6) Install the oil filter rotor and the right crankcase cover in accordance with section 5.B.

8. CAM CHAIN TENSIONER AND A.C. GENERATOR

A friction plate cam chain tensioner is utilized, and a plate spring supports the entire one side of the cam chain to control the slack in the chain. A chain guide is mounted on the opposite side to reduce the chain noise for a quiet operation. (Fig. 76)
The description of the A.C. generator is found in the electrical system section.

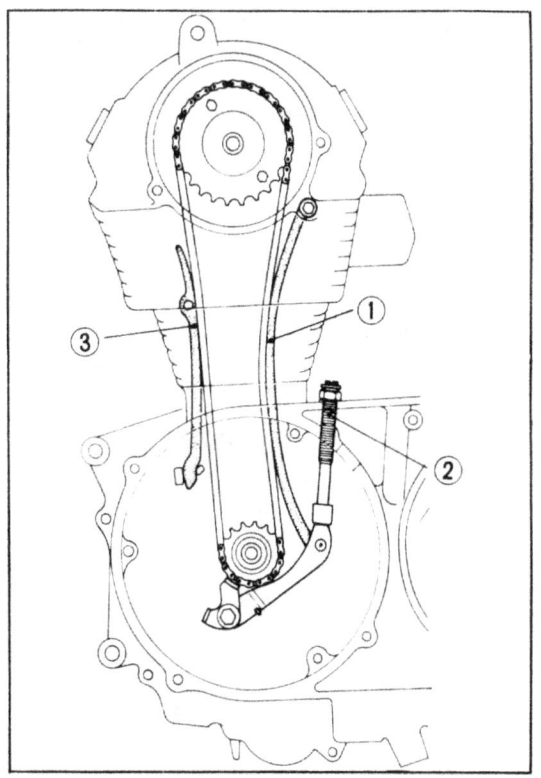

Fig. 76 ① Cam chain tensioner ② Adjusting bolt
③ Cam chain guide

A. Disassembly

1) Loosen four screws and remove the left crankcase cover.
2) Remove generator mounting bolts and remove the rotor assembly. (Fig. 77)
3) Loosen three 6mm A.C. generator mounting screws and remove the generator.
4) Remove the cam chain adjuster nut. (Fig. 78)
5) By removing the tensioner pivot bolt, the cam chain tensioner and the cam chain tensioner arm can be disassembled. (Fig. 78)
6) By removing the tensioner arm and push rod, the tensioner adjusting bolt can be pulled out. (Fig. 78)

Fig. 77 Rotor removal
① Dynamo rotor puller (Tool No. 07011-03001)
② Dynamo rotor

Fig. 78 ① Bolt ② Cam chain tensioner arm
③ Adjusting bolt

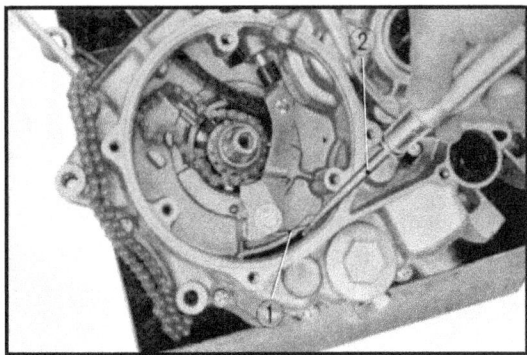

Fig. 79 Cam chain tensioner installation
1 Spring 2 Screwdriver

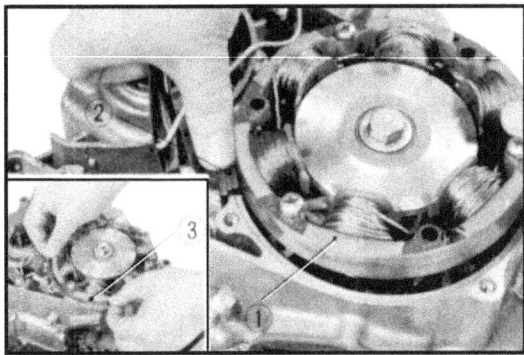

Fig. 80 Generator installation
1 Stator 2 Cord grommet 3 O ring

B. Reassembly

1) Install tensioner adjusting bolt from the outside of the case, install the case, and then install the tensioner arm rubber.
2) Assemble cam chain tensioner on the tensioner arm pin, hook the spring on the arm, and then install the tensioner arm adjusting bolt. (Fig. 79)

Note:
To simplify work, hook the spring only on the tensioner arm and leave the other end unattached.

3) Install the rotor assembly.
   Torque to **2.6–3.2 kg-m (19.0–23.0 ft-lbs)**.
4) Mount the A.C. generator. First install the cord grommet, mount the generator, and then align the screw mounting holes. (Fig. 80)

Note:
Do not forget to install the 70 × 2.4 "O" ring

5) Install the left crankcase cover.

9. CRANKSHAFT

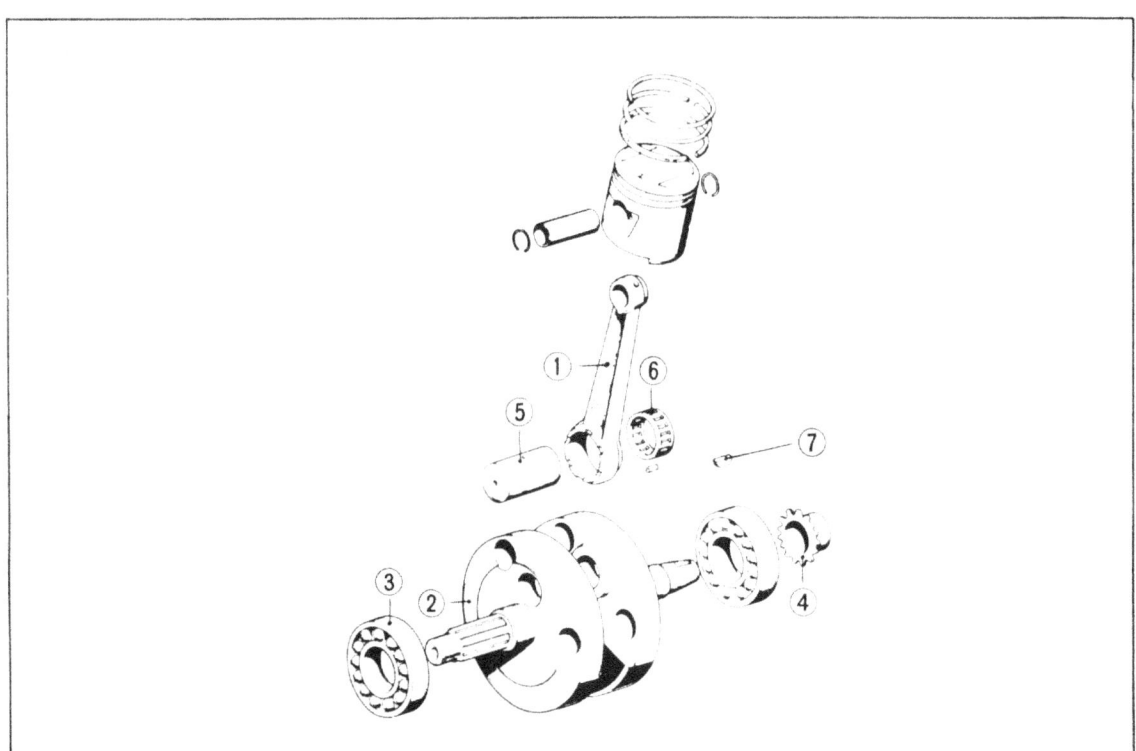

Fig. 81 ① Connecting rod ② Crank shaft ③ 6305 ball bearing ④ Timming sprocket ⑤ Crank pin ⑥ Retainer ⑦ Key

A. Disassembly

1) Remove the cylinder head and cylinder in accordance with section 3.A.
2) Remove the right crankcase cover, oil filter and the oil pump in accordance with section 5.A.
3) Remove the clutch in accordance with section 6.A.
4) Remove the gear shift in accordance with section 7.A.
5) Remove the A.C. generator in accordance with section 8.A.
6) Remove the drive sprocket and unscrew eleven 6 mm crankcase mounting bolts (one screw on the inside is mounted on the right crankcase), tap the crankcase with a wooden hammer and separate the crankcase. (Fig. 82)
7) Support the right crankcase lightly and then gently tap the crankshaft on the right side to loosen and then separate it from the case. (Fig. 83)

B. Inspection

1) Measure the runout of the crankshaft. Support the crankshaft at bearing with V block, and check the amount of runout using a dial gauge. (Fig. 84)

Item	Standard value	Serviceable limit
Crankshaft Right & left side	0.03mm (0.001 in.)	0.1mm (0.004 in.)

Replace if beyond the serviceable limit.

2) Check the clearance of the connecting rod big end. (Fig. 85)

Item	Standard value	Serviceable limit
Side clearance	0~0.01mm (0~0.0004 in.)	0.05mm (0.0020 in.)
Vertical clearance	0.10~0.35mm (0.004~0.014 in.)	0.8mm (0.0032 in.)

Replace if beyond the serviceable limit.

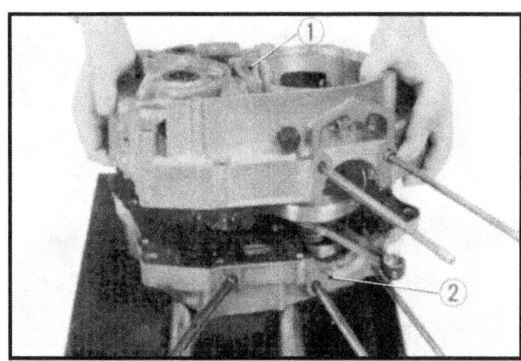

Fig. 82 Crankcase disassembly
1 L. crankcase 2 R. crankcase

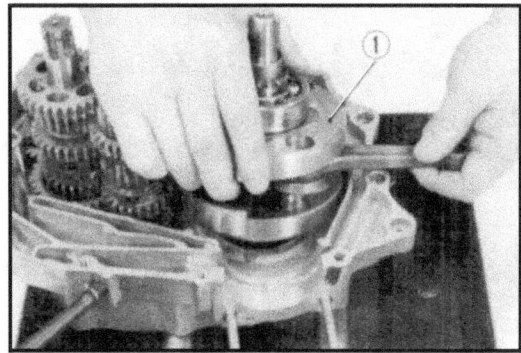

Fig. 83 Crankshaft disassembly
1 Crankshaft

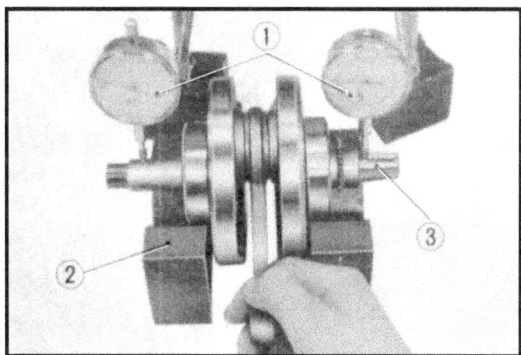

Fig. 84 Crankshaft runout measurement
1 Dial gauge 2 V block

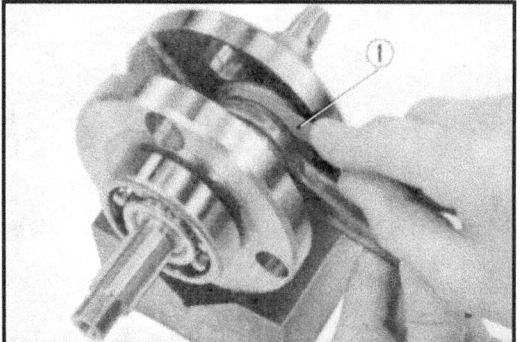

Fig. 85 Connecting rod large end clearance measurement
1 Thickness gauge

Fig. 86 Crankcase tightening
1 Screwdriver

C. Reassembly

1) Assemble the crankshaft into the right crankcase.

Note:

Fit the crankshaft gently into the case. Forcibly handling or hammering may cause damage to ball bearings.

2) Install the left crankcase with the 6 mm attaching screws. (Fig. 86)

Note:

Exercise care not to cause the packing to shift or forget to install the two dowel pins.

10. TRANSMISSION AND PRIMARY KICK STARTER

This series of motorcycles utilize a five speed transmission, but since it incorporates a primary kick, the engine can be started with the gears engaged by disengaging the clutch. The kick gear will directly engage the crankshaft through the primary driven gear which rotates freely on the main shaft.

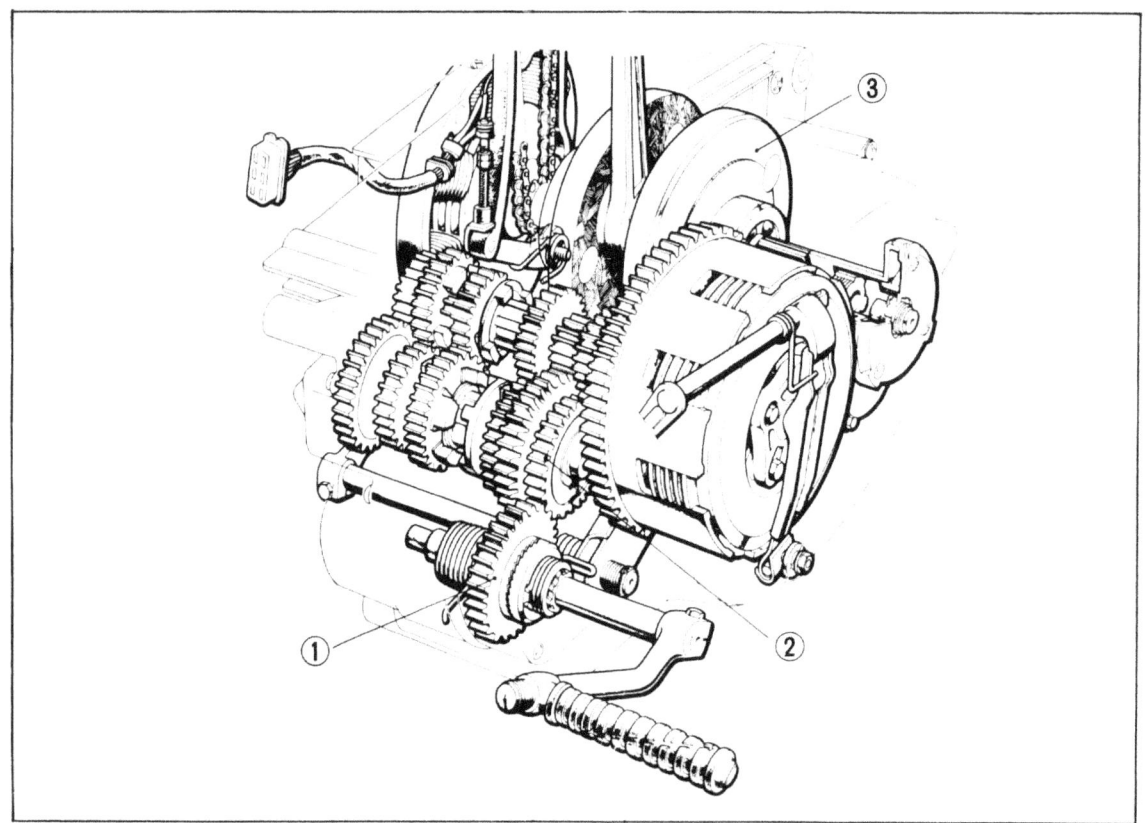

Fig. 87 ① Kick gear ② Primary starter idle gear ③ Crankshaft

A. Disassembly

1) Remove the cylinder head and cylinder in accordance with section 3.A.
2) Remove the right crankcase cover, oil filter and the oil pump in accordance with section 5.A.
3) Remove the clutch in accordance with section 6.A.
4) Remove the gear shift in accordance with 7.A.
5) Remove the A.C. generator in accordance with section 8.A.
6) Separate the case in accordance with section 9.A.
7) Remove the kick starter spindle.
8) Remove the main shaft, counter shaft and shift drum all at the same time.
9) The shift fork can be removed by extracting the shift fork guide shaft.
10) The kick gear can be removed together with the kick spindle and spring by extracting the circlip.

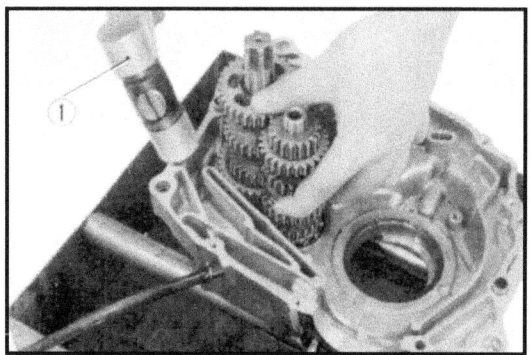

Fig. 88 Transmission gear removal
① Wooden hammer

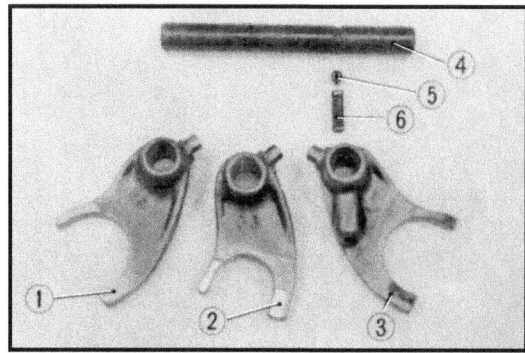

Fig. 89 ① R. shift fork ② Center shift fork ③ L. shift fork
④ Shift fork guide shaft ⑤ 4×10 roller ⑥ Spring

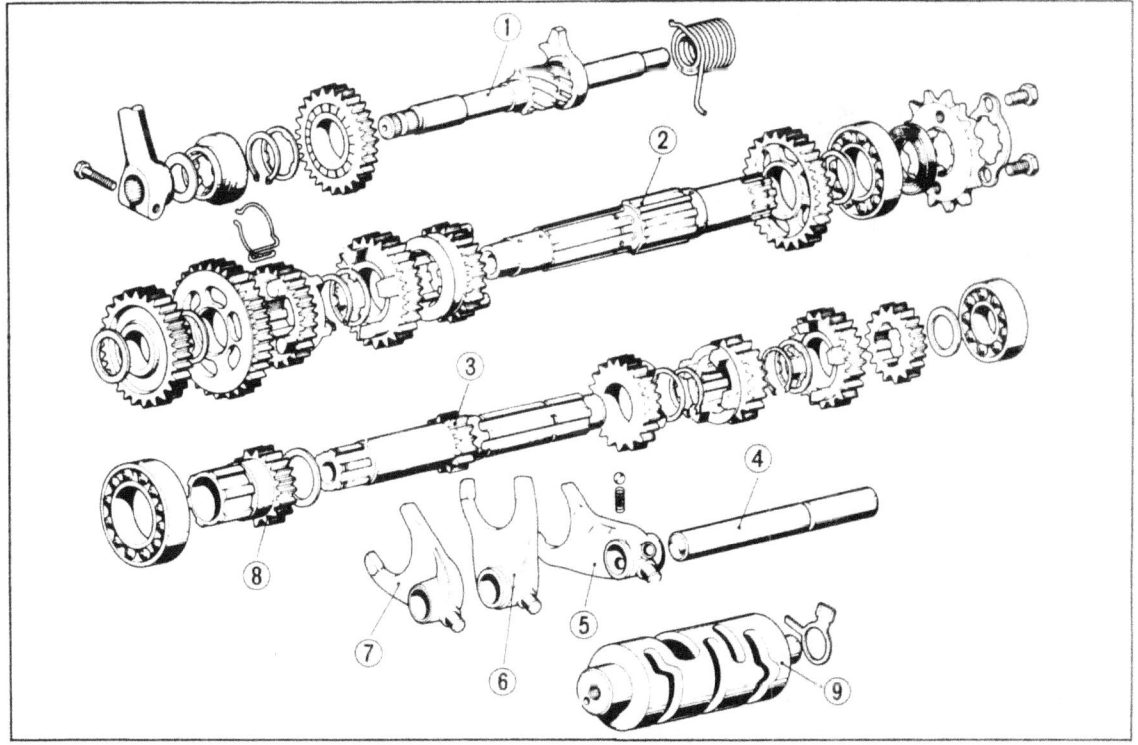

Fig. 90 ① Kick starter spindle ② Counter shaft ③ Main shaft ④ Gear shift fork guide shaft ⑤ L. shift fork ⑥ Center shift fork
⑦ R. shift fork ⑧ Primary starter gear ⑨ Gear shift drum

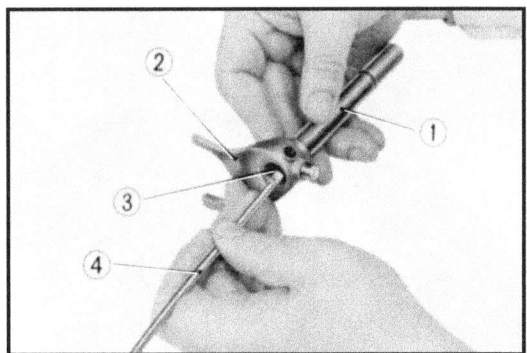

Fig. 91 1 Shift fork guide shaft   2 L. shift fork   3 4×10 roller   4 Screwdriver

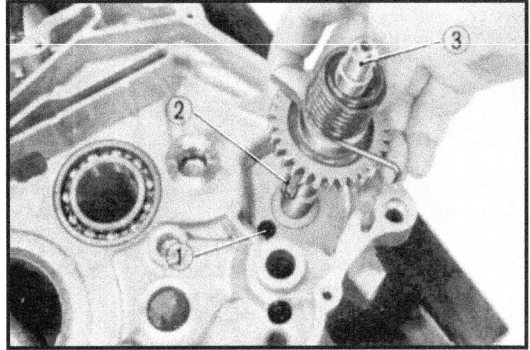

Fig. 92 Kick starter installation
① Hole   ② Spring   ③ Kick starter spindle

Fig. 93 Direction of drum installation
① Gear shift drum   ② Main shaft   ③ Counter shaft

Fig. 94 ① R. shift fork

B. Reassembly

1) Assemble right gear shift fork on the gear shift fork guide shaft. (Fig. 91)

Note:
When installing the spring and 4×10 rollers on the guide shaft, use a thin screwdriver or other pointed tool to make the installation.

2) Assemble the kick starter spindle into the right crankcase. (Fig. 92)

Note:
Insert one end of spring into the hole in the case and then hook the other end on the boss in the case.

3) Subassemble the main shaft and countershaft, and then assemble the subassembly into the case. (Fig.93)

4) Install the gear shift drum

Note:
If neutral switch rotor is positioned in the direction of the cylinder installation, the installation of gear shift fork will be simplified.

5) Assemble the right shift fork into the counter shaft top gear, raise the gear and then assemble guide pin into guide groove on the drum. (Fig. 94)

6) Install the center shift fork in the same manner. (Fig. 95)

Note:
Perform installation from the counter shaft end.

7) Install the left gear shift fork, align the holes in the three shift forks and then insert the shaft in from the top.
8) Install the crankshaft.
9) When installing the left crankcase, make sure that the kick spindle shaft is perpendicular to the hole in the left crankcase. (Fig. 96)

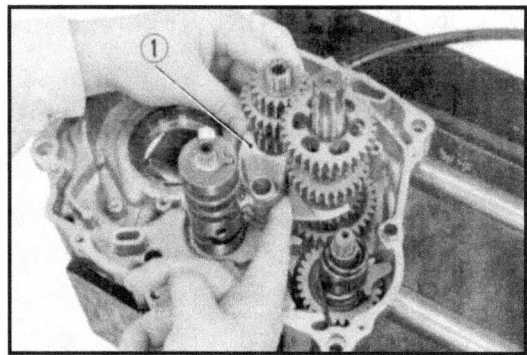
Fig. 95 ① Center shift fork

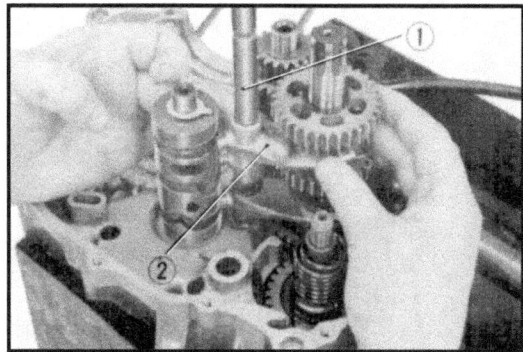
Fig. 96 ① Shift fork guide shaft ② L. shift fork

11. CARBURETOR
Float level adjustment

1) Set the carburetor on its side.
2) Raise the float lightly with the finger tip and locate the position of the float where the float arm and the float valve are either barely touching or provided with a clearance of **0.1 mm (0.003 in.)**
3) In this position, the height of the float above the carburetor body should be **24 mm (0.826 in.)** when measured at the side of the float. If adjustment is necessary, carefully bend the float arm. (Fig. 97)

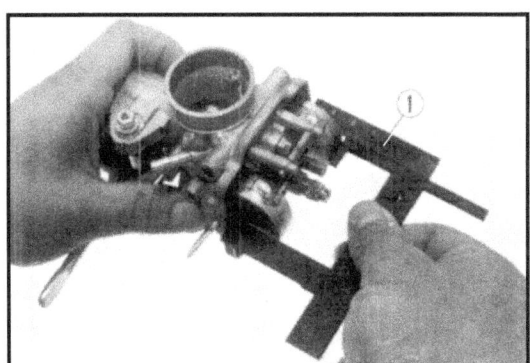
Fig. 97 ① Fuel level gauge

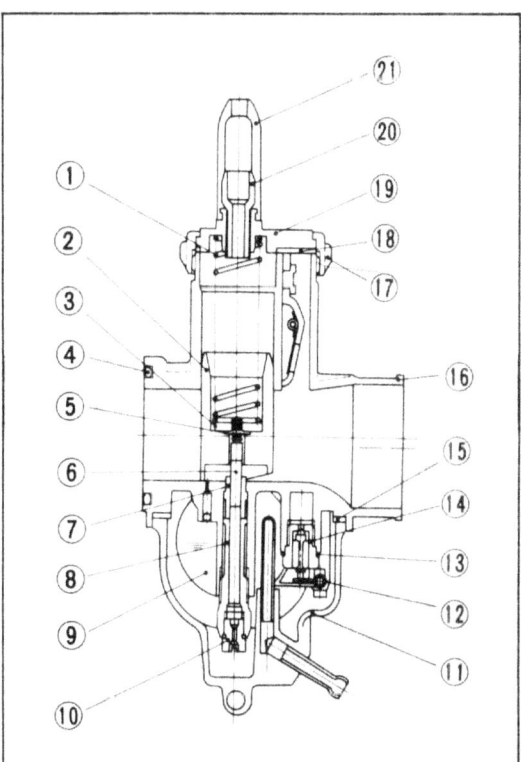
Fig. 98 ① Coil spring ② Throttle valve ③ Needle clip plate ④ O ring ⑤ Bar clip ⑥ Jet needle ⑦ Needle jet ⑧ Needle jet holder ⑨ Float ⑩ Main jet ⑪ Float chamber body ⑫ Arm pin ⑬ Valve seat ⑭ Slow jet ⑮ Float chamber washer ⑯ Body ⑰ Cap ⑱ Top washer ⑲ Top ⑳ Cable adjuster ㉑ Rubber cap

CARBURETOR SETTING TABLE

Item	CB100, CL100, SL100	CB125S, CD125S, SL125S
Main jet	#110	#105
Air jet	#100	
Needle jet	2.6φ×3.8φ length 10	
Needle jet holder	5.0φ	
Jet needle	2°30″×3 step 2.495φ	2°30″×5 step 2.495φ
Air screw	11/2±1/8	
Throttle valve	#2.5 cutaway width 1.2 depth 0.2	#2.5 cutaway width 1.8 depth 0.2

Slow jet	#38 1 0.8φ×2
	      2 0.8φ×2
	      3 0.8φ×2
		#38 0.9φ×2×4

Fuel level	24mm (0.9449 in.)	

IV. CHASSIS

1. FRONT BRAKE AND FRONT WHEEL

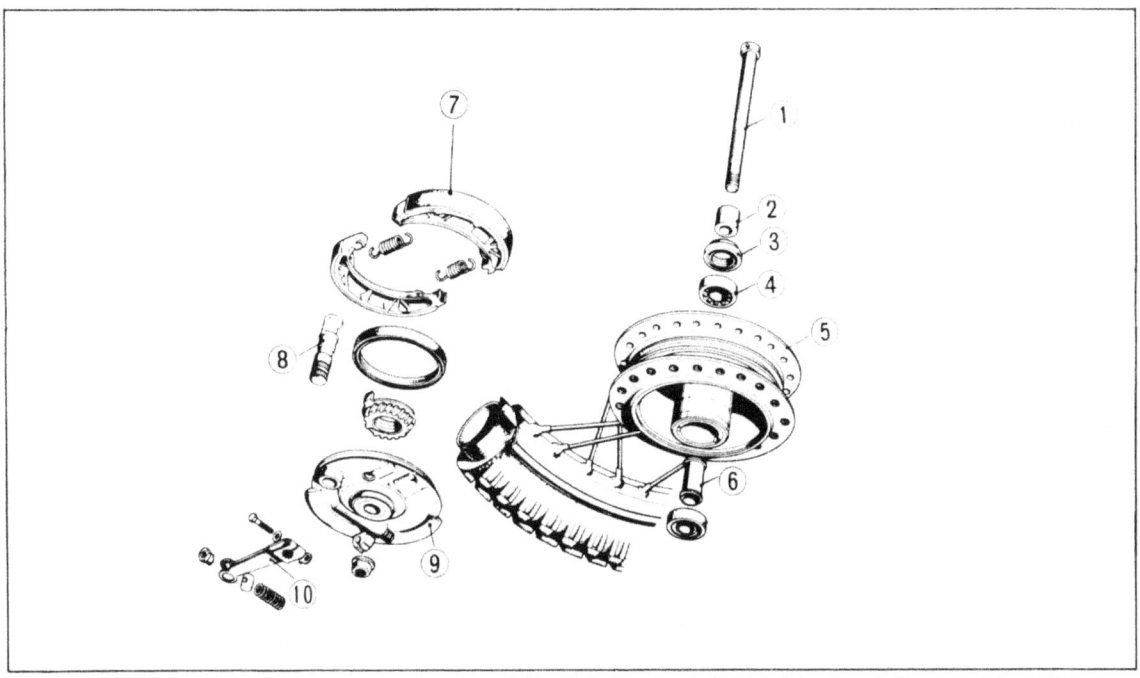

Fig. 99 ① Front wheel axle ② Front wheel side collar ③ 21×37×7 oil seal ④ 6301R ball bearing ⑤ Front wheel hub ⑥ Front axle distance collar ⑦ Brake shoe ⑧ Front brake cam ⑨ Front brake panel ⑩ Front brake arm

A. Disassembly

1) Place an appropriate stand under the engine.
2) Disconnect the front brake cable.
3) Disconnect the speedometer cable.
4) Remove front wheel axle nut, extract the front wheel axle and then drop the wheel (Fig. 100)
5) Remove the brake arm, unhook the two brake shoe springs and then disassemble the brake shoes from the brake panel. (Fig. 101)
6) Remove the oil seal, the two ball bearings (#6301R), and then pull out the front axle distance collar.

Fig. 100 Front wheel removal
① Front wheel axle

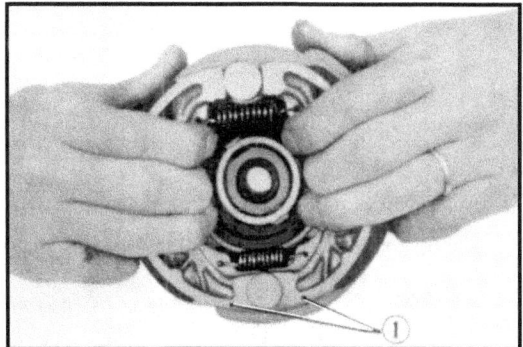

Fig. 101 Brake shoe removal
① Brake shoe

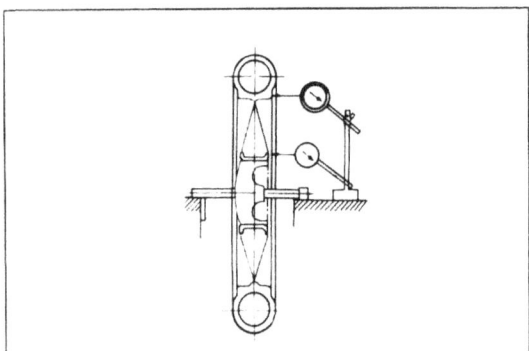

Fig. 102 Rim runout measurement

Fig. 103 Front brake drum measurement

Fig. 104 Spoke retightening

B. Inspection

1) Check for bend in the front axle.
2) Check for worn bearing (#6301R).
3) Check rim runout using a dial gauge. (Fig. 102)

Item	Standard value	Serviceable limit
Side runout	0.5mm Max. (0.020 in.) Max.	3.0mm (0.120 in.)

True the wheel rim by tightening the spokes if beyond the serviceable limit. If damaged or excessively bent, replace with new one.

4) Check wear of brake drum using a caliper. (Fig. 103)

Item	Standard value	Serviceable limit
Inside diameter of drum	109.8~110.2mm (4.3229-4.3385 in.)	112mm (4.4094 in.)

Replace if beyond the serviceable limit.

5) Check wear of brake lining.

Item	Standard value	Serviceable limit
Lining thickness	3.9~4.1mm (0.1535-0.1614 in.)	2mm 0.07874 in.)

Replace if beyond the serviceable limit.

6) Check spokes for damage, bent and loosening. Tighten the loose spokes, straghten the bent spokes and replace the broken spokes with new one. (Fig. 104)
7) Check brake panel for buckling and other damages. If damaged, replace with new one.
8) Check speedometer gears for wear. If worn, replace with new one.
9) Check oil seal for damage, buckling and wear. If worn or damaged, replace with new one.
10) Check both the exterior and interior of tire for damage, and imbedding of stones or nails. If worn or damaged, replace with new one. When replacing the tire, fit a new inner tube together. Measure tire pressure with pressure gauge. Correct tire pressure is **1.8 kg/cm² (26 psi)** for front.
11) Check for air leaks around the valve stem and tube. If leaking, repair or replace with new one.

C. Reassembly

1) Inflate the tube with small amount of air and install the tire on the rim by forcing the bead of the tire on the inside of the rim (Fig. 105)

Note:
- **After the tire has been assembled, inflate with air to about 1/3 the specified pressure and then tap the tire all around with a wooden hammer to relieve pinching of folds in the tube.**
- **After assuring that the valve stem is in alignment with the wheel axle, tighten the stem lock nut, being careful not to cause leak around the stem.**

2) Apply grease to the wheel ball bearings (#6301R) and the inside of the wheel hub. Assemble distance collar and ball bearings into the wheel hub.

Note:
The ball bearings are equipped with a dust seal, therefore, make sure that it is installed in the proper direction.
(Fig. 106)

3) Assemble the brake cam into the front brake panel, hook the brake shoe springs on to the brake shoes and then assemble the brake shoes on the brake panel.

4) Install the brake arm.

5) Assemble the brake panel on the front wheel. Align the recessed section of the panel to the protruding section of the front fork. Assemble the oil seal and side collar on the side of the bearing retainer and then mount it on the front axle with a nut. (Fig. 107)

6) Connect the speedometer cable.

7) Connect the front brake cable to the brake arm and adjust the play in the brake lever. (Fig. 108)

Fig. 105 Tire assembly

Fig. 106   ① #6301R ball bearing

Fig. 107   Front brake wire adjustment
① Recessed section of pannel ② Adjuster nut

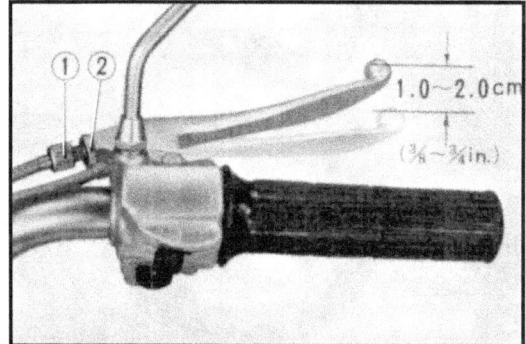
Fig. 108 Brake lever play
① Adjuster nut ② Lock nut

2. REAR BRAKE AND REAR WHEEL

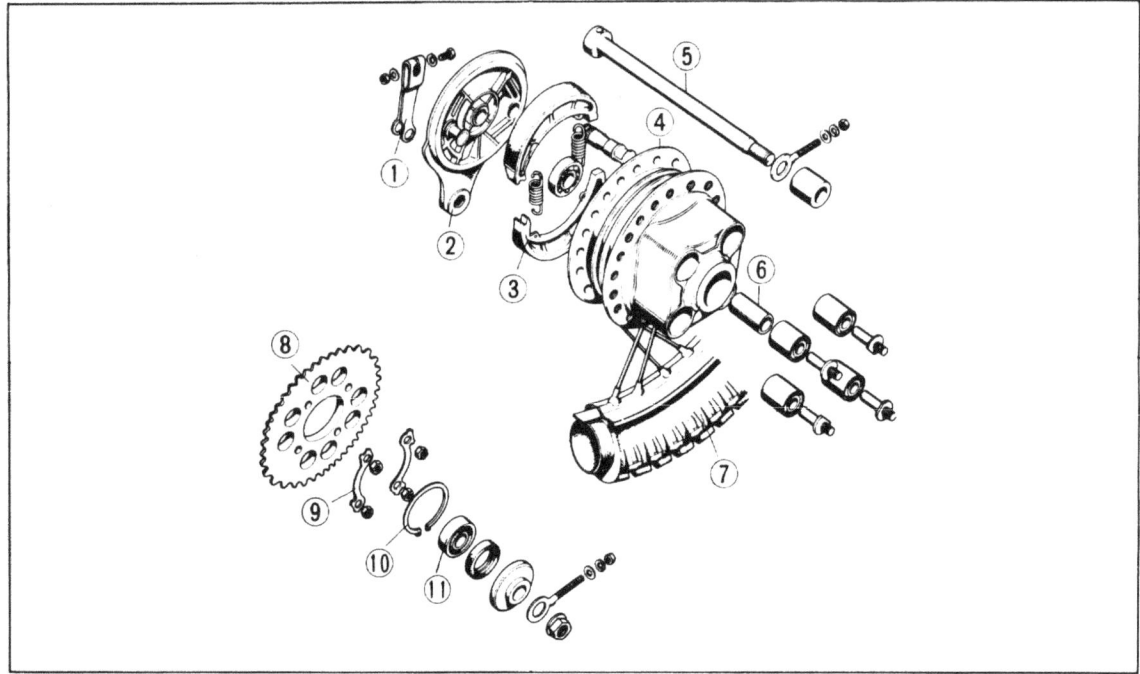

Fig. 109 ① Rear brake arm ② Rear brake pannel ③ Brake shoe ④ Rear wheel hub ⑤ Rear wheel axle ⑥ Rear axle distance collar ⑦ Rear wheel tire ⑧ Final driven sprocket ⑨ 8 mm tongued washer ⑩ 58 mm circlip ⑪ 6302R ball bearing

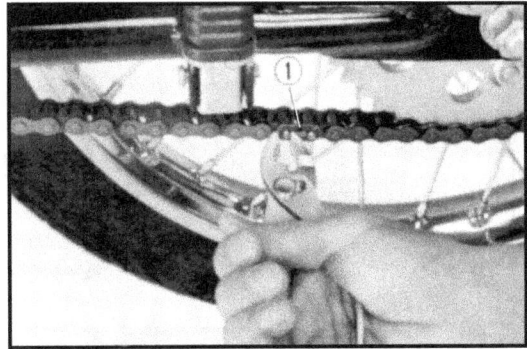

Fig. 110 Drive chain disassembly
① Drive chain link

Fig. 111 Rear wheel removal

A. Disassembly

1) Place an appropriate stand under the engine.
2) Remove the rear brake rod.
3) Unfasten the drive chain link and disconnect the chain.
   (Fig. 110)
4) Remove the rear brake arm bolt and then remove the rear brake arm from the brake panel.
5) Loosen the nut from the rear axle and remove the rear axle.
6) Remove the rear wheel. (Fig. 111)
7) Disassemble the brake panel from the wheel hub.
   Remove the brake arm from the panel, pull out the brake cam, disconnect the spring and then remove the brake shoes.
8) Straighten the tongued washer on the final driven sprocket, loosen the four mounting bolts. unfasten the circlips and then remove the final driven sprocket.

9) Remove the oil seal, ball bearings (see below), and the distance collar from the rear wheel hub.

Ball bearings
CB100, CD100   #6202R and 6302R one
CB125S, CD125S each
SL100, SL125   #6302R two each

B. Inspection

1) Check for bend in the rear axle.
2) Check bearing for wear.
3) Check rim runout using a dial gauge.

Item	Standard value	Serviceable limit
Side runout	0.5mm max. (0.0197 in.) max.	3.0mm (0.1181 in.)

True the wheel rim by tightening the spokes if beyond the serviceable limit. If damaged or excessively bent, replace with new one.

4) Check wear of brake drum using a caliper. (Fig. 112)

Item	Standard value		Serviceable limit
Drum inside diameter	CB100 CL100 CB125S CD125S	109.8~110.2mm (4.3229-4.3385in)	112mm (4.4094in.)
	SL100 SL125	110.0-110.3mm (4.3307-4.3425)	

Replace if beyond the serviceable limit.

5) Check wear of brake lining. (Fig. 113)

Item	Standard value	Serviceable limit
Lining thickness	3.9-4.1mm (0.1535-0.1614 in.)	2mm (0.0787 in.)

Replace if beyond the serviceable limit.

6) Check the spokes for damage, bent and loosening. Tighten the loose spokes, straghten the bent spokes and replace the broken spokes with new one. (Fig. 114)
7) Check the brake panel for buckling and other damages. If damaged, replace with new one.
8) Check the oil seal for damage, buckling and wear. If worn or damaged, replace with new one.
9) Check the tire for damage, and imbedding of stones or nails on both the exterior and interior. If worn or damaged, replace with new one. The tire pressure should be **2.0 kg/cm² (28 psi)**.
10) Check for air leaks around the valve stem and tube. If leaking, repair or replace with new one.

Fig. 112 Rear brake drum measurement

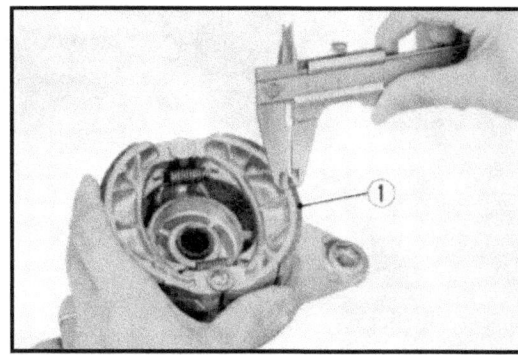
Fig. 113 Brake lining measurement
1 Brake lining

Fig. 114 Spoke retightening

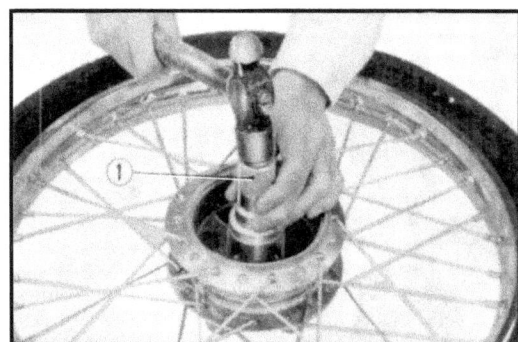
Fig. 115 Ball bearings installation
1 Ball bearing driver

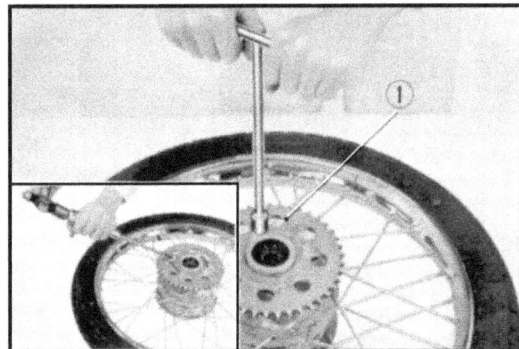

Fig. 116 Final driven sprocket assembly
1 Final driven sprocket

Fig. 117 Brake stopper arm installation
1 Brake stopper arm

Fig. 118 Drive chain adjustment
1 Index mark and side scale 2 Adjuster nut
3 Drive chain link

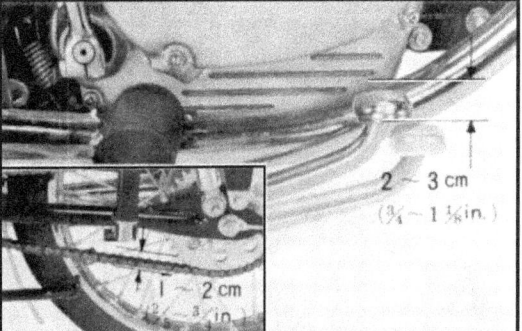

Fig. 119 Chain slack and brake pedal play

C. Reassembly

1) Inflate the tube with a small amount of air and install the tire on the rim by forcing the bead of the tire on the inside of rim.

Note:
- After the tire has been assembled, inflate with air to about 1/3 the specified pressure and then tap tire all around with a wooden hammer to relieve any pinching or folds in the tube.
- After assuring that the valve stem is in alignment with wheel axle, tighten stem lock nut being careful not to cause leaks around the stem.

2) Apply grease to the wheel ball bearings and the inside of the wheel hub.
Assemble distance collar and ball bearings into the wheel hub. (Fig. 115)

3) Mount the final drive sprocket on the rear wheel hub, install the tongued washers, and nuts. After torquing the nuts, bend the tab on tongued washer to lock it. Finally, install the circlip. (Fig. 116)

4) Mount the brake panel assembly on the rear wheel hub.

5) Assemble the right and left side collars on each side of oil seal and then install rear wheel on the rear fork with the axle.

6) Mount the rear brake stopper arm on the rear brake panel. (Fig. 117)

7) Install and connect drive chain, and after completing the adjustment, tighten the rear axle nut. Chain should be adjusted so that there is **1–2 cm (2/5–3/4 in)** slack in the chain (Fig. 119).

Note:
The chain joint link must be installed so that the cutout is pointing in the opposite direction to the direction of rotation. When chain is finally adjusted, the chain adjuster indicator on both right and left sides should be at indentical locations. (Fig. 118)

8) Connect rear brake rod to the brake arm and then make brake adjustments.

Note:
The play in the brake pedal should be 2–3 cm (1/4–1-1/8 in.). (Fig. 119).

3. STEERING UNIT

A. Disassembly

1) Disconnect the front brake cable from brake lever.
2) Disconnect the clutch cable at the handle clutch lever. (Fig. 120)

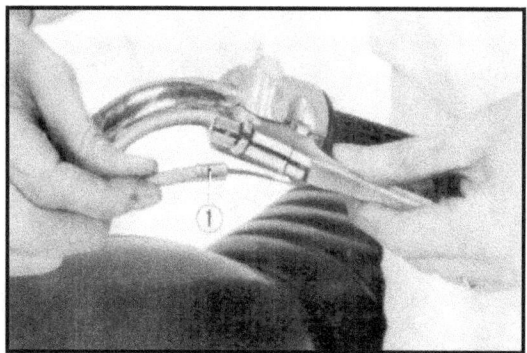

Fig. 120 Clutch cable removal
① Clutch cable

3) **(SL100, SL125 U.S.A. Type)**
   Remove the combination headlight control and emergency switch by unscrewing two mounting screws. (Fig. 121).
4) Disconnect the throttle cable from the throttle grip.

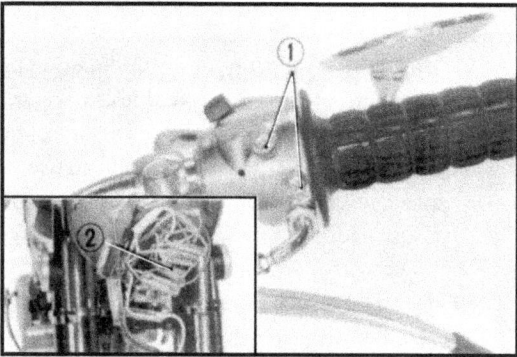

Fig. 121 Emergency switch removal
① Mounting screws ② Wire harness

5) Remove the headlight and disconnect the wire harness in the headlight case. (Fig. 121)
6) Loosen four 6mm bots and remove the handle bar upper holder and handle bar. (Fig. 122)
7) Remove the front wheel in accordance with section 1.A.
8) Remove the headlight case and front fender.
9) **(CB100, CL100, CB125S, CD125S)**
   Remove the fork bolt, loosen the steering stem mounting bolt, and then drop front fork out the bottom.
   (SL100, SL125)
   Remove four fork top and bottom bridge mounting bolts and drop front fork out the bottom.
10) Loosen the steering stem nut and remove the fork top bridge. (Fig. 123)

Fig. 122 Handle bar removal
1 6 mm bolts 2 Handle bar upper holder

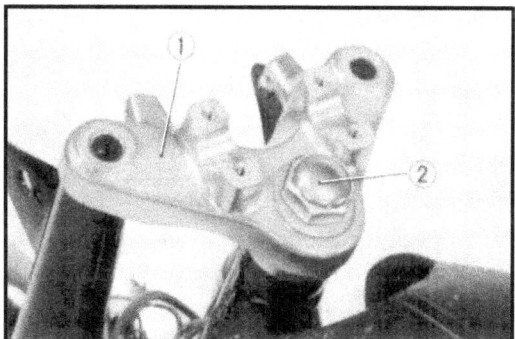

Fig. 123 Fork top bridge removal
1 Fork top bridge 2 Steering stem nut

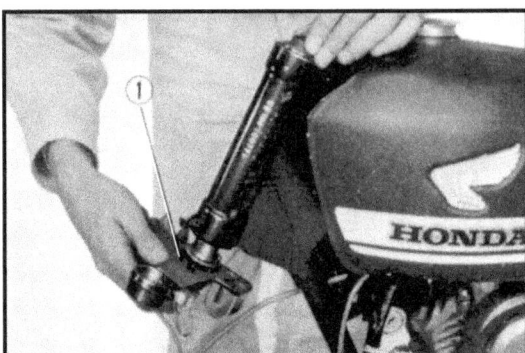

Fig. 124 Steering stem removal
1 Steering stem

B. Inspection

1) Check the condition of both inner cable and casing of the control cables for operation, action and damages. If the cable does not move smoothly, apply grease or replace with new one. If the outer cable is damaged, repair with the plastic tape or replace with new one.
2) Check the operation of the throttle grip. If the throttle grip does not move smoothly, apply grease to the inside of the throttle grip. If worn, replace with new one.
3) Check the condition of the handle bar for bend and twist. If bent or twisted, straighten or replace with new one.
4) Inspect the steel balls for wear and cracks. If worn or damaged, replace with new ones.
5) Inspect the steering top cone, bottom cone, and the other ball races for galling and wear condition. If worn, replace the cones, races and steel ball together.
6) Inspect the steering head dust seal for wear and damage. If worn or damaged, replace with new one.
7) Check the steering stem for bend and twist. If slightly bent or twisted, repair with the press. If badly bent or twisted, replace with new one.
8) Inspect the threads for damage and deformation. If damaged, replace with new one.
9) Check the action of the handle lock return spring. If it does not work properly, replace with new one.

11) Loosen the steering head top nut and then drop steering stem out the bottom. (Fig. 124)
    When removing steering stem, exercise care not to drop and lose the steel balls (21 pcs. each).
12) Remove the two 6mm bolts and separate handle lock from steering stem. Insert engine key into the lock, turn counter clockwise and remove the lock cylinder.

C. Reassembly

1) Mount the handle lock on the steering stem.
2) Apply grease on the ball races and on it set the steel balls. Insert the steering stem into steering head and assemble the top cone race and head top nut.

Note:
- **Wash the cone race, ball race and steel balls, and apply new grease on the friction surfaces. When assembling parts, exercise care not to drop the steel balls.**

- To adjust the headstock top nut, assemble the fork top bridge, front fork, headlight case, front fender and the front wheel in that order; tighten top nut so that the steering handle is neither too tight nor too loose when it is moved fully to the right and left.
3) Install the fork top bridge, front fork and wheel.
4) Reconnect the throttle, clutch and front brake cables.
5) Route the wire harnesses and control cables through their respective positions and then install the steering handle.

Note:
Check to make sure that the harnesses and cables are not binding when the steering handle is moved fully to both sides.
6) Reconnect all wire harnesses.
7) Adjust the play in all the cables. (Fig. 125, 126)

   Throttle cable
     (twist grip to full travel)   90°—100°
     (play)   10°— 15°
   Front brake cable (at end of lever)
     1–2 cm (3/8–3/4 in.).
   Clutch cable (at end of lever)
     1–2 cm (3/8–3/4 in.).

4. FRONT SUSPENSION

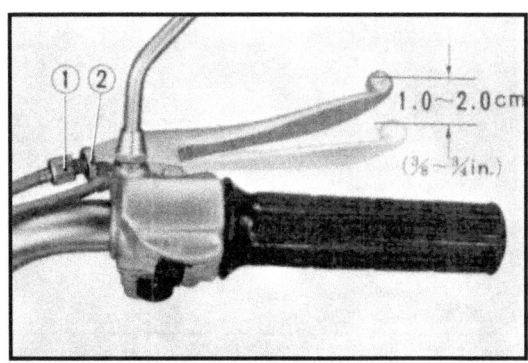
Fig. 125 Brake cable play adjustment
1 Adjuster nut 2 Lock nut

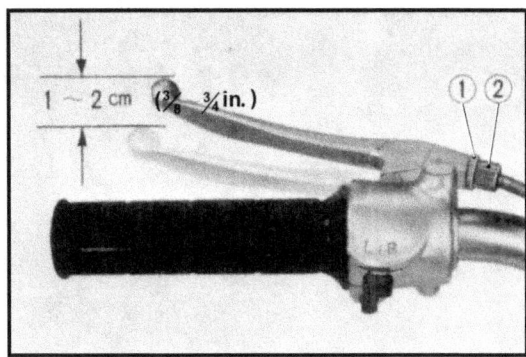
Fig. 126 Clutch cable play adjustment
1 Lock nut 2 Adjuster nut

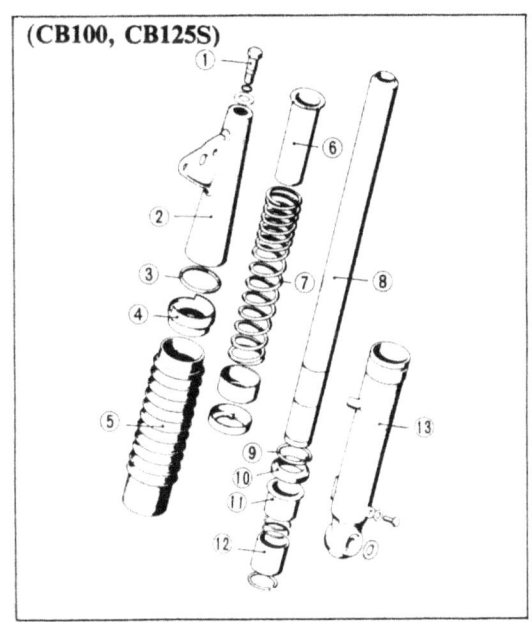
(CB100, CB125S)

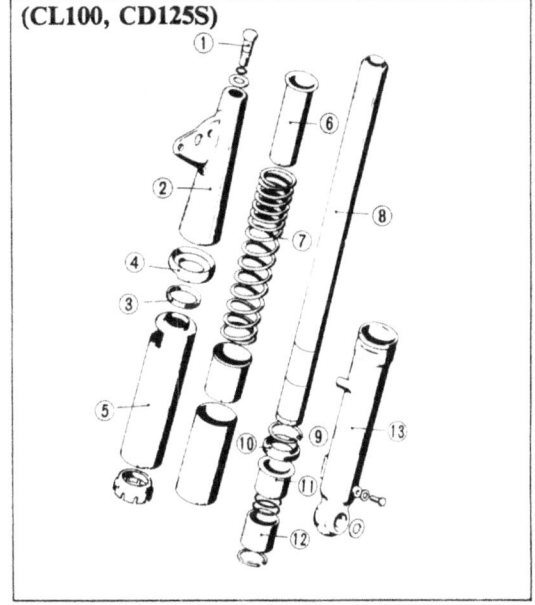
(CL100, CD125S)

Fig. 127 CB100, CL100
1 Front fork bolt 2 Front fork upper cover 3 Fork cover lower seat packing 4 Fork cover lower seat 5 Front fork under cover (CB100), Front fork boot (CL100) 6 Front fork spring guide 7 Front fork spring 8 Front fork pipe 9 37 mm circlip 10 Front fork oil seal 11 Front fork pipe guide 12 Front fork piston 13 Front fork bottom pipe

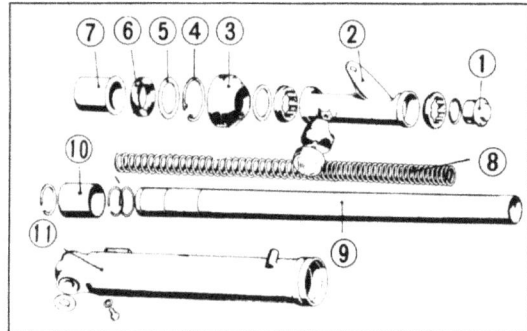

Fig. 128 ① Front fork bolt ② Front fork upper cover
SL100 ③ Front fork dust seal ④ 44 mm circlip ⑤ Back up ring ⑥ 31×43×10 oil seal ⑦ Front fork pipe guide ⑧ Front fork spring ⑨ Front fork pipe ⑩ Front fork piston ⑪ Front fork bottom case

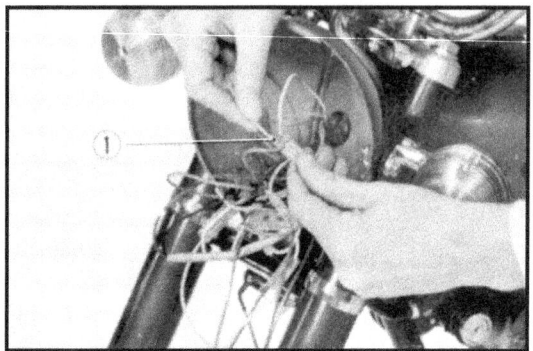

Fig. 129 ① Turn signal connector

Fig. 130 Front fork removal
① Front fork bolt ② Fork mounting bolt

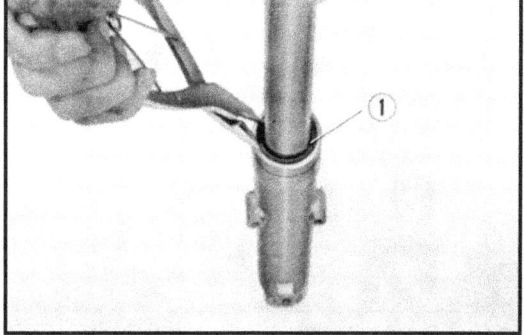

Fig. 131 Circlip removal
① Circlip

A. Construction

It is of a telescopic design with bottom case made of alluminium alloy to reduce unspring weight. The long stroke provides good stability and handling on rough roads.
The damper is filled with SAE 10W-30 oil.

Item	CB100, CL100	SL100	CB125S, CD125S	SL125
Stroke	108.5mm (4.2716 in.)	160mm (6.2992 in.)	114.3mm (4.5000 in.)	142mm (5.5118 in.)

B. Disassembly

1) Remove the front wheel in accordance with section 1.A

2) **(CB100, CL100, CB125S, CD125S)**
Remove the headlight case, disconnect the turn signal connector within the case and remove the turn signal. (Fig. 129)

3) Loosen the headlight case mounting bolts from both sides and remove the case from the fork upper case.

4) **(CB100, CL100, CB125S, CD125S)**
Unscrew four fender mounting bolts and remove the fender from the fork.

5) **(CB100, CL100, CB125S, CD125S)**
Remove the front fork bolt, loosen the steering stem fork mounting bolt and then remove the fork. (Fig. 130)
(SL100, SL125)
Loosen the fork top bridge and steering stem front fork mounting bolt and then remove the fork out the bottom.

6) Loosen oil drain plug from the bottom case and drain oil.

7) **(CB100, CL100, CB125S, CD125S)**
Remove the front fork under cover or front fork boot, circlip (37 mm dia.), and then disassemble the fork bottom case. (Fig. 131)
(SL100, SL125)
Remove the dust seal, circlip (44mm dia.), and then disassemble the fork bottom case.

C. Inspection

1) Front fork spring. (Fig. 132)

Item	Standard value		Serviceable limit
Free length	CB100 CL100	184mm (7.2440 in.)	160mm (6.2992 in.)
	SL100	484.2mm (19.0629 in.)	460mm (18.1102 in.)
	CB125S CD125S	205.5mm (8.0905 in.)	180mm (7.0866 in.)
	SL125	482.3mm (18.9881 in.)	460mm (18.1102 in.)

Replace if beyond the serviceable limit.

2) Wear of front fork piston.

Item	Standard value		Serviceable limit
Outside diameter	CB100 CL100 CB125S CD125S	30.936–30.975mm (1.2174–1.2194 in.)	30.9mm (1.2165 in.)
	SL100 SL125	35.425–35.450mm (1.3946–1.3956 in.)	35.4mm (1.2937 in.)

Replace if beyond the serviceable limit.

3) Check the front fork oil seal for damage. If damaged, replace with new one.
4) Check the front fork pipe and bottom case for bend or crank. If badly damaged, replace with new one.

D. Reassembly

1) Assemble piston stopper and piston on the front fork pipe.
2) Fill front fork bottom case with **SAE 10W-30**.
   CB100, CL100, CB125S, CD125S:
   130–140cc (4.4–4.7 ozs)
   SL100, SL125: 180–190cc (6.1~6.4 ozs)
3) **(CB100, CL100, CB125S, CD125S)**
   Insert the front fork pipe assembly into the bottom case, install the oil seal and circlip, and assemble the front fork spring into the fork pipe so that the end with the large pitch is at the bottom. (Fig. 134)
   (SL100, SL125)
   Place the large pitch end of the front fork spring into the bottom case, insert the front fork pipe and assemble the oil seal and circlip.
4) **(CB100, CL100, CB125S, CD125S)**
   Attach the front fork upper and lower covers or fork boots, and install the front fork as a unit. Tighten the front fork bolt and mounting bolt. Attach the front fender to the front fork. (Fig. 135)

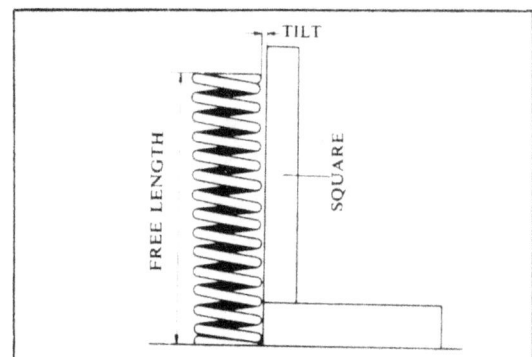

Fig. 132 Spring free length measurement

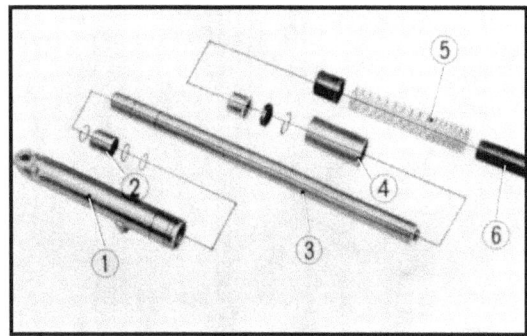

Fig. 133 ① Front fork bottom pipe ② Fork piston
③ Front fork pipe ④ Bottom case cover
⑤ Front fork spring ⑥ Front fork spring guide

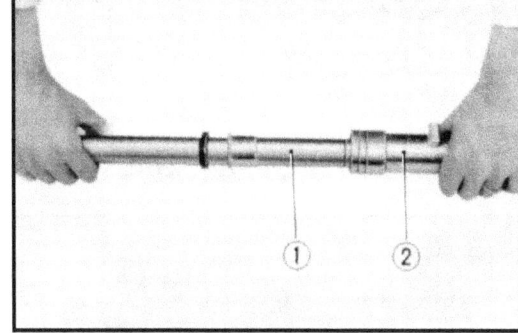

Fig. 134 Front fork assembly
① Front fork pipe ② Front fork bottom pipe

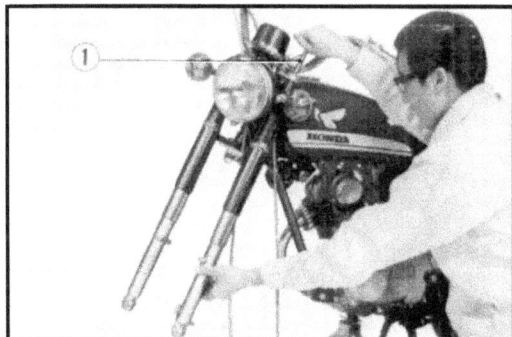

Fig. 135 Front fork installation
① Front fork puller

(SL100, SL125)

Attach the headlight case stay between the fork top bridge and steering stem and install the front fork as a unit.

Tighten the front fork mounting bolts.

5) Install the headlight case.

5. REAR SUSPENSION

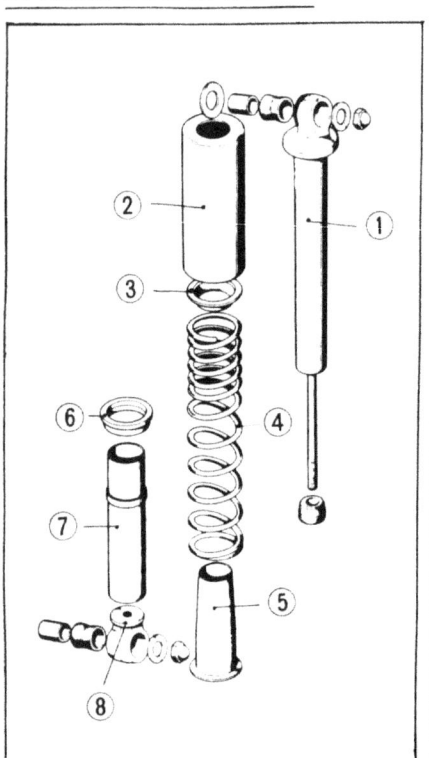
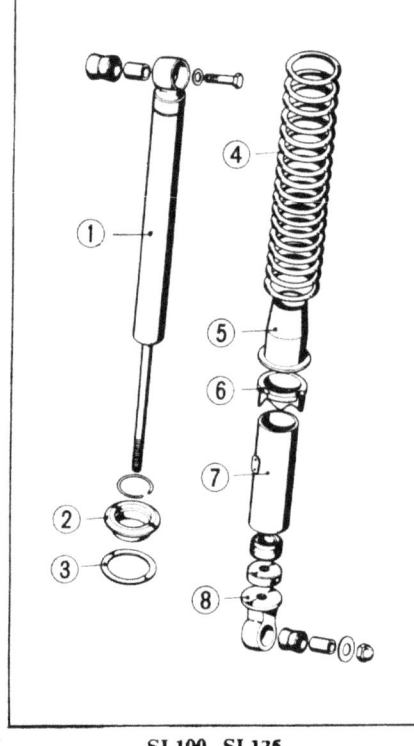

CB100, CL100, CB125S, CD125S
① Rear shock absorber
② Rear shock absorber upper case
③ Rear shock absorber upper seat
④ Rear shock absorber spring
⑤ Rear shock absorber spring guide
⑥ Rear shock absorber spring seat
⑦ Rear shock absorber under seat
⑧ Rear shock absorber bottom metal

SL100, SL125
① Rear shock absorber
② Rear shock absorber spring seat stopper
③ Rear shock absorber spring upper seat
④ Rear shock absorber spring
⑤ Rear shock absorber spring guide
⑥ Rear shock absorber spring adjuster
⑦ Rear shock absorber end case
⑧ Rear shock absorber bottom metal

Fig. 136 CB100, CL100, CB125S, CD125S   SL100, SL125

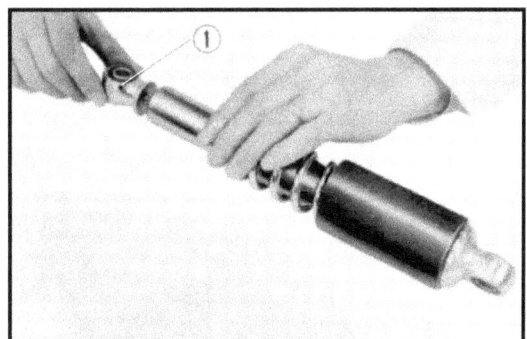

Fig. 137 Rear shock absorber disassembly
① Bottom metal

A. Disassembly

1) Remove the rear wheel in accordance with section 2.A.

2) Unscrew the two rear shock absorber mounting cap nuts and remove the shock absorber from the frame and rear fork.

3) Remove the rear shock absorber bottom metal and then separate the spring and upper case (Fig. 137)

4) Remove the chain case.

5) Loosen the rear fork pivot nut, extract the rear fork pivot bolt and then remove the rear fork.

6) Remove the cotter pin and nut and then remove the rear brake stopper arm from the rear fork.

B. Inspection

1) Rear shock absorber spring.

Item	Standard value	Serviceable limit
Free length	CB100 CL100 CB125S CD125S — 180.9mm (7.1200 in.)	160mm (6.2992 in.)
	CL100 SL125 — 190mm (7.4803 in.)	170mm (6.6929 in.)

Replace if beyond the serviceable limit.

2) Check the shock absorber for oil leaks. If leaks from inside of body, replace the body with new one.
3) Check the main damper body for damage or deformation and damper action. If damaged or shock absorber action is not satisfactory, replace with new one. The shock absorber cannot be disassembled and repaired.
4) Check the shock absorber case and stopper for damage. Replace if damaged.
5) Clearance between the rear fork pivot bushing and bolt.

Item	Standard value	Serviceable limit
Clearance	0.1–0.3mm (0.0031 0.0118 in.)	0.5mm (0.0196 in.)

Replace if beyond the serviceable limit.

6) Check the pivot shaft for bends or damage. Straighten the bent shaft and check with the dial gauge. If damaged, replace with new one.
7) Check the rear fork swing arm for bend, twist and crack. If slightly bent or twisted, straighten with press and check the swinging arm with the dial gauge. If damaged, replace with new one.

C. Reassembly

1) Install the rear brake arm stopper on the rear fork.
2) Insert the grease coated pivot bushing into the rear fork and install into the frame with the rear fork pivot bolt. (Fig. 139)
3) Install the chain case on the rear fork, join the rear shock absorber complete to the frame and fork, install and tighten cap nuts.
4) Install the rear wheel.

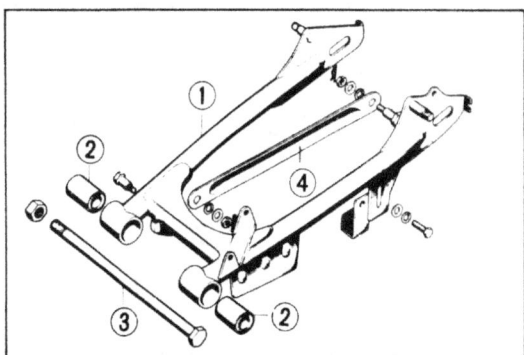

Fig. 138 ① Rear fork ② Rear fork pivot rubber bush ③ Rear fork pivot bolt ④ Rear brake stopper arm

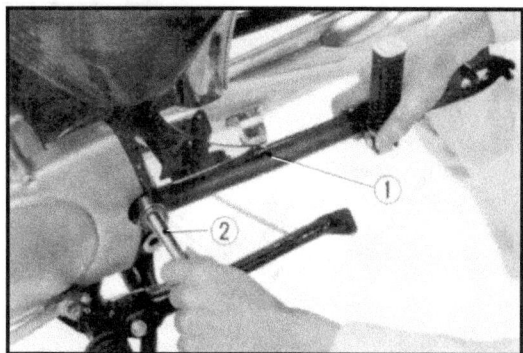

Fig. 139 Rear fork assembly
① Rear fork ② Rear fork pivot bolt

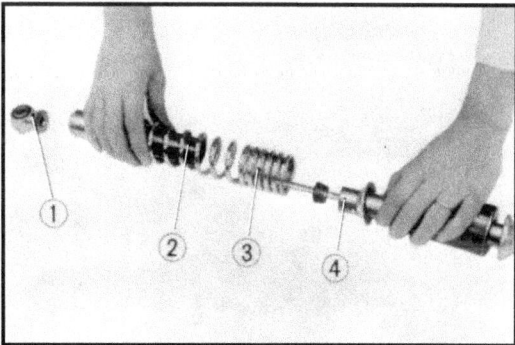

Fig. 140 Rear shock absorber assembly
① Bottom metal ② Spring guide
③ Shock absorber spring ④ Shock absorber body

Note:
- When assembling the rear shock absorber complete, the large pitch end of spring goes toward the top. (Fig. 140)
- After completing installation, adjust the tension of drive chain and the rear brake.

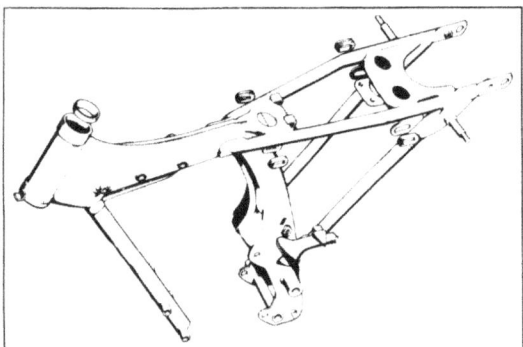

Fig. 141 CB100, CL100, CB125S, CD125S Diamond frame

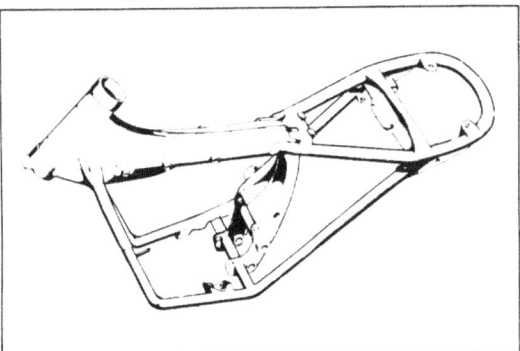

Fig. 142 SL100, SL125 Double cradle frame

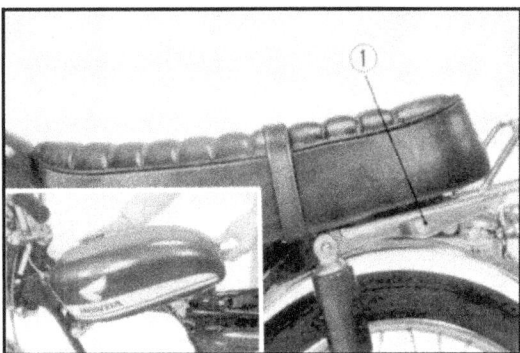

Fig. 143 Seat and fuel tank removal
1 Sub-carrier mounting bolt

Fig. 144 Air cleaner and tool box removal

6. FRAME BODY

A. Construction

Half frame, half pillar, is made of high strength press steel sheet. The CB100, CL100, CB125S and CD125S are designed with the aim for light weight. It utilizes a diamond frame. The SL100 and SL125 are designed with a sporty double cradle frame.

B. Disassembly

1) Remove the engine in accordance with section engine removal and installation.
2) Remove the steering handle in accordance with section 3.A.
3) **(CB100, CL100, CB125S, CD125S)**
   Detach the sub-carrier and then remove the seat. (Fig. 143)
   (SL100, SL125)
   Loosen the seat mounting nuts and remove the seat.
4) Position the fuel cock lever to STOP position, disconnect the fuel tube from carburetor, and then remove the fuel tank by pulling toward the rear and slightly upward. Remove the strainer cup, take out the strainer screen and packing and remove the mounting screws to detach it from the fuel tank. (Fig. 143)
5) Disassemble the air cleaner and tool box. (Fig. 144)

6) Remove the front wheel and front suspension in accordance with section 1.A and 4.B.
7) Remove the rear wheel and rear cushion in accordance with section 2.A and 5.A and then remove the rear fender.
8) Disassemble the electrical system.
9) **(CB100, CL100, CB125S, CD125S)**
Extract the cotter pin in the main stand pivot pipe, pull out the pivot pipe and remove the stand from the frame. (Fig. 145)

C. Inspection

1) Inspect the welded joints for cracks, damage or twist to the pipe. Straighten the minor dent or twisting, weld the cracks and paint the worn or scratched parts. Replace twisted or badly dented frame with new one.
2) Inspect the top and bottom races for damage and wear.

Note:
The ball race can be driven out easily by using a wooden drift from the inside. Exercise care when installing the race so that it is driven in straight and to the full depth. (Fig. 146)

3) Check the angle of head pipe and lock for any damage. If damaged, replace with new one.
4) Check damage to the seat leather upholstery. If damaged, repair or replace with new one.
5) Check for fuel tank leak, clogged fuel filler cap vent, damage or deformed cock valve packing, strainer cup packing and aging or damage to the fuel tube. Flush out interior of the tank with clean gasoline.
6) Clean the air cleaner element by blowing off dust with compressed air or wash in soap water. (Fig. 147)
7) Replace any exhaust pipe gasket which is damaged.
   Check the muffler for cracks and deformation. If badly damaged, replace with new one. Remove the carbon from the diffuser pipe and clean.
8) Check the stand spring for deformation and damage. If the part has lost tension or damaged, replace with new one.

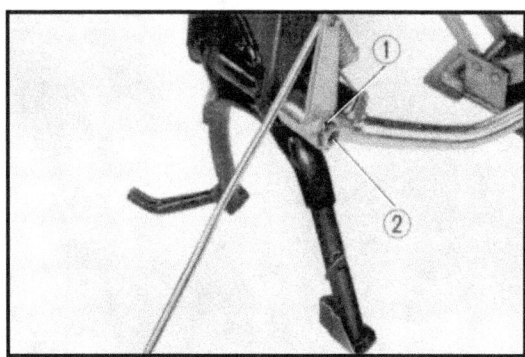

Fig. 145 Stand removal
① Cotter pin ② Main stand pivot pipe

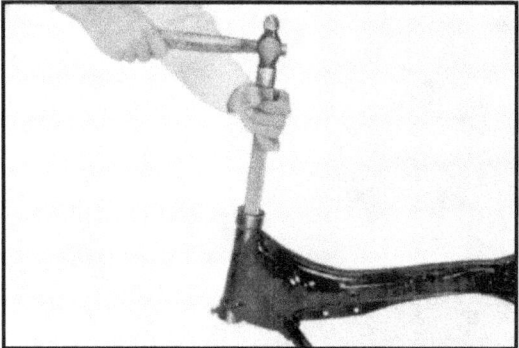

Fig. 146 Ball race removal

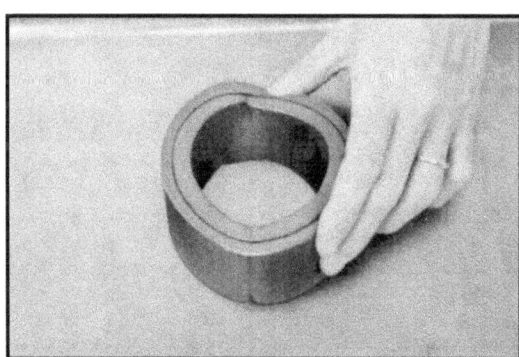

Fig. 147 Air cleaner element cleaning

D. Reassembly

1) **(CB100, CL100, CB125S, CD125S)**
   Mount the main stand and brake pedal to the frame together
   (SL100, SL125)
   Mount the brake pedal on the main stand pivot pipe.
2) Mount the rear fender on the frame and install the electrical equipment.
3) Install the rear fork, rear shock absorber, and rear wheel.
4) Install the steering stem, front fork and the front wheel.
5) **(CB100, CL100, CB125S, CD125S)**
   Install the fuel tank, seat and sub-carrier on the frame.
   (SL100, SL125)
   Install the fuel tank and seat on the frame.
6) Mount the engine on the frame.
7) Route the respective control cables, and wire harnesses through the specified positions and complete the connections.

Note:

Adjust the brakes, clutch and drive chain slack and check the steering operation.

V. ELECTRICAL

1. GENERATING SYSTEM

The charging system is an A.C. generator (magnetic single phase A.C. generator) which consists of the stator and rotor. The A.C. generator is rectified by the selenium rectifier and is used to charge the battery.

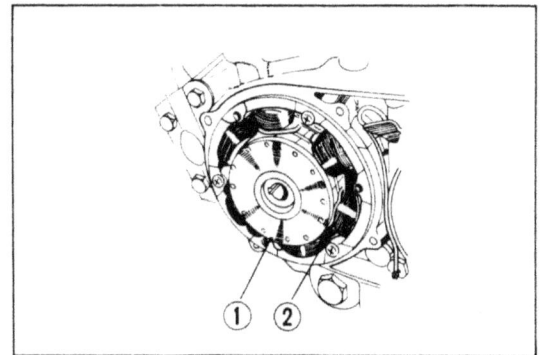

Fig. 148 ① Rotor ② Stator

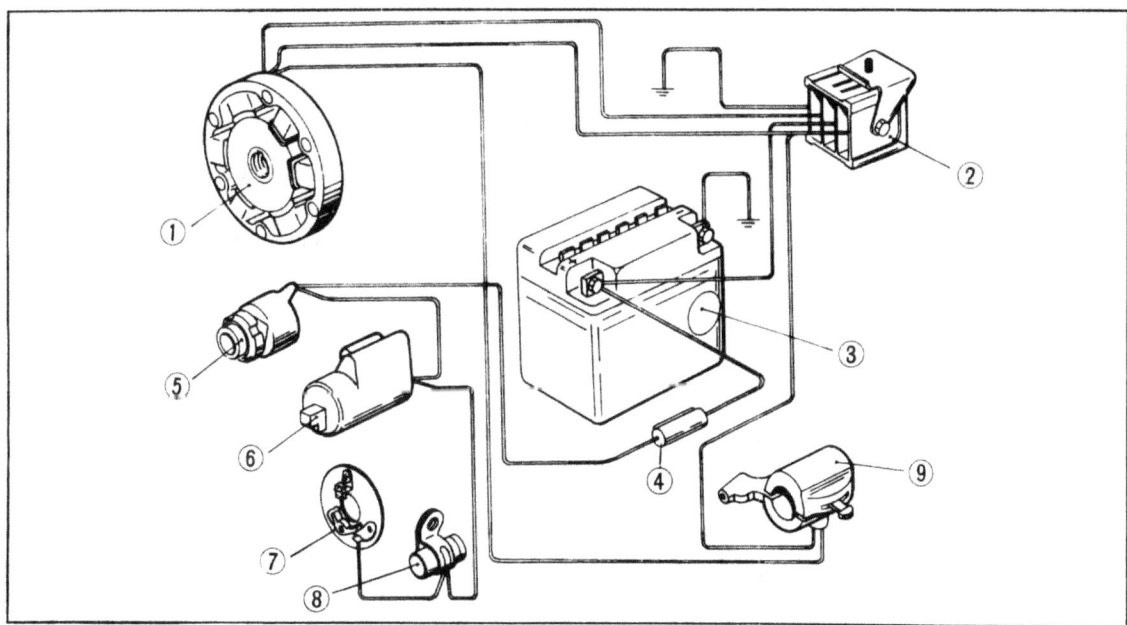

Fig. 149 ① A.C. generator ② Selenium rectifier ③ Battery ④ Fuse ⑤ Combination switch ⑥ Ignition coil ⑦ Braker points ⑧ Condenser ⑨ Lighting switch

A.G. GENERATING SPECIFICATIONS

Type & manufacturer	Rotary type. Kokusan Denki or Nippon Denki
Output	6V 50W (at 5,000 rpm in night)
Battery voltage	6V-6A
Changing rpm	500-12,000 rpm
Polarity of ground	⊖
weight	1.45kg (3.20 lbs)

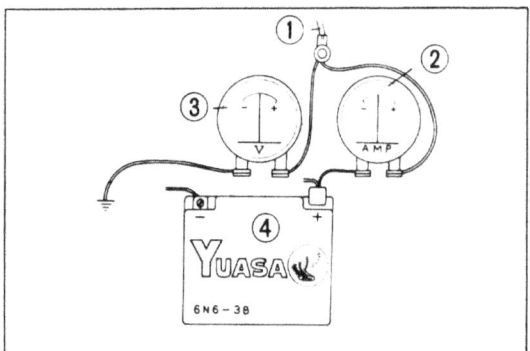

Fig. 150 Charging test
① Red/white wire harness ② Ammeter
③ Voltmeter ④ Battery

2. CHARGING SYSTEM
A. Charging test
1) Use the ammeter-and-voltmeter.
2) Measure the specific gravity of the electrolyte in battery. If it is below 1.26 (corrected to 20°C.), recharge the battery. Its normal value is 1.28 (corrected to 20°C) Perform the following test.
3) Disconnect the red/white wire harness terminal from the ⊕ terminal of the battery and connect it to the ⊖ terminal of the ammeter. Connect the ⊕ terminal of battery to the ⊖ terminal of ammeter. Connect the red/white wire harness to the ⊕ terminal of the voltmeter and ground the ⊖ terminal of the voltmeter to earth.
4) Start the engine and perform the following two tests in both the day and night operation mode. (Fig. 150)
5) Measure the battery voltage and charging current. If they are less than values shown in the following table, check or replace the stator, selenium rectifier, ignition coil and condenser with new one.

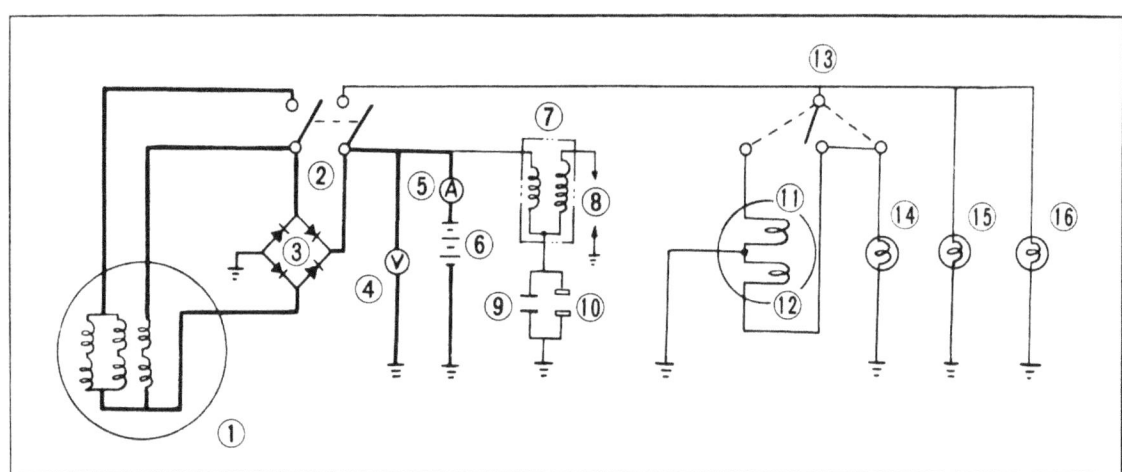

Fig. 151 ① A.C. generator ② Lighting swith ③ Selenium rectifeier ④ Voltage meter ⑤ Ammeter ⑥ Battery 6V—6AH ⑦ Ignition coil ⑧ Spark plag ⑨ Condenser ⑩ Contact breaker ⑪ Headlight high beam ⑫ Headlight low beam ⑬ Dimmer switch ⑭ Highbeam pilot light ⑮ Tail/stop light ⑯ Meter light

			Initial charging r.p.m.		5000 r.p.m.	
	Lighting switch	Dimmer switch	r.p.m.	Battery Voltage	Charging current	Battery Voltage
100cc Series	Day	OFF	OFF	1000 r.p.m.	6.8 V	1.3 A	7.8 V
	Night	ON	HB (high beam)	3500 r.p.m.	6.8 V	1.3 A	7.8 V
		ON	LB (low beam)	2200 r.p.m.	6.8 V	1.3 A	7.2 V
125cc Series	Dry	OFF	OFF	1000 r.p.m.	6.8 V	1.7 A	7.9 V
	Night	ON	LB (low beam)	2000 r.p.m.	6.8 V	1.3 A	7.8 V

B. Inspection

1) Stator coil test

   Perform a continuity test on the three stator coil harnesses (orange, white, yellow) with a tester to determine the condition of the coil and also inspect for exterior damage. Replace with new one if there is no continuty or it is damaged. (Fig. 152)

Note:

Do not test on a metal bench.

2) Selenium rectifier test

   Check the continuity in the normal direction and also in the reverse direction by applying tester lead probes to green and pink leads, pink and red/white leads, green and yellow leads, and yellow and red/white leads respectively and alternately as shown in the figure. The rectifier is in good condition if continuity exists only in one direction. If there is continuity in both directions or no continuity in either direction when tested, the rectifier is defective and should be changed. (Fig. 153-154)

Fig. 152 Stator coil test
1 Stator coil

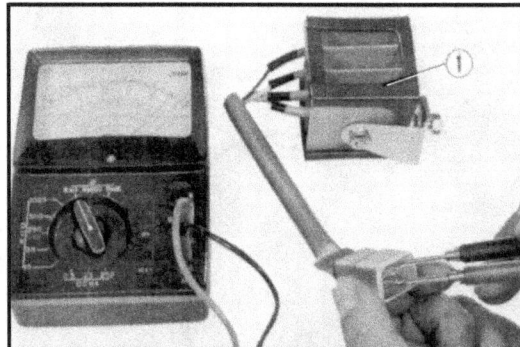

Fig. 153 Selenium rectifier continuity test
① Selenium rectifier

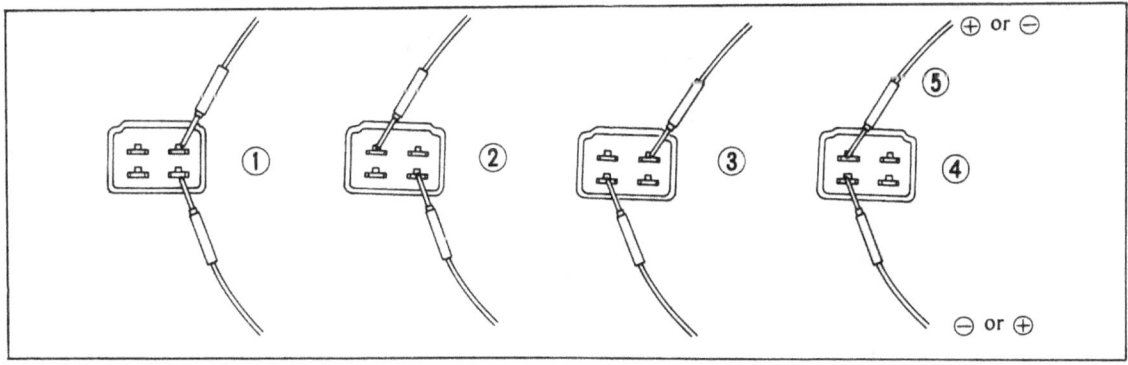

Fig. 154 ① Green and pink leads ② Pink and red/white leads ③ Green and yellow leads ④ Red/white and yellow leads
⑤ Tester leads

3. IGNITION SYSTEM

1) Ignition coil test

   ① Perform functional test of the ignition coil to determine its condition. When poor starting is experienced, the cause may also be found by testing the spark plug, contact breaker points, condenser, etc.

   ② Check the ignition coil using the service tester.

   ③ Connect the battery power source to the tester and ground the grounding lead. (Fig. 156)

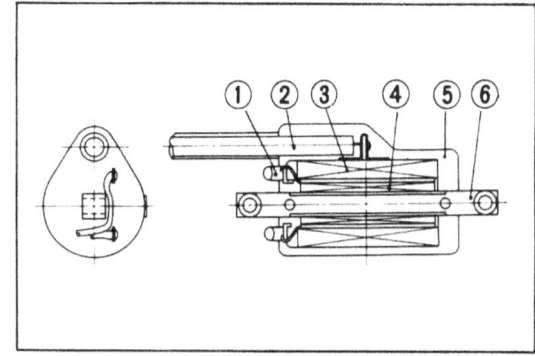

Fig. 155 ① Secondary coil terminal ② Ignition cord ③ Secondary coil ④ Primary coil ⑤ Body ⑥ Core

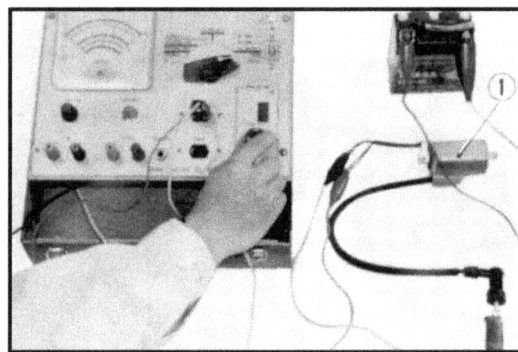

Fig. 156 Ignition coil test
① Ignition coil

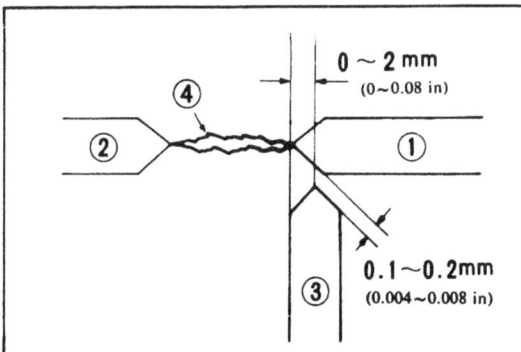

Fig. 157 ① No.1 electrode ② No.2 electrode
③ No.3 electrode ④ Spark

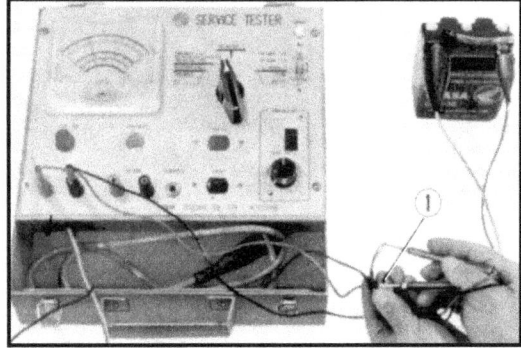

Fig. 158 Condenser test
① Condenser

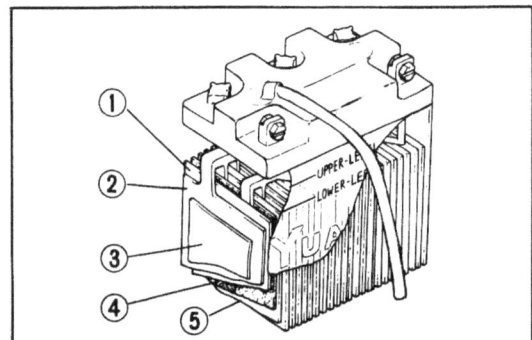

Fig. 159 Battery construction
① Separator plate ② Cathode plate ③ Separator plate ④ Glass mat ⑤ Anode plate

4) Connect the ignition primary cord to the tester and connect the opposite terminal end to the primary terminal of the coil. Connect the white lead with (√) type plug to the blue terminal of the ignition coil (primary side) and the red tester lead to the black terminal of the ignition coil. (Fig. 156)

⑤ Connect the red tester high tension cord to the high tension cord of the ignition coil.

⑥ Turn the slector knob to the COIL TEST position.

⑦ Adjust the three point spark tester to maintain maximum distance of spark by turning the control knob while observing the spark condition and then measure the spark distance.

⑧ If the spark plug distance is less than **6 mm (0.24 in.)**, the spark plug is unserviceable.

2) Condenser test (Fig. 158)
   1) Connect the 6V battery power source to the tester.
   2) Turn the selector knob to the "CONDENSER" position.
   3) Apply one of the tester lead probes to the condenser body, and then read the meter indication. If it measures between **0.21–0.26 μF**, the condenser is satisfactory. Condenser indicating less than 0.21 μF should be replaced.

4. BATTERY

A. Construction

The construction and name of the component parts are shown in the figure. The type of battery having the specifications shown below is installed in these models. (Fig. 159)

Type	6N6–3B
Voltage	6V
Capacity	6AH (at 10 hr rate)
Changing current	0.6A
Specific gravity of electrolyte (when fully charged)	1.260–1.280 at 20°C (68°F)

B. Inspection and Servicing

1) Measure the specific gravity of the battery electrolyte with a hydrometer and if it is below 1.200 (corrected to 20°C), the battery should be recharged. The specific gravity is calibrated on the stem of the float and the reading is taken at the fluid level with the float buoyant. (Fig. 160)

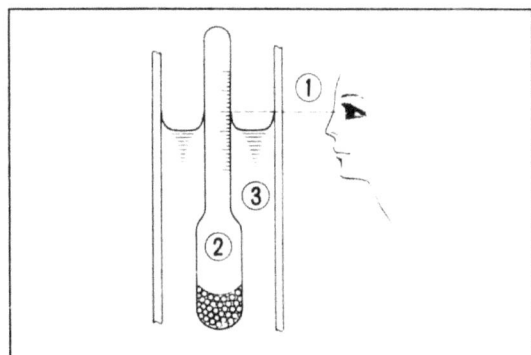

Fig. 160 ① Eye level ② Hydrometer ③ Battery electrolyte

2) If any cell is found to be below the lower level mark on the battery case, add distilled water to bring the level up to the upper level mark. If the electrolyte evaporation rate is unusually great, the charging system should be checked for possible malfunction. If the battery case is cracked or damaged, replace with new one.

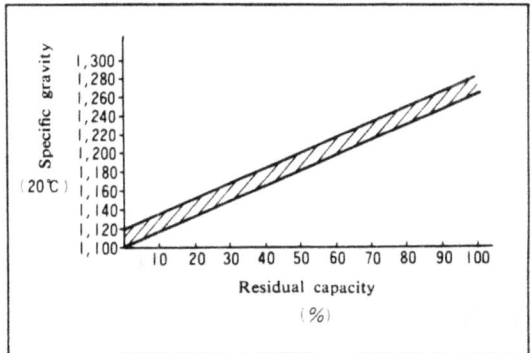

Fig. 161 Relation between specific gravity of battery electrolyte and electrical capacity

3) Check the poor battery connection due to corrosion of the connector and terminal, flaking of the paste from vibration and sulfation. The flaked paste remains on bottom and will eventually short circuit the battery, if so, replace with new one. (Fig. 162)

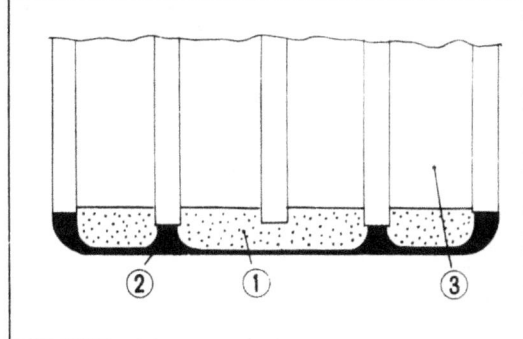

Fig. 162 ① Flaked paste ② Bottom ③ Cathode plate

C. Battery Charging

1) Quick-charge method of charging the battery will seriously effect the battery service life, therefore, it is recommended that this method not be used. When the rapid charge is required, the battery should be recharged at a rate of **0.2 AH**.
2) During the charging process, hydrogen gas will be generated, therefore, open flame should be kept away.
3) After the recharging is completed, the battery should be washed with water to remove spilled electrolyte and the terminals coated with grease.

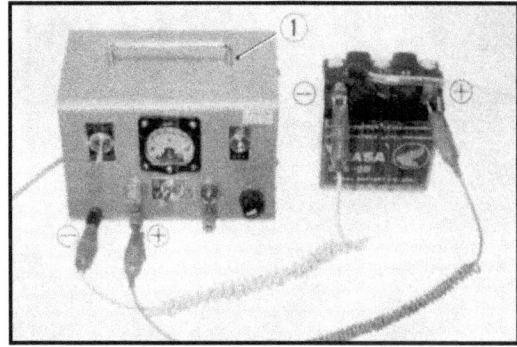

Fig. 163 Battery charging
① Battery charger

	Normal charge	Rapid charge
Charging current rate	0.6AH	2.0AH max.
Checking for full charge	(1) Specific gravity: 1.260–1.280 (20°C: 68°F) maintained constant (2) 0.2AH→0.6AH (3) 7.5V→8.3V	(1) Specific gravity: 1.260–1.280 maintained at 20°C (68°F) (2) Voltage: When large volume of gas is emitted from the battery (in about 2–3 hours for fully discharged battery), reduce charging rate to 0.2A. Battery is fully charged when a voltage of 7.5V is maintained.
Charging duration	By this method, a battery with specific gravity of electrolyte below 1.220 at 20°C (68°F) will be fully charged in approximately 12–13 hours.	By this method, battery with specific gravity of electrolyte below 1.220 at 20°C (68°F) will be fully charged approximately 1–2 hours.
Remarks		When the charging is urgent, quick charging method may be used, however, the recommended charging current rate should be under 2.0A.

Note: Battery should not be charged near open flame.
Terminals should be cleaned with clean water. Apply grease.

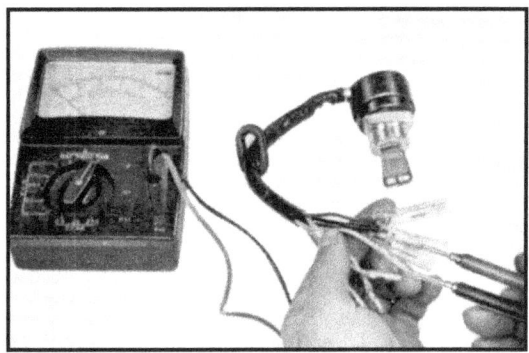

Fig. 164 Combination switch continuty test

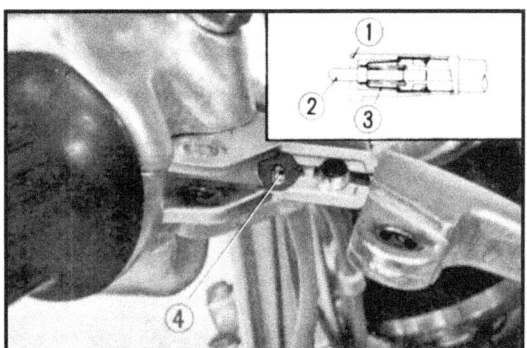

Fig. 165 １ Switch case ２ Shaft ３ Contact plate
４ Front stop switch

5. AUXILIARY ELECTRICAL EQUIPMENT

A. Inspection

1) Combination switch (Fig. 164)

If continuty exists in any other leads than those shown below, first make sure the wiring harness is connected correctly. If the wiring is correct, the switch is defective. Check by the testing conductivity of wires with the switch in each positions. Replace with new one if the conductivity is not correct.

CB100, CL100, CB125S, CD125S, SL100, SL125

	BAT	IG$_1$	IG$_2$	HO	SW	WL$_1$	WL$_2$	BAT	IG
OFF					O—O—O				
ON	O—O—O			O—O				O—O	

2) Front stoplight switch (Fig. 165)

Check the front stop light switch for continuity by applying the tester lead probe to the black and green/yellow-green switch lead and depress the brake lever. If there is no continuity, the switch is defective.

Also check the action of switch manually.

Note:
- Check brake lever for excess play.
- Light should only operate by the brake lever.

3) Rear stop switch

Check the rear stop switch spring for disengagement. Apply tester lead probes to the green/yellow and black lead to check continuity.

The light should come on when the brake pedal is depressed 2cm (0.78 in.).

Turning the adjuster nut clockwise will delay the switch engagment. (Fig. 166)

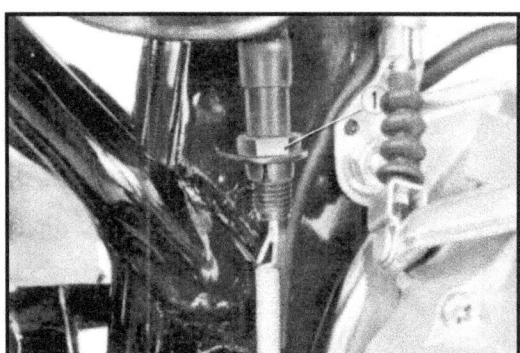

Fig. 166 Rear stop switch
1 Adjuster nut

4) Horn

Connect a 6V battery to the horn to test its operation.

The sound volume can be adjusted with the adjusting screw provided on the back of the horn. (Fig. 167)

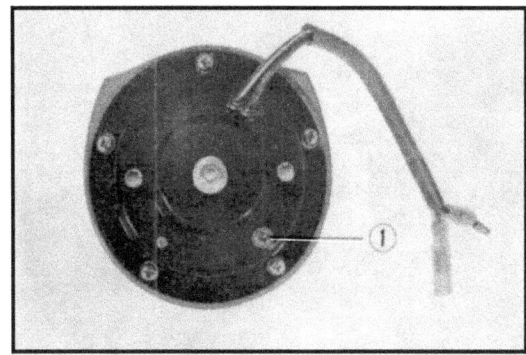

Fig. 167 Horn
1 Volume adjusting screw

5) Horn button switch

Check the continuity of the switch by applying the tester lead probes to the light green cord within the headlight case and to the handle bar. Continuity should exist when the button is pressed. (Fig. 168)

6) Turn signal siwtch

Disconnect the turn signal switch leads in the headlight case and check the continuity by connecting the gray switch lead to one of the tester probes and appling the other tester lead probe to the blue and orange switch leads alternately and operating the switch. If continuity exist in both positions, the switch is satisfactory. However, if there are continuity in the position other than shown on the chart, the switch is defective. If the both turn signal lamps on one side do not light up or if all lamps on both side light up, the switch or wiring is defective. If the switch and wiring are not defective and no turn signal lamps turn on, the relay is defective. Replace the relay with new one. (Fig. 169)

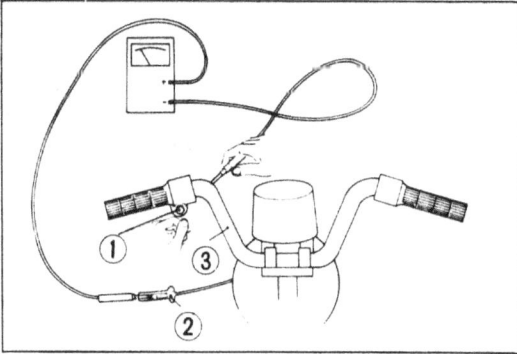

Fig. 168 1 Horn button switch 2 Horn button switch lead
3 Handle bar

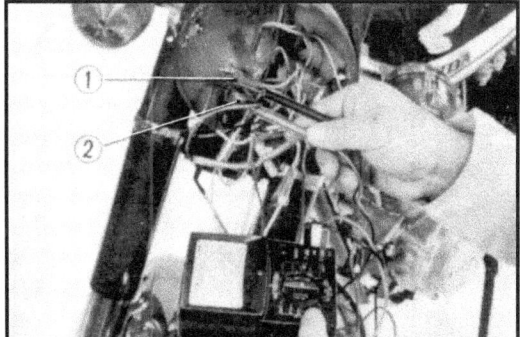

Fig. 169 Turn signal switch continuty test
1 Gray lead 2 Blue lead

Knob position	Blue cord	Gray cord	Orange cord
Right side	○—○		
Left side		○—○	

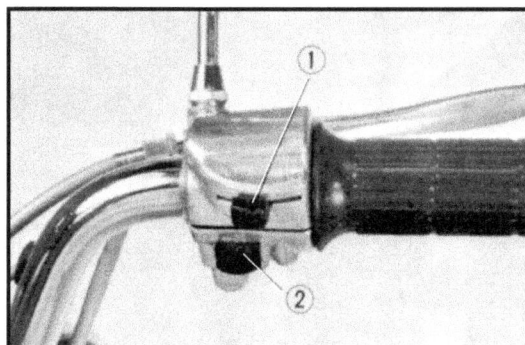

Fig. 170 ① Dimmer switch ② Lighting switch

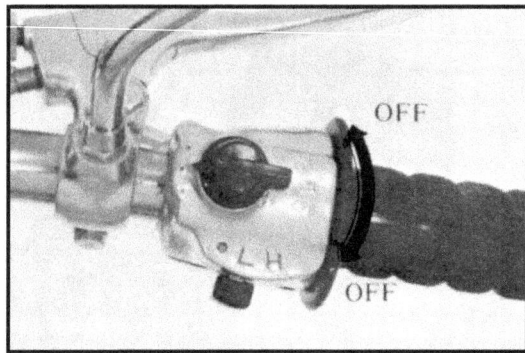

Fig. 171 Emergency switch

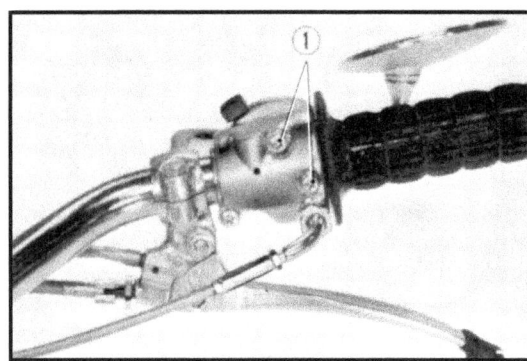

Fig. 172 Emergency switch removal
① Switch mounting screws

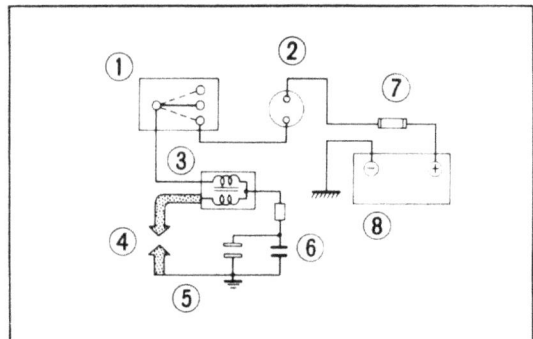

Fig. 173 Emergency switch operation
① Emergency switch ② Main switch ③ Ignition coil ④ Spark plug ⑤ Contact breaker ⑥ Condenser ⑦ Fuse 15A ⑧ Battery 6V-6AH

7) Lighting and dimmer switch

Check the continuity of switch with the tester in accordance with the table below. (Fig. 170)

	H	TL	L	IG	DY	SE
Off Low		O—O—O			O—O	
(N)	O—O—O—O				O—O	
High	O—O—O—O				O—O	
Color of	Blue	Brown	White	Black	White/Yellow	Yellow

8) Emergency switch (SL 100 U.S.A. Type). Construction

The emergency ignition switch (kill button) is provided to insure safe riding and shutting off the engines operation when the motorcycle is overturned or when trouble develops in the throttle system. (Fig. 171)

Disassembly

① Loosen two switch mounting screws and separate the upper and lower halves. (Fig. 172)

② Disconnect the throttle cable from the throttle cable connector on the bottom of the switch housing.

③ Disconnect the wiring within the headlight case and remove the switch assembly.

Inspection

Start the engine, first make sure the engine can be stopped by switching off the emergency switch. If the respective switch positions are not functioning properly, the switch or wiring is defective.

If the wiring is correct, check by the testing conductivity of wires with the switch. If the conductivity is not correct, replace with new one.

Reassembly

Perform assembly in the reverse order of disassembly. Check switch operation.

Operation

The operational principle of the emergency ignition switch is shown by the illustration. Even if ignition switch is ON, the primary circuit can be opened by operation of the switch. (Fig. 173)

VI. DISK BRAKE

1. M. K. DISK
● Features of CB125S mechanical disc brake
1) Fully enclosed caliper
    The body of the caliper is constructed in the form of a box to accommodate the brake arm shaft, improving the rigidity of the caliper and protecting each operating point from dust and dirt, sand, mud, etc.
    A boot was added to each handlebar lever to prevent water from entering from the handlebar side through the cable, resulting in the improved durability of the cable.
2) Automatic adjuster for pad-to-disc clearance
    On a hydraulic type disc brake, the adjuster is very simple in the construction by using the rollback of piston seal. On the mechanical type, the construction of the adjuster is complicated and the brake dragging may be caused from the over-adjustment. This automatic adjuster uses the twisting force of the arm return spring to simplify the construction and prevent the over-adjustment.
3) Great transmitting efficiency of braking force
    Generally a mechanical disc brake is poor in the transmitting efficiency of braking force. The M.K. disc brake is improved in the transmitting efficiency by using steel balls (cam mechanism) and a thrust needle bearing. The brake cable is also coated to assist in greater transmitting efficiency of braking force.
4) Employment of disc cover
    A disc cover was newly employed to protect the pads from dust and dirt, mud or other foreign materials, resulting in the longer service life of pads.

2. EXPLODED VIEW OF DISC TYPE PRONT WHEEL

① Front wheel axle
② Front wheel side collar
③ Front wheel hub
④ Front axle spacer collar
⑤ Speedometer gearbox retainer
⑥ Gearbox retainer cover
⑦ Front wheel rim
⑧ Front wheel tire (2.50−18)
⑨ Tube
⑩ Tire flap
⑪ Speedometer gearbox assembly
⑫ Front brake disc
⑬ 6×28 stud bolts
⑭ Front axle nut
⑮ 6 mm lock plate
⑯ 42×2.5 O-ring
⑰ 23×37×7 oil seal
⑱ 5×16 cross recessed pan head screws
⑲ 5×16 cross recessed oval head screw
⑳ 6 mm hex nuts
㉑ Spring washers
㉒ 3.0×25 cotter pin
㉓ 6301R boll bearings
㉔ 10×200.5 spoke B
㉕ 10×200 spoke B

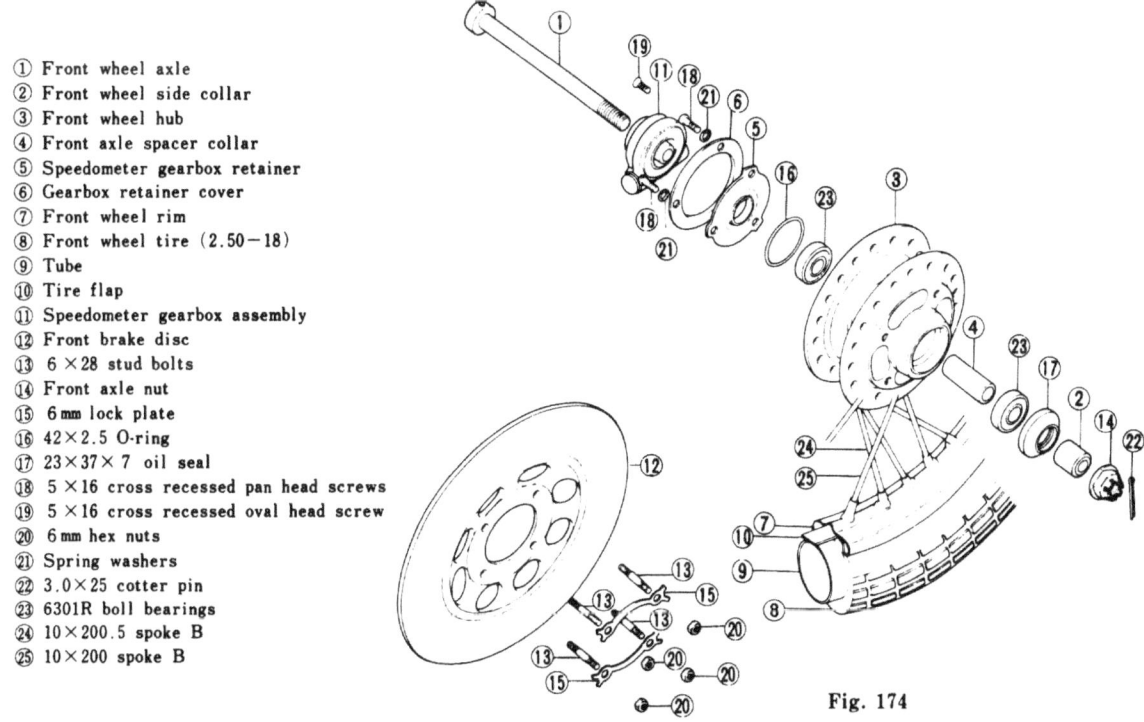

Fig. 174

3. EXPLODED VIEW OF CALIPER

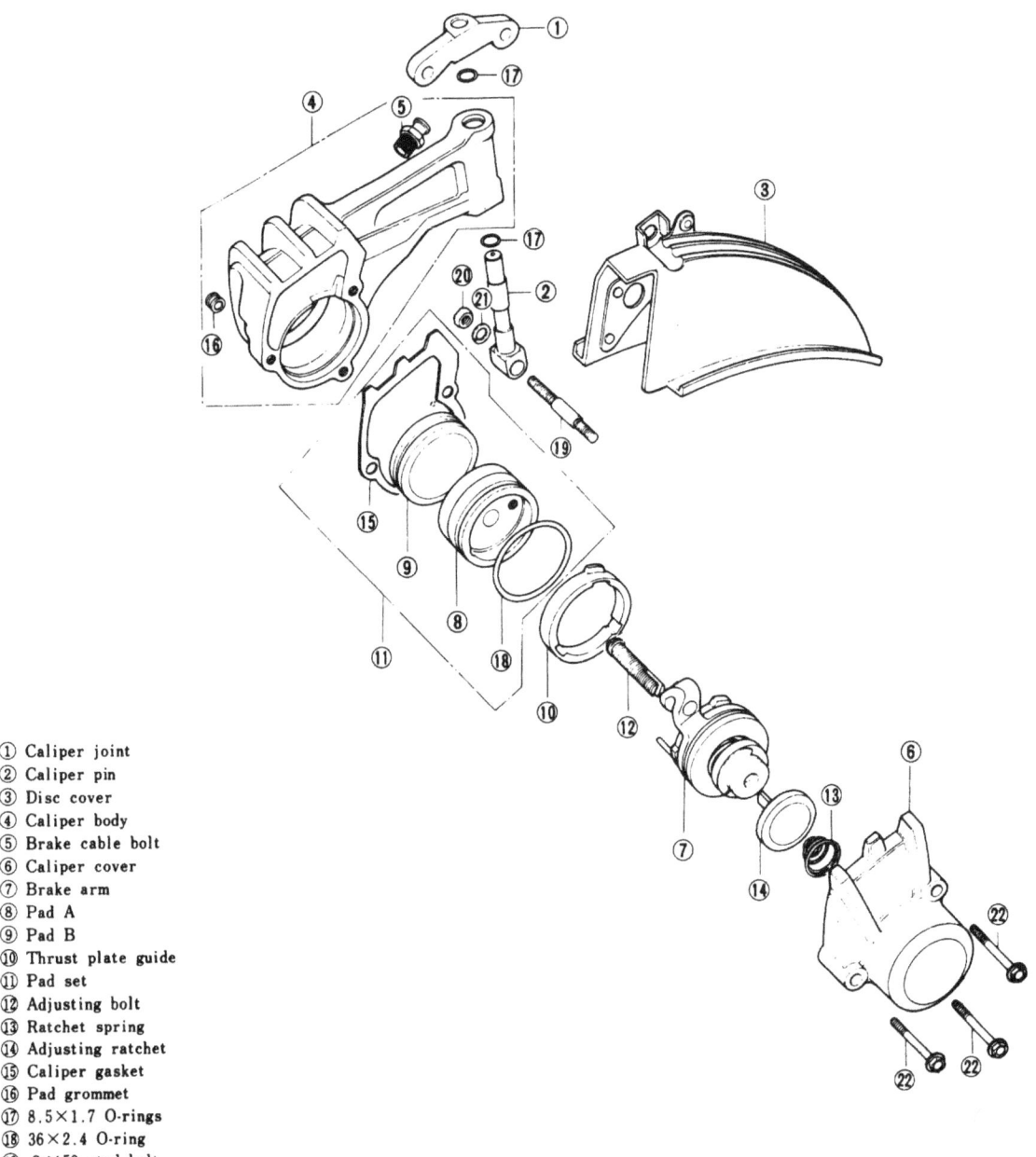

① Caliper joint
② Caliper pin
③ Disc cover
④ Caliper body
⑤ Brake cable bolt
⑥ Caliper cover
⑦ Brake arm
⑧ Pad A
⑨ Pad B
⑩ Thrust plate guide
⑪ Pad set
⑫ Adjusting bolt
⑬ Ratchet spring
⑭ Adjusting ratchet
⑮ Caliper gasket
⑯ Pad grommet
⑰ 8.5×1.7 O-rings
⑱ 36×2.4 O-ring
⑲ 8×50 stud bolt
⑳ 8 mm hex nut
㉑ 8 mm spring washer
㉒ 6×35 flange bolts

Fig. 175

4. FRONT DISK BRAKE AND FRONT WHEEL

A. Mechanical disc

● Disassembly

1) Place a service stand under the engine.
2) Disconnect the speedometer cable.
3) Remove the front wheel axle nut and pull out the axle. Then remove the front wheel.

CAUTION:

Do not operate the brake lever frequently with the front wheel removed. If the brake lever is operated under such a condition, the automatic adjuster advances to make it impossible to install the disc into between the caliper pads. If the disc cannot be re-installed between the pads, remove the caliper cover and back off the adjusting bolt as necessary. (For one turn of the bolt the clearance between the pads is increased 1mm or 0.039in.) When this operation has been performed, squeeze the brake lever several times to cause the automatic adjuster to operate after assembly.

4) Remove the front wheel side collar and 27×37×7 oil seal from the wheel hub.
5) The brake disc can be removed from the wheel by removing the nuts and lock plates.

6) Remove the speedometer gearbox, 42×2.5 O-ring, gearbox retainer cover and gearbox retainer from the opposite side.
7) Remove the front wheel bearings and front wheel axle spaeer collar.

Fig. 176 ① Front wheel axle

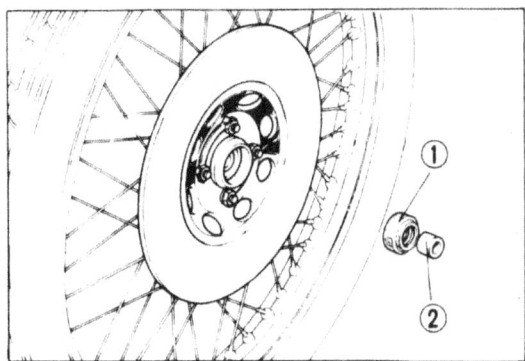

Fig. 177 ① 27×37×7 oil seal ② Side collar

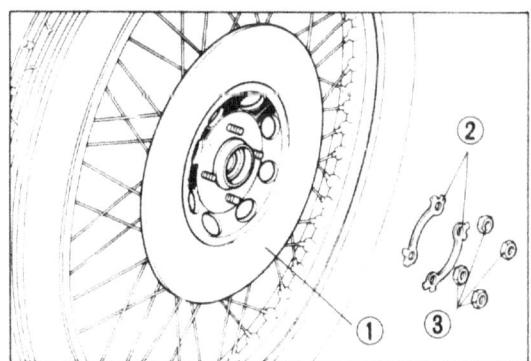

Fig. 178 ① Brake disc ② Lock plates
③ 6 mm hex nuts

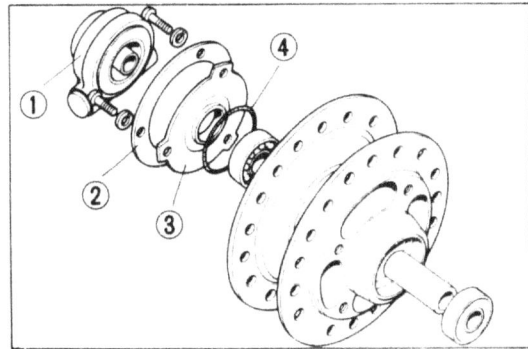

Fig. 179 ① Speedometer gearbox
② Gearbox retainer cover
③ Gearbox retainer
④ 42×2.5 O-ring
⑤ Front wheel bearings
⑥ Front wheel axle spacer collar

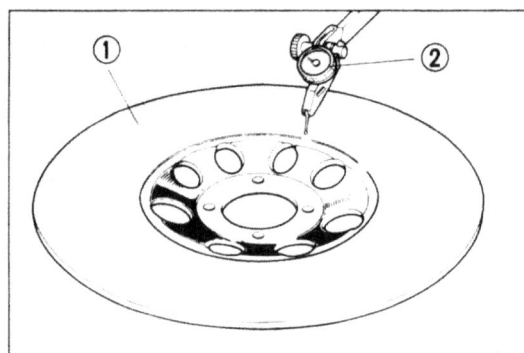

Fig. 180 ①Brake disc ②Dial gauge

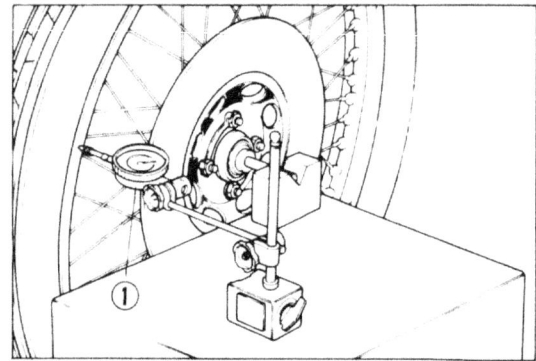

Fig. 181 ①Dial gauge

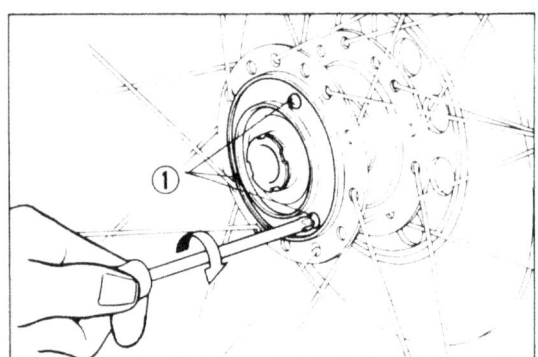

Fig. 182 ① 5 mm screws

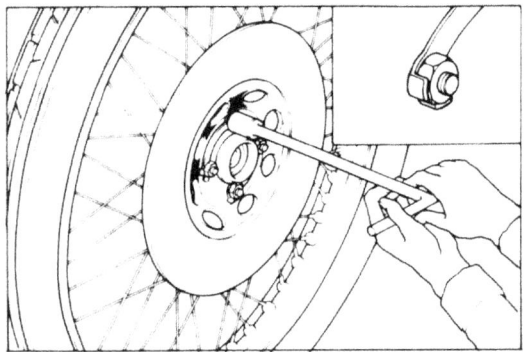

Fig. 183

- **Inspection**
  1) Brake disc
     Place the disc on a level surface and measure it at several points using a dial gauge. If the amount of wear exceeds 0.2 mm (0.008 in.), replace the disc.
     With the disc installed to the wheel, the disc run-out should be within 0.3 mm (0.012 in.) (provided that the front wheel axle and bearings are not loose).
     If the disc thickness is below 4 mm (0.157 in.), replace the disc.
  2) Wheel rim
     While rotating the wheel, check the disc radial runout using a dial gauge.

Item	Assembly standard	Service limit
Axial runout	0.5 mm (0.020 in.), max.	2.0 mm (0.079 in.), min.
Radial runout	0.5 mm (0.020 in.), max.	2.0 mm (0.079 in.), min.

- **Assembly**
  1) Drive in the 6301R ball bearings into the wheel hub.
  2) Install 23×37×7 mm oil seal and install the cover to the speedometer gearbox retainer with three 5 mm screws.
  3) Install the brake disc to the wheel.
     NOTE:
     After tightening the lock plates with the nuts, bend the locking tabs.

4) Install the speedometer gearbox from the right side and insert the front axle. When tightening the axle nut, be careful of the installation position of the gearbox.
5) After assembly, operate the motorcycle and check the wheel for proper operation and the brake for effectiveness.

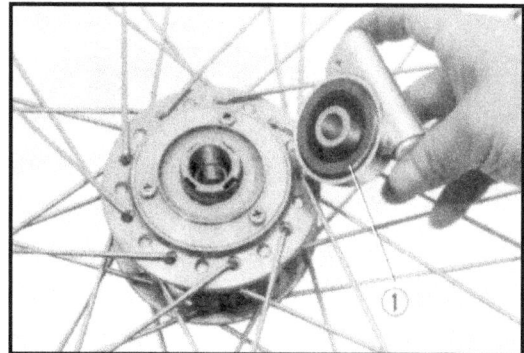

Fig. 184 ① Speedometer gearbox

B. Pads, caliper and brake cable
● Disassembly
   Precautions for disassembly:

1) Pads
   ● Replace the pads A and B as a set, if necessary. At this time replace the caliper gasket and O-rings.
   ● Do not disassemble the brake arm.
2) Brake cable
   ● When replacing the brake cable, also replace the caliper gasket.

1) Wash the caliper and disc clean. Turn over the cable boot and screw in the cable adjusting bolt fully.

Fig. 185 ① Cable boot ② Cable adjusting bolt

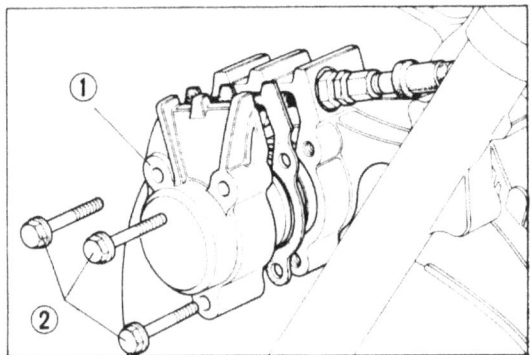

Fig. 186 ①Caliper cover ②6mm bolts

Fig. 187 ①Brake cable ②Brake arm

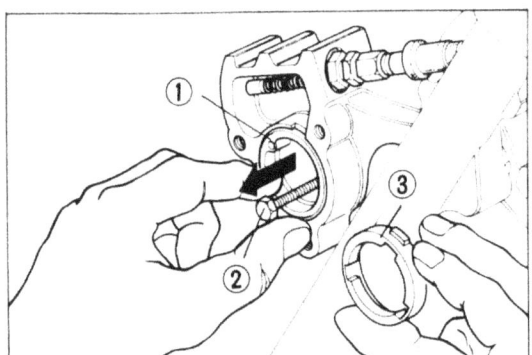

Fig. 188 ①Pad A ②6mm bolt

Fig. 189

2) Remove the caliper cover by loosening three 6mm bolts.

3) Disconnect the brake cable at the brake arm.

4) Remove the thrust plate guide. Screw in a caliper cover 6mm bolt in the back plate of the pad A and pull out the pad.

NOTES:
1) When replacing only the pads, it is unnecessary to disconnect the cable.
2) After separating the brake arm, wrap it up in a clean waste cloth to keep dirt and dust off the part.

5) Jack up the front of the motorcycle and remove the front wheel.

6) Push the pad B lock pin area of the rear side of the caliper body using a wire and remove the pad B.

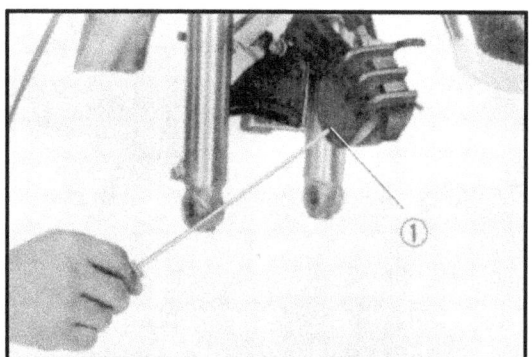
Fig. 190 ① Lock pin area

7) The pad B is removed from the pad A side. However, if the pad B is worn down to the red mark, it can be removed as shown.

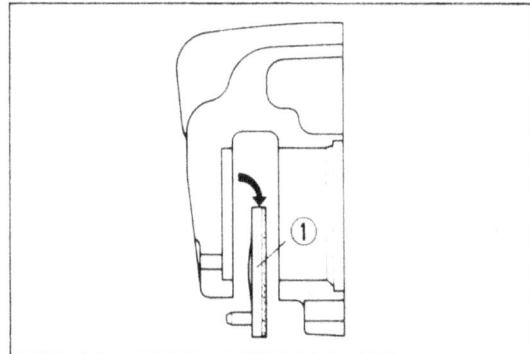
Fig. 191 ① Pad B

8) Remove the brake lever boot, then the brake cable. Pull the cable backward (toward the caliper).
NOTE:
When replacing only the brake cable, it is unnecessary to remove the wheel. Disconnect the cable end at the brake arm.

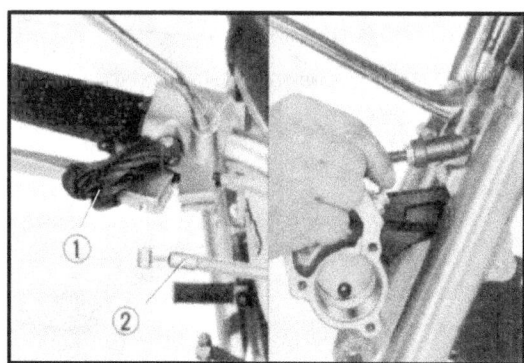
Fig. 192 ① Brake lever boot ② Brake cable

9) Remove two 6 mm bolts and one 8 mm nut and separate the disc cover, caliper body, caliper joint and caliper pin.

Fig. 193 ① Disc cover   ② Caliper body
         ③ Caliper joint ④ Caliper pin

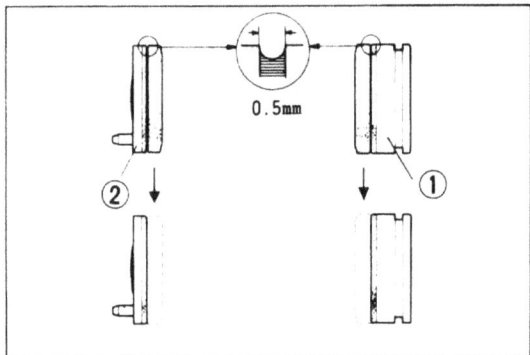

Fig. 194 ① Pad A ② Pad B

- **Inspection**

1. **WEAR OF PADS**

   The pads are respectively marked with a red slit. If the pads are worn down to the red mark, replace. Especially, after operating the motorcycle in deep mud and water or on extremely rough surfaces, clean the pads and check for wear.

- **Assembly**

Precautions for assembly:

1) Caliper
   - After disassembling the caliper, wash the brake arm, if dirty, in gasoline or cleaning solvent and apply machine grease. Repeat this procedure to replace the brake cable.
2) Pads
   - Apply a coat of silicon grease KS62M (common with CB500 and CB750) to the back plates. Take special care not to allow oil or grease to come in contact with the pads and disc. Remove oil or grease by washing the parts in gasoline or cleaning solvent.
   - When assembling, be careful not to allow foreign materials to enter the parts.

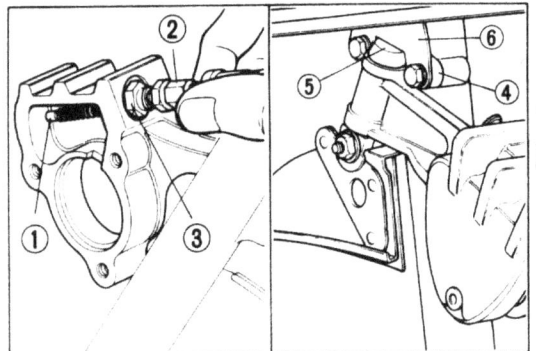

Fig. 195 ① Cable end ② Adjusting bolt ③ Brake cable bolt
         ④ Caliper joint ⑤ Caliper pin ⑥ Fender stay

1) Install the caliper body, caliper pin, disc cover and caliper joint.

NOTE:

Install the caliper joint between the fender stay and fork pipe and tighten to specification (see Page 1 - torque settings).

2) Connect the brake cable. Insert the cable end into the brake cable bolt and screw in the adjusting bolt fully.

3) Wipe the mating surfaces of the pads A and B with a clean cloth. Gasoline or cleaning solvent may be used for the purpose.

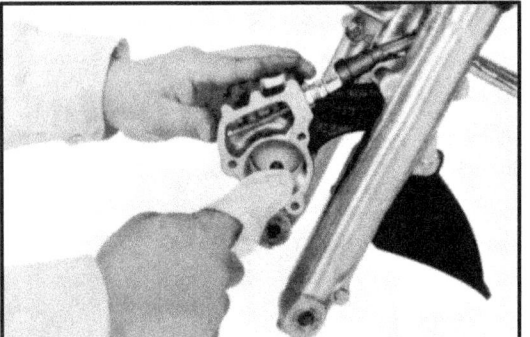

Fig. 196

4) Apply a coat of 0.6~1g (0.021~0.035oz) silicon grease KS62M (common with CB750 and CB500) to the back plate of the pad B and set to the caliper body. Install the front wheel.

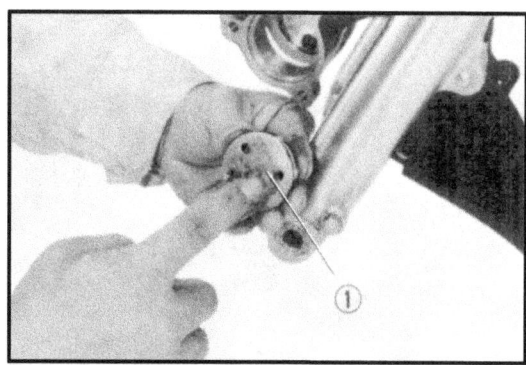

Fig. 197 ① Apply grease to pad B

5) Install the O-ring onto the pad A. Apply a coat of about 0.5g (0.018oz) silicon grease KS62M to the outer circumference of the pad, align the punch mark with that of the caliper body and then press in the pad in the body.
NOTE:
Use a new O-ring.

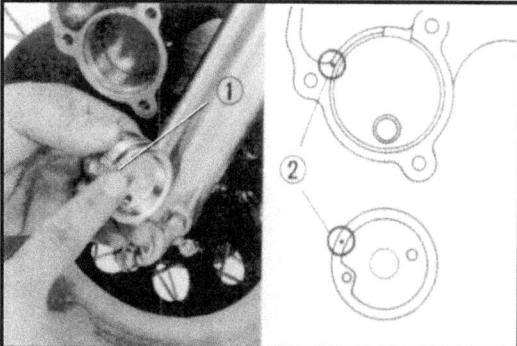

Fig. 198 ① Pad A ② Punch marks

6) Set the brake cable end and thrust plate guide to the brake arm.

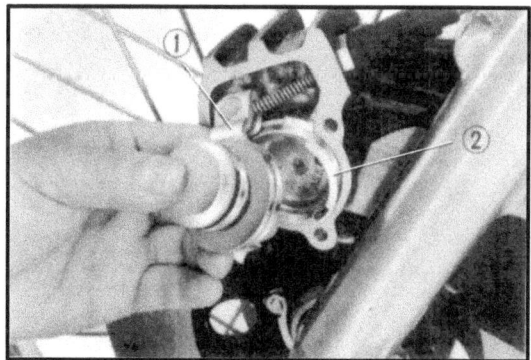

Fig. 199 ① Brake arm ② Thrust plate guide

7) Remove the ratchet from the brake arm and back off the adjusting bolt, using a standard screwdriver, as far as it will go.
NOTE:
This procedure is unnecssary when replacing the brake cable only.

8) Install the ratchet and make sure the pawl engages properly.
9) Set the brake arm complete in the caliper.

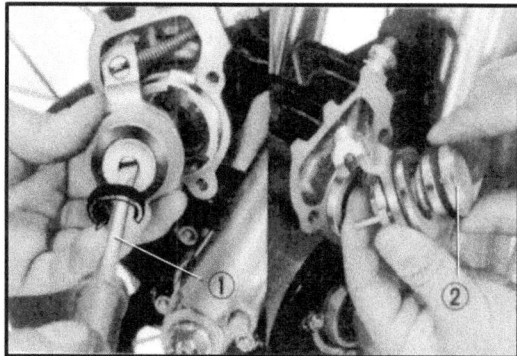

Fig. 200 ① Standard screwdriver ② Retchet

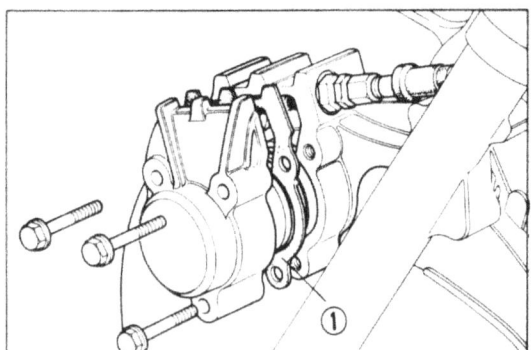

Fig. 201　①Caliper cover gasket

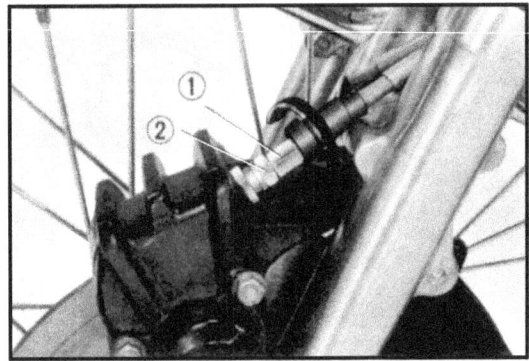

Fig. 202　①Brake cable adjusting bolt　②Lock nut

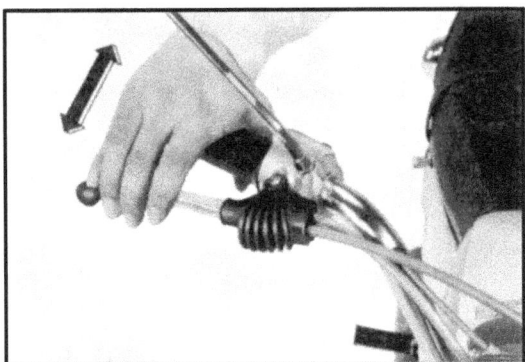

Fig. 203

Fig. 204

10) Install the caliper gasket and cover with three 6mm bolts.

NOTE:

Use a new gasket.

11) In order to eliminate the excessive clearance of the brake lever, loosen the brake cable adjusting bolt. Upon noting that the clearance is completely eliminated, loosen the bolt two or three turns more and lock it with the lock nut. Then make sure the brake lever is completely returned by the spring force.

NOTE:

The brake lever clearance does not mean the lever free play but the condition where the brake lever does not return completely.

12) Squeeze the brake lever about ten times so that the automatic adjuster can properly operate. At this time slightly squeeze the lever as in the braking operation. Now the lever free play is automatically adjusted to 20～30mm (0.787～1.181 in.).

13) After adjustment, install the boot onto the cable adjusting bolt. With the front wheel raised check if it can be turned by hand. (Check for dragging.)

TROUBLE SHOOTING

Troubles	Probable causes	Corrective action
Engine does not start or hard starting	1. Lack of compression (1) Tappet stuck open (2) Worn valve guide (3) Valve timing out of adjustment (4) Worn piston rings (5) Worn cylinder 2. No spark produced from spark plug electrodes (1) Fouled spark plug (2) Wet spark plug (3) Fouled breaker contact points (4) Improper point gap (5) Ignition timing out of adjustment (6) Defective ignition coil (7) Open or shorted circuit in ignition cord (8) Shorted condenser 3. Fuel does not flow to carburetor (1) Clogged fuel tank cap vent hole (2) Clogged fuel cock (3) Defective carburetor float valve (4) Clogged fuel tube	 Adjust tappet clearance, Replace Repair Replace Replace Clean Clean Clean Adjust Adjust Replace Replace Replace Clean Clean Replace Clean
Engine suddenly stalls while running	1. Fouled spark plug 2. Fouled breaker contact points 3. Ignition timing out of adjustment 4. Clogged fuel line 5. Clogged carburetor jets	Clean Clean Adjust Clean Clean
Engine noise	1. Tappet noise (1) Excessive tappet clearance (2) Weakened or broken valve spring 2. Knocking noise from piston (1) Worn piston and cylinder noise (2) Carbon accumulation in combination chamber (3) Worn piston pin or connecting rod small end 3. Cam chain noise (1) Stretched cam chain (2) Worn cam sprocket or timing sprocket	 Repair Replace Replace Clean Replace Replace or shorten the chain Replace

Troubles	Probable causes	Corrective action
Engine noise	4. Knocking noise from clutch	
	(1) Looseness of clutch center spline	Replace
	(2) Excessively worn friction disc or clutch	Replace
	(3) Distorted friction disc or clutch plate	Replace or repair
	5. Crankshaft	
	(1) Excessive runout of crankshaft	Repair
	(2) Excessively worn crankshaft bearing	Replace
	(3) Excessively worn connecting rod, large end	Replace
	6. Gear noise	
	(1) Worn or binding transmission gear teeth	Replace
	(2) Worn transmission spline	Replace
	(3) Worn or binding primary transmission gear	Replace
Clutch slips	1. Improper adjustment of clutch (no free play)	Readjust
	2. Weakened clutch spring	Replace
	3. Worn or distorted pressure plate.	Replace
	4. Distorted clutch plate	Replace
	5. Worn or distorted friction plate	Replace
Clutch disengages improperly	1. Improper adjustment of clutch (excessive play)	Readjust
	2. Uneven clutch spring tension	Readjust
	3. Distorted clutch plate	Replace
Gear does not engage	1. Broken center gear shift fork pawl	Replace
	2. Broken gear shift cam	Replace
	3. Deformed gear shift fork	Repair or replace
Change pedal does not return to its position	1. Broken or dislocated gear shift return spring	Repair or replace
	2. Shifting spindle hits crankcase hole	Repair
Gear jumps out while running	1. Worn shifting gears on main shaft and counter shaft	Replace
	2. Distorted or worn gear shift fork	Repair or replace
	3. Weakened shift drum stopper spring	Replace

Troubles	Probable causes	Corrective action
Poor engine performance at low speed	1. Improper adjustment of tappet	Readjust
	2. Poor cylinder head valve seating	Replace
	3. Defective valve guide	Replace
	4. Ignition timing out of adjustment	Readjust
	5. Improper breaker contact points	Repair
	6. Excessive spark plug gap	Readjust
	7. Weak ignition spark (defective condenser and ignition coil)	Replace
	8. Improper adjustment of carburetor float level	Readjust
	9. Improper adjustment of carburetor air screw	Readjust
Poor engine performance at high speed	1. Weak valve spring	Replace
	2. Valve timing out of adjustment	Readjust
	3. Too small spark plug gap	Readjust
	4. Ignition timing is retarded	Readjust
	5. Weak point arm spring	Replace
	6. Defective ignition coil	Replace
	7. Improper adjustment of carburetor float level	Readjust
	8. Clogged air cleaner element	Clean
	9. Insufficient fuel flow to carburetor	Clean or replenish
Hard steering	1. Broken steering ball bearings	Replace
	2. Bent steering stem	Repair or replace
	3. Excessively tightened steering cone race	Retighten to specified torque
	4. Low tire pressure	Inflate to specified pressure
Front and rear suspension function too soft	1. Weakened main spring	Replace
	2. Insufficient front damper oil	Refill to specified amount
Front and rear suspension function too hard	1. Front damper oil viscosity is too high	
	2. Excessive damper oil	
	3. Improper adjustment of rear cushion	
Ineffective brake	1. Worn brake lining	Replace
	2. Foreign objects adhered on brake lining surface	Clean
	3. Improper engagement of brake arm serration	Repair
	4. Worn brake cam	

Troubles	Probable Causes	Corrective Action
Exhaust smoke from muffler	1. Excessive engine oil	Check oil level with oil level gauge
	2. Excessively worn cylinder and piston rings	Replace
	3. Worn valve guide	Replace
	4. Damaged cylinder	Replace
Insufficient horsepower	1. Improper adjustment of tappet (valve stuck open)	Readjust
	2. Weakened valve spring	Replace
	3. Valve timing out of alignment	Repair
	4. Worn cylinder and piston rings	Replace
	5. Poor valve seating	Replace
	6. Ignition timing out of adjustment	Readjust
	7. Poor breaker contact points	Repair or replace
	8. Defective plug gap	Repair
	9. Clogged carburetor fuel passage	Clean
	10. Improper adjustment of float level	Readjust
	11. Clogged air cleaner	Clean
Overheating	1. Excessive carbon accumulation on cylinder head	
	2. Insufficient oil	Refill up to specified oil level
	3. Defective oil pump and clogged oil passage	Clean
	4. Too low float level	Readjust
	5. Too early ignition timing (causes knocking)	Readjust

ELECTRICAL SYSTEM

Troubles	Probable Causes	Corrective Action
Engine does not start	1) Battery • Discharged • Poor contact of battery terminals	Recharge or replace Repair
	2) Combination switch • Open or shorted circuit, disconnected connections • Poor contact between combinanation switch wire and wire harness	Repair Repair
	3) Ignition coil • Improperly insulated high tension coil • Open or shorted circuit in ignition coil	Replace Replace
	4) Contact breaker • Open circuit in the primary coil • Dirty ground point with oil or dust • Point gap out of adjustment • Improperly charged condenser	Repair Clean Readjust Replace

Troubles	Probable Causes	Corrective Action
Battery problems	1) Wiring • Open or shorted circuit in battery or disconnected battery terminals	Replace or retighten
	2) Generator • Open or shorted circuit in stator coil or ground • Broken or shorted leads • Demagnetization of rotor	Repair or replace Repair Replace
	3) Battery • Poor contact of battery terminals • Insufficient battery electrolyte • Shorted battery electrode	Repair Add distilled water Repair
Winker lamp blinks too fast or too slow	1) Bulb Blinks unusually fast improperly connected relay	Replace
	2) Wiring • Blinks too fast: bulb with unsuitable wattage • Blinks too slow: Burnt or broken bulb filament Defective relay	Replace Replace Replace
Winker lamp inoperative	1) Winker lamp switch • Poor contact of winker relay • Open circuit in winker relay coil 2) Bulb • Bulb wattage is smaller than rated wattage 3) Relay • Poor contact of winker relay • Improperly connected leads	Replace Replace Replace Replace Replace
Horn inoperative, poor sound or too weak sound	1) Horn • Cracked diaphragm 2) Horn button • Poor grounding 3) Wiring • Poor contact 4) Adjusting screw • Out of adjustment	Replace Repair Readjust Readjust
Tail light and head light inoperative	1) Fuse • Blown fuse or burnt bulb filament 2) Bulb • Poor contact of lighting switch 3) Switch • Poor contact of dimmer switch 4) Wiring	Replace Readjust Readjust
Stop light inoperative	1) Bulb • Burnt or broken bulb filament 2) Front & tail stop light switch • Malfunction of switch 3) Wiring • Poor contact of leads	Replace Readjust Readjust

PERIODICAL MAINTENANCE

Maintenance Schedule

The milage intervals shown in the MAINTENANCE SCHEDULE are intended as a guide for establishing regular maintenance and lubrication periods by which the best and most safe riding conditions are assured.

The operating procedures for individual items are described in the section of MAINTENANCE OPERATION.

After 12 months or 10,000 km (6,000 miles) perform repeatedly all items which are described in the column at every 6 months or 5,000 km (3,000 miles) intervals.

Sustained severe or high speed operation under adverse conditions may necessitate more frequent servicing.

Service Required	Months or Miles, whichever occurs first					Page Reference
	First	Second	Third	Thereafter Repeat Every		
	Month —	6	12	6	12	
	km 300	5,000	10,000	5,000	10,000	
	Mile 200	3,000	6,000	3,000	6,000	
Engine Oil-change	○	Every 1,000 Miles (1,600 km)				8
Oil Filter-clean	○		○		○	8
Spark Plug-clean and adjust or replace		○	○	○		7
Contact Breaker Points-check or service		○	○	○		6
Ignition Timing-check or adjust	○	○	○	○		6
Valve Tappet Clearance-check or adjust	○	○	○	○		5
Cam Chain-adjust	○	○	○	○		9
Air- Cleaner-clean		○		○		9
Throttle Operation-check		○	○	○		45
Carburetor-check or adjust		○	○	○		5
Fuel Valve Strainer-clean		○	○	○		50, 51
Fuel Tank and Fuel Lines-check		○	○	○		50, 51
Clutch-check or adjust	○	○	○	○		7
Drive Chain and Sprockets-adjust and lubricate or replace	○	○	○	○		11
Front and Rear Brake-adjust	○	○	○	○		10
Front and Rear Brake Shoes-check or replace			○		○	38, 41
Front and Rear Brake Links-check		○	○	○		38, 41
Wheel Rims and Spokes-check	○	○	○	○		38, 41
Tires-check or replace		○	○	○		38, 39, 41
Front Fork Oil-check and		○		○		11
change			○		○	11
Steering Head Bearings-check or adjust			○		○	44
Steering Handle Lock-check for operation			○		○	44
Side Stand Spring-check		○	○	○		51
Battery Electrolyte Level-check and replenish if necessary	○	○	○	○		11, 56–58
Lights, Horn and Speedometer-check for operation or adjust		○	○	○		58–60

TECHNICAL DATA

ITEM	CB100	CL100	SL100
DIMENSION			
Overall length	74.2 in. (1,885mm)	71.6 in. (1,820mm)	75.4 in. (1,915mm)
Overall width	29.5 in. (750mm)	32.5 in. (825mm)	31.9 in. (810mm)
Overall height	40.0 in. (1,015mm)	40.5 in. (1,030mm)	42.9 in. (1,090mm)
Wheel base	47.4 in. (1,205mm)	47.8 in. (1,215mm)	49.4 in. (1,255mm)
WEIGHT			
Dry weight	191.8 lbs (87 kg)	191.8 lbs (87 kg)	211.7 lbs (96 kg)
CAPACITIES			
Engine oil	2.1 US pt (1.0 liter)	2.1 U.S. pt (1.0 liter)	2.1 U.S. pt. (1.0 liter)
Fuel tank	2.0 US gal. (7.5 liter)	2.0 U.S. gal. (7.5 liter)	2.0 U.S. gal. (7.5 liter)
Fuel reserve tank	2.5 US pt (1.2 liter)	2.5 U.S. pt (1.2 liter)	2.5 U.S. pt. (1.2 liter)
ENGINE			
Bore and stroke	1.988 × 1.944 in. (50.5 × 49.5mm)	1.988 × 1.949 in. (50.5 × 49.5mm)	1.988 × 1.949 in. (50.5 × 49.5mm)
Compression ratio	9.5 : 1	9.5 : 1	9.5 : 5
Displacement	6.04 cu in. (99 cc)	6.04 cu in. (99 cc)	6.04 cu in. (99 cc)
Horse power	11.5 ps/11,000 rpm	11.5 ps/11,000 rpm	11.5 ps/11,000 rpm
Contact breaker point gap	0.012~0.016 in. (0.3~0.4mm)	0.012~0.016 in. (0.3~0.4mm)	0.012~0.016 in. (0.3~0.4mm)
Spark plug gap	0.024~0.028 in. (0.6~0.7mm)	0.024~0.028 in. (0.6~0.7mm)	0.024~0.028 in. (0.6~0.7mm)
Valve tappet clearance	0.002 in. (0.05mm)	0.002 in. (0.05mm)	0.002 in. (0.05mm)
CHASSIS AND SUSPENSION			
Caster	64°	63°40′	61.5°
Trail	2.95 in. (75mm)	3.07 in. (78mm)	3.7 in. (95mm)
Tire size, front	2.50~18 (4 PR)	2.50-18 (4 PR)	2.75-19 (4 PR)
Tire size, rear	2.75~18 (4 PR)	3.00-18 (4 PR)	3.25-17 (4 PR)
POWER TRANSMISSION			
Primary reduction	4.055	4.055	4.055
Final reduction	2.857	3.071	3.142
Gear ratio, 1 st.	2.500	2.500	2.500
2 nd.	1.722	1.722	1.722
3 rd.	1.333	1.333	1.333
4 th.	1.083	1.083	1.083
5 th.	0.923	0.923	0.923
ELECTRICAL			
Battery	6V-6AH	6V-6AH	6V-6AH
Generator	A.C. generator	A.C. generator	A.C. generator
Fuse	15 amp	15 amp	15 amp
LIGHTS			
Headlight	6V-35/25W	6V-35/25W	6V-35/25W
Tail/stoplight	6V-5.3/17W	6V-5.3/17W	6V-5.3/17W
Turn signal light	6V-18W	6V-18W	---
Meter light	6V-1.5W	6V-1.5W	6V-1.5W
Neutral indicator light	6V-1.5W	6V-1.5W	6V-1.5W
Turn signal indicator light	6V-1.5W	6V-1.5W	---
High beam indicator light	6V-1.5W	6V-1.5W	6V-1.5W

ITEM	CB125S	CD125S	SL125
DIMENSION			
Overall length	74.8 in. (1,900mm)	74.8 in. (1,900mm)	78.5 in. (1,995mm)
Overall width	29.5 in. (750mm)	29.5 in. (750mm)	31.9 in. (810mm)
Overall height	40.0 in. (1,015mm)	39.4 in. (1,000mm)	44.3 in. (1,115mm)
Wheel base	47.4 in. (1,205mm)	47.2 in. (1,200mm)	50.2 in. (1,275mm)
WEIGHT			
Dry weight	202.0 lbs (91.5 kg)	196.2 lbs (89 kg)	209.5 lbs (95.0 kg)
CAPACITIES			
Engine oil	1.0 U.S. qt. 0.9 Imp. qt (1.0 l)	1.0 U.S. qt., 0.9 Imp. qt. (1.0 l)	1.0 U.S. qt., 0.9 Imp. qt. (1.0 l)
Fuel tank	2.0 U.S. gal. 1.6 Imp. gal. (7.5 l)	2.0 U.S. gal., 1.6 Imp. gal. (7.5 l)	1.8 U.S. gal. 1.6 Imp. gal. (7.0 l)
Fuel reserve tank	1.3 U.S. qt. 1.1 Imp. qt. (1.2 l)	1.3 U.S. qt., 1.1 Imp. qt. (1.2 l)	0.4 U.S. gal. 0.3 Imp. gal. (1.5 l)
ENGINE			
Bore and stroke	2.205 × 1.949 in. (56 × 49.5mm)	2.205 × 1.949 in. (56 × 49.5mm)	2.205 × 1.949 in. (56 × 49.5mm)
Compression ratio	9.5 : 1	9.5 : 1	9.5 : 1
Displacement	7.44 cu in. (122 cc)	7.44 cu in. (122 cc)	7.44 cu in. (122 cc)
Horse power	12.0 ps/9,000 rpm	12.0 ps/9,000 rpm	12.0 ps/9,000 rpm
Contact breaker point gap	0.012~0.016 in. (0.3~0.4mm)	0.012~0.016 in. (0.3~0.4mm)	0.012~0.016 in. (0.3~0.4mm)
Spark plug gap	0.024~0.028 in. (0.6~0.7mm)	0.024~0.028 in. (0.6~0.7mm)	0.024~0.028 in. (0.6~0.7mm)
Valve tappet clearance	0.002 in. (0.05mm)	0.002 in. (0.05mm)	0.002 in. (0.05mm)
CHASSIS AND SUSPENSION			
Caster	63°45′	63°45′	60°
Trail	3.15 in. (80mm)	3.15 in. (80mm)	3.15 in. (80mm)
Tire size, front	2.75-18 (4 PR)	2.50-18 (4 PR)	2.75-21 (4 PR)
Tire size, rear	3.00-17 (4 PR)	2.75-18 (4 PR)	3.25-18 (4 PR)
POWER TRANSMISSION			
Primary reduction	4.055	4.055	4.055
Final reduction	3.267	2.800	3.267
Gear ratio, 1 st.	2.500	2.769	2.769
2 nd.	1.722	1.722	1.722
3 rd.	1.333	1.272	1.272
4 th.	1.083	1.000	1.000
5 th.	0.923	—	0.815
ELECTRICAL			
Battery	6V-6 AH	6V-6 AH	6V-6 AH
Generator	A.C. generator	A.C. generator	A.C. generator
Fuse	10 amp	10 amp	15 amp
LIGHTS			
Headlight	6V-25/25W	6V-25/25W	6V-25/35W
Tail/stoplight	6V-3/10w	6V-3/10W	6V-5.3/17W
Turn signal light	6V-8W	6V-8W	—
Meter light	6V-1.5W	6V-1.5W	6V-1.5W
Neutral indicator light	6V-1.5W	6V-1.5W	6V-1.5W
Turn signal indicator light	6V-18W	6V-1.5W	6V-1.5W
High beam indicator light	6V-1.5W	6V-1.5W	6V-1.5W

WIRING DIAGRAM

(CB100)

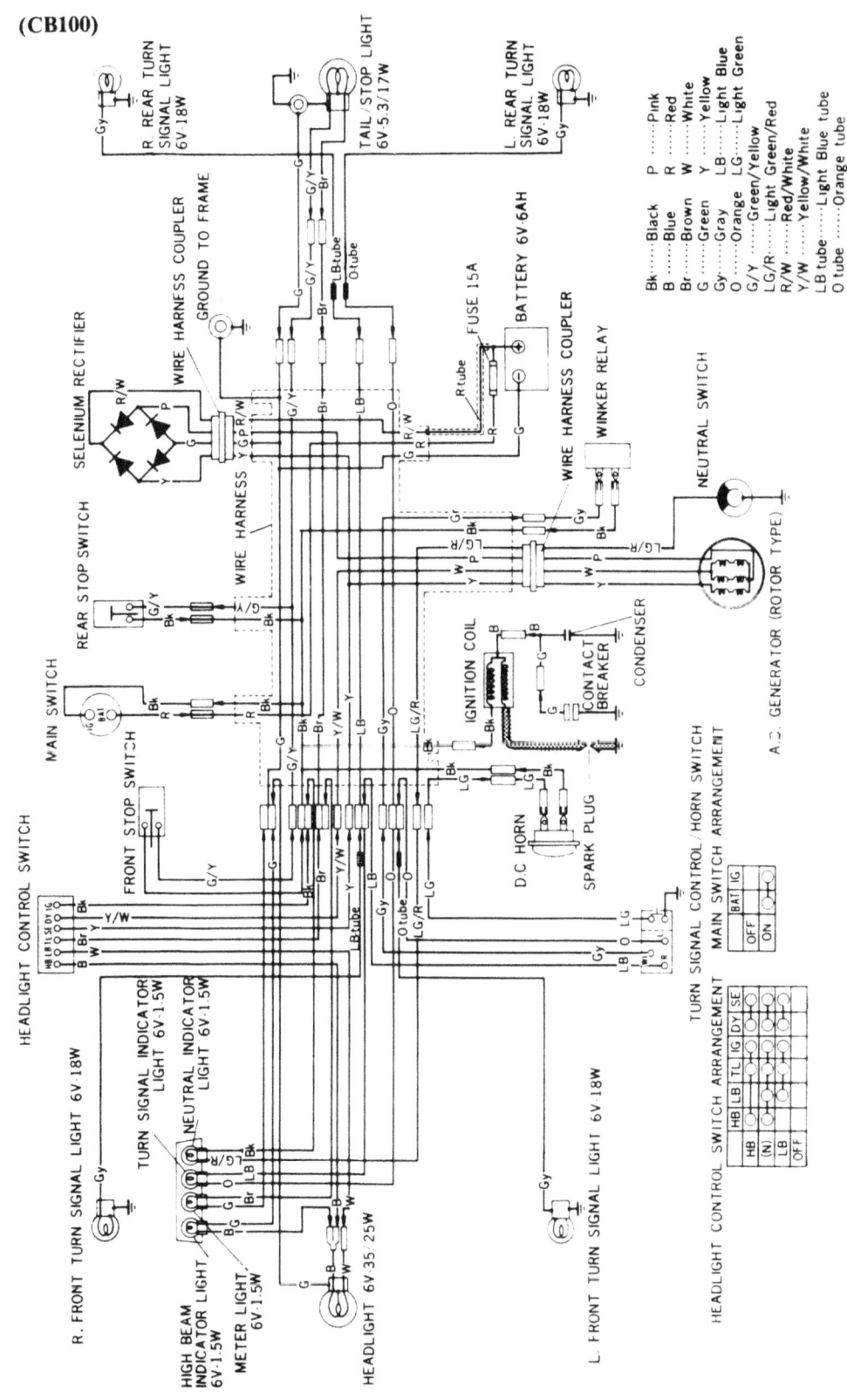

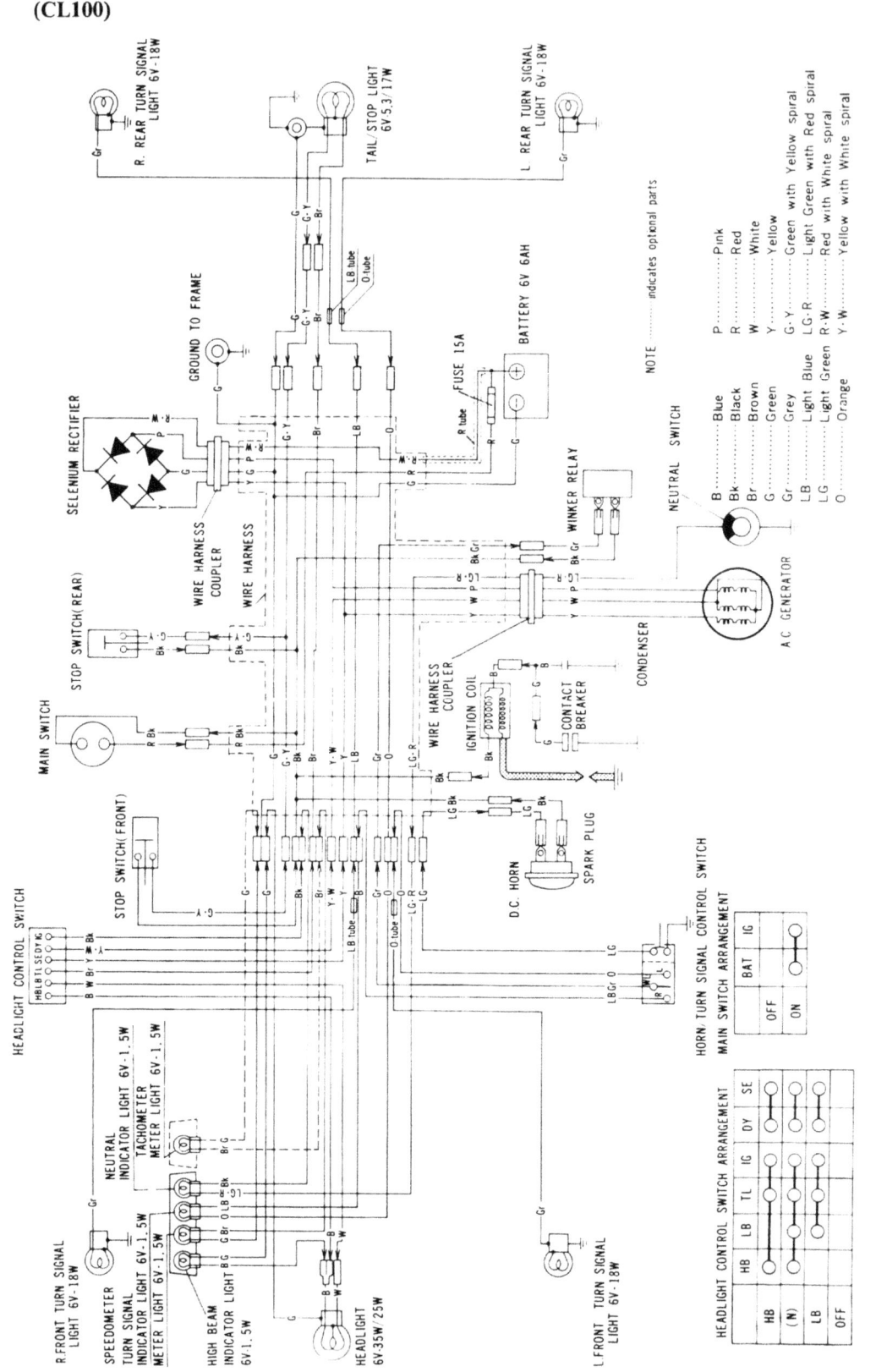

(SL100)

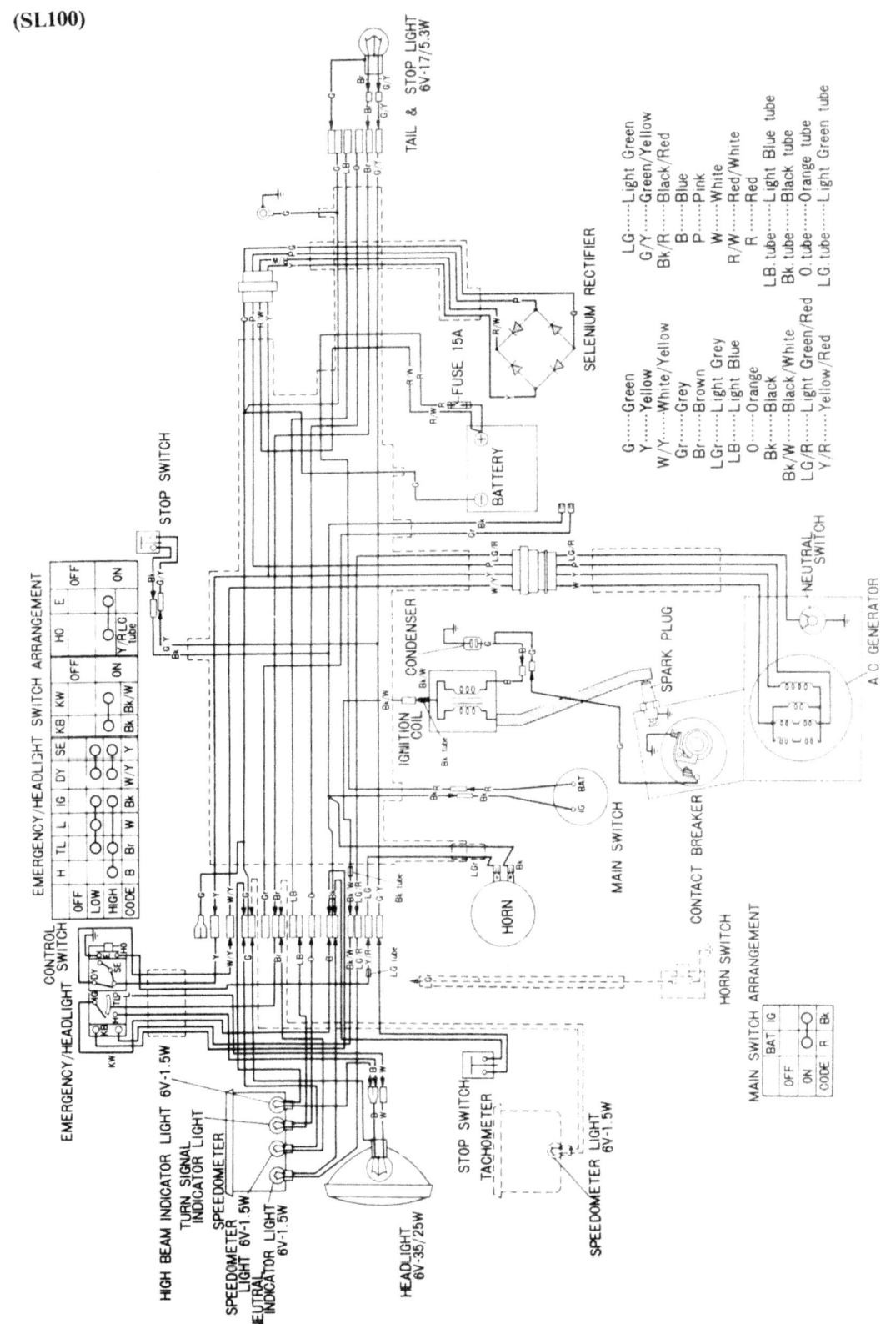

(CB125S)

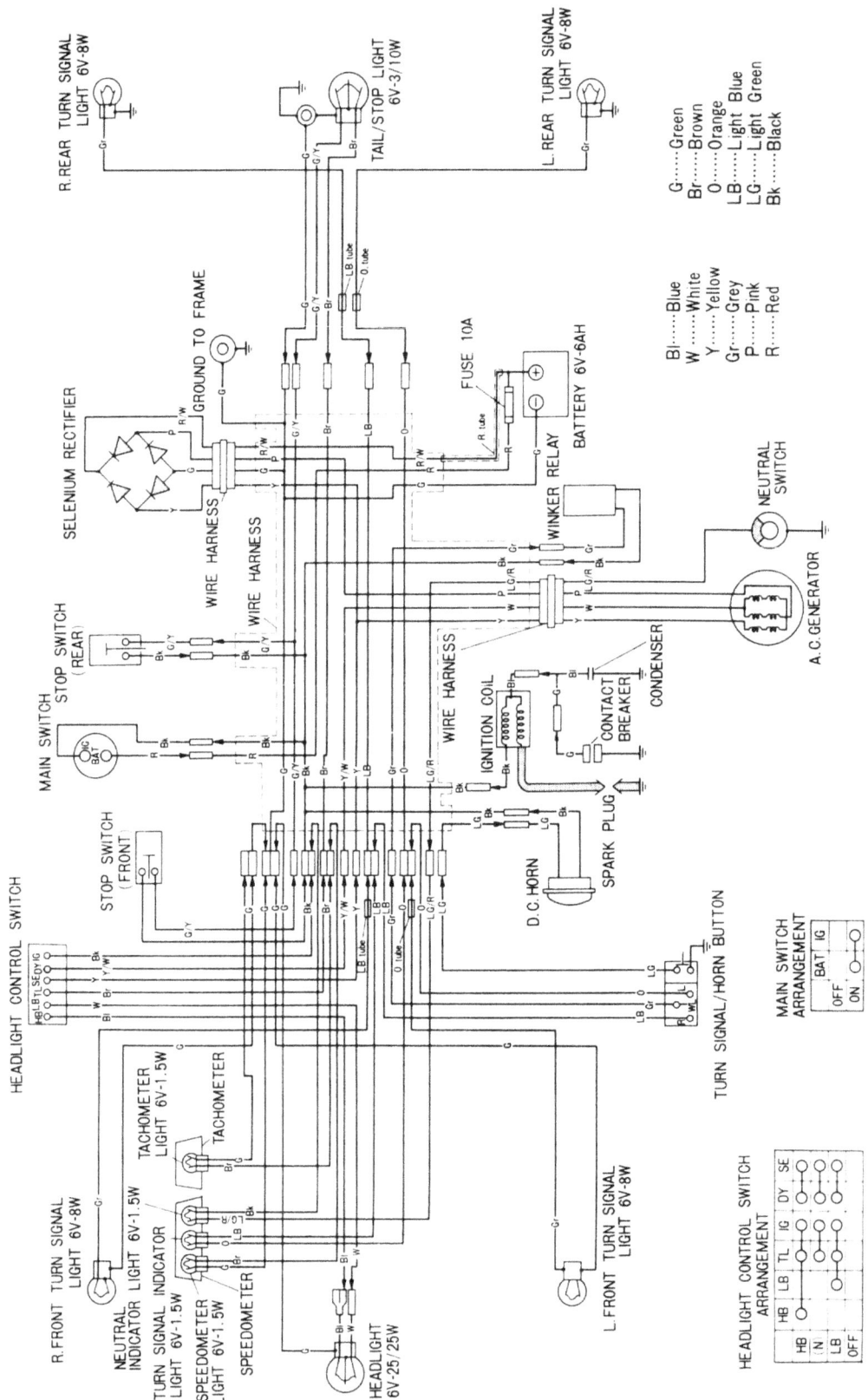

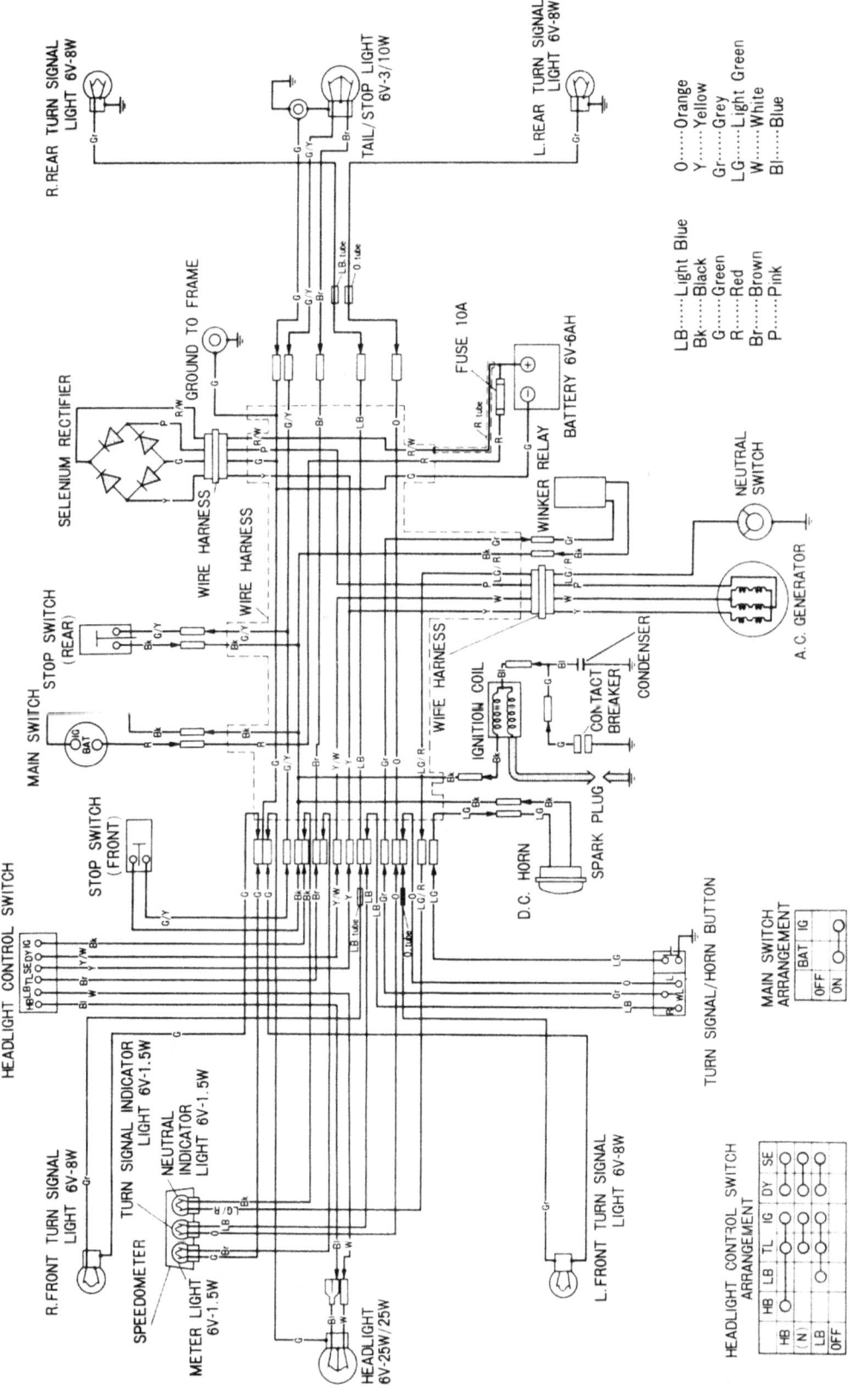

(SL125)

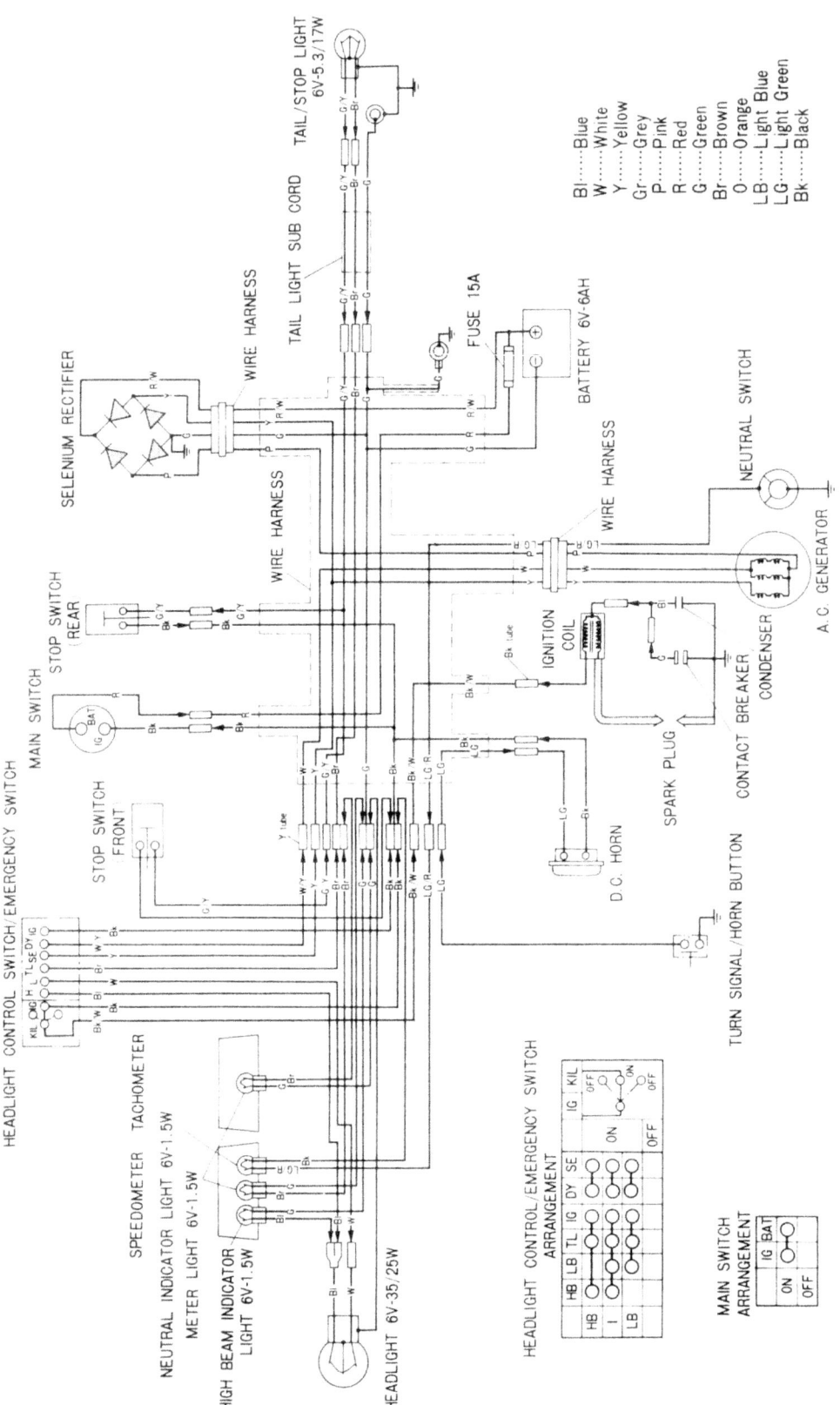

SUPPLEMENTS & ADDENDUMS

The original manual (pages 1-84) included overhaul, repair and maintenance information for the 1970-1974 CB100, CL100, SL100, CB125S, CD125S & SL125 models. However, due to modifications to existing models and/or the introduction of a new model within the series, Honda published a number of 'supplements' and 'addendums' in order to update the data in that original manual through the end of the series in 1985.

The balance of this manual (pages 85-257) consists of the following supplements and addendums:

1973 TL125K0	Supplement (pages 85-106)
1975 CB125S2	Supplement (pages 107-111)
1975 TL125K2	Supplement (pages 112-114)
1976 TL125'76	Supplement (pages 115-118)
1976 CB100K3 / CB125J / CB125S'76	Supplement (pages 119-135)
1978 CB125S'78	Addendum (pages 136-138)
1979 CB125S'79	Addendum (pages 139-176)
1980 CB125S'80	Addendum (pages 177-188)
1981 CB125S'81	Addendum (pages 189-216)
1982 CB125S'82	Addendum (pages 217-224)
1984 CB125S'84	Addendum (pages 225-257)

These supplements and addendums are intended to be used in conjunction with the original manual (pages 1-84) for items that are 'common' with the later models. For example, the CB125S was fitted with a front disc brake from 1974 to 1978, that information is included in the original manual and not the later updates.

INDEX - TL 125 SUPPLEMENT

TL125 SUPPLEMENT
- SERVICE TOOL 85
- I MAINTENANCE OPERATIONS 87
  1. Tappet clearance adjustment 87
  2. Carburetor adjustment 87
  3. Breaker point and ignition 87
  4. Oil filter cleaning 87
  5. Engine oil change 88
  6. Cam chain adjustment 88
  7. Fuel system inspection 88
  8. Air cleaner maintenance 88
  9. Clutch wire adjustment 89
  10. Drive chain adjustment 89
  11. Front brake adjustment 90
  12. Rear brake adjustment 90
  13. Brake pedal height adjustment 91
  14. Gear change pedal height adjustment . 91
  15. Front suspension spring adjustment .. 91
  16. Front fork oil change 91
  17. Cylinder compression inspection ... 92
- II ENGINE 93
  1. In-motorcycle 93
  2. Engine removal and installation 93
  A. Engine removal 93
  B. Engine installation notes 94

III ENGINE, CHASSIS AND ELECTRICAL 95
- ENGINE 95
  1. Clutch 95
  2. Transmission 96
- CHASSIS 97
  1. Brake arm 97
  2. Handlebar 97
  3. Cables and wires 97
  4. Front suspension 98
  A. Disassembly notes............ 98
  B. Inspection 99
  C. Assembly 99
- ELECTRICAL SYSTEM 100
  1. A.C. generator 101
  A. Removal 102
  B. Stator inspection 102
- INSPECTION OF ELECTRICAL ACCESSORIES 102
- TABLE OF OPTIONAL PARTS 103
- SPECIFICATIONS 104
- MAINTENANCE SCHEDULE 105
- TL125 WIRING DIAGRAM 106

TL125

• TL125 SPECIAL TOOLS
(ENGINE)

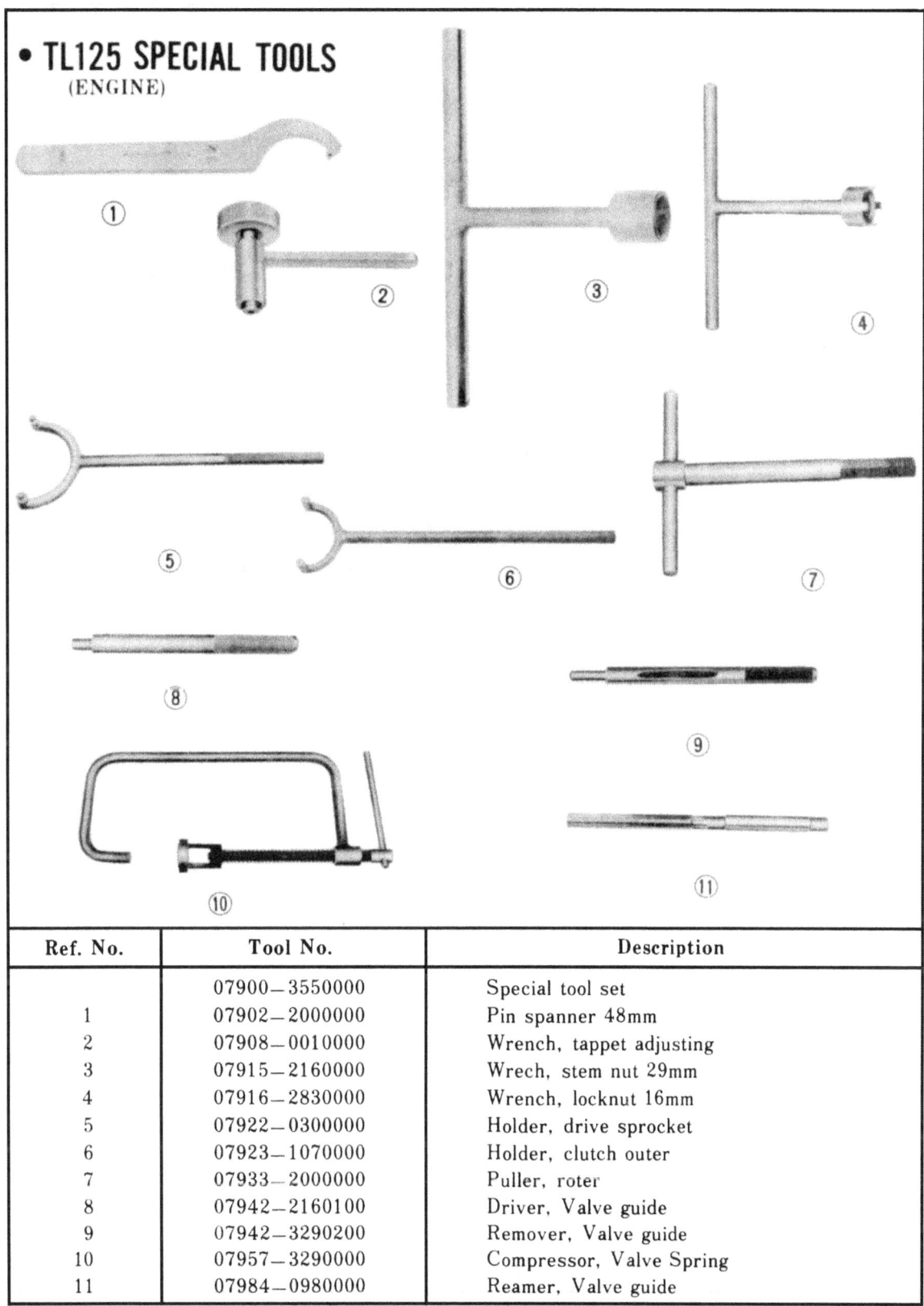

Ref. No.	Tool No.	Description
	07900−3550000	Special tool set
1	07902−2000000	Pin spanner 48mm
2	07908−0010000	Wrench, tappet adjusting
3	07915−2160000	Wrech, stem nut 29mm
4	07916−2830000	Wrench, locknut 16mm
5	07922−0300000	Holder, drive sprocket
6	07923−1070000	Holder, clutch outer
7	07933−2000000	Puller, roter
8	07942−2160100	Driver, Valve guide
9	07942−3290200	Remover, Valve guide
10	07957−3290000	Compressor, Valve Spring
11	07984−0980000	Reamer, Valve guide

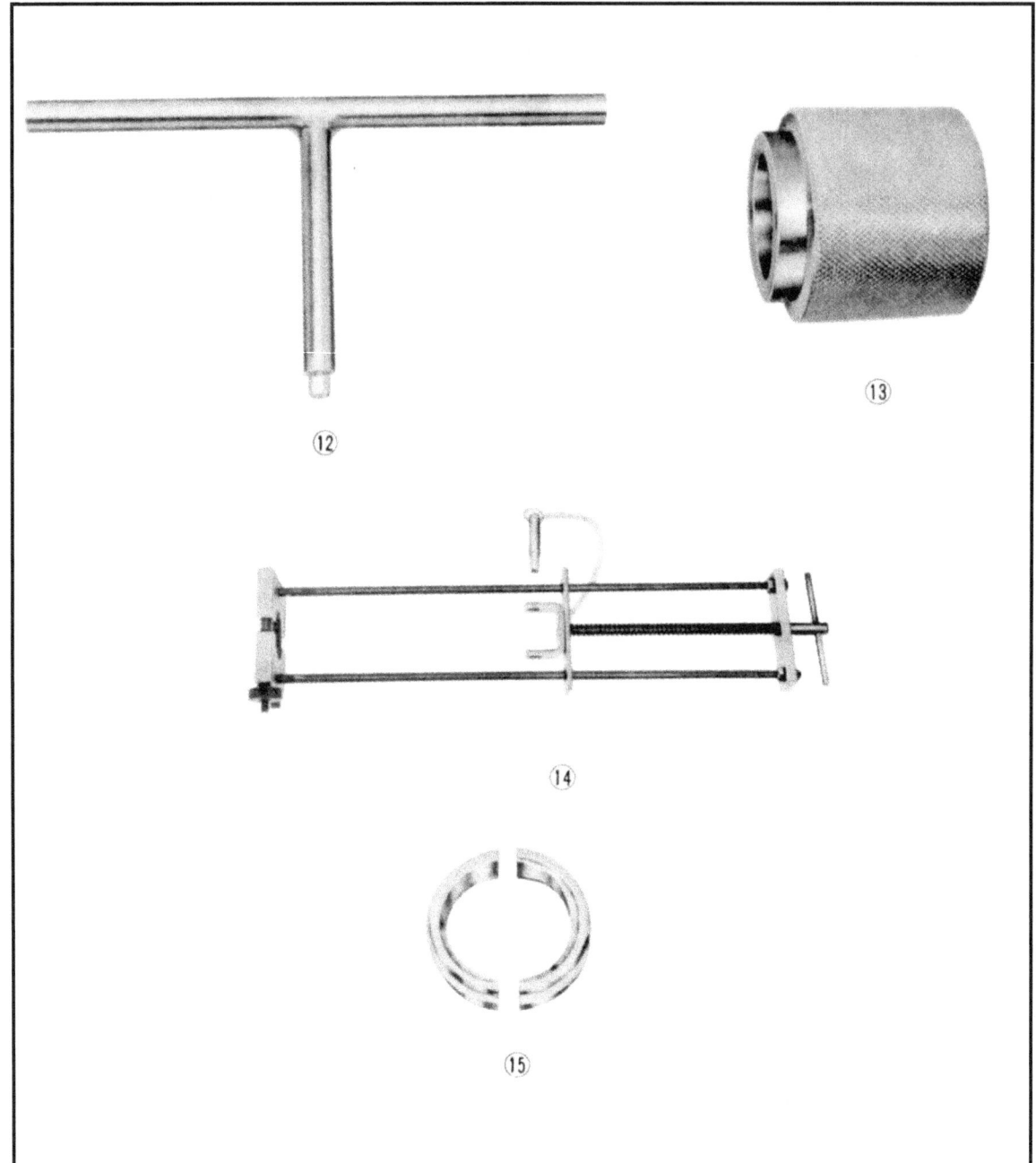

Ref. No.	Tool No.	Description
12	07917-3230000	Wrench, hollow set 6mm
13	07947-3550000	Driver, fork seal
14	07957-3290000	Tool disassembling (Rear cushion)
15	07967-1180100	Holder, spring attachment (**Rear cushion**)

I. MAINTENANCE OPERATIONS

1. TAPPET CLEARANCE ADJUSTMENT

Tappet clearance check and adjustment should be made the with engine is cold.

1) For adjustment, refer to page 5.

Remove the ACG caps A and B to observe whether or not the T mark is lined up with the index mark on the left crankcase cover. Specified tappet clearance:
(Fig. 1) Intake 0.002in (0.05mm)
         Exhaust 0.002in (0.05mm)

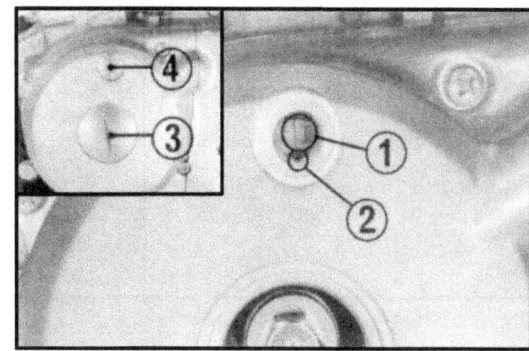

Fig. 1 ① T mark ② INDEX mark
③ ACG Cap A. ④ ACG Cap B.

2. CARBURETOR ADJUSTMENT

1) Refer to page 5.
  (Fig. 2)

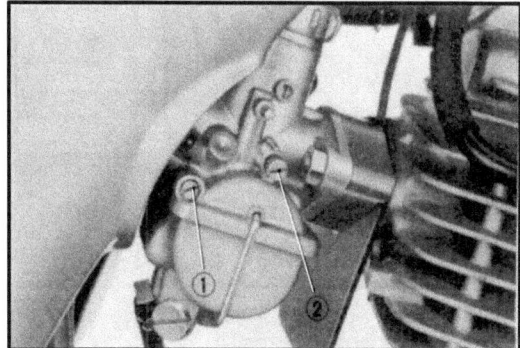

Fig. 2 ① Air screw ② Throttle stop screw

3. BREAKER POINT AND IGNITION TIMING ADJUSTMENT

1) Refer to page 6.

Fig. 3 ① Right crankcase cover

4. OIL FILTER CLEANING

1) Drain the engine.
2) Remove the kick starter pedal.
3) Disengage the clutch cable from the clutch lever.
4) Remove the right crankcase cover. (Fig. 3)
5) Remove the oil filter rotor cover.
6) Clean any sludge off the center of the oil filter rotor. (Fig. 4) Reassemble the filter.

Fig. 4 ① Oil filter rotor cover ② Oil filter rotor

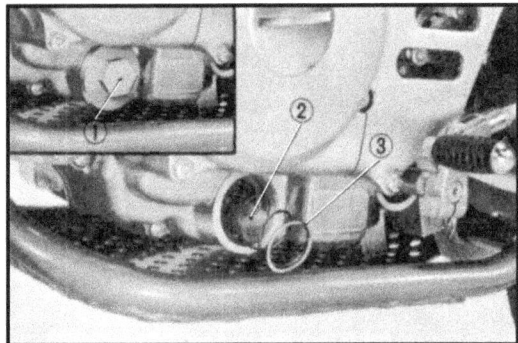

Fig. 5　① Oil filter cap　② Screen filter　③ Spring

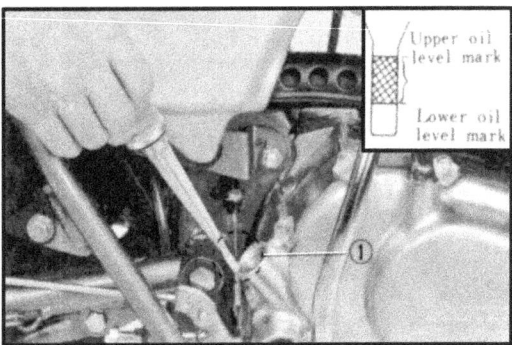

Fig. 6　① Oil level gauge

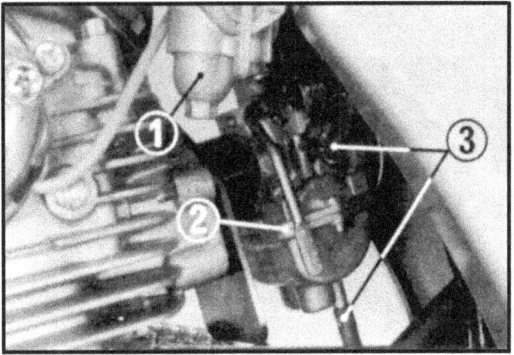

Fig. 7　① Fuel cock　② Carburetor　③ Fuel pipe

Fig. 8　① Air cleaner connecting band　② Nut
　　　　③ Air cleaner element

5. ENGINE OIL CHANGE

Start engine and run until the normal operating temperature is reached. This facilitates complete and rapid draining.

1) Apply the side stand. With the oil filter cap removed, operate the kick pedal several times. Use caution to avoid dropping the screen on the floor.
2) Check both the screen filter and spring for presence of dust and dirt; if necessary, clean in solvent or gasoline and dry with compressed air. (Fig. 5)
3) Replace the cap and refill with fresh oil up to the upper level mark on the dip stick.
　Specified oil viscosity :　　　　　(Fig. 6)
　General, all temperatures　　SAE10W-40
　Extreme, high temperature　SAE20W-50
　　　　　　　Capacity.........1l(1.05 qt)

Alternate :

Above 59° F	SAE30
32° to 59° F	SAE20W
Below 32° F	SAE10W

6. CAM CHAIN ADJUSTMENT
1) Refer to page 9.

7. FUEL SYSTEM INSPECTION
1) Refer to page 9. (Fig. 7)
Note :
Do not spill gasoline on the floor since it is highly flammable and may catch fire very easily. Place oily rags or waste in containers provided for them.

8. AIR CLEANER MAINTENANCE
1) Remove the right side cover.
2) Unfasten the band securing the cleaner to the carburetor. Remove three nuts and take out the filter element. Clean the element in solvent or gasoline and dry with compressed air. Refer to page 10. (Fig. 8)

9. CLUTCH WIRE ADJUSTMENT

1) Fine adjustment is made by loosening lock nut and turning the adjuster in or out until the proper play is obtained at the lever tip.

   To decrease play...Turn clockwise

   To increase play...Turn counter clockwise
   (Fig. 9)

   The normal play at the tip of clutch lever should be: 10～20mm (0.4～0.8in)

Note:
Check the adjustment of the clutch with the engine running. If there is excessive play, even full movement of the clutch lever will not release the clutch fully, resulting in engine stall or creeping of the motorcycle. Also check to be sure that the lever operates smoothly.

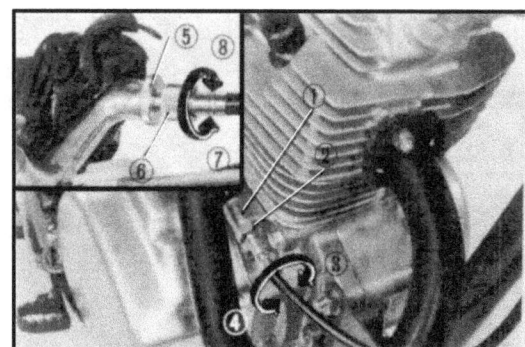
Fig. 9　① Adjuster　② Lock nut　③ To decrease play
　　　　④ To increase play　⑤ Nut　⑥ Adjuster
　　　　⑦ To decrease play　⑧ To increase play

10. DRIVE CHAIN ADJUSTMENT

1) Check the tension of the drive chain. This is done by moving either the top or bottom side of the chain up and down with fingers midways between the sprockets. Drive chain tension should be adjusted to allow approximately ¾" inch vertical movement at this point. (Fig. 10)
   Rotate the rear wheel and check drive chain tension throughout its length.

2) To adjust, remove the cotter pins from the axle nuts on both side of the rear fork and turn the adjuster plates in either direction until the specified chain tension is obtained. The adjusters on both side must be in the same setting. To secure them, tighten the nuts to specification and install the cotter pins securely. (Fig. 11)

3) Should you experience difficulty in rotating the adjuster, hold it with a hand and rotate while tapping on side of the tire with the other. (Fig. 12)

Fig. 10　① Drive chain

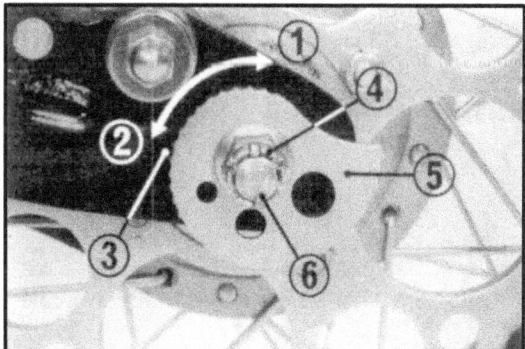
Fig. 11　① To increased tension　② To decrease tension
　　　　③ Stopper　④ Axle nut　⑤ Adjuster　⑥ Cotter pin

Fig. 12

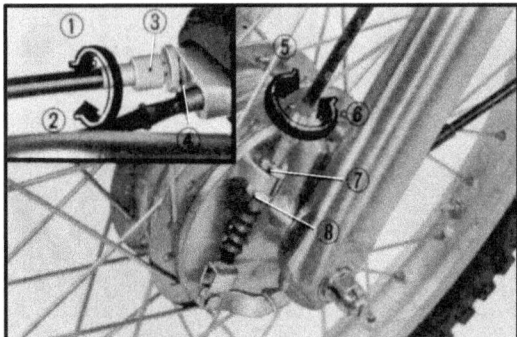

Fig. 13　① To decrease play　② To increase play
　　　　　③ Adjuster　④ Nut　⑤ To decrease play
　　　　　⑥ To increase play　⑦ Adjuster　⑧ Lock nut

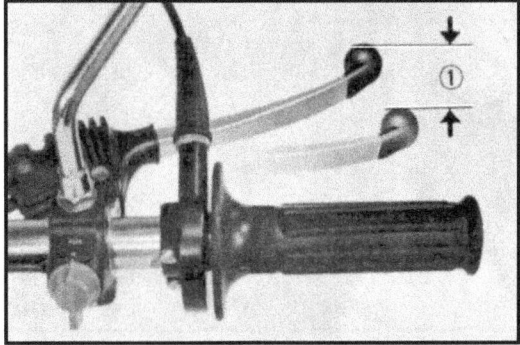

Fig. 14　① 20~30mm (0.8~1.2 in)

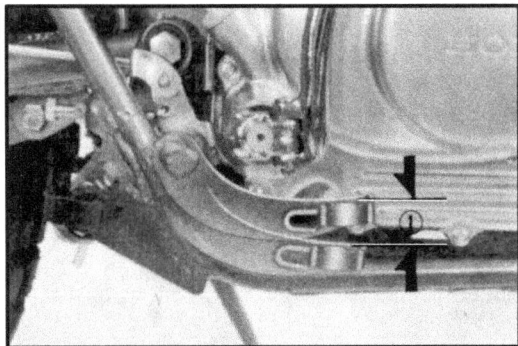

Fig. 15　① 20~30mm (0.8~1.2 in)

Fig. 16　① To increase play　② To decrease play
　　　　　③ Adjusting nut

11. FRONT BRAKE ADJUSTMENT

1) To set the free play adjustment, loosen the lock nut and turn the adjuster in or out located at the front wheel. Minor adjustments should be made on the adjuster at the handlebar. Do not rotate the adjuster without first loosening the lock nut.

(Fig. 13)

2) Free play at the tip of the brake lever tip should be 20~30mm (0.8~1.2 in)

(Fig. 14)

Note:

To avoid brake lever breakage in case of an accident, the tightening torque of the ignition and brake lever braket is a little less than the standard torque limit to allow it to slip.

Make sure to use the specified torque.

Tightening torque 0.2kg-m

(1.4lbs-ft)

12. REAR BRAKE ADJUSTMENT

1) Rear brake pedal free play, measured at the tip of the rear brake pedal ①, should be maintained at 20~30 mm (0.8~1.2 in). Free play is the distance the brake pedal moves until the brake starts to engage.

(Fig. 15)

2) Adjust the pedal free play by turning the rear brake adjusting nut ③. Turning the adjusting nut in direction ② will decrease the brake pedal free play and turning the nut in the direction ① will increase the play. (Fig. 16)

13. BRAKE PEDAL HEIGHT ADJUSTMENT

1) Brake pedal height can be adjusted to suit an individual rider. To adjust, loosen the lock nut and turn the stopper in or out as required. (Fig. 17)

Note:
Always make pedal play adjustment after the pedal height is changed.

Fig. 17 ① Raise ② Lower ③ Lock nut ④ Stopper

14. GEAR CHANGE PEDAL HEIGHT ADJUSTMENT

1) The gear change pedal can be also adjustable in height to suit the riding position of an individual rider. This adjustment is made by turning the adjuster after loosening the lock nut. After adjustment, tighten the lock nut firmly. (Fig. 18)

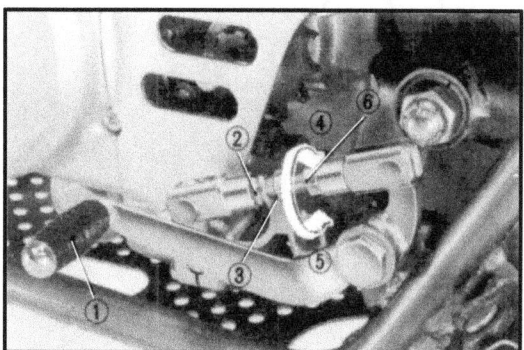

Fig. 18 ① Gear change pedal ② Lock nut (lefthand thread) ③ Adjuster ④ Raise ⑤ Lower ⑥ Lock nut

15. FRONT SUSPENSION SPRING ADJUSTMENT

1) Front suspension spring tension can be adjustable to meet the rider's weight or different road condition. Use the following procedure.
2) Remove the rubber cap from the top of the front fork.
3) Using a screwdriver, adjust the spring tension.
   To obtain hard suspension, turn the adjuster clockwise, and turn counter-clockwise to make it soft. (Fig. 19)

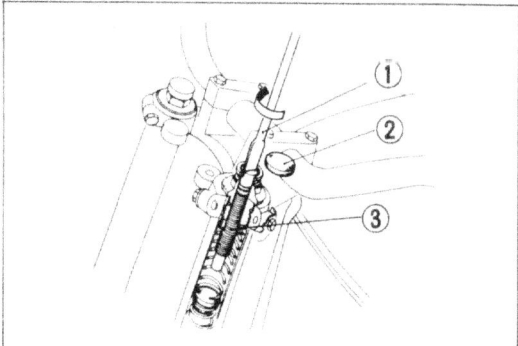

Fig. 19 ① Screwdriver ② Rubber cap ③ Adjuster

16. FRONT FORK OIL CHANGE

1) Regular oil change is required to keep the front suspension operating efficiently.
2) Remove the suspension spring adjuster from top of the fork. Loosen off the drain plugs from each fork leg and pump the fork several times to encourage oil to drain thoroughly. (Fig. 20)

Fig. 20 ① Suspension spring adjuster

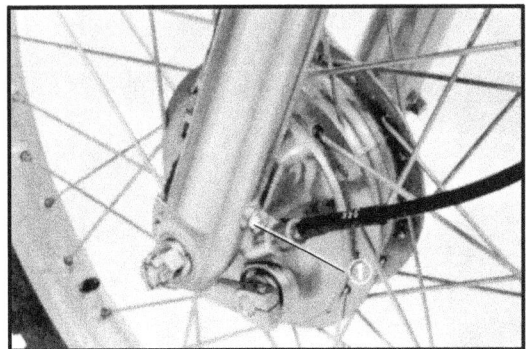

Fig. 21 ① Drain plug

Note:
The fork should be flushed using an approved solvent. Do not use gasoline to avoid damaging rubber parts.

3) Reinstall the drain plugs and refill with fresh oil. (Fig. 21)

Specified oil............ (automobile automatic transmission oil)

Quantity.................. (4.4 to 4.770 ozs) 130 to 140cc

Note:
Tighten the plugs firmly.

17. CYLINDER COMPRESSION INSPECTION

1) Refer to page 12.

II. ENGINE

1. In-motorcycle service items

Items to be serviced	Page
1. Oil filter and oil pump	22
2. Clutch	25
3. Gear shift mechanism	32

2. ENGINE REMOVAL AND INSTALLATION

A. Engine Removal
1) With the aid of a suitable hollow set wrench, loosen the bolt at the muffler band securing the muffler to the exhaust pipe joint. (Fig. 23)

Fig. 23 ① Socket bolt

2) To disassemble the exhaust pipe, remove the two exhaust pipe retaining nuts. (Fig. 24)

Fig. 24 ① 6mm hex. head nut

3) Separate the carburetor from the air cleaner.
4) Take of the seat.
5) Remove the fuel tank.
6) Remove the throttle valve from the carburetor. (Fig. 25)

Fig. 25 ① Throttle valve

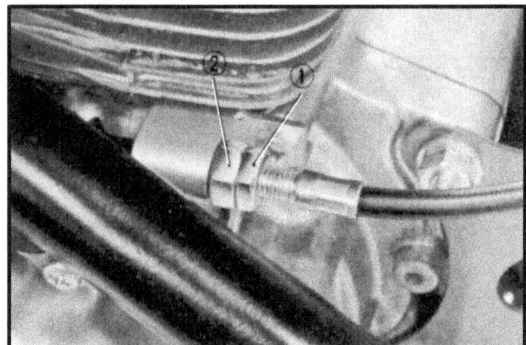

Fig. 26 ① Lock nut ② adjuster

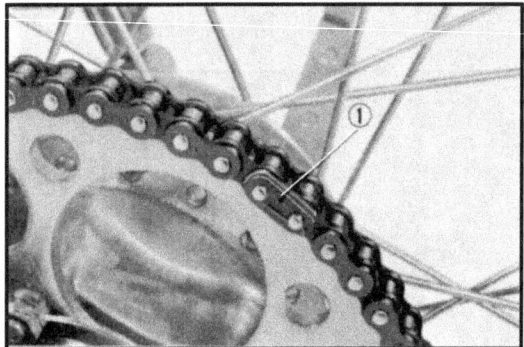

Fig. 27 ① Retaining clip and master link

Fig. 28 ○ — Engine hanger bolts

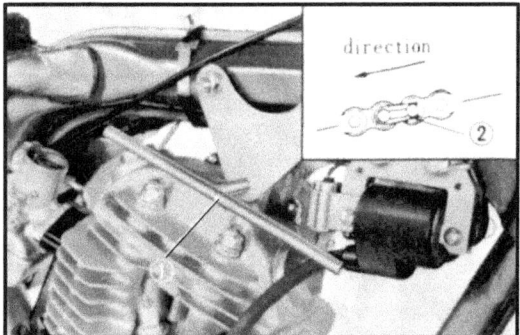

Fig. 29 ① T-screwdriver ② Retaining clip and master link

7) Loosen the clutch wire lock nut and adjuster just enough to slacken the wire; disconnect the wire from the clutch lever. (Fig. 26)

8) Remove the noise suppresor cap.
9) Remove the left side cover. Disconnect the drive chain by removing the clip from the master link. Take off the chain from the motorcycle. (Fig. 27)
10) Disconnect the coupler from the wiring harness.
11) Remove the primary wire.
12) Remove the nuts from the engine hanger bolts. Lift the rear of the engine just enough to remove load from the hanger bolts; pull out the bolts. (Fig. 28)
Place the engine on a clean surface or work bench.

B. Engine Installation

1) To facilitate installation, line up eye on the cylinder head with holes in the top hanger bracket on the frame. Install a T-screwdriver with the end through these holes. The hanger bolts can then be installed easily. (Fig. 29)

2) Tighten the exhaust pipe joint to the muffler in two steps; first fingertight and then to the specified torque using a suitable torque wrench.
3) In installing a drive chain, note the direction of the master link retaining clip.
4) Adjust the clutch as per the instructions described earlier in this manual.

III. ENGINE, CHASSIS AND ELECTRICAL

● ENGINE

1. CLUTCH

In the clutch assembly of TL125, four friction discs and four clutch plates are incorporated, one plate less than those of CB/CL/SL100 and CB/CL/SL 125 S models.

The following shows an exploded view of the clutch so that the relative positions of the parts can be seen. (Fig. 30)

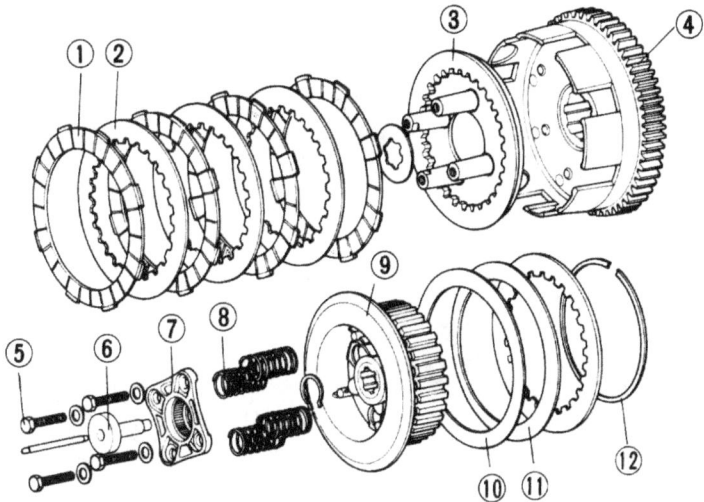

Fig. 30 ① Friction disc ② Clutch plate ③ Clutch pressure plate ④ Clutch outer ⑤ Clutch lifter rod
⑥ Clutch lifter guide pin ⑦ Clutch lifter plate ⑧ Clutch spring ⑨ Clutch center ⑩ Disc spring seat
⑪ Clutch spring disc ⑫ Set ring (82.5mm)

Removal

1) Remove the kick pedal and right crankcase cover as shown in (Fig. 3).
2) Disengage the clutch wire end at the crankcase cover.
3) Remove the split pin; take out the clutch lifter cam, clutch spring and clutch lever.

(Fig. 31)

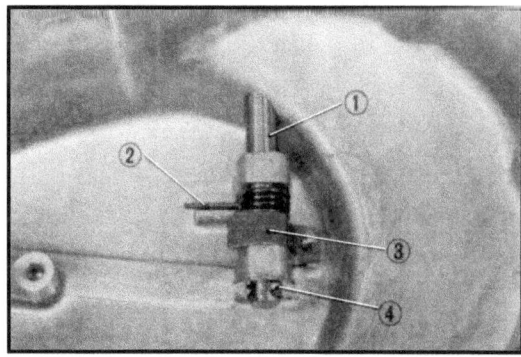

Fig. 31 ① Clutch lever ② Clutch spring
③ Clutch lifter cam ④ Split pin

4) Remove the clutch lifter rod. Follow the items listed on page 25.

Reverse the order of the removal to install the clutch lever.

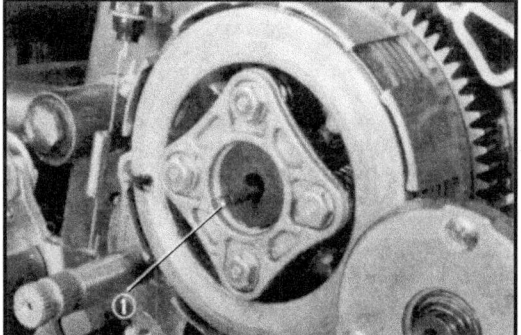

Fig. 32 ① Clutch lifter rod

2. TRANSMISSION

The transmission used on TL 125 is essentially the same as those used on CB/CL/SL100 and CB/CD/SL 125S except for the gear arrangement on the main shaft and the resultant changes in the shift drum groove. (Fig. 33)

Disassembly, inspection and assembly procedures will not be shown here since these are identical to those of CB100. See pages 32 thru 35.

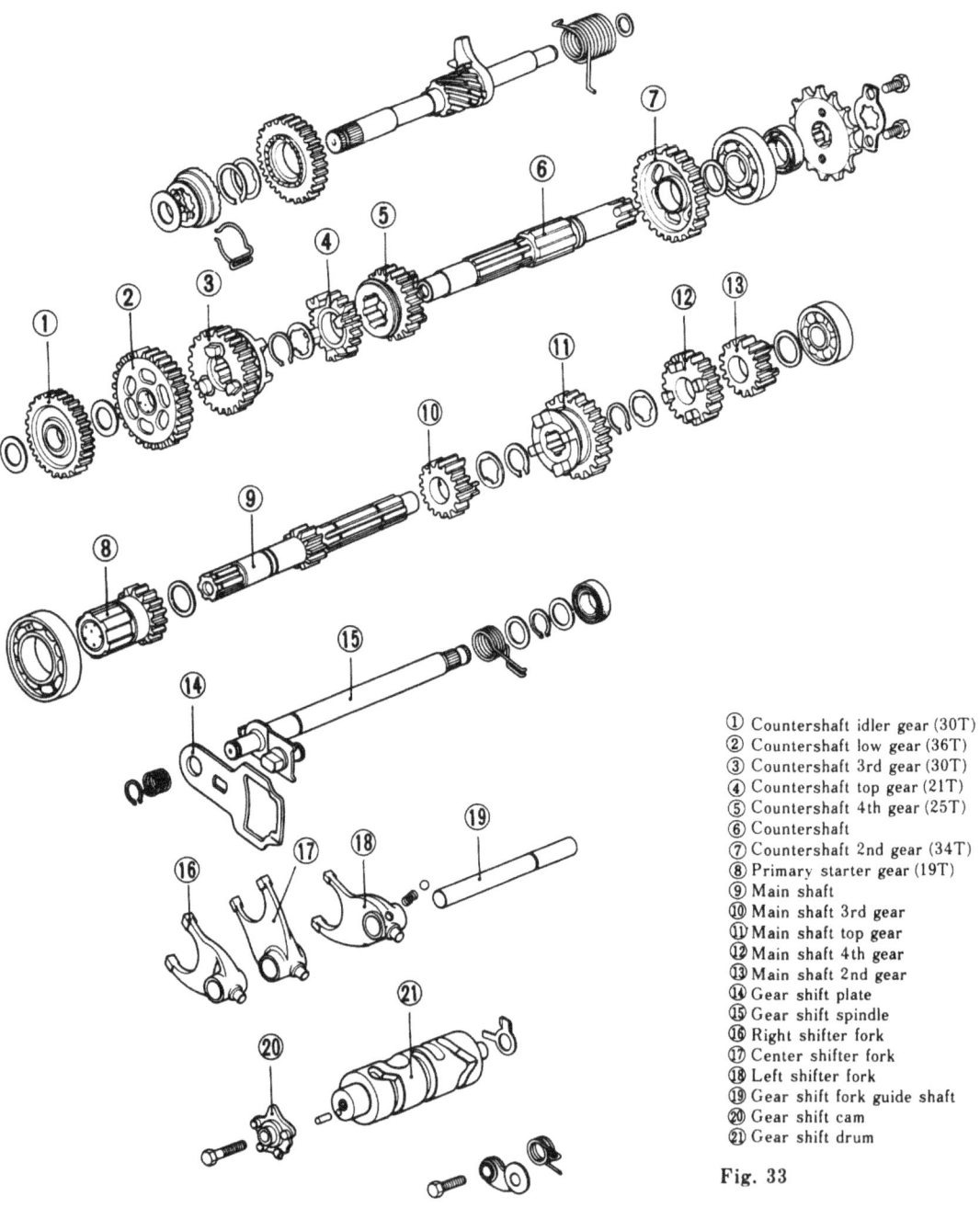

① Countershaft idler gear (30T)
② Countershaft low gear (36T)
③ Countershaft 3rd gear (30T)
④ Countershaft top gear (21T)
⑤ Countershaft 4th gear (25T)
⑥ Countershaft
⑦ Countershaft 2nd gear (34T)
⑧ Primary starter gear (19T)
⑨ Main shaft
⑩ Main shaft 3rd gear
⑪ Main shaft top gear
⑫ Main shaft 4th gear
⑬ Main shaft 2nd gear
⑭ Gear shift plate
⑮ Gear shift spindle
⑯ Right shifter fork
⑰ Center shifter fork
⑱ Left shifter fork
⑲ Gear shift fork guide shaft
⑳ Gear shift cam
㉑ Gear shift drum

Fig. 33

● CHASSIS

1. BRAKE ARM

After putting the brake panel assembly on the wheel hub, install the brake arm on the brake camshaft, aligning the mark on the arm with index on the shaft. (Fig. 34)

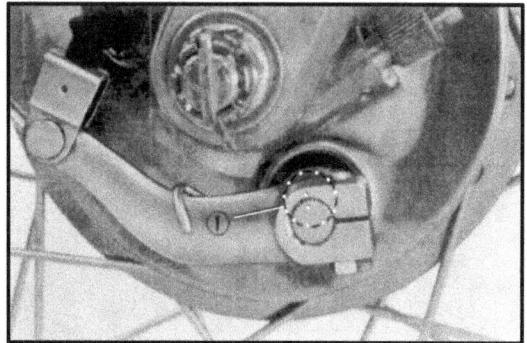

Fig. 34 ① Aligning marks

2. HANDLEBAR

Be sure and keep the punch mark on the handlebar flush with the top face of the holder as shown. (Fig. 35)

Note:
After making sure that the punch mark and top face of the holder match up, tighten the holder firmly, starting with the front then the rear.

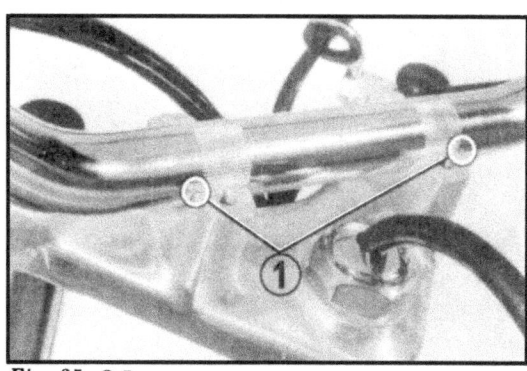

Fig. 35 ① Punch mark

3. CABLES AND LEAD WIRES

All cables and lead wires should be positioned as per the instructions given in Figs. 36 and 37.

Note:
Be sure that cables and wires are not binding or stressed when the handle is operated between two extremes.

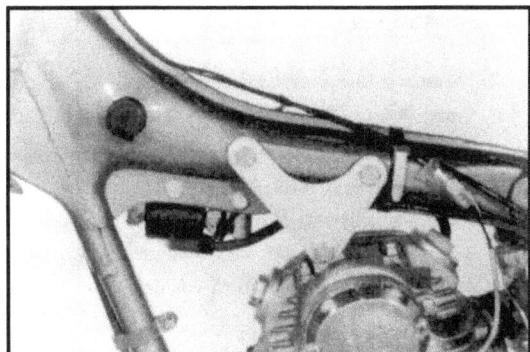

Fig. 36

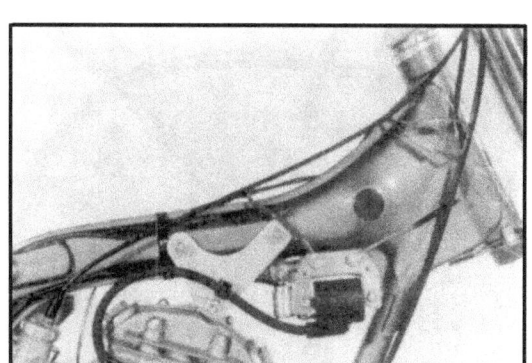

Fig. 37

4. FRONT SUSPENSION

	stroke	damping force
TL125	152mm	15~20kg/0.5m/sec

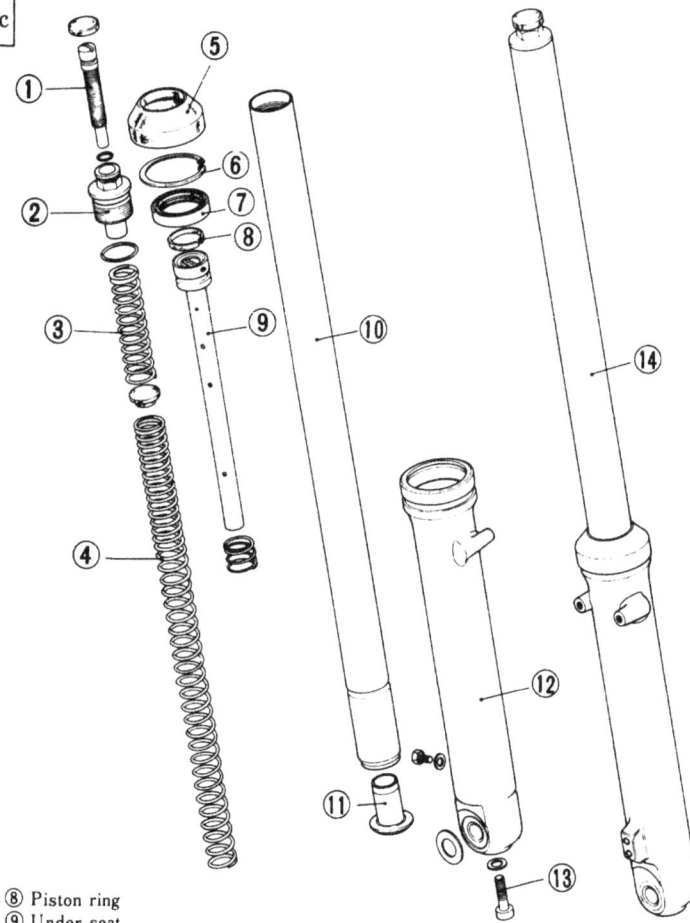

Fig. 38

① Spring adjuster
② Fork bolt
③ Front cushion spring "A"
④ Front cushion spring "B"
⑤ Front fork dust seal
⑥ Inner snap ring (45mm)
⑦ Oil seal (31×43×12.5)
⑧ Piston ring
⑨ Under seat
⑩ Front fork pipe
⑪ Oil lock piece
⑫ Front fork bottom case
⑬ Fork bolt cap
⑭ Front fork Assy

Fig. 39 ① Front fork bolt ② Clamp bolts

A. DISASSEMBLY NOTES

1) Remove the front wheel. For details, see page 37.
2) Before removing each front fork, remove the fork bolt and drain bolt.
3) Pump the front fork to drain the oil.
4) Loosen the upper and lower clamp bolts and pull the front fork legs down.

5) Separate the bottom case from the front fork pipe by removing the fork bolt cap. To remove, use tool "Hollow set Wrench 07917-3230000."
6) Remove the dust seal. Remove the snap ring by using pliers. (**Fig. 40**)
7) Separate the fork pipe from the bottom pipe.
8) Separate the lower section from the front fork pipe.
9) Remove the oil seal.

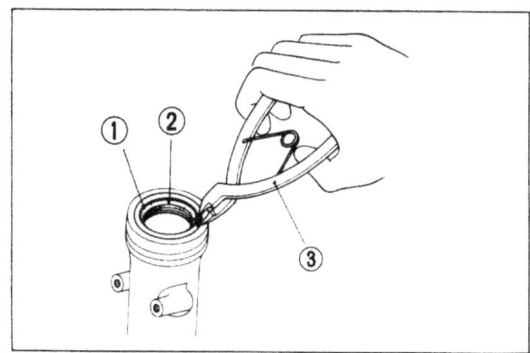

Fig. 40 ① Snap ring ② Oil seal ③ Snap ring plier

B. INSPECTION
1) Check the front fork piston ring is not worn.
2) Check the suspension spring for free length and as-installed tension.
3) Inspect the front bottom case for wear.
4) Determine if the fork pipe is not cracked or damaged excessively beyond use.

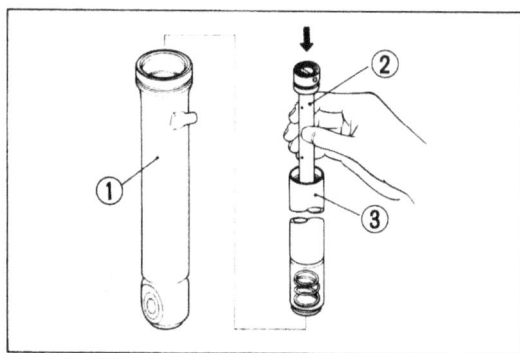

Fig. 41 ① Front fork bottom pipe ② Bottom pipe ③ Fork pipe

C. ASSEMBLY
1) Wash all parts thoroughly in cleaning solvent.
2) Slide the lower section into place in the fork pipe; insert the suspension spring. (**Fig. 41**)

Note:
Before installation, apply Automobile automatic transmission fluid.

3) Assemble the fork pipe with the bottom case.

Note:
Use suitable sealer to the fork bolt cap

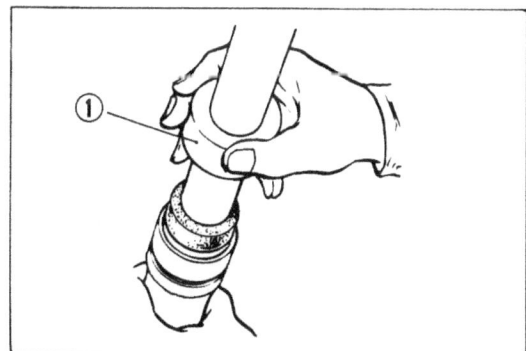

Fig. 42 ① Oil seal installer

4) Drive the oil seal into place in the bottom case. Use tool "Oil Seal Installer. 07947-3550000. (**Fig. 42**)
5) Place the snap ring in the groove in the bottom case. Make sure it seats properly.
6) Pour the specified amount of HONDA automobile automatic transmission fluid oil in the front fork. (**Fig. 43**)
Specified quantity............ 4.4~4.70 ozs (130~140cc)

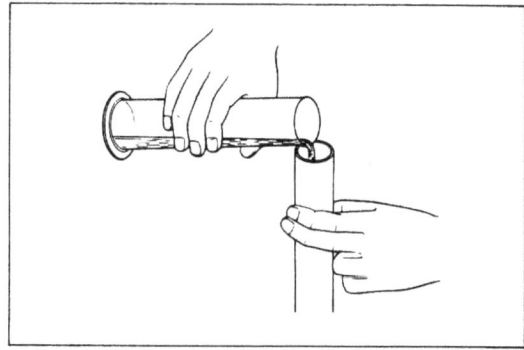

Fig. 43

Note:
The fork should be filled with the fluid before it is installed into the steering stem.

● ELECTRICAL SYSTEM

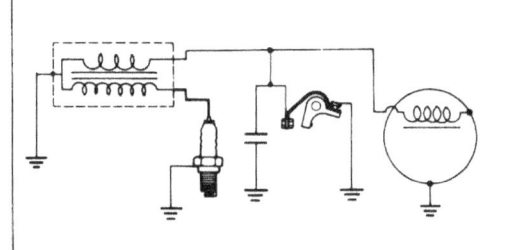

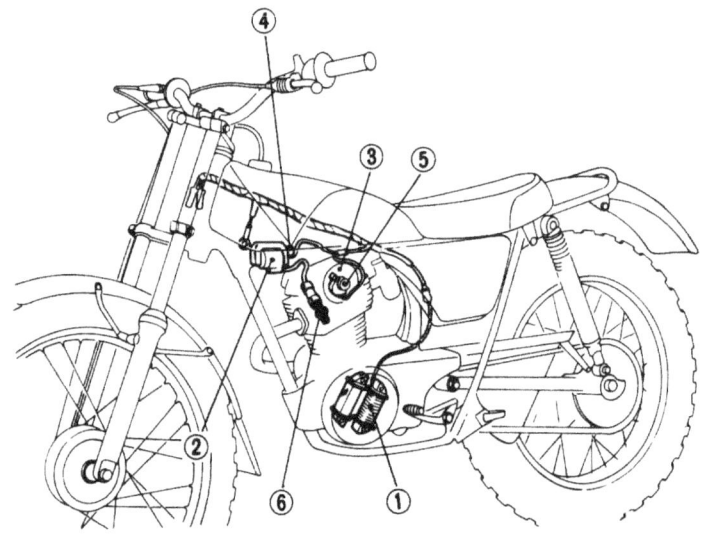

Fig. 44
① Generator coil
② Ignition coil
③ Contact breaker
④ Condenser
⑤ Spark advancer
⑥ Spark plug

Referring to the illustration above, the ignition system consists of the generator, ignition coil, contact breaker, condenser, spark advance mechanism and spark plug to ignite the air-fuel mixture in the engine cylinder.

Technical Data

Ignition coil	Spark length (3-needle)	7mm min @ 500 rpm
Spark plug	Type	D-8ESL (NGK) X-24ES (DENSO)
	Gap	0.6 to 0.7mm
Contact breaker	Point pressure	800 ± 100g
	Point gap	0.35mm ± 0.05mm
Condenser	Capacity	0.24 μF
	Insulation resistance	10MΩ (by 1000V Megger)
Spark advancer	Advance angle	8.5° ± 1.5°
	Camshaft rpm at 1° advance	1100 ± 100 rpm
	Engine rpm at full advance	2000 ± 100 rpm

1. GENERATOR

The generator is fundamentally an A.C. generator, with the rotor driven by the crankshaft. The design is essentially the same as that used on SL250S. Current available at the generator operates the ignition system to supply high-voltage surges to the spark plug.

2. A.C. GENERATOR

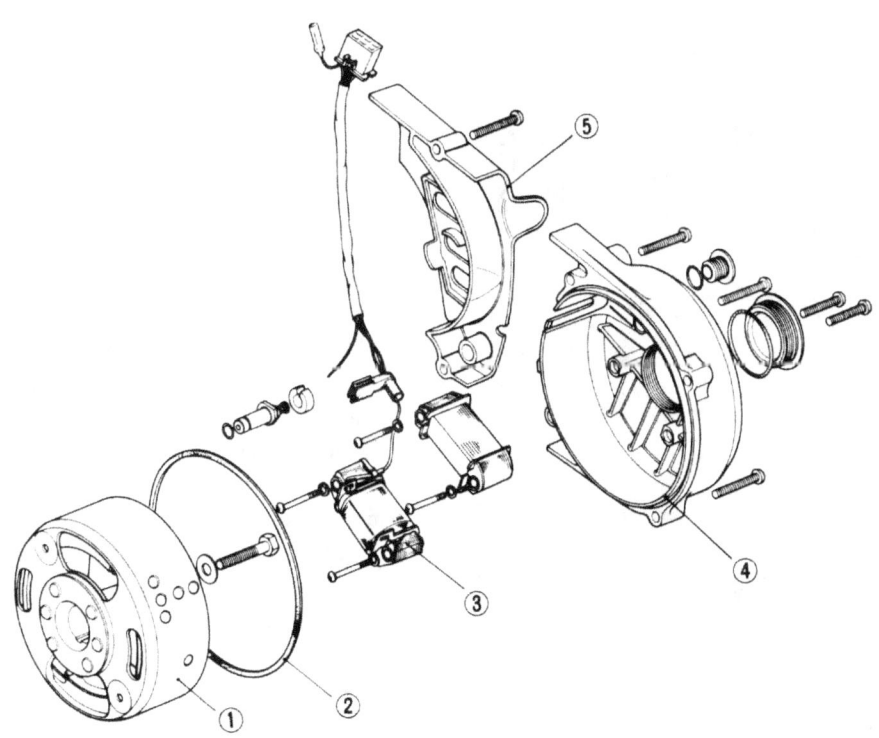

Fig. 45
① Flywheel
② Oil seal
③ Primary coil
④ Left crankcase cover
⑤ Left crankcase rear cover

Fig. 46 ① Stator mounting bolt

A. Removal
1) Remove the two crankcase covers, front and rear, from the left side of the engine.
2) Remove the stator by loosening the attaching bolts.
3) Remove the primary coil by loosening the Stator mounting bolt (Fig. 46)

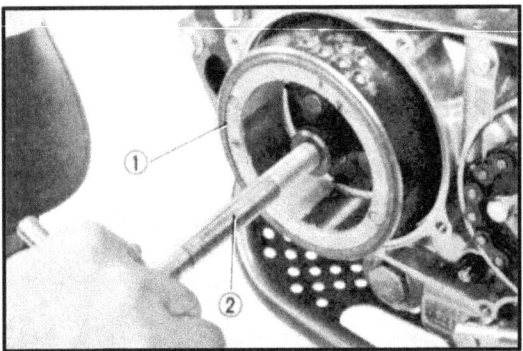

Fig. 47 ① Flywheel ② Flywheel extractor

4) With the help of tool "Flywheel Extractor 07011-20001," remove the rotor. (Fig. 47)

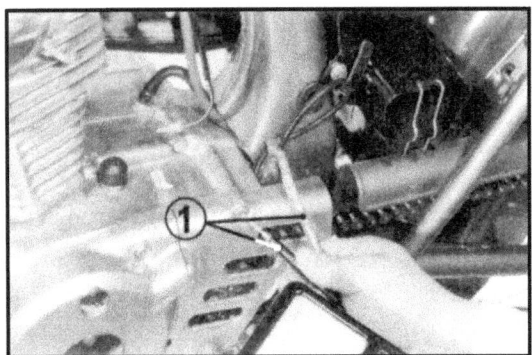

Fig. 48 ① Tester probes

B. Stator Inspection
When failure to start is due to broken stator coil, this can be checked with a tester. To make this check, disconnect the stator cord, black stripes on white ground, at the wiring connector. Hold a test prod against the connector, and the other against the metal part of the stator. If continuity exists, it indicates the stator coil is not broken or disconnected.

● INSPECTION OF ELECTRICAL ACCESSORIES

1. MAIN SWITCH

If the engine fails to stop with the ignition switch in OFF, the likelihood is that the switch is internally short-circuited. The ignition switch test is made by first disconnecting the primary lead (black/white) and that of the neutral switch and then checking continuity between the leads with a tester. If continuity exists when the kill switch is turned on, it is probable that the switch is defective, calling for replacement.

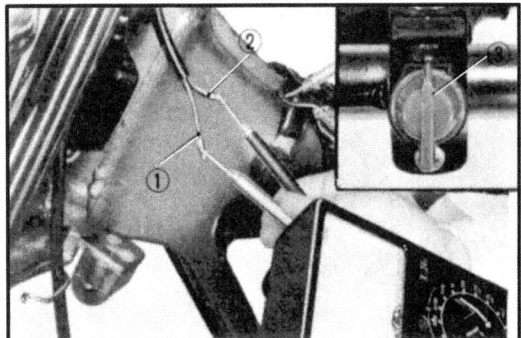

Fig. 49 ① Black/White ② Green ③ Mainswitch

TABLE OF OPTIONAL PARTS

No.	Part Name	Description	Application	Remarks
1	Rear wheel tire	1) New, wider tread tire with special tread pattern (about 10mm wider than standard specification) 2) Tire size same as standard type 3) Featuring more bite on swampy underfoot conditions or on slopes	1) Chain case to be removed 2) Trial race only	Off-road use only
2	Tire gauge (psi)	1) For measuring tire pressure in pound-inch system 2) Gauge dial: 5 to 35 psi		
3	Air pump	1) Portable air pump to inflate tires to standard pressure when driving on public road after racing		
4	Air pump brackets	1) Air pump lower bracket 2) Air pump upper bracket	1) Tightened with left upper of engine hanger plate 2) Fastened with 12mm bolt along with frame body downtube	
5	Front fork stiffener	1) To improve structural rigidity of front fork for racing	**(Mounting location)** Left of bottom bridge on the bottom, and right of top bridge on the upper, as viewed from front of motorcycle	
6	Number plate	1) For number or code assigned during race	1) Fastened with band to front fork stiffener	
7	Number plate band		1) Tightened to front fork stiffener with two 6mm bolts	
8	Direct type gear change pedal	For use in trial racing	1) Directly attached to gear change pedal spindle in place of link type pedal	

MAINTENANCE SCHEDULE

The maintenance intervals shown in the following schedule are based upon average riding conditions. Machines subjected to severe use, or ridden in unusually dusty areas, require more frequent servicing.
Items marked with* should be serviced by an authorized Honda dealer, unless the owner has proper tools and is mechanically proficient.
Other maintenance items are simple to perform and may be serviced by the owner.

INITIAL SERVICE PERIOD **FIRST WEEK OF OPERATION**	• ENGINE OIL—Change. • *CONTACT POINTS AND IGNITION TIMING—Clean, check, and adjust or replace if necessary. • *VALVE TAPPET CLEARANCE—Check and adjust if necessary. • *CARBURETOR—Check and adjust if necessary. • THROTTLE OPERATION—Inspect cable. Check and adjust free play. • *CLUTCH—Check operation and adjust if necessary.	• DRIVE CHAIN—Check, lubricate, and adjust if necessary. • BRAKE CONTROL LINKAGE—Check linkage and adjust if necessary. • TIRES—Inspect and check air pressure. • ALL NUTS, BOLTS, AND OTHER FASTENERS—Check security and tighten if necessary. • *WHEELS, RIMS, AND SPOKES—Check. Tighten spokes and true wheels if necessary.
EVERY 30 OPERATING DAYS **NOTE** Change oil every 30 operating days or every 3 months, whichever occurs first.	• ENGINE OIL—Change. • SPARK PLUG—Clean and adjust gap, or replace if necessary. • *CONTACT POINTS AND IGNITION TIMING—Clean, check, and adjust or replace if necessary. • *VALVE TAPPET CLEARANCE—Check and adjust if necessary. • POLYURETHANE FOAM AIR • FILTER ELEMENT—Clean and oil. Service more frequently if operated in dusty areas. • *CARBURETOR—Check and adjust if necessary. • *WHEELS, RIMS, AND SPOKES—Check. Tighten spokes and tire wheels if necessary.	• *CAM CHAIN TENSION—Adjust (only initial service). • THROTTLE OPERATION—Inspect cable. Check and adjust free play. • *CLUTCH—Check operation and adjust if necessary. • DRIVE CHAIN—Check, lubricate, and adjust if necessary. • BRAKE CONTROL LINKAGE—Check linkage and adjust if necessary. • TIRES—Inspect and check air pressure. • ALL NUTS, BOLTS, AND OTHER FASTENERS—Check security and tighten if necessary.
EVERY YEAR	• FUEL FILTER SCREEN—Clean. • FUEL LINE—Check. • FRONT FORK OIL—Drain and refill. • *OIL FILTER SCREEN—Clean. • *CENTRIFUGAL OIL FILTER—Clean. • *FRONT AND REAR SUSPENSION—Check operation. • *STEERING HEAD BEARINGS—Adjust. • *BRAKE SHOES—Inspect and replace if worn. • *CAM CHAIN TENSION—Adjust.	

SPECIFICATIONS

	Item	English	Metric
Dimension	Overall length	78.5 in.	1,995 mm
	Overall width	33.1 in.	840 mm
	Overall height	43.1 in.	1,095 mm
	Wheel base	50.4 in.	1,280 mm
	Seat height	30.7 in.	780 mm
	Foot peg height	13.2 in.	335 mm
	Ground clearance	10.2 in.	260 mm
	Dry weight	194 lbs.	88 kg
Frame	Type	Semi double cradle	
	F. suspension, travel	Telescopic fork, travel 6.0 in. (152mm)	
	R. suspension, travel	Swing arm, travel 3.7 in. (94mm)	
	F. tire size, pressure	2.75–21 (4PR), Semi-Knobby, tire air presure 1.5kg/cm² 21psi	
	R. tire size, pressure	4.00–18 (4PR), Semi-Knobby, tire air presure 1.5kg/cm² 21psi	
	F. brake, lining area	Internal expanding shoes, swept area 13.4 sq·in (86.4 sq-cm)	
	R. brake, lining area	Internal expanding shoes, swept area 13.4 sq·in (86.4 sq-cm)	
	Fuel capacity	1.2 US gal.	4.5 lit.
	Fuel reserve capacity	0.1 US gal	0.5 lit.
	Caster angle	61° 30'	
	Trail length	4.1 in.	105 mm
Engine	Type	Air cooled, 4-stroke OHC engine	
	Cylinder arrangement	Single cylinder 15° inclined from vertical	
	Bore and stroke	2.204 × 1.949 in.	56.0 × 49.5 mm
	Displacement	7.44 cu-in	122 cc
	Compression ratio	8.0 : 1	
	Valve train	Chain driven over head camshaft	
	Maximum horsepower	8.0 BHP/8,000 rpm	
	Maximum torque	5.55 lb-ft/4,000 rpm	0.83 kg-m/4,000 rpm
	Oil capacity	1.1 US qt.	1.0 lit.
	Lubrication system	Forced and wet sump	
	Cylinder head compression pressure	12 kg/sq-cm at 1,000 rpm	
	Intake valve Opens	BTDC 0°	
	Intake valve Closes	ABDC 30°	
	Exhaust valve Opens	BBDC 35°	
	Exhaust valve Closes	ATDC 0°	
	Valve tappet clearance	0.0002 in.	0.05 mm
	Idle speed	1,300 rpm	
Drive train	Clutch	Wet, multi plates	
	Transmission	5-speed constant mesh	
	Primary reduction	4.055	
	Gear ratio I	2.769	
	Gear ratio II	2.125	
	Gear ratio III	1.578	
	Gear ratio IV	1.000	
	Gear ratio V	0.724	
	Final reduction	4.000, drive sprocket 15T, driven sprocket 60T	
	Gear shift pattern	Left foot operated return system	
Electrical	Ignition	Flywheel magneto	
	Starting system	Kick starter	
	Alternator	A. C. generator	
	Spark plug	NGK D 8ES–L or ND X 24ES	

TL 125 WIRING DIAGRAM

1. FUEL COCK

The indication marks and their positions on the fuel cock were changed to a new type.

Fig. S2-1 ①Fuel cock ②Lever

2. HEADLIGHT AND ENGINE STOP SWITCH

The dimmer switch, previously offered on the switch case at the right side of the steering handlebar, was relocated to the left switch case. This also necessitated changes in the design of the switch case.

The engine stop switch is also new for the revised model.

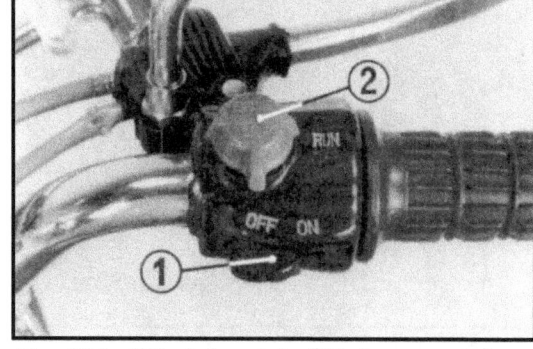

Fig. S2-2 ①Headlight switch ②Engine stop switch

3. TURN SIGNAL, HORN AND DIMMER SWITCH

A new dimmer switch is added to the turn signal and horn switch case at the left side of the handlebar.

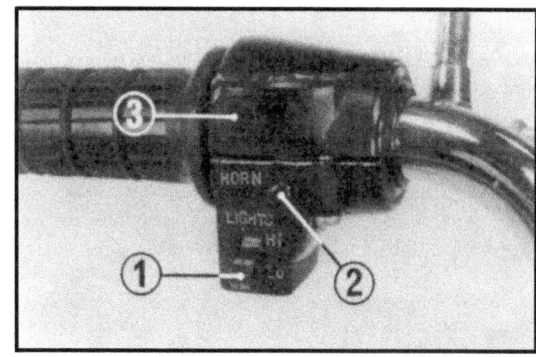

Fig. S2-3 ①Dimmer switch ②Horn switch ③Turn signal control switch

Fig. S2-4 ①Lower adjuster

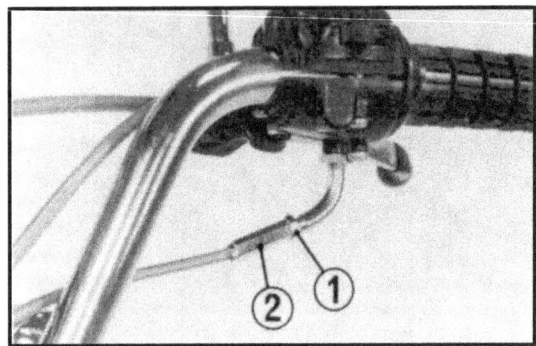

Fig. S2-5 ①Lock nut ②Upper adjuster

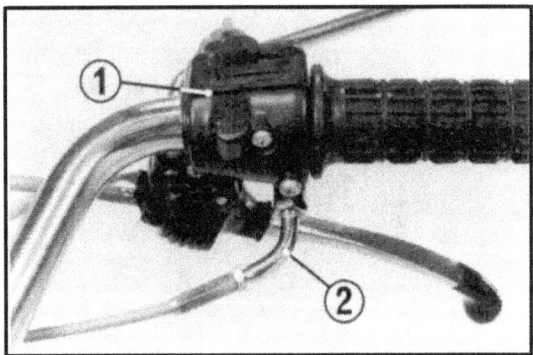

Fig. S2-6 ①Switch case ②Throttle cable

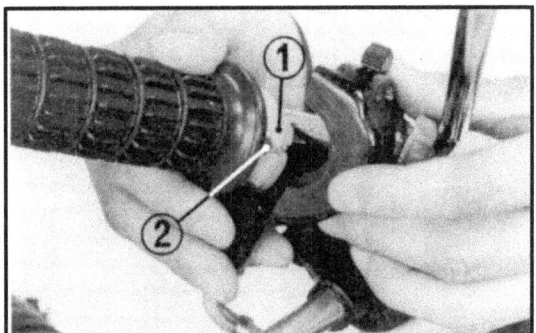

Fig. S2-7 ①Grip pipe ②Throttle cable end

4. THROTTLE GRIP

The throttle grip was changed.

Inspection and adjustment

1) Check the free play of the throttle grip. It should be 10-15 degrees of the grip rotation.
2) This play can be adjusted at either end of the throttle cable. Major free play adjustments are made with the lower adjuster (such as after replacing a throttle cable or removing the carburetor).

    Minor free play adjustments are made with the upper adjuster. To adjust, loosen the lock nut and turn the adjuster. Tighten the look nut after adjustment.
3) Check the throttle cable for twisting, or interference with adjacent parts; also for proper routing, while turning the handlebar to each extreme.

    Repair or, if necessary, replace the cable with a new one.

Disassembly and assembly

1) Loosen off the screws securing the switch housing to the handlebar; separate the housing.
2) Disconnect the throttle cable end from the throttle grip pipe.
3) Withdraw the throttle grip from the handlebar.
4) Disconnect the throttle cable from the switch housing.
5) Assemble the throttle grip in the reverse order of disassembly.

5. SIDE STAND

The side stand was changed to a new type with a shock absorbing rubber pad.

The stand must be inspected periodically to determine that it is in good condition.

Inspection

1) Check the entire stand assembly (side stand bar, bracket and rubber pad) for installation, deformation or otherwise excessive damage.
2) Check the spring for freedom from damage or other defects.
3) Check the side stand for proper return operation
   a. With the side stand applied, raise the stand off the ground by using the main stand.
   b. Attach a spring balance to the lower end of the stand and measure the force with which the stand is returned to its original position.
   c. The stand condition is correct if the measurement falls within 2–3kg (4.4–6.6 lbs.).

   If the stand requires force exceeding the above limit, this might be due to neglected lubrication, overtightened side stand pivot bolt, worn stand bar or bracket, or otherwise excessive tension. Repair as necessary.

4) Check the rubber pad for deterioration or wear.

   When the rubber pad wear is excessive so that it is worn down to the wear line, replace it with a new one.

Rubber pad replacement

1) Remove the 6mm bolt; separate the rubber pad from the bracket at the side stand.
2) After making sure the collar is installed, put a new rubber pad in place in the bracket with the arrow mark out.

Note:

Use rubber pad having the mark "BELOW 259 lbs ONLY".

3) Secure the rubber pad with the 6mm bolt.

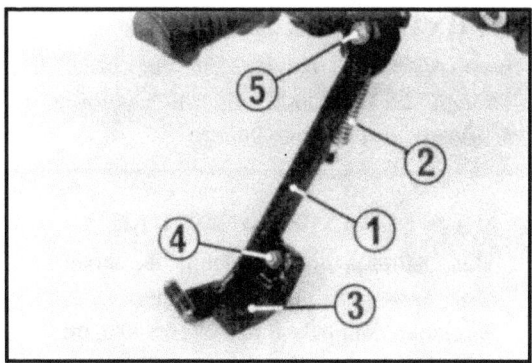

Fig. S2-8 ①Side stand bar ②Spring ③Rubber pad ④6mm bolt ⑤Side stand pivot bolt

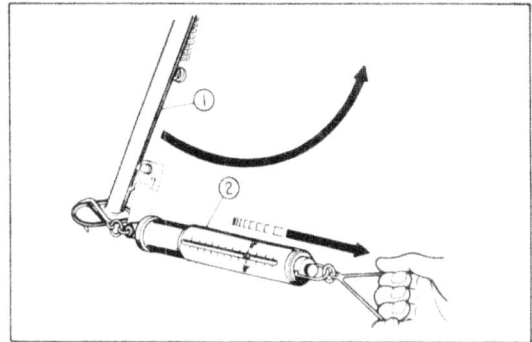

Fig. S2-9 ①Side stand bar ②Spring balance

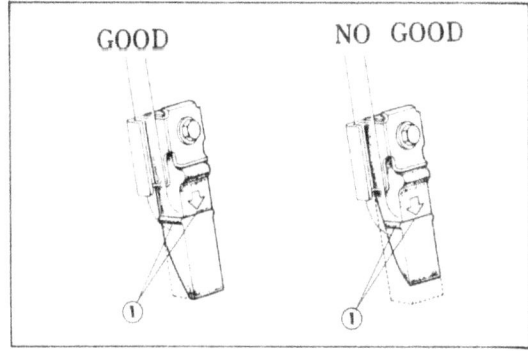

Fig. S2-10 ①Wear line

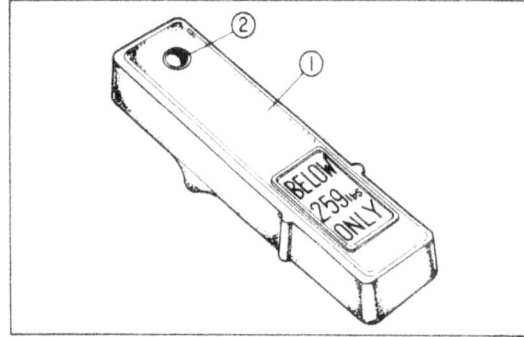

Fig. S2-11 ①Rubber pad ②Collar

6. MAINTENANCE SCHEDULE

Some additions occured in the MAINTE-NANCE SCHEDULE, of which details are as shown immediately below:

MAINTENANCE SCHEDULE This maintenance schedule is based upon average riding conditions. Machines subjected to severe use, or ridden in unusually dusty areas, require more frequent servicing.	Initial Service Period	Regular Service Period Perform at every indicated month or mileage interval, whichever occurs first.			
	500 miles	1 month	3 months	6 months	12 months
		500 miles	1,500 miles	3,000 miles	6,000 miles
* Side Stand — check installation, operation, deformation, damage and wear.				○	

Items marked * should be serviced by an authorized Honda dealer, unless the owner has proper tools and is mechanically proficient. All other maintenance items are simple to perform and may be serviced by the owner.

7. WIRING DIAGRAM
(CB125S2)

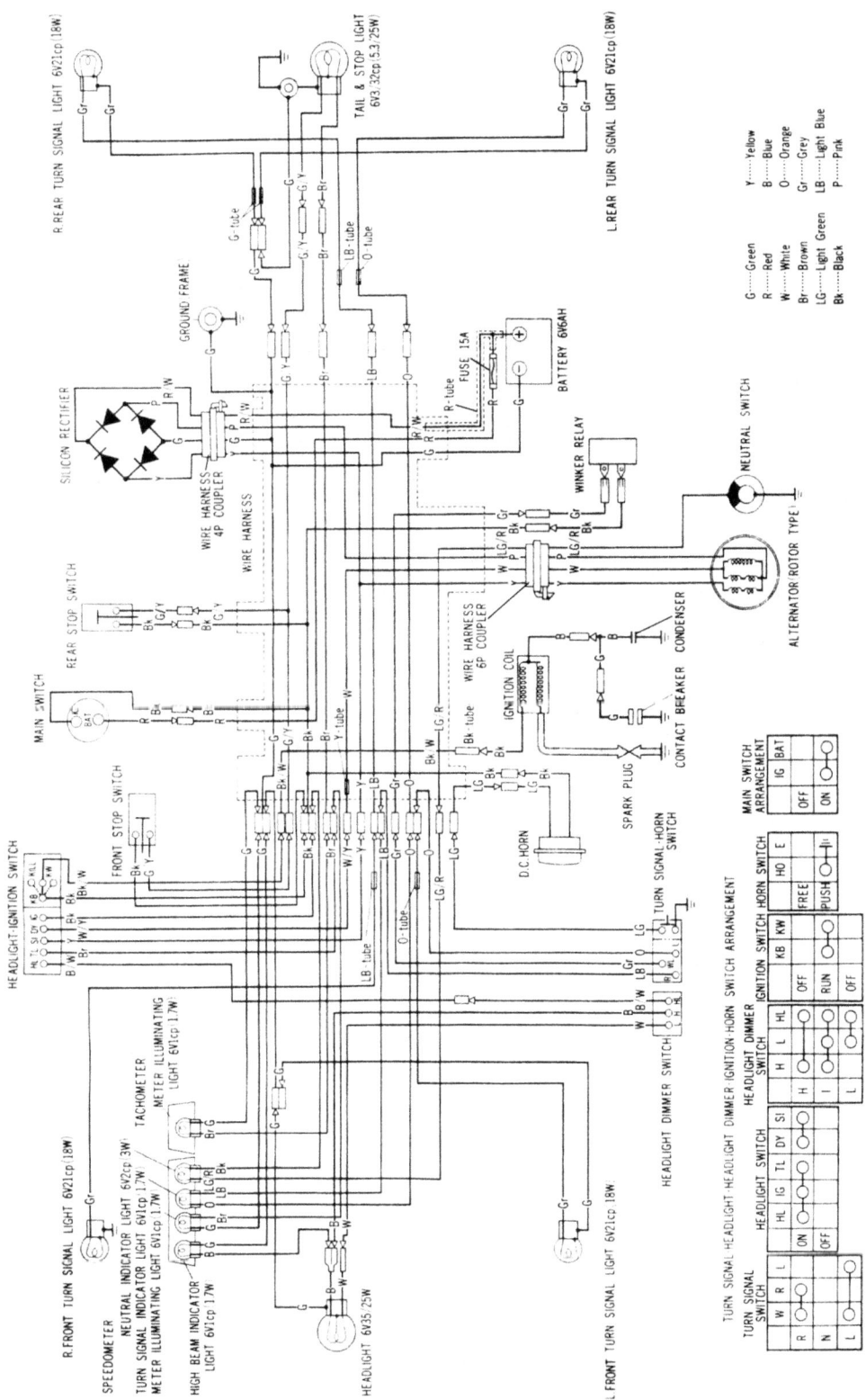

1. GEAR CHANGE PEDAL

The revised model now features a direct gear change pedal in place of those previously offered.

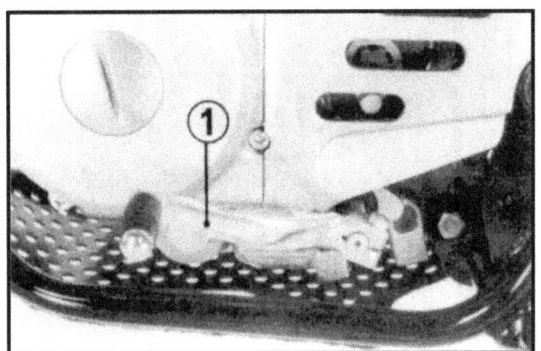

Fig. K2-1　①Gear change pedal

2. BRAKE WEAR INDICATOR

On the TL125K2, there are wear indicators provided for the front and rear brakes. When the brake is applied, the arrow, adjacent to the brake arm, moves toward the reference mark on the brake panel. The distance between the arrow and the reference mark, on full application of the brake, indicates brake lining thickness. If the arrow aligns with the reference mark on full application of the brake, replace the brake shoes.

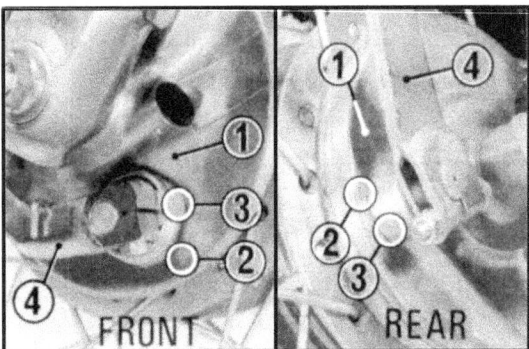

Fig. K2-2　①Brake panel　②Reference mark　③Arrow　④Brake arm

3. FRONT SUSPENSION

The tension adjustment mechanism of the front shock absorber was discontinued. Concurrent with this change, the absorber was changed in design. See Fig. K2-3

Changing front fork oil

1) Remove the drain plugs from both forks. Grasp the handlebar and bounce up and down several times to aid in draining the remaining oil.
2) Replace the drain plugs. Place a suitable stand under engine the to raise the front wheel off the ground.
3) Remove the rubber cap from the top of the shock absorber.

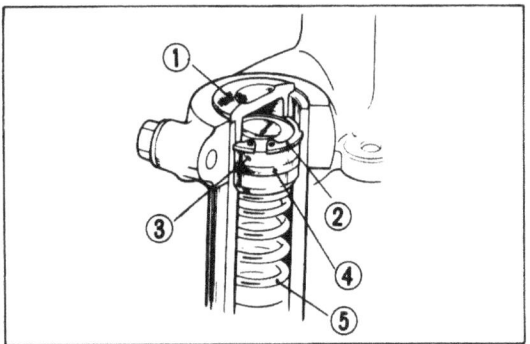

Fig. K2-3　①Rubber cap　②Snap ring　③Plug　④O-ring　⑤Shock absorber spring

4) Pry out the snap ring with snap ring pliers while pushing the plug down with a screwdriver.
5) Take out the plug.
6) Pour the specified amount of ATF (automatic transmission fluid) into the vacant holes.
   Specified amount : 130-140cc (4.4-4.8 ozs.)
7) Install the plug, snap ring and rubber cap.

Note:
Make sure the snap ring is fully seated in the groove.

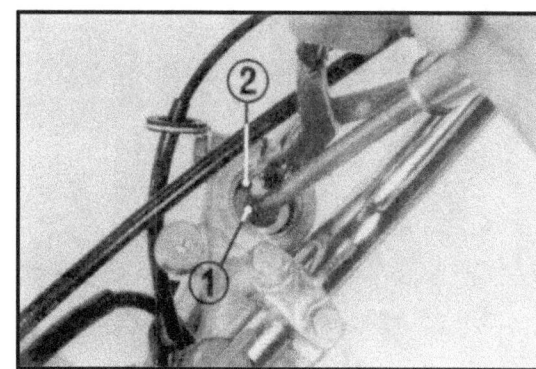

Fig. K2-4 ①Plug ②Snap ring

4. REAR SUSPENSION

The damping characteristic of the rear shock absorber was changed for smoother ride on rough surfaces.

	TL125K2	TL125K1
Ten.	79-101kg/0.5m/s (174-223lbs./1.64ft/s)	30kg/0.5m/s (66lbs./1.64ft/s)
Comp.	16-24kg/1.0m/s (35-53lbs./3.28ft/s)	30kg/1.0m/s (66lbs./1.64ft/s)

5. MUFFLER MOUNTING

The muffler of the new model was mounted on the frame with two bolts and one rubber pad at the bottom instead of three bolts for the previous model.

6. IGNITION SWITCH

The ignition switch was changed in location. It is now at the center of the steering handlebar as shown in Fig. K2-6

Fig. K2-5 ①Rubber pad ②Bolt

7. MAINTENANCE SCHEDULE

Some additions occured in the MAINTENANCE SCHEDULE, of which details are as shown immediately below:

REGULAR SERVICE PERIOD EVERY 30 OPERATING DAY	● SIDE STAND – Check installation, operation, deformation, damage and wear.

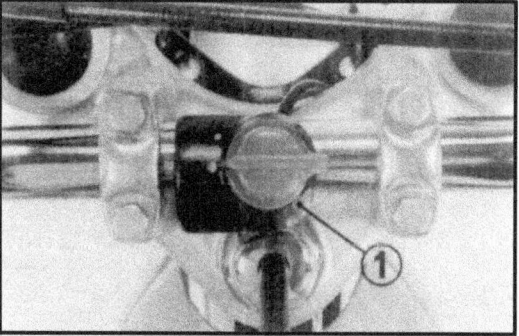

Fig. K2-6 ①Ignition switch

8. WIRING DIAGRAM
(TL 125 K2)

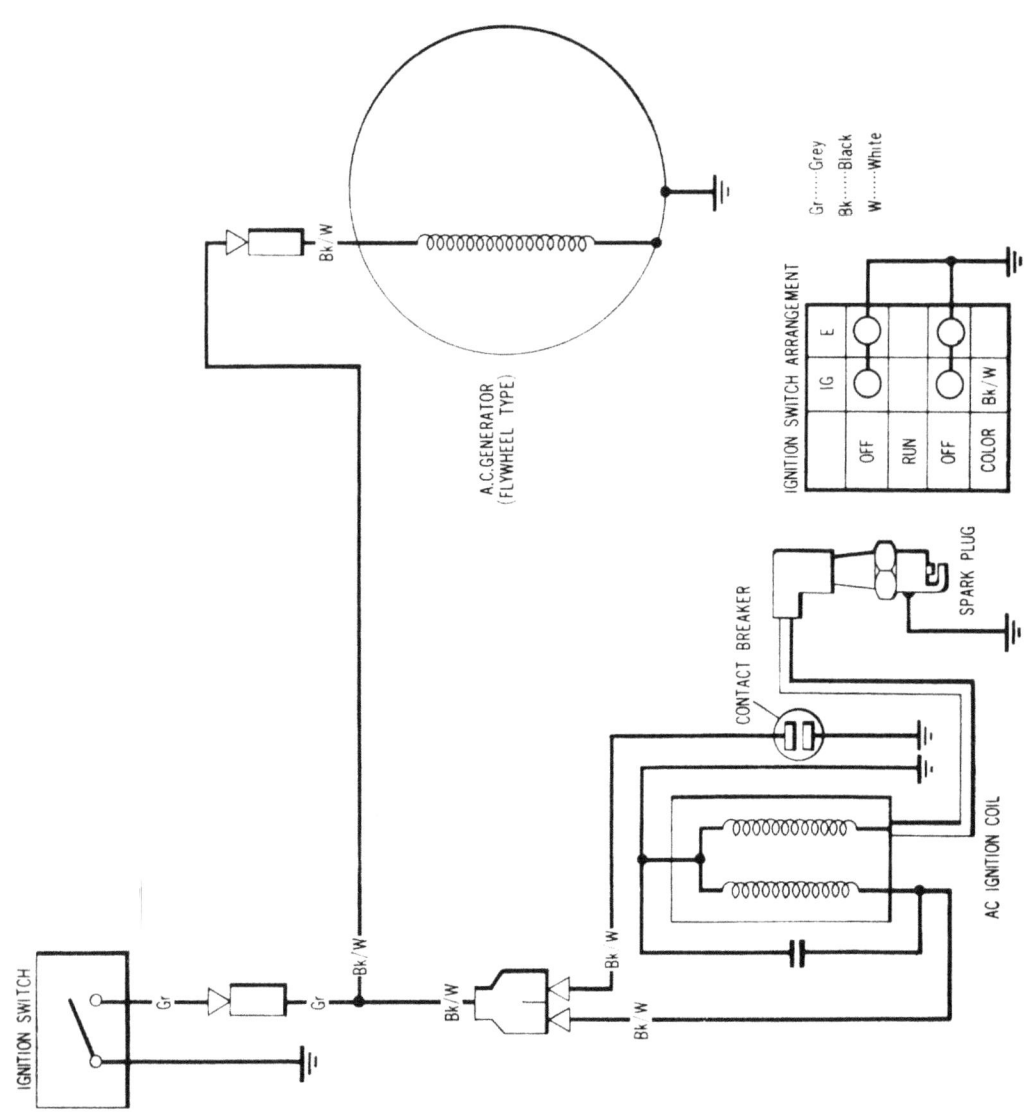

'76 SUPPLEMENT TL125

SUPPLEMENT TO TL125 '76
Engine No. TL125SE-1000001 and subsequent.
Frame No. TL125S-1000001 and subsequent.

Headlight
A. Disassembly
1) Remove the headlight attaching screw and remove the headlight.

Fig. 1 ① Headlight attaching screw

2) Remove each connector.
3) Remove the two 8mm bolts and remove the headlight case.

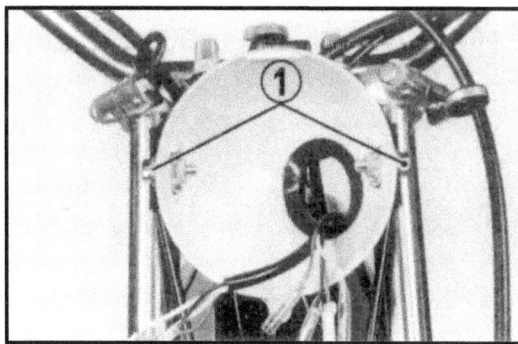

Fig. 2 ① 8mm bolt

4) Remove the two 6mm bolts and remove the headlight bracket.

B. Reassembly
1) To reassemble the headlight reverse the disassembly procedures.

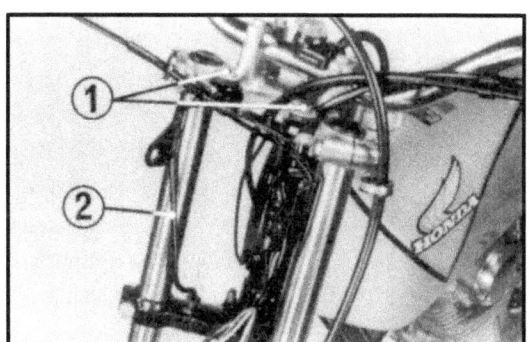

Fig. 3 ① 8mm bolt ② headlight bracket

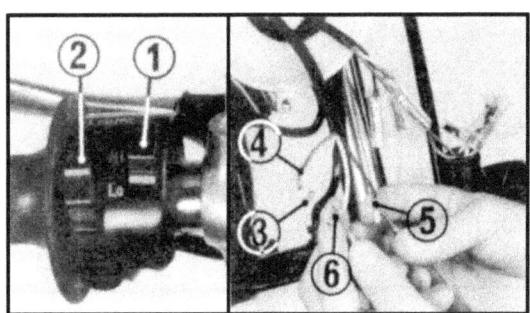

Fig. 4 ①Headlight switch ②Headlight Dimmer switch ③Yellow ④Brown ⑤Blue ⑥White

Lighting dimmer switch

Check for continuity between the respective terminals of the switch leads in the headlight case. The switch is in good condition if there is continuity in the circuits (0-0) with the switch selector knob set in the appropriate positions.

		C	TL	Hi	Lo
Wire color		Yellow	Brown	Blue	White
OFF					
ON	Hi	0——	——0——	——0	
ON	Lo	0——	——0——	——	——0

Carburetor setting

Item	
Setting No	04A
Main jet	#92
Slow jet	#35
Jet needle setting	2nd groove
Pilot screw opening	7/8 (standard)
Float level	24mm

SUPPLEMENT TO TL125 '76

SPECIFICATIONS

	Item	Metric	English
Dimension	Overall length	1,995mm	78.7in.
	Overall width	840mm	33.1in.
	Overall height	1,095mm	43.1in.
	Wheel base	1,280mm	50.4in.
	Seat height	780mm	30.7in.
	Ground clearance	260mm	10.2in.
	Dry weight	88kg	194lbs
Frame	Type	Semi couble cradle	
	F. Suspension, travel	Telescopic fork, tradel 152mm (6.0in.)	
	R. Suspension, travel	Swing arm, travel 94mm (3.7in.)	
	F. Tire size, type	2.75-21-4PR Semi-knobby, tire air pressure 1.5kg/cm² (21 psi.)	
	R. Tire size, type	4.00-18-4PR Semi-knobby, tire air pressure 1.5kg/cm² (21 psi.)	
	F. Brake	Internal expanding shoe	
	R. Brake	Internal expanding shoe	
	Fuel capacity	4.5 lit.	1.19 US. gal., 0.99Imp. gal.
	Fuel reserve capacity	0.5 lit.	0.13 US. gal., 0.11Imp. gal.
	Caster angle	61°30'	
	Trail length	105 mm	4.1in.
Engine	Type	Air cooled 4 stroke O.H.C engine	
	Cylinder arrangement	Single cylinder 15° inclined from vertical	
	Bore and stroke	56.5×49.5 mm	2.224×1.949in.
	Displacement	124 cc	7.57 cu. in.
	Compression ratio	9.0 : 1	
	Valve train	Chain driven over head camshaft	
	Oil capacity	1.0 lit.	1.1 US. qt., 0.9 Imp. qt.
	Lubrication System	Forced and wet sump	
	Valve tappet clearance	IN, EX : 0.05 mm	0.002in.
	Idle speed	1,300 rpm	
Drive train	Clutch	Wet multi-plate	
	Transmission	5-speed constant mesh	
	Primary reduction	4.055	
	Gear ratio I	2.769	
	Gear ratio II	2.125	
	Gear ratio III	1.450	
	Gear ratio IV	1.000	
	Gear ratio V	0.724	
	Final reduction	4.000, Drive sprocket 15T, driven sprocket 52T	
	Gear shift	Left foot operated return system	
Electrical	Ignition	Flywheel magneto and ignition coil	
	Starting system	Kick starter	
	Alternator	A.C. generator, 0.036 kW/5,000rpm	
	Battery capacity		
	Spark plug	NGK D8ES-L, NDX24ES	

TL125 WIRING DIAGRAM

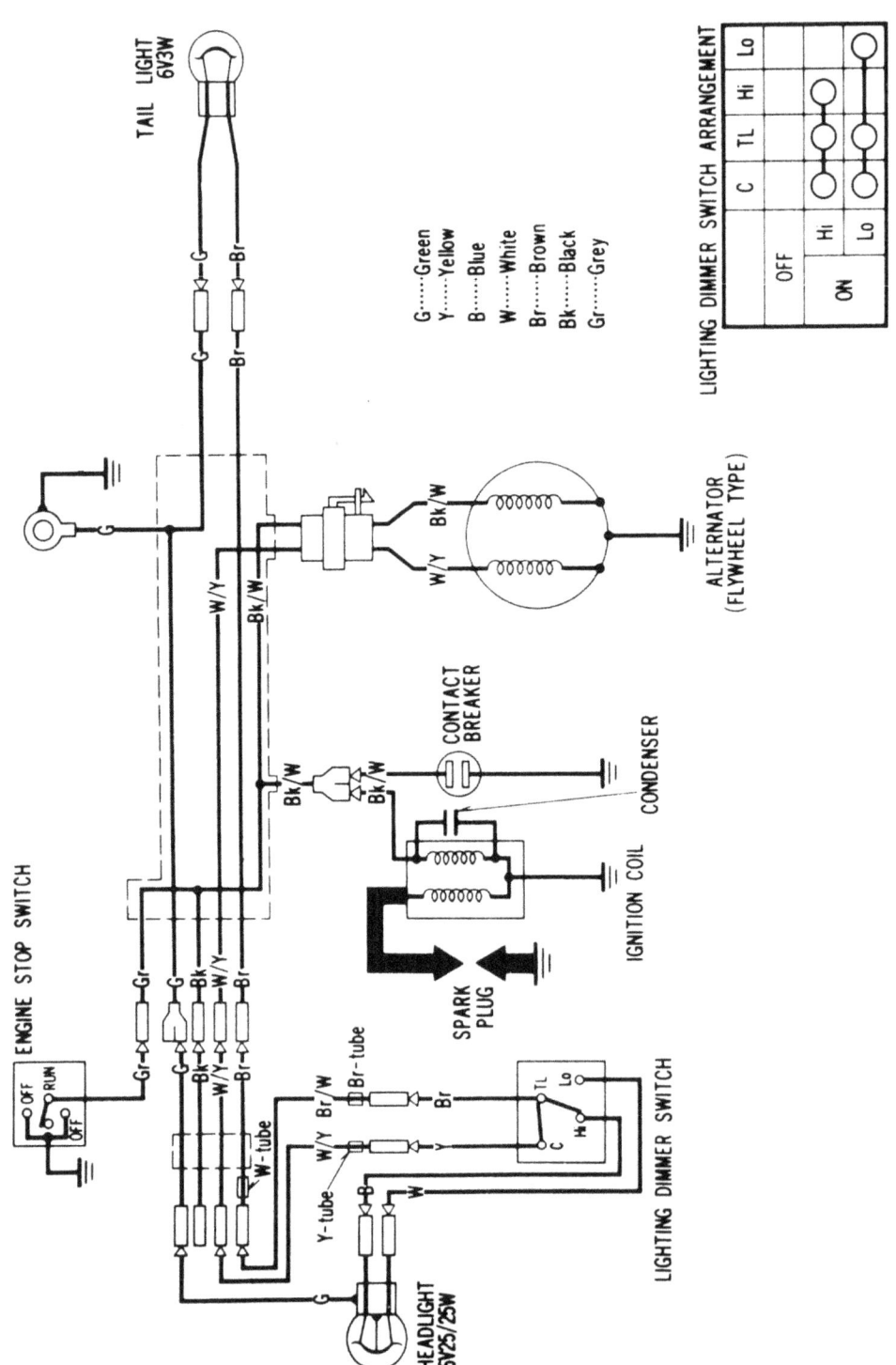

'76 SUPPLEMENT CB100K3/CB125J/CB125S

SUPPLEMENT TO CB100K₃/CB125J/CB125S '76
Engine No. CB100E-1300001 and subsequent.
Engine No. CB125SE-1300001 and subsequent.
Frame No. CB100-1300001 and subsequent.
Frame No. CB125S-1300001 and subsequent.

1. **Engine**
   Cylinder head and cylinder

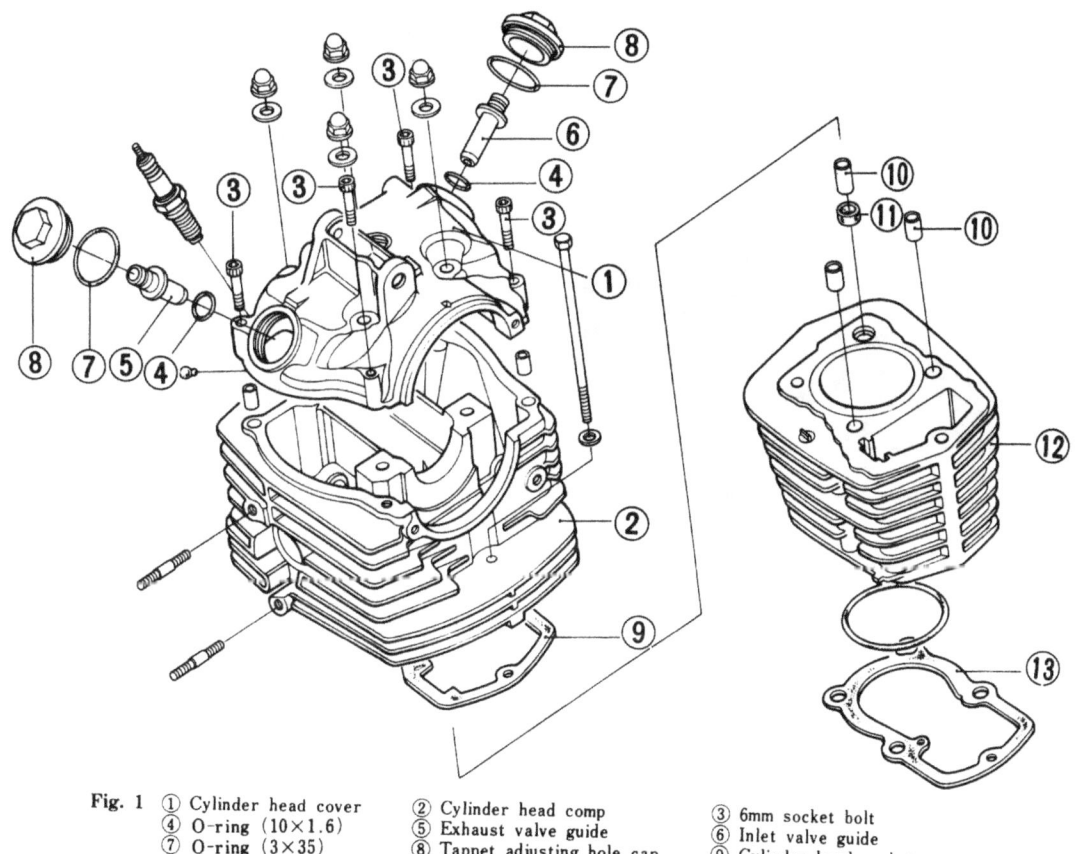

Fig. 1
① Cylinder head cover ② Cylinder head comp ③ 6mm socket bolt
④ O-ring (10×1.6) ⑤ Exhaust valve guide ⑥ Inlet valve guide
⑦ O-ring (3×35) ⑧ Tappet adjusting hole cap ⑨ Cylinder head gasket
⑩ Dowel pin (10×14) ⑪ Cylinder stud gasket ⑫ Cylinder comp
⑬ Cylinder gasket

A. Disassembly

1) Refer to item A on pages 14 and 15 for procedure to be followed in disassembling the head and cylinder.
2) The camshaft, rocker arms and valve springs can be removed without removing the cylinder head cover.
3) To remove the cylinder head cover, remove the four socket bolts.

Fig. 2 ① Cylinder head cover ② Cylinder head

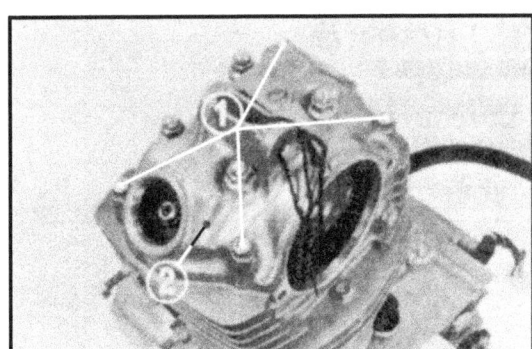

Fig. 3　① Socket bolt　② Cylinder head cover

Fig. 4　Oil seal rubber

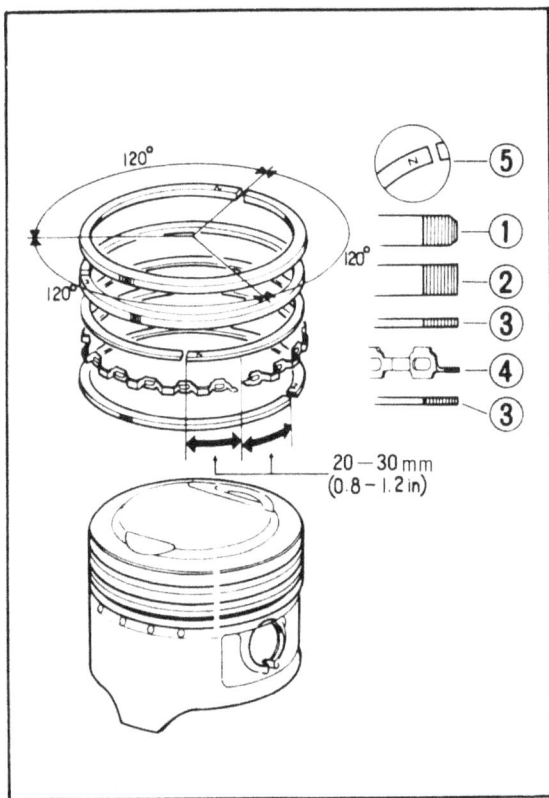

Fig. 5　① Top ring　② 2nd ring　③ Rail　④ Spacer
　　　　⑤ Ring mark

B. Inspection

1) Cylinder bore　　　　Unit : mm (in.)
(CB125J/CB125S '76)

Item	Standard value	Service limit
Cylinder I.D.	56.50–56.51 (2.2244–2.2247)	56.60 max (2.2283)

2) Piston (CB125J/CB125S '76) Unit : mm (in.)

Item	Standard value	Service limit
Piston O.D.	56.46–56.48 (2.2228–2.2236)	56.35 min. (2.2184)

3) Valve stem clearance　Unit : mm (in.)

Item	Standard value	Service limit
Valve stem O.D.		
IN	5.450–5.465 (0.2146–0.2152)	5.42 max. (0.2134)
EX	5.430–5.445 (0.2138–0.2144)	5.400 max. (0.2126)
Valve guide I.D.	5.475–5.485 (0.2155–0.2519)	5.5 min (0.2165)

4) Valve spring　　　　Unit : mm (in.)

Item	Standard value	Service limit
Free length		
OUTER	44.85 (1.7658)	40.5 (1.5945)
INNER	39.2 (1.5433)	35.2 (1.3858)
As-installed tension/length (kg/mm)(lb/in)		
OUTER	21.0/38.4 (46.2/1.5118)	17.8/38.4 (39.16/1.5118)
INNER	8.3/33.7 (18.26/1.3268)	7.0/33.7 (15.4/1.3268)

C. Assembly

1) Assembly is in the reverse order of removal.

2) Check to make sure that the oil seal rubber is in place. Apply gasket cement to both sides before installation.
Tighten cover with four socket bolts.

Piston ring

1) To install the oil control ring, install the spacer and the rails in the order listed. Stagger the spacer and rail gaps 20–30 cm apart from each other.

2) Install the second and top rings with the ring marks facing up.

NOTE :

1) Do not interchange the top and second rings between ring lands.

2) After installing all rings on the piston, hand-rotate them and check to ensure that they move smoothly without any sign of binding.

3) The ring gaps must be staggered 120 deg. and not be parallel with or at right angles to the piston pin.

NOTE :

On three-piece type oil ring, stagger spacer gaps.

Crankshaft runout

1) Crankshaft runout Unit : mm(in.)

Item	Standard value	Service limit
R & L	0.02 max. (0.00079)	0.05 (0.00197)

2) Connecting rod Unit : mm(in.)

Item	Standard value	Service limit
Side clearance on journal	0.05–0.35 (0.00197–0.01378)	0.8 (0.03150)
Bearing clearance	0–0.08 (0–0.00315)	0.05 (0.00197)

Cam chain tensioner

1) Drain the oil from the engine.
2) Remove the cylinder head.
3) Remove the cam chain guide retainer.
4) Remove the generator rotor and stator.
5) Remove the adjusting bolt and the tensioner arm.
6) Remove the tensioner set arm; then, take out the tensioner.

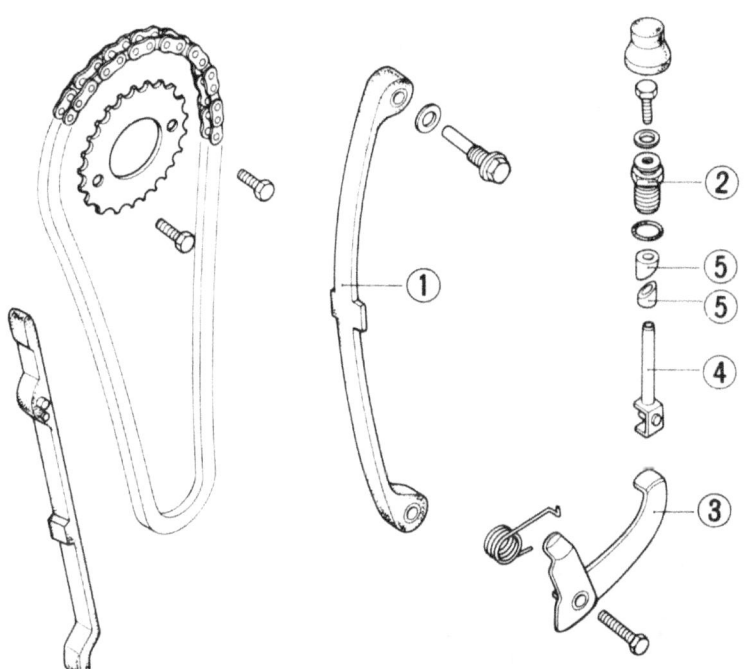

Fig. 6 ① Cam chain tensioner ② Adjusting bolt ③ Tensioner arm ④ Tensioner set bar ⑤ Set bar lock collar

Cam chain adjustment

1) Start the engine and run it at idle speed.
2) Loosen the adjusting bolt.
3) Tighten the adjusting bolt.

NOTE:
The chain tension will be adjusted automatically when the adjusting bolt is loosened. Do not loosen the 6 x 10mm bolt.

Fig. 7 ① 16mm special bolt ② 6×10mm bolt

Clutch

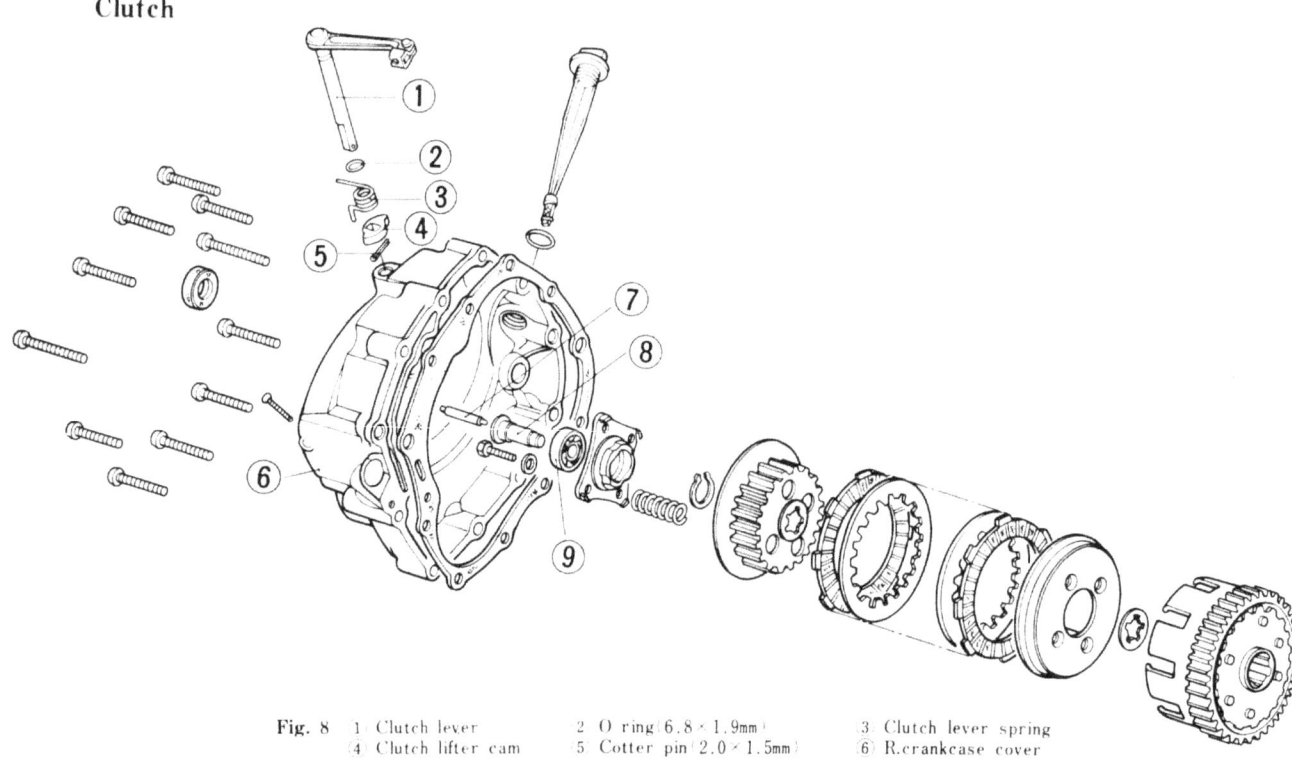

Fig. 8 1) Clutch lever 2) O ring (6.8 × 1.9mm) 3) Clutch lever spring 4) Clutch lifter cam 5) Cotter pin (2.0 × 1.5mm) 6) R.crankcase cover 7) Clutch lifter rod 8) Clutch lifter guide pin 9) Ball bearing (6001)

Fig. 9 1) Clutch lifter rod 2) Clutch lifter guide pin 3) Ball bearing

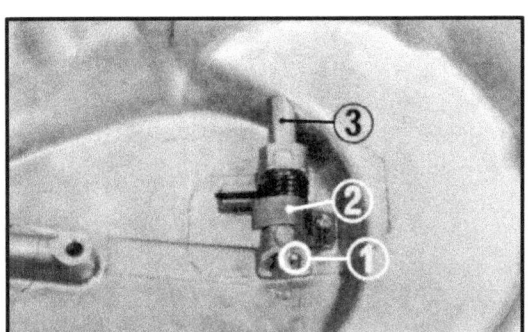

Fig. 10 1) Cotter pin 2) Clutch lifter cam 3) Clutch arm

A. Disassembly

1) Drain the engine oil by removing the 12mm drain plug.
2) Remove the muffler and the kick starter in the order listed.
3) Remove the foot pegs.
4) Disconnect the clutch and tachometer cables; remove the R crank case cover.
5) Pry off the cotter pin and remove the clutch lifter cam and the clutch arm from the R crankcase cover.
6) Remove the clutch lifter rod, the guide pin and the ball bearing. For subsepuent operation, follow the procedure given on page 25.

B. Clutch cuble adjustment

1) Refer to page 89.

Atomizer plate

A plate has been placed in the carburetor insulator so as to divide the air passage into tow halves of different cross-sectional areas. When the throttle is 60 - 70 per cent open, the mixture flows through the lower passage. This causes the mixture to flow faster due to the restricted passage (by 30%). The design provides finer mixture atomization and better engine response during part-throttle operation.

NOTE:

The plate should be reassembled in the same direction to insure proper carburetor performance.

Carburetor Setting

Item	CB100K₃	CB125S '76
Setting No.	658 A	066 A
Main jet	#105	#110
Slow jet	#38	#45
Jet needle setting	2nd groove	2nd groove
Pilot screw opening	$1\frac{5}{8} \pm \frac{1}{8}$	$1\frac{1}{2}$ (standard)
Float level	24mm	24mm

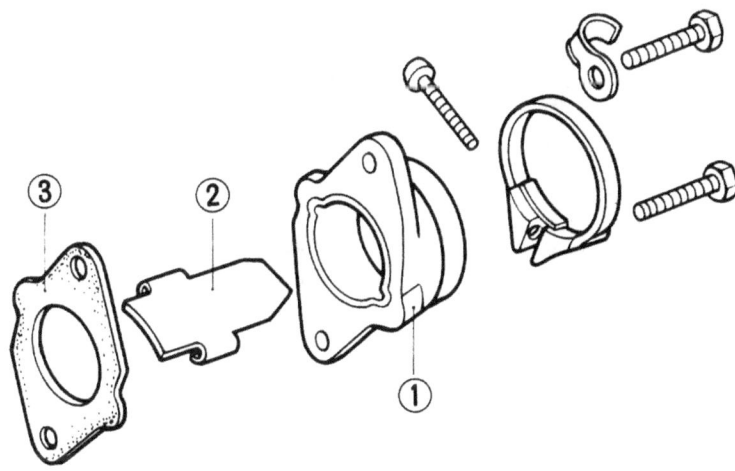

Fig. 11 ① Carburetor insulator ② Atomizer plate
③ Carburetor insulator gasket

2. Frame
Front suspension

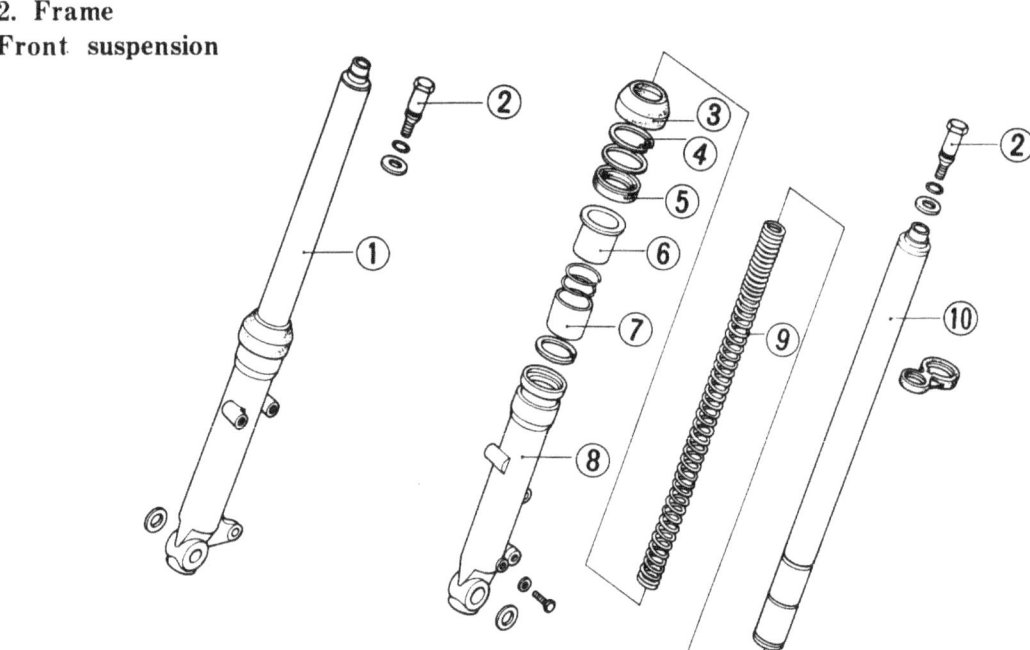

Fig. 12 ① Right front fork ② Front fork bolt ③ Front fork dust seal ④ Internal snap ring ⑤ Front fork oil seal ⑥ Front fork pipe guide ⑦ Front fork piston ⑧ Front fork bottom case ⑨ Front cushion spring ⑩ Front fork pipe

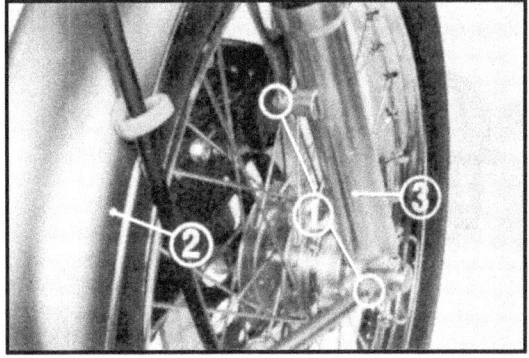

Fig. 13 ① Bolt ② Front fender ③ Front fork

Disassembly

1) Remove the front wheel calipper. See page 65
2) Loosen the six fender bolts and remove the front fender from the front fork.
3) Remove the four **handlebar** bolts and remove the upper holders and the handlebar.
4) Remove the front reflector.
5) Remove the front fork bolt. Remove the fork by loosening the fork attaching bolt at the steering stem
6) Drain the oil from the front fork bottom case by removing 6mm bolt.
7) Remove the front fork dust seal. Disassemble the fork bottom case by removing the snap ring.

Fig. 14 ① Fork bolt ② Fork attaching bolt ③ Front reflector

Inspection

1) Front fork spring

Item	Standard value	Service limit
Free length	411.6 (16.2046)	390 (15.3543)

2) Front fork stroke

Item	Stroke	Attenuation
	104mm	10±4kg/0.5m/sec.

3) Front fork oil quantity
   Oil : SS8 (ATF)
   Quantity : 105-110cc

4) Front fork piston   Unit : mm(in.)

Item	Standard value	Service limit
O D	30.936-30.975 (1.21795-1.2195)	309 (1.2165)

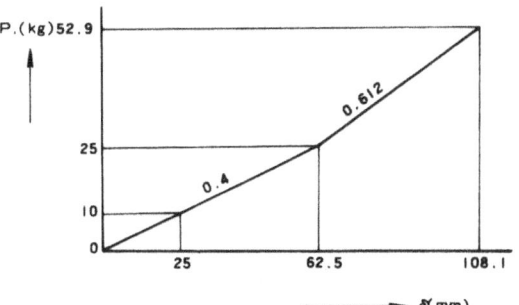

Fig. 15 Performance curve of front cushion spring

Air cleaner element

1) Remove R-side cover
2) Remove air cleaner case by removing two securing nuts.

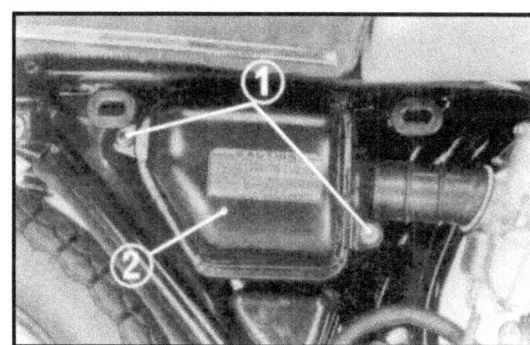

3) To remove the air cleaner element, pull off the set spring.
4) Wash the element in solvent and dry.
   NOTE :
   Do not wash in gasoline, kerosene or mineral spirits. Use only approved solvents commercially available for the purpose.
5) Immerse element in clean engine oil (10W-30) and squeeze to remove excess.
6) Install element in holder and set in case with set spring. Install cover.

Fig. 16 ① Nut ② Air cleaner case cover

Fig. 17 ① Air cleaner element ② Set spring

SUPPLEMENT TO CB100K₃/CB125J/CB125S '76

Fig. 18 ① Headlight case bolt
② Case attaching bolt

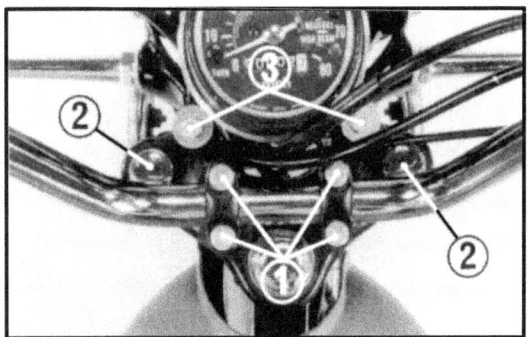

Fig. 19 ① Bolt ② Front fork bolt
③ Speedometer holder attaching bolt

Headlight case bracket
Disassembly

1) Remove the headlight and disconnect the wire leads in the case.
2) Remove the right and left headlight case bolts; separate the case from the wire harness.
3) Disconnect the speedometer cable at the speedometer.
4) Remove the four handlebar clamp bolts and remore the handlebar and the front fork bolts.
5) Separate the speedometer holder by loosening two bolts.
6) Remove the headlight case bracket from the steering stem.

3. Electrical
Charging test

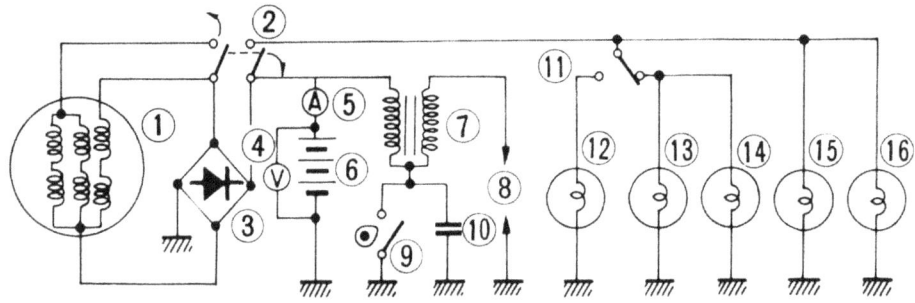

Fig. 20 ① A.C.Generator ② Combination switch ③ Silicon rectifier ④ Voltage meter
⑤ Ammeter ⑥ Battery ⑦ Ignition coil ⑧ Spark plug
⑨ Contact breaker ⑩ Condenser ⑪ Dimmer switch ⑫ Headlight low beam
⑬ Headlight high beam ⑭ High beam pilot light ⑮ Tail light ⑯ Position light

	Initial charging r.p.m		5,000 r.p.m		10,000 r.p.m	
	r.p.m	Battery Voltage	Charging Current	Battery Voltage	Charging Current	Battery Voltage
Day	1,000	6.8V min.	1.3A min.	7.8V min.	3.5A max.	8.8V max.
Night	2,800	6.8V min.	1.0A min.	7.2V min.	3.0A max.	8.8V max.

SUPPLEMENT TO CB100K₃/CB125J/CB125S '76

WIRING

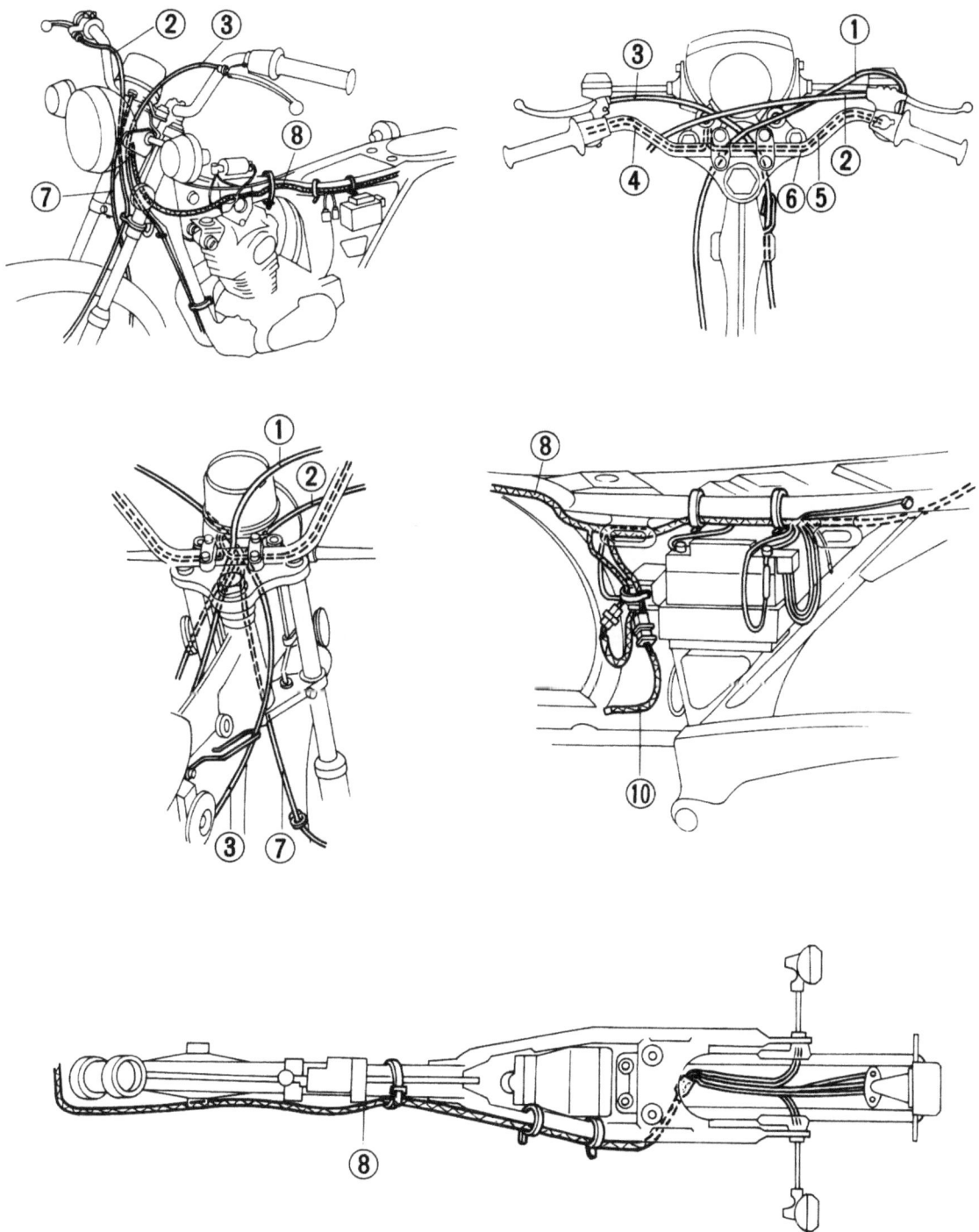

Fig. 21 ① Throttle cable ② Front brake cable ③ Clutch cable ④ Handle switch (L) cord ⑤ Handle switch (R) cord ⑥ Engine stop switch ⑦ Speed meter cable ⑧ Main wire harness ⑨ Battery breather tube ⑩ A.C.Generator cord

SPECIFICATIONS CB100K₃

	Item	Metric	English
Dimension	Overall length	1,885 mm	74.2 in.
	Overall width	750 mm	29.5 in.
	Overall height	1,015 mm	40.0 in.
	Wheel base	1,195 mm	47.0 in.
	Seat height	765 mm	30.1 in.
	Ground clearance	170 mm	6.7 in.
	Dry weight	87 kg	192 lb.
Frame	Type		Diamond frame
	F. Suspension, travel	Telescopic fork, travel 104 mm (4.1 in.)	
	R. Suspension, travel	Swing arm, travel 62 mm (2.4 in.)	
	F. Tire size, type	2.50-18-4PR Block, tire air pressure 1.8 kg/cm² (26 psi.)	
	R. Tire size, type	2.50-17-4PR Block, tire air pressure 2.25 kg/cm² (32 psi.)	
	F. Brake	Disk brake	
	R Brake	Internal expanding shoe	
	Fuel capacity	7.5 lit.	2.0 U.S. gal., 1.6 Imp. gal.
	Fuel reserve capacity	2.2 lit.	0.6 U.S. gal., 0.5 Imp. gal.
	Caster Angle	62°50'	
	Trail length	96 mm	3.8 in.
Engine	Type	Air cooled 4 stroke O.H.C. engine	
	Cylinder arrangement	Single cylinder 15° inclined from vertical	
	Bore and stroke	50.5 × 49.5 mm	1.988 × 1.949 in.
	Displacement	99 cc	6.04 cu. in.
	Compression ratio	9.0 : 1	
	Valve train	Chain driven over head camshaft	
	Oil capacity	1.1 U.S. qt., 1.0 lit.	0.9 Imp. qt.
	Lubrication system	Forced and wet sump	
	Valve tappet clearance	IN, EX : 0.05 mm	0.002 in.
	Idle speed	1,300 rpm	
Drive train	Clutch	Wet multi-plate	
	Transmission	5-speed constant mesh	
	Primary reduction	4.055	
	Gear ratio I	2.769	
	Gear ratio II	1.882	
	Gear ratio III	1.450	
	Gear ratio IV	1.173	
	Gear ratio V	1.000	
	Final reduction	2.642, Drive sprocket 15T, driven sprocket 35T	
	Gear shift	Left foot operated return system	
Electrical	Ignition	Battery and ignition coil	
	Starting system	Kick starter	
	Alternator	A.C. generator, 0.076 kw/5,000 rpm	
	Battery capacity	6V-6AH	
	Spark plug	NGK D8ES-L, ND X24ES	

SPECIFICATIONS CB125S '76

	Item	Metric	English
Dimension	Overall length	1,860 mm	73.2 in.
	Overall width	750 mm	29.5 in.
	Overall height	1,050 mm	41.3 in.
	Wheel base	1,205 mm	47.4 in.
	Seat height	765 mm	30.1 in.
	Ground clearance	170 mm	6.7 in.
	Dry weight	93 kg	205 lb.
Frame	Type		Diamond frame
	F. Suspension, travel	Telescopic fork, travel (104 mm) 4.1 in.	
	R. Suspension, travel	Swing arm, travel (62 mm) 2.4 in.	
	F. Tire size, type	2.75-18-4PR Block, tire air pressure $1.8 kg/cm^2$ (26 psi.)	
	R. Tire size, type	3.00-17-4PR Block, tire air pressure $2.25 kg/cm^2$ (32 psi.)	
	F. Brake	Disk brake	
	R Brake	Internal expanding shoe	
	Fuel capacity	9.5 lit.	2.5 U.S. gal., 2.1 Imp. gal.
	Fuel reserve capacity	2.2 lit.	0.6 U.S. gal., 0.5 Imp. gal.
	Caster Angle	62°50'	
	Trail length	96 mm	3.8 in.
Engine	Type	Air cooled 4 stroke O.H.C. engine	
	Cylinder arrangement	Single cylinder 15° inclined from vertical	
	Bore and stroke	56.5×49.5 mm	2.224×1.949 in.
	Displacement	124 cc	7.6 cu. in.
	Compression ratio	9.4 : 1	
	Valve train	Chain driven over head camshaft	
	Oil capacity	1.1 U.S. qt., 1.0 lit.	0.9 Imp. qt.
	Lubrication system	Forced and wet sump	
	Valve tappet clearance	IN, EX : 0.05 mm	0.002 in.
	Idle speed	1,300 rpm	
Drive train	Clutch	Wet multi-plate	
	Transmission	5-speed constant mesh	
	Primary reduction	4.055	
	Gear ratio I	2.769	
	Gear ratio II	1.882	
	Gear ratio III	1.450	
	Gear ratio IV	1.173	
	Gear ratio V	1.000	
	Final reduction	2.333, Drive sprocket 15T, driven sprocket 35T	
	Gear shift	Left foot operated return system	
Electrical	Ignition	Battery and ignition coil	
	Starting system	Kick starter	
	Alternator	A.C. generator, 0.076 kw/5,000 rpm	
	Battery capacity	6V-6AH	
	Spark plug	NGK D8ES-L, ND X24ES	

SUPPLEMENT TO CB100K₃/CB125J/CB125S '76

WIRING DIAGRAM CB100₃

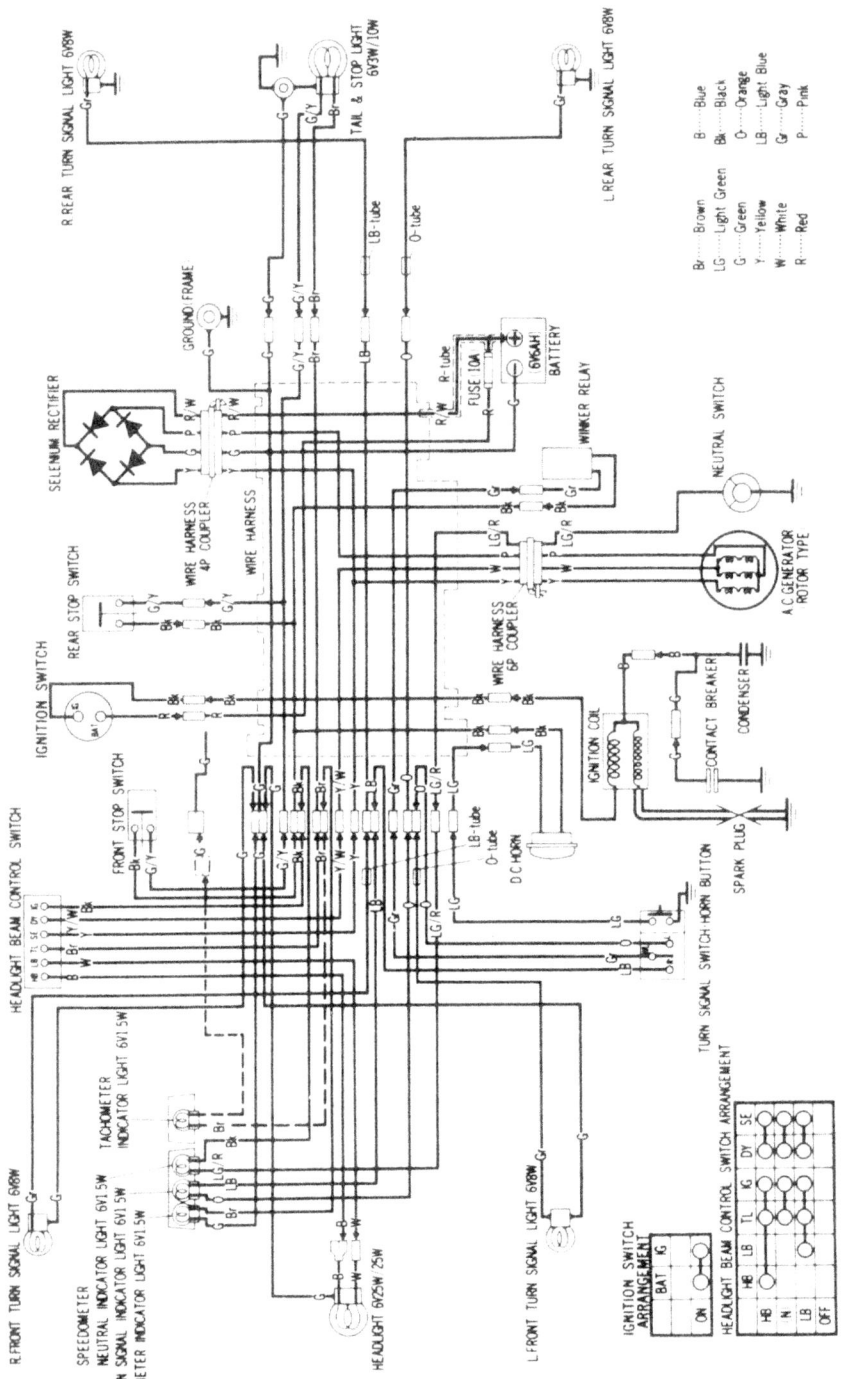

WIRING DIAGRAM CB125S '76

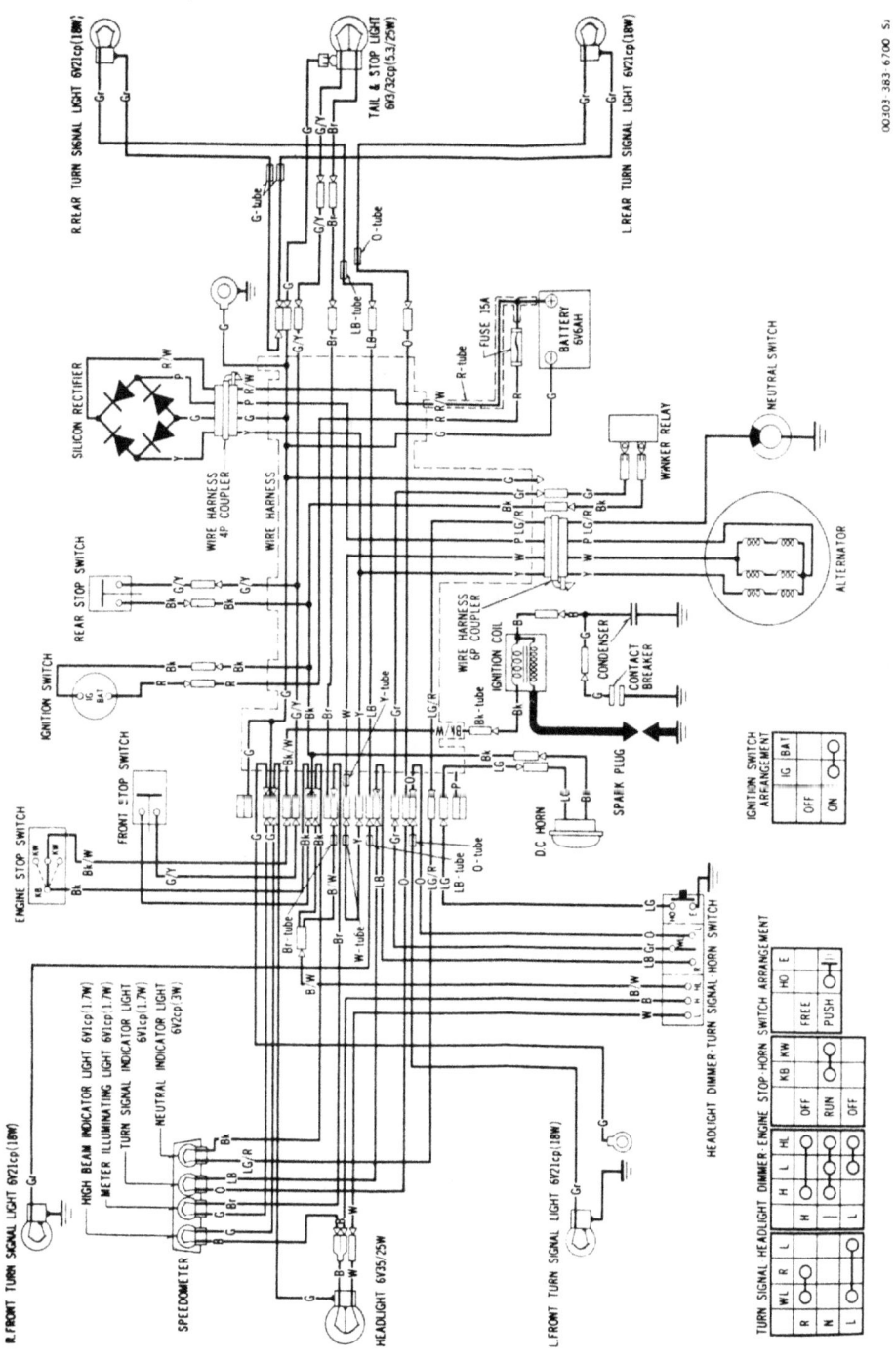

WIRING DIAGRAM CB125J (AUSTRALIA TYPE)

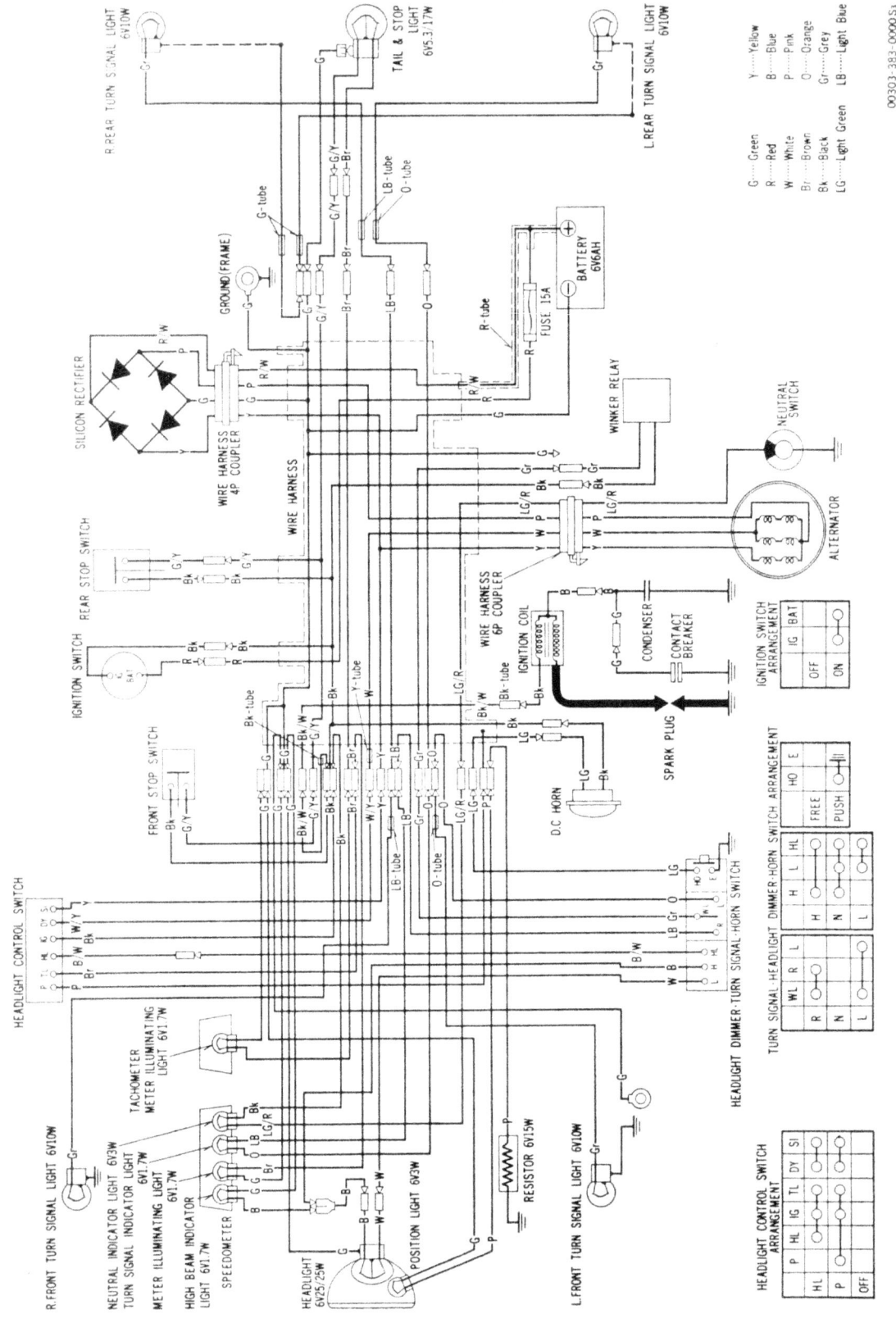

WIRING DIAGRAM CB125J (GERMANY TYPE)

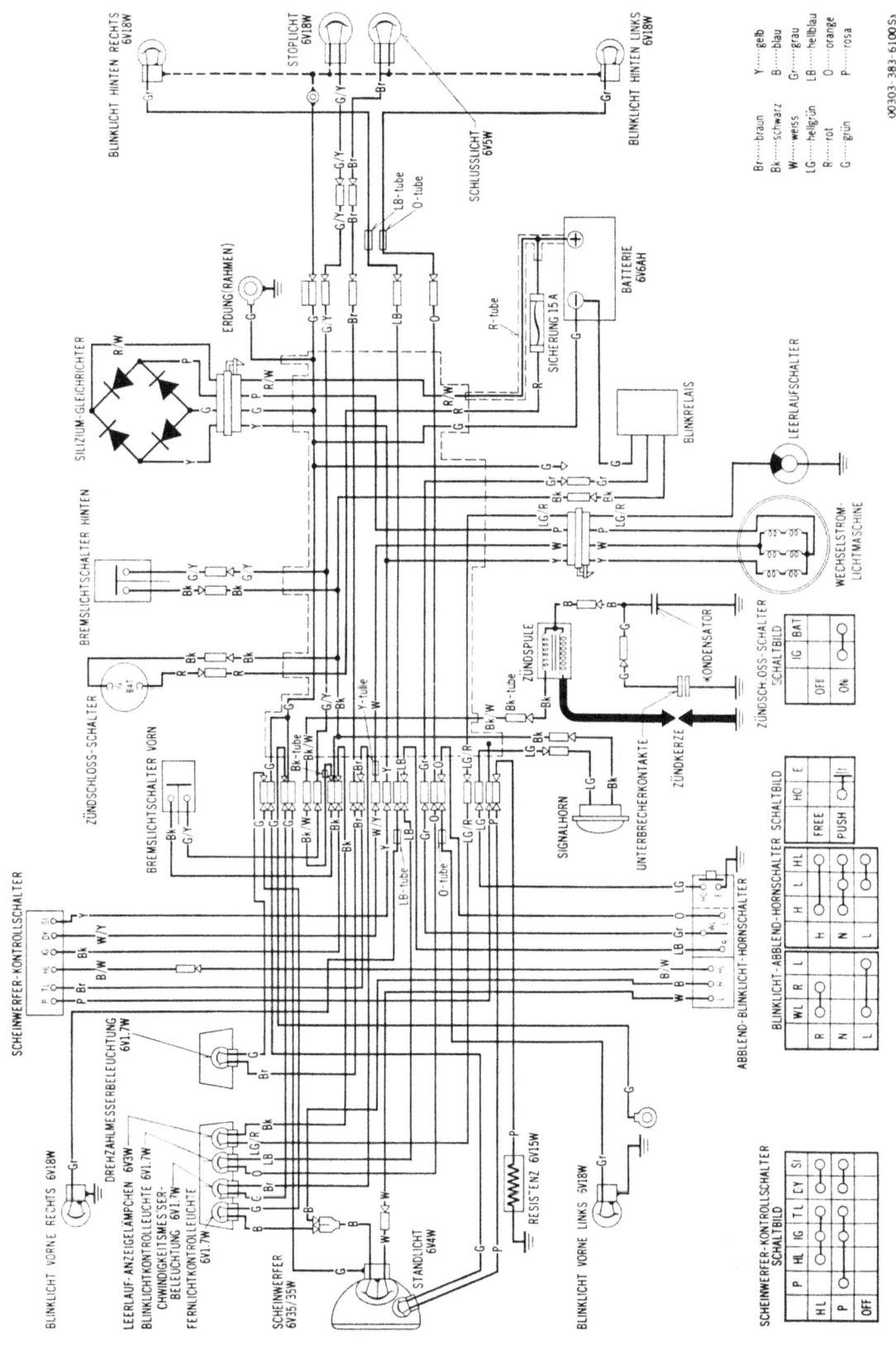

WIRING DIAGRAM CB125J (FRENCH TYPE)

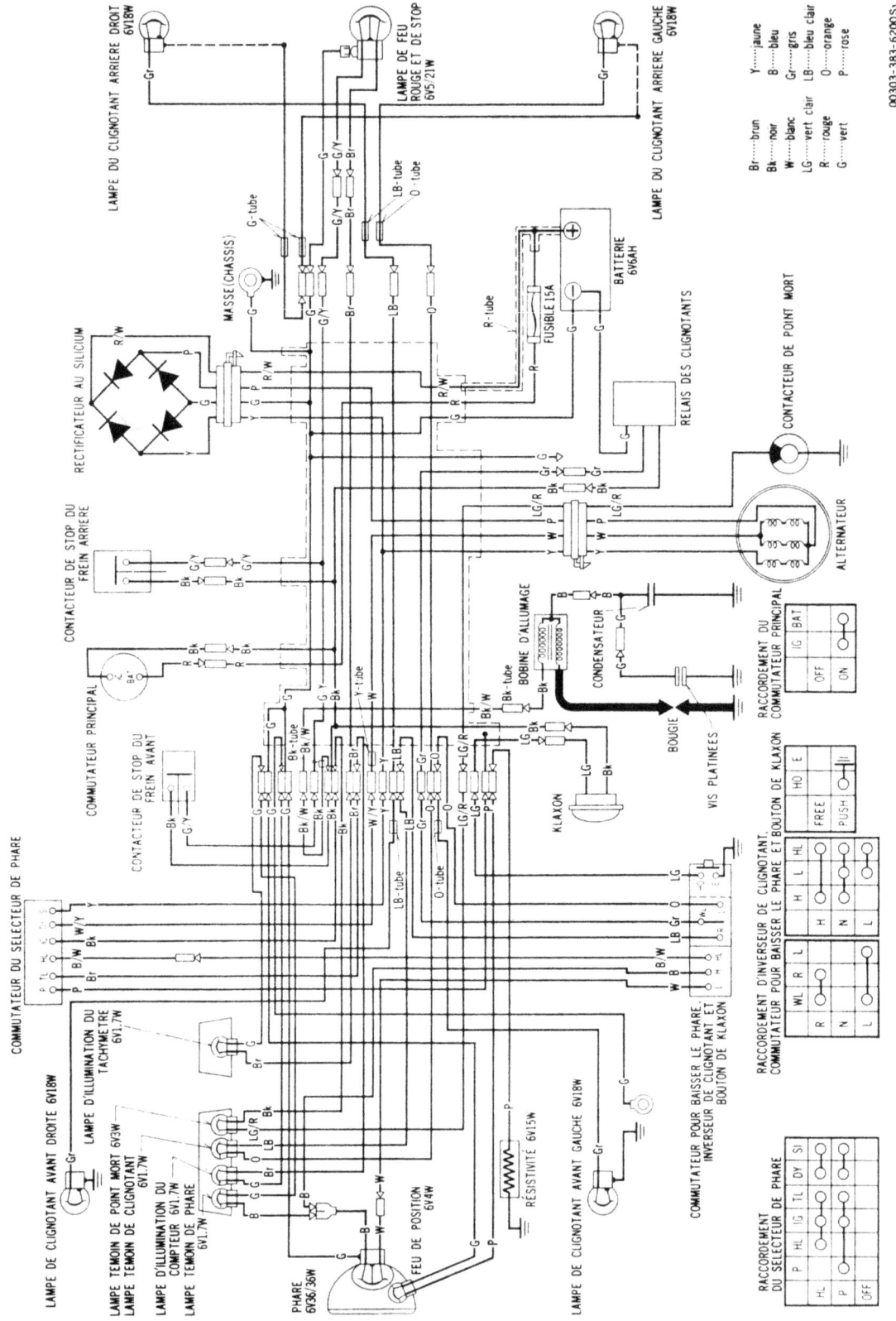

WIRING DIAGRAM CB125J (U.K. EUROPPEAN TYPE)

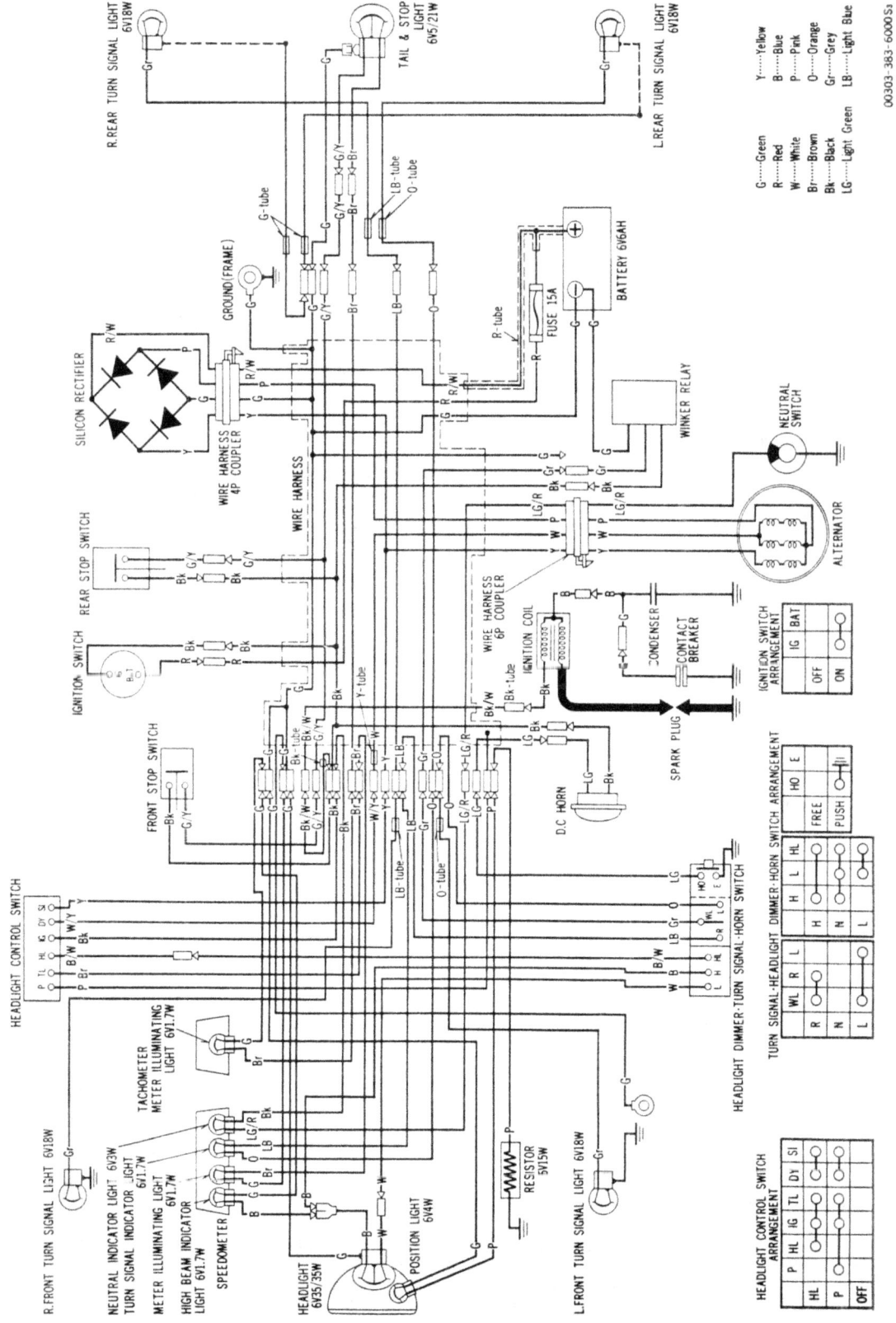

ADDENDUM SHEET CB125S '78

> This addendum applies to CB125S('78).
> Frame No. CB125S-1500001 and subsequent,
> manufactured before January 1, 1978.

1. CARBURETOR

Carburetor Setting Table

Setting number	PD66B
Main jet	No. 110
Jet needle setting	3rd groove
Pilot screw opening	1
Float height	18.5mm (0.728 in.)

2. MAINTENANCE SCHEDULE

Perform the Pre-Ride Inspection described in the Owner's Manual at each maintenance period.

I: INSPECT, CLEAN, ADJUST, OR REPLACE IF NECESSARY.   C: CLEAN   R: REPLACE   A: ADJUST

FREQUENCY ITEM	WHICHEVER COMES FIRST EVERY	600 mi. (1000km)	2400 mi. (4000km)	4800 mi. (8000km)	7200 mi. (12000km)	REFER TO
ENGINE OIL	YEAR	R	REPLACE EVERY 1200 mi. (2000km)			Page 8
* ENGINE OIL FILTER ROTOR				C		Page 9
* ENGINE OIL FILTER SCREEN				C		Page 9
AIR CLEANER	NOTE (1)		C	C	C	Page 125
* FUEL LINES			I	I	I	
SPARK PLUG			I	I	R	Page 8
* VALVE CLEARANCE		I	I	I	I	Page 5
* CONTACT BREAKER POINTS		I	I	I	I	Page 6
* IGNITION TIMING		I	I	I	I	Page 6
* CAM CHAIN TENSION		A	A	A	A	Page 121
* THROTTLE OPERATION		I	I	I	I	
* CARBURETOR IDLE SPEED		I	I	I	I	
* CARBURETOR CHOKE			I	I	I	
DRIVE CHAIN	NOTE (3)	INSPECT EVERY 600 mi. (1000km)				Page 11
BATTERY ELECTROLYTE	MONTH	I	I	I	I	Page 11
BRAKE SHOE/PAD WEAR			I	I	I	
BRAKE FREE PLAY		I	I	I	I	Page 10
* BRAKE LIGHTING SWITCH		I	I	I	I	Page 59
* HEADLIGHT AIM		I	I	I	I	
CLUTCH FREE PLAY		I	I	I	I	Page 122
SIDE STAND			I	I	I	Page 109
* SUSPENSION		I	I	I	I	
* NUTS, BOLTS, FASTENERS		I	I	I	I	
** WHEELS/SPOKES		I	I	I	I	
** STEERING HEAD BEARING		I		I		

** IN THE INTEREST OF SAFETY, WE RECOMMEND THESE ITEMS BE SERVICED ONLY BY AN AUTHORIZED HONDA DEALER.

* SHOULD BE SERVICED BY AN AUTHORIZED HONDA DEALER, UNLESS THE OWNER HAS PROPER TOOLS AND SERVICE DATA, AND IS MECHANICALLY QUALIFIED.

NOTES: (1) More frequent service may be required when riding in dust areas.
(2) For higher odometer readings, repeat at the frequency interval established here.
(3) Initial service period 200 miles.

ADDENDUM SHEET CB125S '78

3. SPECIFICATIONS

	Item	Metric	English
Dimension	Overall length	1,860 mm	73.2 in.
	Overall width	750 mm	29.5 in.
	Overall height	1,050 mm	41.3 in.
	Wheel base	1,205 mm	47.4 in.
	Seat height	765 mm	30.1 in.
	Ground clearance	170 mm	6.7 in.
	Dry weight	93 kg	205 lb.
Frame	Type	Diamond frame	
	F. Suspension, travel	Telescopic fork, travel 104mm (4.1 in.)	
	R. Suspension, travel	Swing arm, travel 62 mm (2.4 in.)	
	F. Tire size, type	2.75-18-4PR Block, tire air pressure 1.8 kg/cm² (26 psi.)	
	R. Tire size, type	3.00-17-4PR Block, tire air pressure 2.25 kg/cm² (32 psi.)	
	F. Brake	Disk brake	
	R. Brake	Internal expanding shoe	
	Fuel capacity	9.5 lit.	2.5 U.S. gal., 2.1 Imp. gal.
	Fuel reserve capacity	2.2 lit.	0.6 U.S. gal., 0.5 Imp. gal.
	Caster Angle	62°50′	
	Trail length	96 mm	3.8 in.
Engine	Type	Air cooled 4 stroke O.H.C. engine	
	Cylinder arrangement	Single cylinder 15° inclined from vertical	
	Bore and stroke	56.5 x 49.5 mm	2.224 x 1.949 in.
	Displacement	124 cc	7.6 cu. in.
	Compression ratio	9.4 : 1	
	Valve train	Chain driven over head camshaft	
	Oil capacity	1.0 lit.	1.1 U.S. qt., 0.9 Imp. qt.
	Lubrication system	Forced and wet sump	
	Valve clearance	IN, EX ; 0.05 mm	0.002 in.
	Intake valve Opens	5° BTDC	
	Intake valve Closes	40° ATDC	
	Exhaust valve Opens	40° BBDC	
	Exhaust valve Closes	5° ATDC	
	Idle speed	1,300 rpm	
Drive train	Clutch	Wet multi-plate	
	Transmission	5-speed constant mesh	
	Primary reduction	4.055	
	Gear ratio I	2.769	
	Gear ratio II	1.882	
	Gear ratio III	1.450	
	Gear ratio IV	1.173	
	Gear shift V	1.000	
	Final reduction	2.333, Drive sprocket 15T, driven sprocket 35T	
	Gear shift	Left foot operated return system	
Electrical	Ignition	Battery and ignition coil	
	Ignition advance "F" mark	10° BTDC	
	Ignition advance Max. advance	30°	
	Ignition advance RPM from "F" to max. advance	1,600 - 4,000 rpm	
	Dwell angle	105° ± 2.5°	
	Condenser capacity	0.22 - 0.26 μF	
	Starting system	Kick starter	
	Alternator	A.C. generator. 0.076 kw/5,000 rpm	
	Battery capacity	6V - 6 AH	
	Spark plug	NGK D8EA, ND X24ES-U (U.S.A. model) NGK DR8ES-L, ND X24ESR-U (Canadian model)	

MEMO

1979 CB125S ADDENDUM

INTRODUCTION

This addendum contains mandatory emissions maintenance for CB125S's manufactured after December 31, 1977 (USA only).

Follow the Maintenance Schedule recommendations (Page 144) to ensure that the vehicle is always in peak operating condition and the emission levels are within the standards set by the Federal Clean Air Act. Performing the first scheduled maintenance is very important. It compensates for the initial wear that occurs during the break-in period (USA only).

Refer to the base CB125S Shop Manual for service data and procedures not included in this addendum.

CONTENTS

I.	SPECIFICATIONS	140
II.	EMISSION CONTROL SYSTEM (USA only)	142
	1. CONTROL SYSTEM	142
	2. EMISSION CONTROL INFORMATION LABEL	143
III.	MAINTENANCE SCHEDULE	144
IV.	INSPECTION AND ADJUSTMENT	145
	1. ENGINE OIL	145
	2. ENGINE OIL FILTER ROTOR	146
	3. ENGINE OIL FILTER SCREEN	146
	4. CRANKCASE BREATHER (USA only)	147
	5. AIR CLEANER	147
	6. FUEL LINE	148
	7. SPARK PLUG	148
	8. VALVE CLEARANCE	149
	9. CONTACT BREAKER POINTS	150
	10. IGNITION TIMING	150
	11. SPARK ADVANCER	151
	12. CAM CHAIN TENSION	152
	13. THROTTLE OPERATION	152
	14. CARBURETOR CHOKE	153
	15. CARBURETOR IDLE SPEED	153
	16. DRIVE CHAIN	153
	17. BATTERY	155
	18. BRAKE SHOE WEAR	156
	19. BRAKE SYSTEM	156
	20. BRAKE LIGHT SWITCH	158
	21. HEADLIGHT AIM	159
	22. CLUTCH FREE PLAY	159
	23. SIDE STAND	160
	24. SUSPENSION	161
	25. NUTS, BOLTS, FASTENERS	161
	26. WHEELS/SPOKES	162
	27. STEERING HEAD BEARING	162
V.	CARBURETOR	163
	1. CARBURETOR SPECIFICATIONS	163
	2. DISASSEMBLY AND ASSEMBLY	163
	3. PILOT SCREW ADJUSTMENT	163
	4. HIGH ALTITUDE ADJUSTMENT	164
VI.	WHEEL/SUSPENSION	167
	1. FRONT WHEEL REMOVAL	167
	2. REAR WHEEL REMOVAL	167
	3. REAR SHOCK ABSORBERS	168
	4. FRONT FORK	169
	5. BRAKE DRUM AND BRAKE SHOES	170
VII.	TROUBLESHOOTING	171
VIII.	CABLE AND HARNESS ROUTING	173
IX.	SPECIAL TOOLS	175
X.	WIRING DIAGRAM	176

Date of Issue: Sep., 1978

1. SPECIFICATIONS

Item	Metric	English
DIMENSIONS		
Overall length	1,855 mm	73.0 in
Overall width	745 mm	29.3 in
Overall height	1,045 mm	41.1 in
Wheel base	1,205 mm	47.4 in
Seat height	760 mm	29.9 in
Ground clearance	170 mm	6.7 in
Dry weight	94 kg	207.2 lb
FRAME		
Type	Diamond	
Front suspension, travel	Telescopic fork, 115 mm (4.5 in)	
Rear suspension, travel	Swing arm, 64 mm (2.5 in)	
Front tire size, type	2.75–18–4PR Block, (Tire air pressure: 1.75 kg/cm, 24 psi)	
Rear tire size, type	3.00–17–4PR Block, (Tire air pressure: 2.25 kg/cm, 32 psi)	
Front brake	Internal expanding shoes	
Rear brake	Internal expanding shoes	
Fuel capacity	9.5 lit	2.5 US gal
Fuel reserve capacity	2.2 lit	0.6 US gal
Caster angle	62°40'	
Trail length	98 mm	3.9 in
Front fork oil capacity	80–85 cc	2.7–2.9 US oz.
To fill dry fork assembly		
ENGINE		
Type	Air cooled 4-stroke OHC engine	
Cylinder arrangement	Single cylinder 15° inclined from vertical	
Bore and stroke	56.5 x 49.5 mm	2.224 x 1.949 in
Displacement	124 cc	7.57 cu in
Compression ratio	9.4 : 1	
Compression pressure	13 kg/cm² (1,000 rpm)	185 psi (1,000 rpm)
Carburetor, venturi dia.	Piston valve type, 24 mm (0.94 in)	
Valve train	Chain driven over head camshaft	
Oil capacity	1.0 lit	1.1 US qt
Lubrication system	Forced pressure and wet sump	
Fuel required	Any automotive gasoline with a pump octane number ($\frac{R + M}{2}$) of 86 or higher, or research octane number of 91 or higher may be used.	
Air filtration	Oiled polyurethane foam filter	
Valve timing IN Opens	10° BTDC (at 1 mm lift), 53° BTDC (at 0 lift)	
Closes	40° ABDC (at 1 mm lift), 102° ABDC (at 0 lift)	
EX Opens	40° BBDC (at 1 mm lift), 85° BBDC (at 0 lift)	
Closes	10° ATDC (at 1 mm lift), 72° ATDC (at 0 lift)	

1979 CB125S ADDENDUM

Item	Metric	English
Valve clearance IN/EX	0.05 mm	0.002 in
Engine dry weight	26 kg	57.3 lb
Idle speed	1300 ± 100 rpm	
DRIVE TRAIN		
Clutch	Wet multi-plate	
Transmission	5-speed constant mesh	
Primary reduction	4.055	
Gear ratio I	2.769	
II	1.882	
III	1.450	
IV	1.173	
V	1.000	
Final reduction	2.333 (35/15)	
Gear shift pattern	Left foot operated return system	
Drive chain size and links	428D 100 Links	
ELECTRICAL		
Ignition	Battery and coil	
Ignition advance "F" mark	10° BTDC, idle	
Full advance mark/rpm	36°–40° BTDC/3,700–4,000 rpm	
Starting system	Kick starter	
Alternator	AC generator, 76 w/5,000 rpm	
Battery capacity	6 V - 6 AH	
Fuse capacity	15 A	
Spark plug gap	0.6–0.7 mm	0.024–0.028 in
Condenser capacity	0.22–0.26 µF	
Contact breaker point gap	0.3–0.4 mm	0.012–0.016 in

Spark plug — USA model:

Brand \ Usage	For cold climate (below 5°C, 41°F)	Standard	For extended high speed driving
NGK	D7EA	D8EA	D9EA
ND	X22ES-U	X24ES-U	X27ES-U

Canada model: NGK DR8ES-L or ND X24ESR-U

CARBURETOR SPECIFICATIONS

	Standard	High altitude
	2,000m (6,500 ft) max.	1,500m (5,000 ft) min.
Identification number	PD68B	←
Main jet	#110	#100
Jet needle mark	20C	←
Float height	18.5 mm (0.73 in)	←
Pilot screw	See pages 163 ~ 166	←
Idle speed	1,300 ± 100 rpm	←

II. EMISSION CONTROL SYSTEM (USA only)

1. CONTROL SYSTEM

The CB125S is equipped with two Emission Control Systems.

*Exhaust Emission Control System

The exhaust emission control system is composed of a factory pre-set carburetor. No adjustment should be made except to the idle speed with the throttle stop screw.

*Crankcase Emission Control System

The engine is equipped with a "Closed Crankcase System" to prevent Crankcase emissions entering the atmosphere. Blow-by gas is returned to the combustion chamber through the breather tube, separator, air cleaner and carburetor.

Crankcase Emission Control System

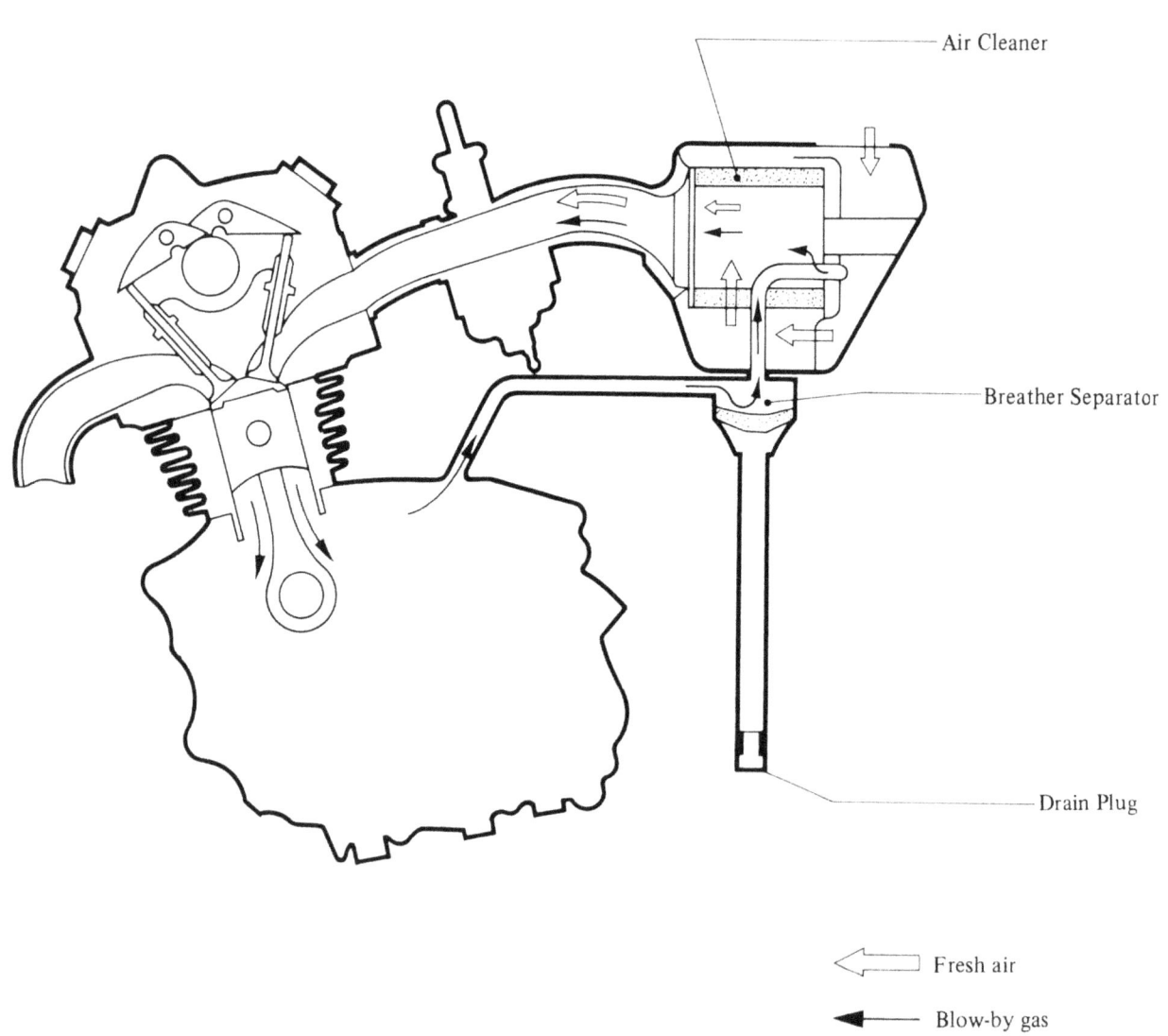

2. EMISSION CONTROL INFORMATION LABEL

CB125S's manufactured after December 31, 1977 have an Emission Control Information Label on the frame as shown. It contains basic tune-up specifications for CB125S manufactured after December 31, 1977. Refer to the base Shop Manual for more details.

III. MAINTENANCE SCHEDULE

Perform the PRE-RIDE INSPECTION in the Owner's Manual at each maintenance period.

I: Inspect, Clean, Adjust, Lubricate or Replace if necessary.
C: Clean
R: Replace
A: Adjust
L: Lubricate

	ITEM	FREQUENCY	WHICHEVER COMES FIRST EVERY	600mi. (1000km)	2500mi. (4000km)	5000mi. (8000km)	7500mi. (12000km)	Refer to
EMISSION RELATED ITEMS	ENGINE OIL		YEAR	R	R EVERY 1250mi. (2000km)			Page 145
	* ENGINE OIL FILTER ROTOR					C		Page 146
	* ENGINE OIL FILTER SCREEN					C		Page 146
	CRANKCASE BREATHER		NOTE (1)		C	C	C	Page 147
	AIR CLEANER		NOTE (2)		C	C	C	Pages 147 - 148
	* FUEL LINE				I	I	I	Page 148
	SPARK PLUG				I	I	R	Pages 148 - 149
	* VALVE CLEARANCE			I	I	I	I	Page 149
	* CONTACT BREAKER POINTS			I	I	I	I	Page 150
	* IGNITION TIMING			I	I	I	I	Pages 150 - 151
	* CAM CHAIN TENSION			A	A	A	A	Page 152
	* THROTTLE OPERATION			I	I	I	I	Page 152
	* CARBURETOR CHOKE				I	I	I	Page 153
	* CARBURETOR IDLE SPEED			I	I	I	I	Page 153
NON EMISSION RELATED ITEMS	DRIVE CHAIN			I, L EVERY 300mi. (500km)				Pages 153 - 155
	BATTERY		MONTH	I	I	I	I	Page 155
	BRAKE SHOE WEAR				I	I	I	Page 156
	BRAKE SYSTEM			I	I	I	I	Pages 156 - 157
	* BRAKE LIGHT SWITCH			I	I	I	I	Page 158
	* HEADLIGHT AIM			I	I	I	I	Page 159
	CLUTCH FREE PLAY			I	I	I	I	Pages 159 - 160
	SIDE STAND				I	I	I	Page 160
	* SUSPENSION			I	I	I	I	Page 161
	* NUTS, BOLTS, FASTENERS			I	I	I	I	Page 161
	** WHEELS/SPOKES			I	I	I	I	Page 162
	** STEERING HEAD BEARING			I			I	Page 162

* Should be serviced by an authorized HONDA dealer, unless the owner has proper tools and service data and is mechanically qualified.
** In the interest of safety, we recommend these items be serviced ONLY by an authorized HONDA dealer.

NOTE:
(1) More frequent service may be required when riding in rain or at full throttle (USA only).
(2) More frequent service may be required when riding in dusty areas.
(3) For higher odometer readings, repeat at the frequency interval established here.

IV. INSPECTION AND ADJUSTMENT

1. ENGINE OIL

ENGINE OIL LEVEL CHECK

1. Place the vehicle upright, and remove the oil filler cap/dipstick and wipe it clean.
2. Insert the dipstick and check the oil level.

NOTE

Do not screw in the dipstick when making this check.

3. If the oil level is below the lower level mark, fill to the upper level mark with the recommended oil.

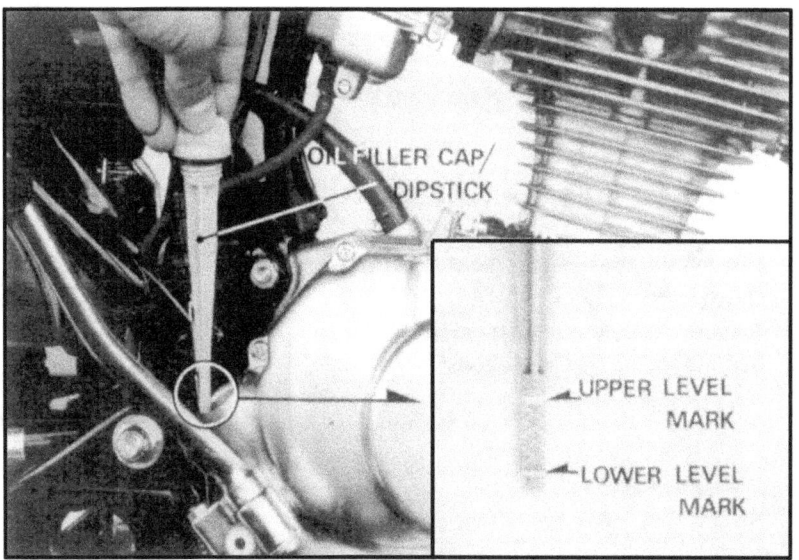

ENGINE OIL CHANGE

NOTE

Drain the oil with the engine warm and the motorcycle upright to assure complete and rapid draining.

1. Remove the oil filler cap/dipstick and drain plug after the engine is warm, and drain the oil.
2. Install the drain plug, and check the sealing washer condition.
   TORQUE: 2.0–3.0 kg-m
   (15–22.3 ft-lb)
3. Fill the crankcase with the recommended oil.
   OIL CAPACITY: 1.0 lit. (1.1 US qt.)
                        approx.

RECOMMENDED OIL:
Use HONDA 4-STROKE OIL or equivalent.
API SERVICE CLASSIFICATION: SE
VISCOSITY:
  General, all temperature; SAE 10W–40
  Alternate;
   Above 15°C (60°F)   SAE 30
   –10° to 15°C
       (15° to 60°F)   SAE 20 or 20W
   Above –10°C (15°F)   SAE 20W-50W
   Below 0°C (32°F)   SAE 10W

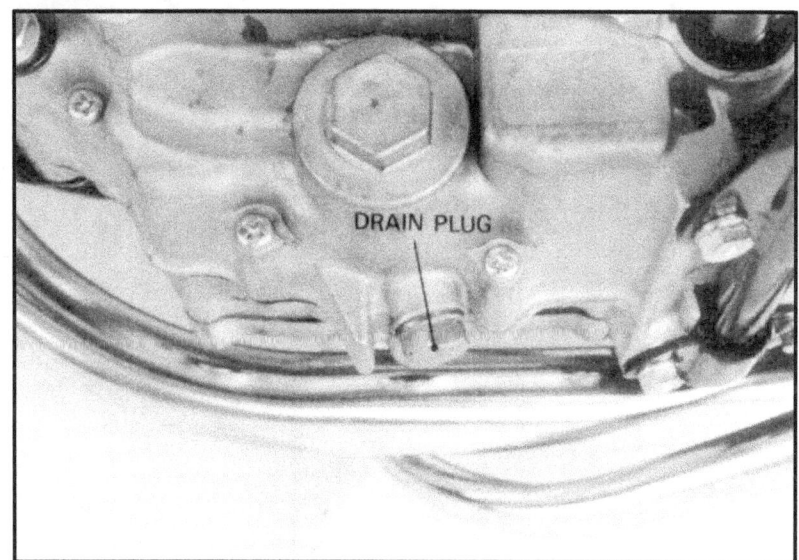

4. Install the oil filler cap/dipstick.
5. Start the engine and allow it to idle for 2–3 minutes.
6. Stop the engine, and make sure that the oil level is at the upper level mark with the vehicle in an upright position, on level ground. Be sure there are no leaks.

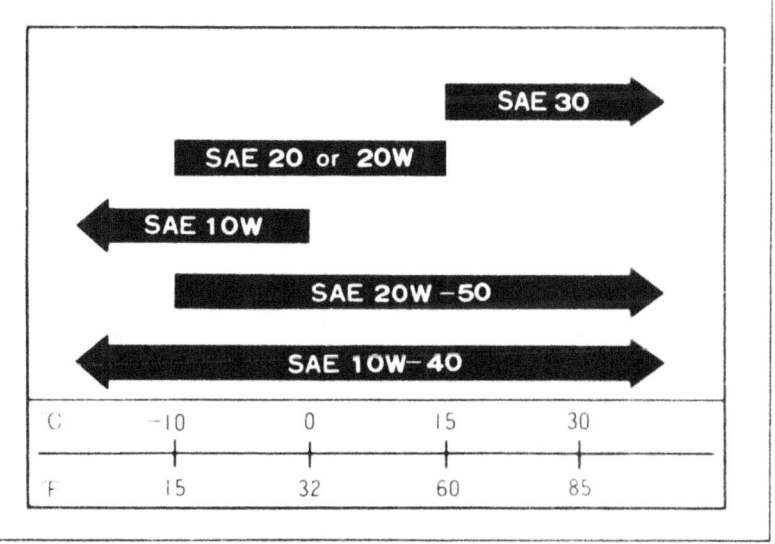

2. ENGINE OIL FILTER ROTOR

NOTE

Perform this maintenance before filling the engine with oil.

1. Remove the kick starter pedal, muffler, and foot peg assembly.
2. Disconnect the clutch cable from the clutch lever.
3. Remove the right crankcase cover.
4. Remove the oil filter rotor cover.

5. Clean the inside of the filter rotor.
6. Install the oil filter rotor cover, right crankcase cover, foot peg assembly, exhaust muffler and kickstarter pedal.
7. Connect and adjust the clutch cable.

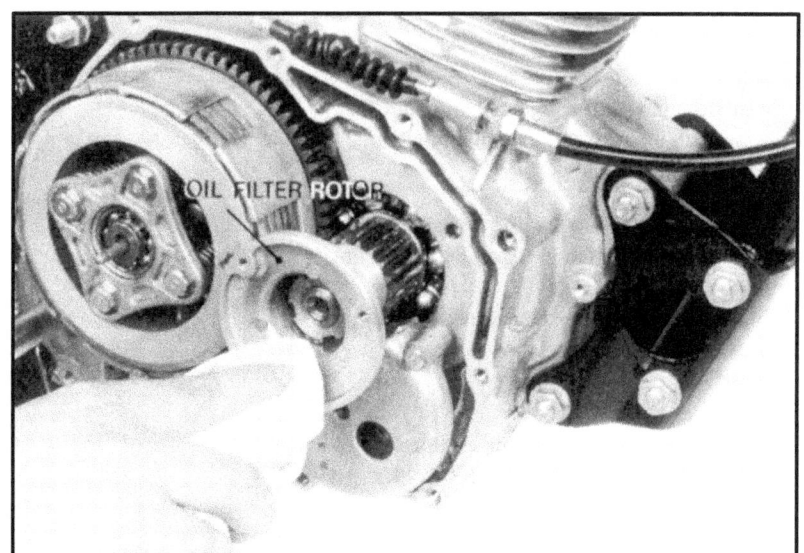

3. ENGINE OIL FILTER SCREEN

NOTE

Perform this maintenance before filling the engine with oil.

1. Remove the filter cap, spring and filter screen.
2. Clean the oil filter screen.
3. Install the oil filter screen, spring and filter cap.
4. Fill the crankcase with the recommended engine oil, and start the engine.
5. Stop the engine and recheck the oil level. Make sure there are no oil leaks.

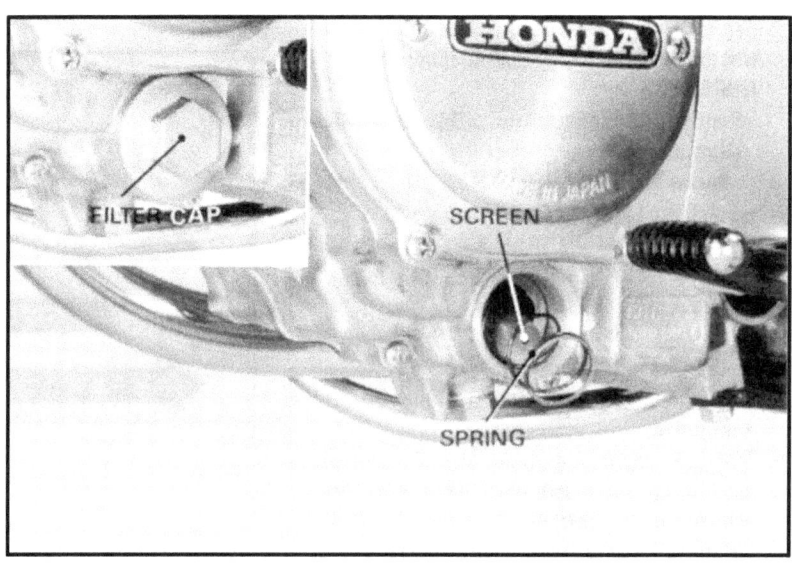

4. CRANKCASE BREATHER (USA only)

1. Remove the drain plug from the drain tube, and drain deposits.
2. Install the drain plug.

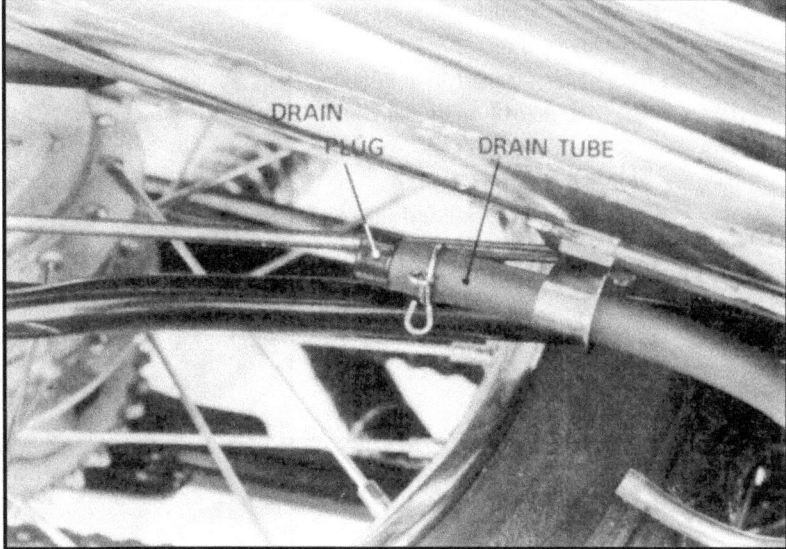

NOTE

Service more frequently than indicated in the maintenance schedule when ridden in the rain or at full throttle, or if deposits can be seen in the transparent section of the drain tube.

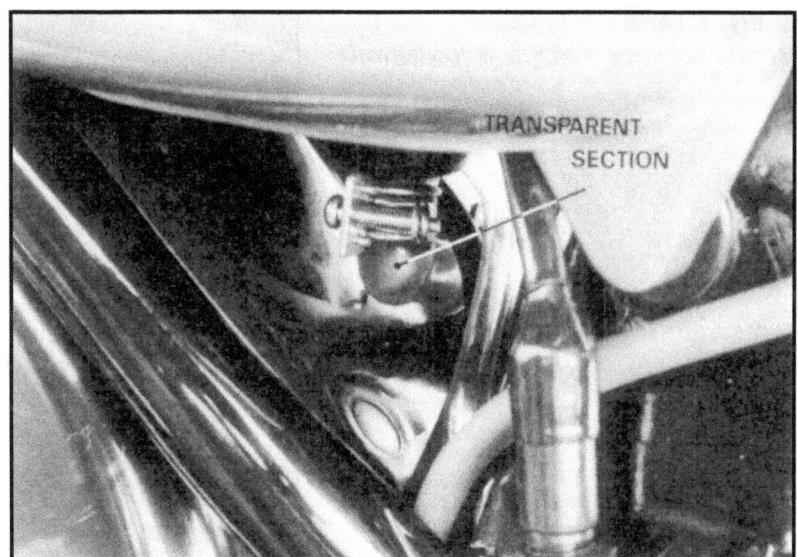

5. AIR CLEANER

1. Remove the right side cover.
2. Remove the air cleaner cover attaching nuts and air cleaner cover.

3. Pull the air cleaner element retainer out and remove the element.
4. Wash the air cleaner element in nonflammable or high flash point solvent and allow to dry.
5. Soak the air cleaner element in gear oil (SAE #80 – #90), and squeeze out the excess.
6. Install the air cleaner element.
7. Install the air cleaner element retainer, air cleaner cover and right side cover.

6. FUEL LINE
Replace any worn, damaged, or leaking parts.

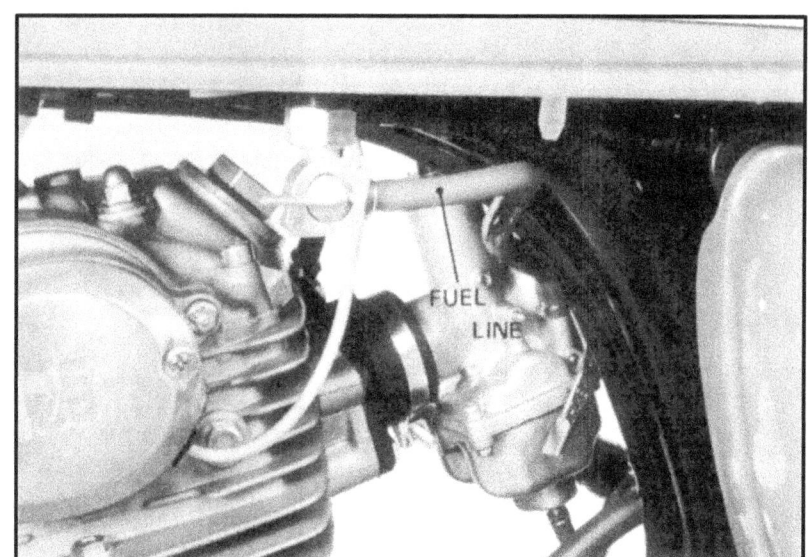

7. SPARK PLUG
1. Disconnect the spark plug cap, and remove the spark plug.
2. Visually inspect the spark plug electrodes for wear.
   The center electrode should have square edges and the side electrode should not be eroded. Discard the spark plug if there is apparent wear or if the insulator is cracked or chipped.

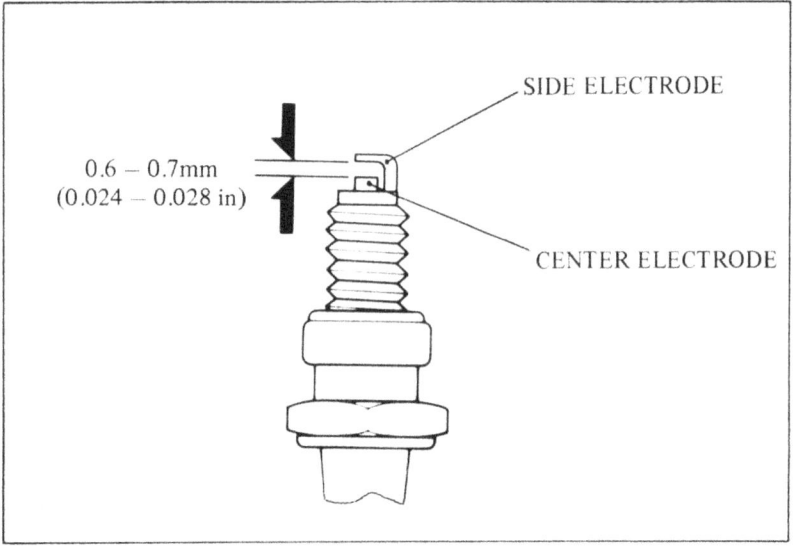

If the spark plug deposits can be removed by sandblasting or wire brush, the spark plug can be reused. The spark plug must be dry before sandblasting, and all grit must be removed before installation.

USA model:

Usage Brand	For cold climate (below 5°C, 41°F)	Standard	For extended high speed driving
NGK	D7EA	D8EA	D9EA
ND	X22ES-U	X24ES-U	X27ES-U

Canada model:

NGK DR8ES-L or ND X24ESR-U

3. Make sure the spark plug gap is 0.6 – 0.7 mm (0.024 – 0.028 in). Adjust by bending the side electrode.
4. Make sure the sealing washer is in good condition. Install the spark plug. First tighten it by hand, then tighten with a spark plug wrench.
5. Connect the spark plug cap.

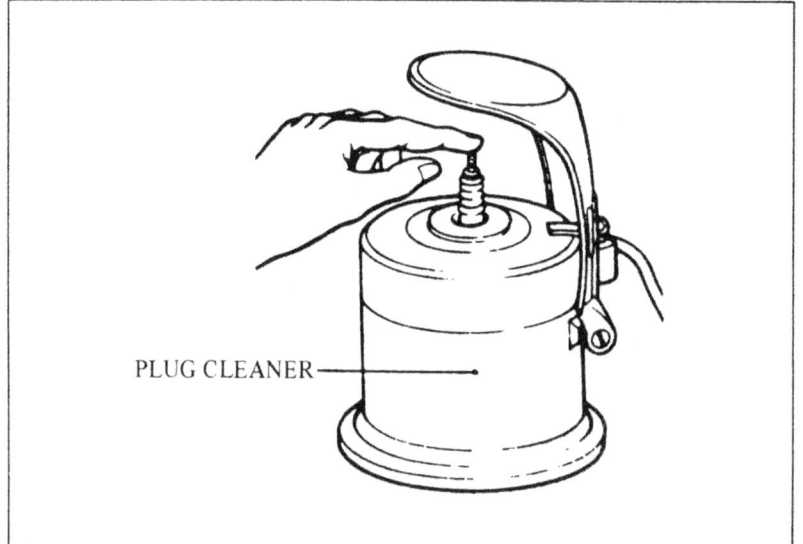

8. VALVE CLEARANCE

NOTE

Valve clearance adjustment must be performed while the engine is cold (below 35°C, 95°F)

1. Remove the generator rotor cover and valve adjusting hole caps.
2. Rotate the generator rotor counterclockwise, and align the "T" mark on the generator rotor with the index mark on the left crankcase cover. The piston must be at T.D.C. of the compression stroke.
3. Measure the intake and exhaust valve clearances with a 0.05mm (0.002 in) feeler gauge. Insert the feeler gauge between the valve adjusting screw and valve stem.
4. Adjust by loosening the valve adjusting screw lock nut and turning the adjusting screw until there is a slight drag on the feeler gauge.
5. Hold the adjusting screw and tighten the lock nut.
6. Recheck the clearance.
7. Install the generator rotor cover and valve adjusting hole caps.

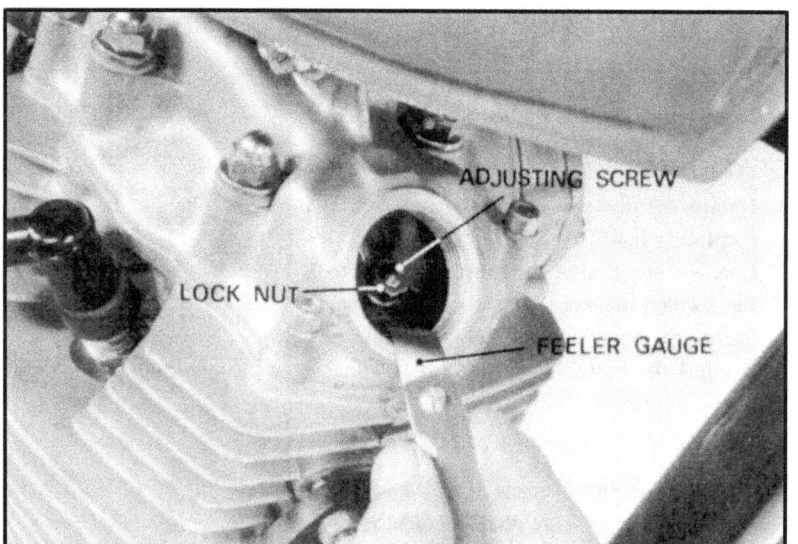

9. CONTACT BREAKER POINTS

1. Remove the generator rotor cover and point cover.
2. Clean the point contact surfaces with an electrical contact cleaner to remove any oil film or dirt. If the contact surfaces are level but grayish in color or are slightly pitted, file them lightly with a point file. If the points have a noticeable transfer of metal from one surface to the other, have evidence of heavy arcing, or are worn at an angle, they should be replaced.

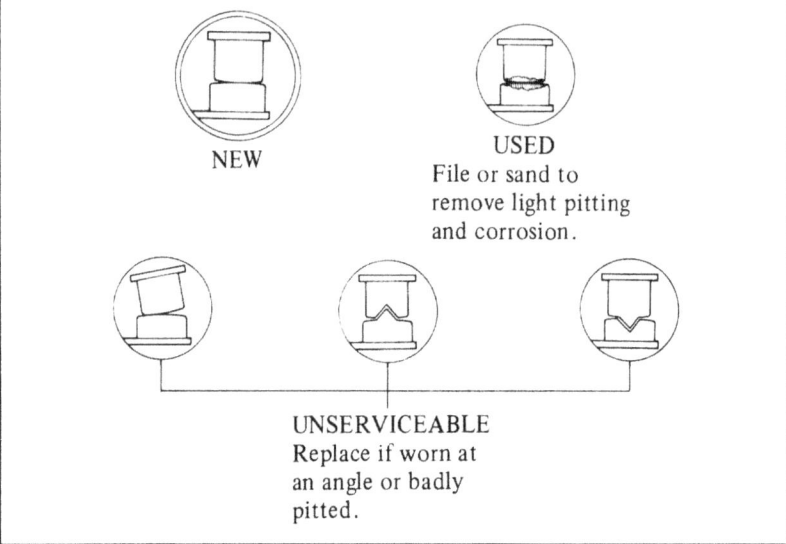

3. Rotate the generator rotor counterclockwise, and measure the maximum point gap with a feeler gauge.
   POINT GAP: 0.3 – 0.4mm (0.012 – 0.016 in)
4. Adjust by loosening the two contact breaker point locking screws, and moving the contact breaker plate.
5. Tighten the locking screws and recheck the point gap.

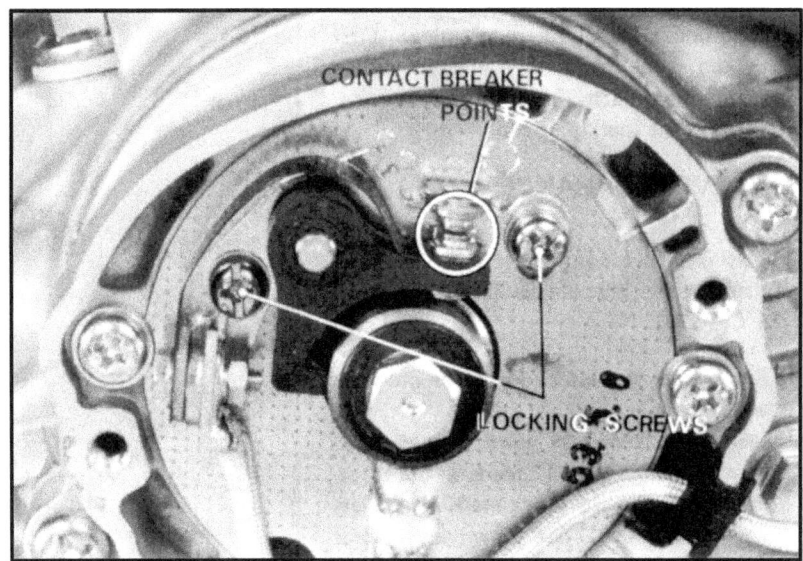

10. IGNITION TIMING

NOTE

Adjust the contact breaker point gap before adjusting ignition timing.

STATIC TIMING

1. Obtain a fully charged 6V battery and a continuity light (6V-3W).
2. Connect one lead of the continuity light to the contact breaker terminal, and the other lead to the battery positive (+) terminal.
3. Ground the battery negative (−) terminal to the motorcycle.

NOTE

This check can also be made using the vehicle battery; make sure that the ignition switch is ON.

4. Rotate the rotor counterclockwise and align the "F" mark on the rotor with the index mark on left crankcase cover. The timing is correct if the light goes out when both marks align.
5. Adjust by loosening the contact breaker base plate locking screws and rotate the plate counterclockwise to retard timing or clockwise to advance timing.
Tighten the locking screws and recheck the timing and point gap.

DYNAMIC TIMING

1. Connect a tachometer and a stroboscopic timing light.
2. Start the engine and adjust the idle speed to 1,300 ± 100 rpm.
3. The timing is correct, if the "F" mark on the rotor aligns with the index mark on the left crankcase cover.
4. Adjust the timing as described for use with a continuity light, step 5.

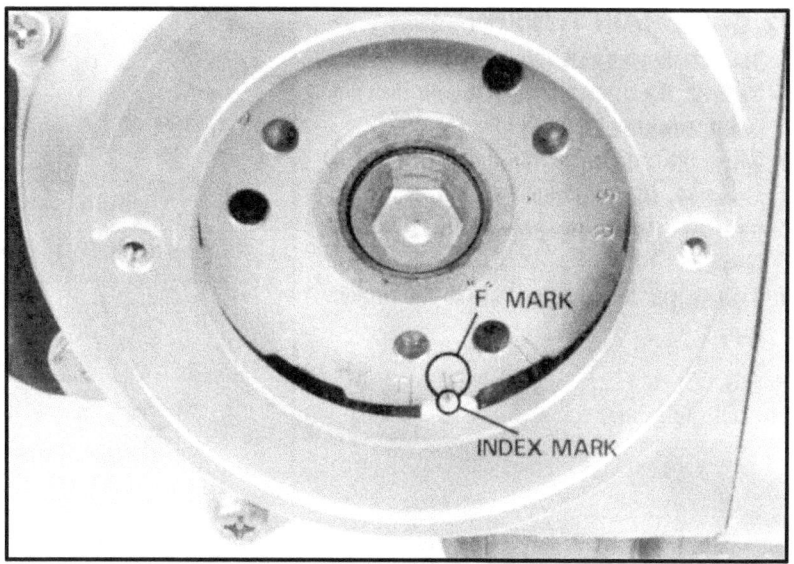

11. SPARK ADVANCER

NOTE

Before performing this test, check and adjust the ignition timing.

1. Connect a tachometer and a timing light.
2. Start the engine.
3. The index mark on the left crankcase cover should be between the full-advance marks on the rotor at 4,000 rpm.
4. If not, check the spark advancer operation.

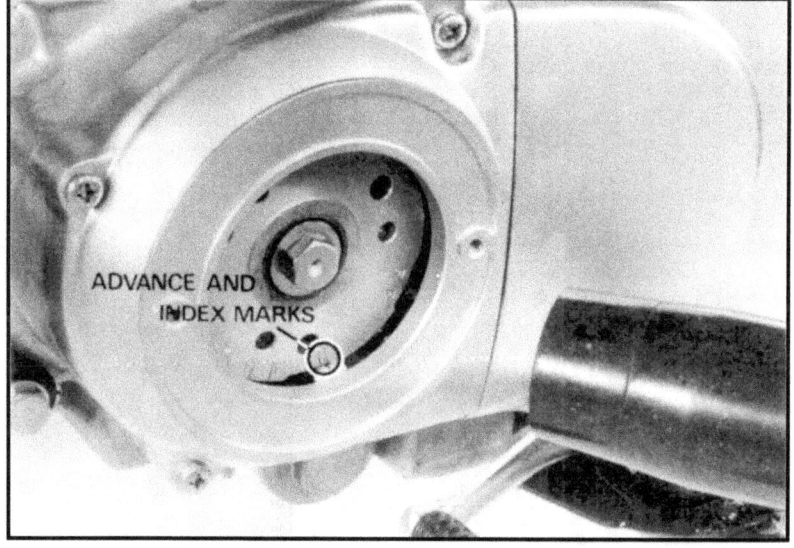

12. CAM CHAIN TENSION

1. Start the engine and allow it to idle.
2. Remove the rubber cap and loosen the cam chain tensioner lock nut.
3. When the cam chain tensioner lock nut is loosened, the tensioner will automatically position itself to provide the correct tension.
4. Tighten the lock nut and install the rubber cap.

NOTE

Install the rubber cap securely after adjustment.

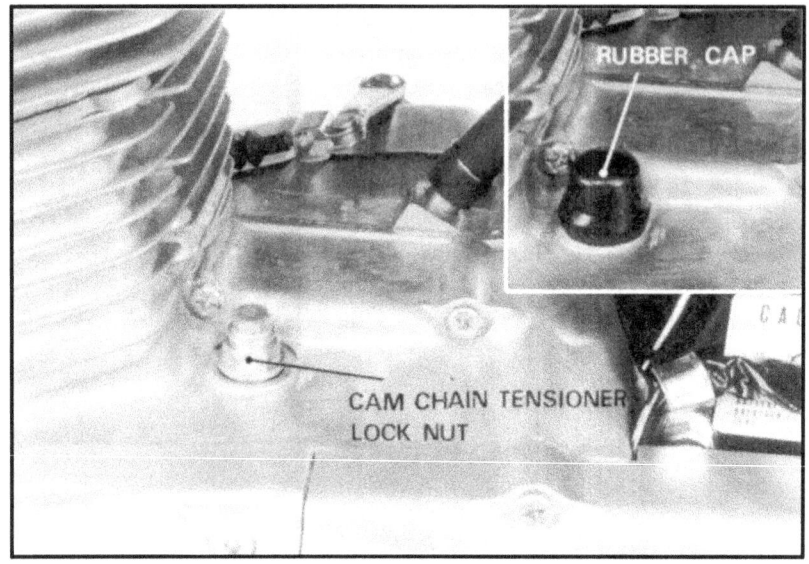

13. THROTTLE OPERATION

1. Check that there is no deterioration, damage or kinks in the throttle cable, and that the throttle grip free play is 2 – 6 mm (1/8 – 1/4 in) at the throttle grip outer flange.
2. Check for smooth throttle grip rotation. Check that the throttle grip returns automatically from the fully open to the fully closed position when released. Check in all steering positions.
3. Adjust with either the upper or lower cable adjuster, or replace if necessary. Tighten the lock nut.

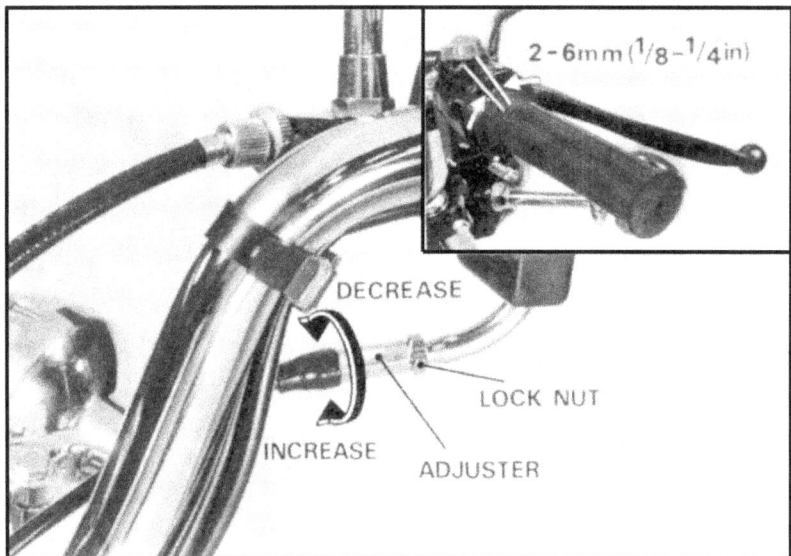

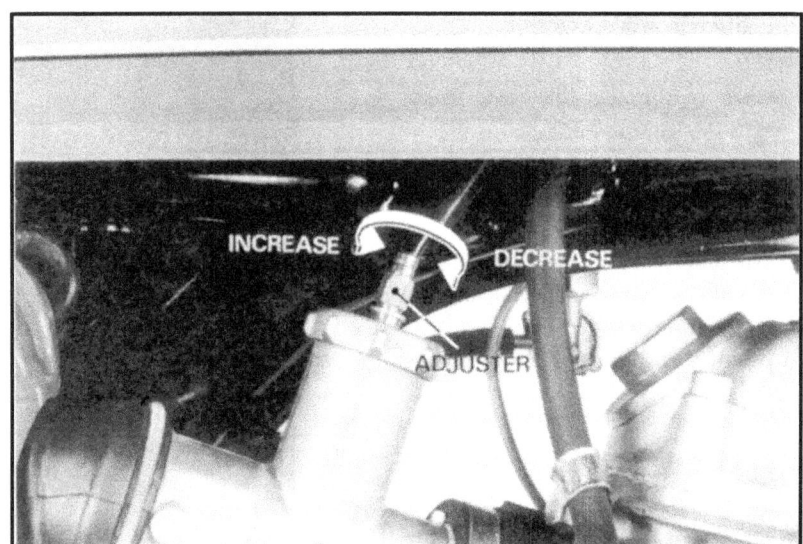

14. CARBURETOR CHOKE

Operate the choke lever and check for smooth operation.

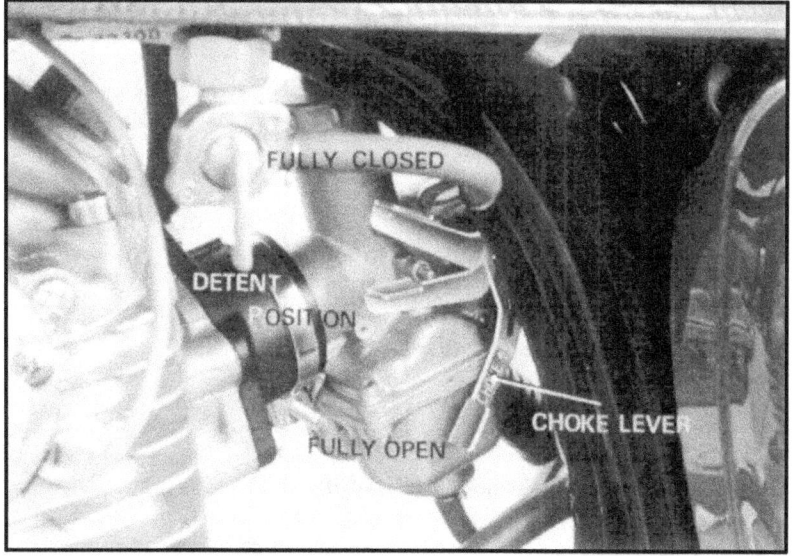

15. CARBURETOR IDLE SPEED

NOTE

Inspect and adjust the idle speed after all other maintenance items have been performed and are within specifications.

NOTE

The engine must be warm for idle adjustment. Ten minutes of stop-and-go driving is sufficient. Hold the motorcycle upright.

1. Warm up the engine and check the idle speed. The correct idle speed is 1,300 ± 100 rpm (in neutral).
2. Adjust the idle speed with the throttle stop screw.

NOTE

The pilot screw is factory pre-set.
Do not adjust the pilot screw except after overhauling the carburetor or if a high altitude main jet is installed (See page 164).

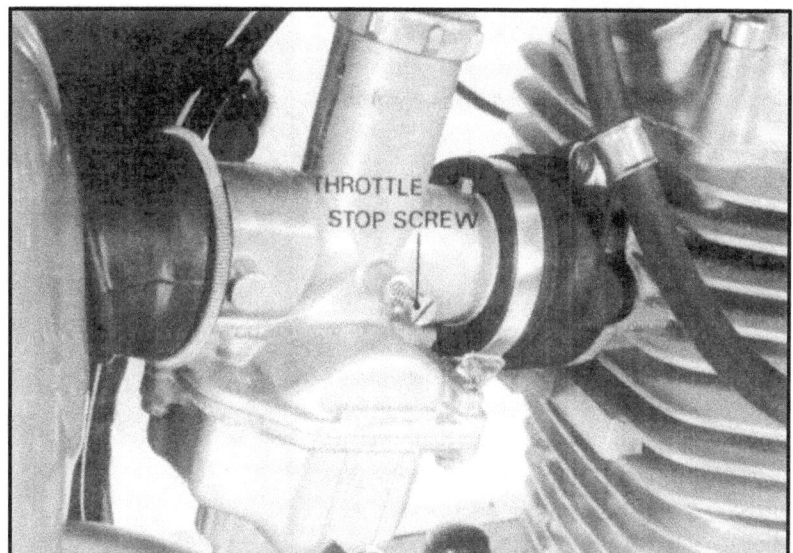

16. DRIVE CHAIN

DRIVE CHAIN SLACK

1. Turn the ignition switch "OFF".
2. Place the vehicle on its side stand and shift the transmission into neutral.
3. Check the drive chain slack midway between sprockets on the lower chain run. Measure the amount of slack.
   SLACK: 15 – 25mm (5/8 – 1 in)

ADJUSTMENT

1. Remove the cotter pin from rear axle nut, and loosen the nut.
2. Turn the adjusting nuts on both sides an equal amount until the correct drive chain slack is obtained.

NOTE
Be sure that the index mark aligns with the same graduation of the scale on both sides.

3. Tighten the axle nut and install a new cotter pin.
   TORQUE: 4.0 – 5.5 kg-m (29 – 40 ft-lb)
4. Lubricate the drive chain.
5. Inspect and adjust brake pedal free play, if necessary.

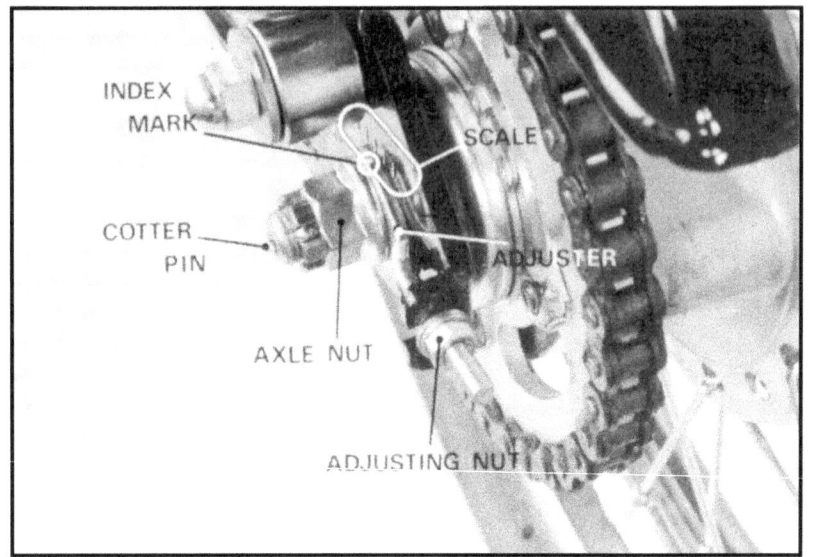

CLEANING/LUBRICATION

When the drive chain becomes extremely dirty, it should be removed and cleaned prior to lubrication.

Remove the master link retaining clip.

NOTE
Do not bend or twist the clip.

Remove the master link and drive chain. Clean the drive chain with nonflammable or high flash point solvent and brush and allow to dry. Inspect the drive chain for possible wear or damage. Replace any chain that is damaged or excessively worn. Inspect the sprocket teeth for excessive wear or damage. Replace if necessary.

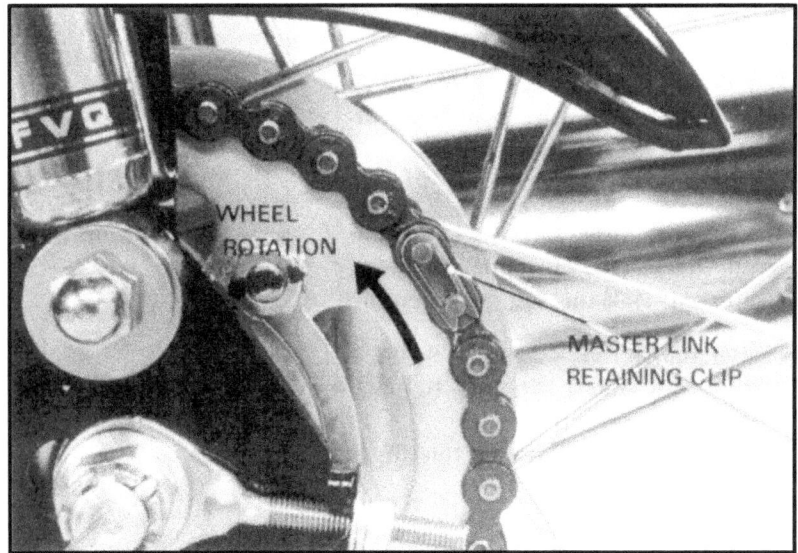

NOTE
* Never install a new drive chain on worn sprockets or a worn chain on new sprockets. Both chain and sprockets must be in good condition, or the new replacement chain or sprockets will wear rapidly.
* Commercial aerosol type drive chain lubricants are recommended.

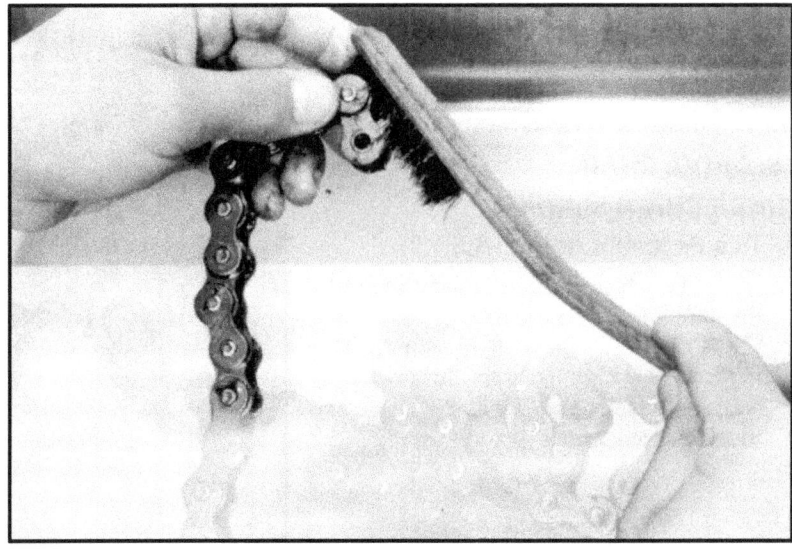

Lubricate the drive chain. Saturate each chain link joint. Install the drive chain. Install the master link. Install the master link retaining clip so that the closed end faces the direction of forward wheel rotation. Master links are reusable, if they remain in excellent condition, but it is recommended that a new master link be installed whenever the drive chain is reassembled.

Adjust the drive chain (See page 154).

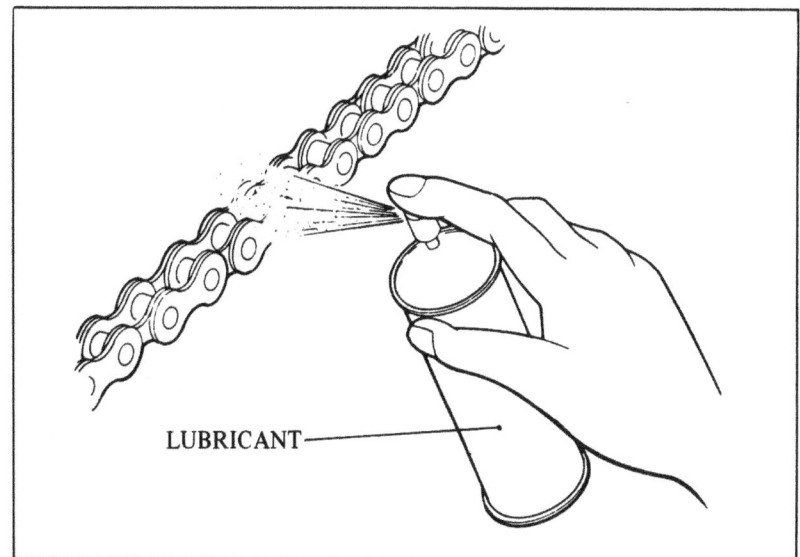

17. BATTERY

1. Remove the left side cover.
2. Check the fluid level. Add distilled water to the upper level mark. The electrolyte level must be maintained between the upper and lower level marks.
3. If sulfation forms or sediments (paste) accumulate on the bottom, replace the battery with a new one.

NOTE

Add distilled water only. Tap water will shorten the service life of the battery.

WARNING

The battery electrolyte contains sulfuric acid. Protect your eyes, skin and clothing. In case of contact, flush thoroughly with water and call a doctor if your eyes were exposed.

4. Route the battery breather tube as shown in the diagram.

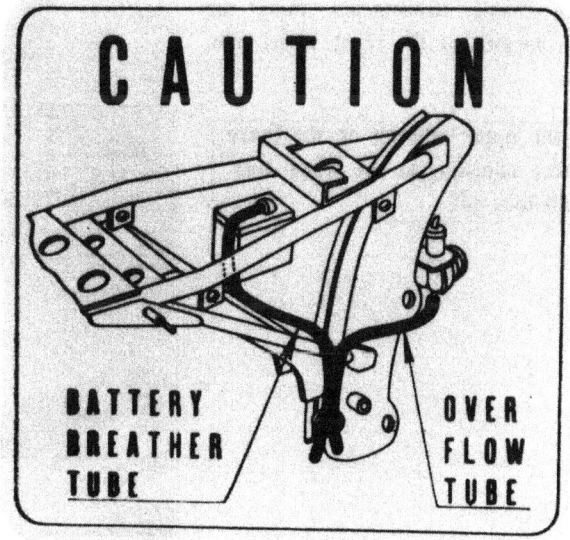

18. BRAKE SHOE WEAR

Replace the brake shoes if the arrow on the brake arm aligns with the reference mark "▲" on the backing plate during full application.

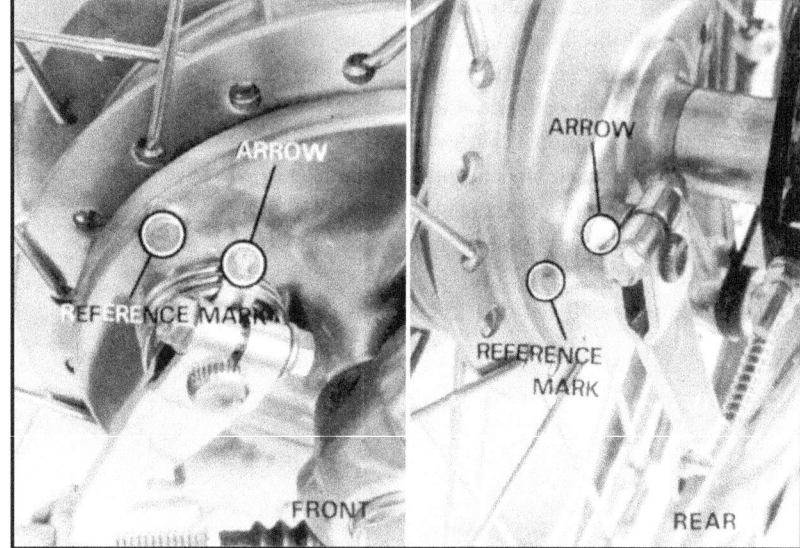

19. BRAKE SYSTEM

FRONT BRAKE FREE PLAY

1. Measure brake lever free play at the lever end.
   FREE PLAY: 20 – 30mm (3/4 – 1 1/4 in.)

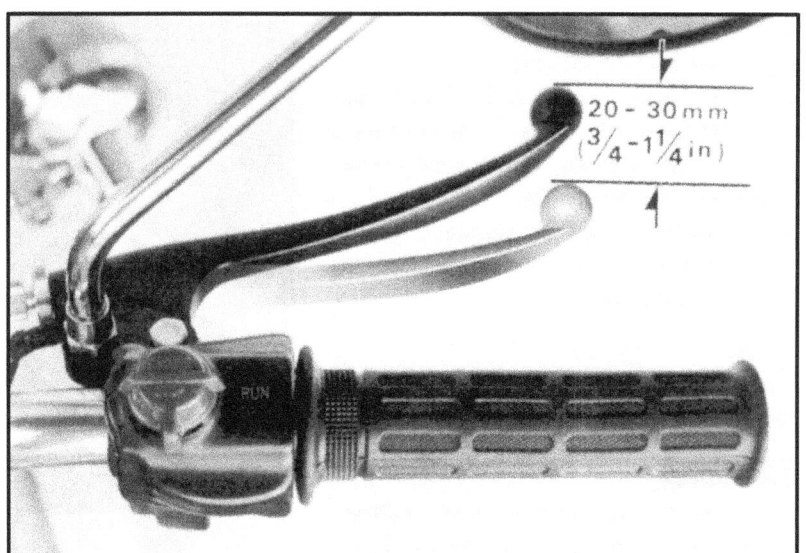

2. Perform major adjustments using the adjuster located at the front wheel hub.

NOTE

Turn in the upper adjuster on the brake lever before adjusting at the wheel hub. Tighten the lock nut.

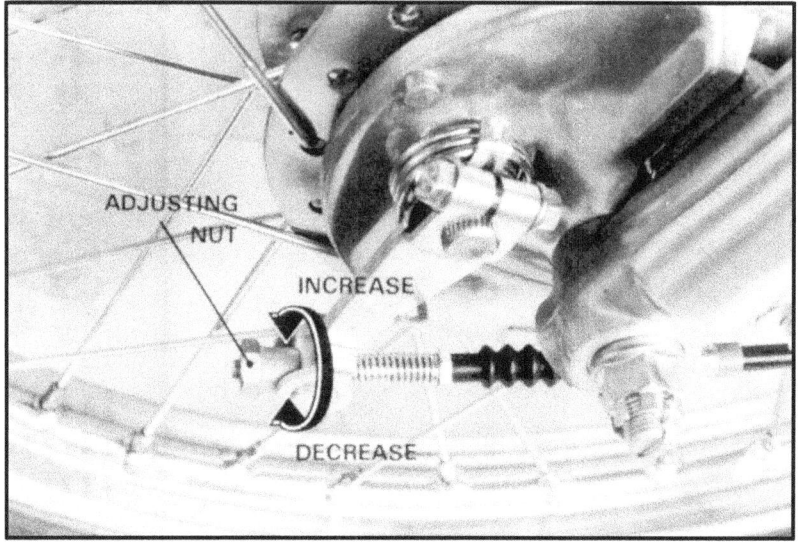

3. Minor adjustment can be made with the upper adjuster located on the brake lever. Loosen the lock nut and turn the adjuster.
4. Recheck brake operation.

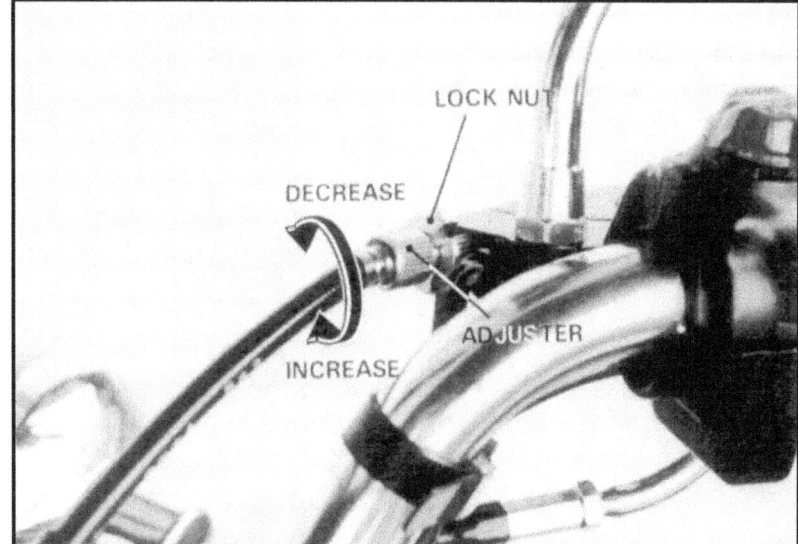

REAR BRAKE FREE PLAY

1. Check brake pedal free play.
   FREE PLAY: 20 – 30mm (3/4 – 1 1/4 in.)

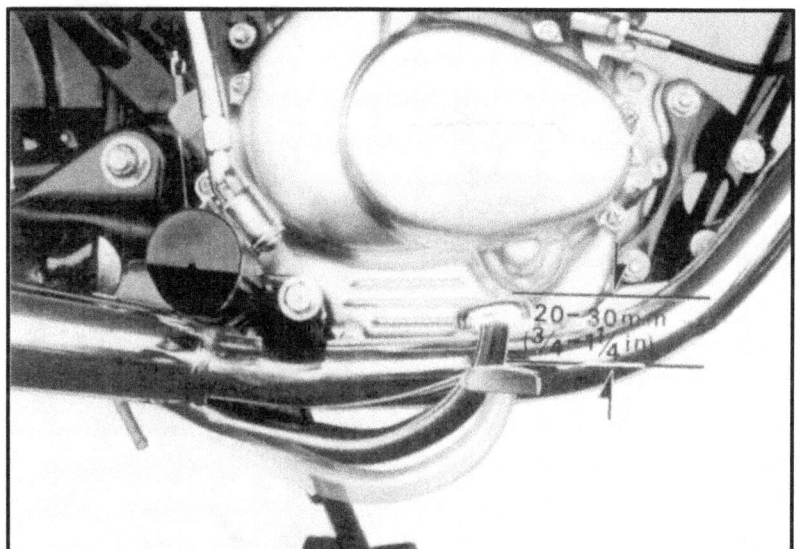

2. If adjustment is necessary, turn the rear brake adjusting nut.

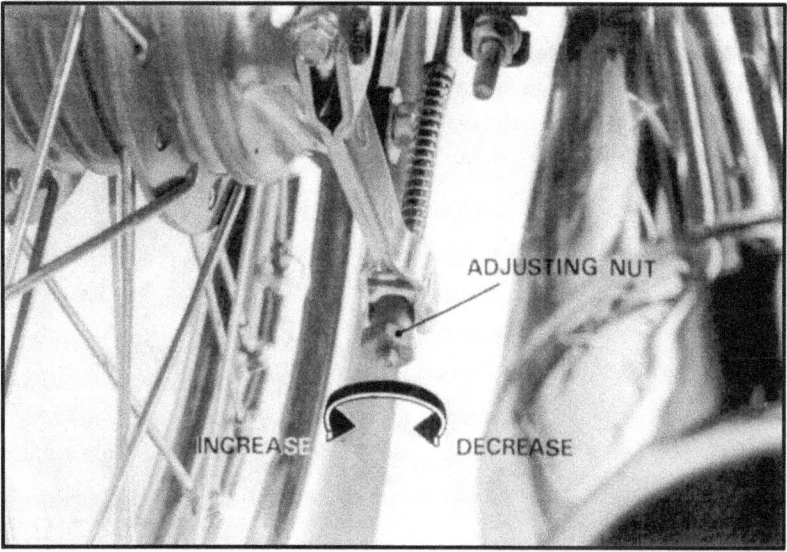

BRAKE LINKAGE INSPECTION

Check the brake rod and brake lever for loose connections, excessive play, bending or damage. Replace or repair if necessary. Inspect the brake and stopper arms for loose connections or damage. Check that the cotter pin is installed properly.

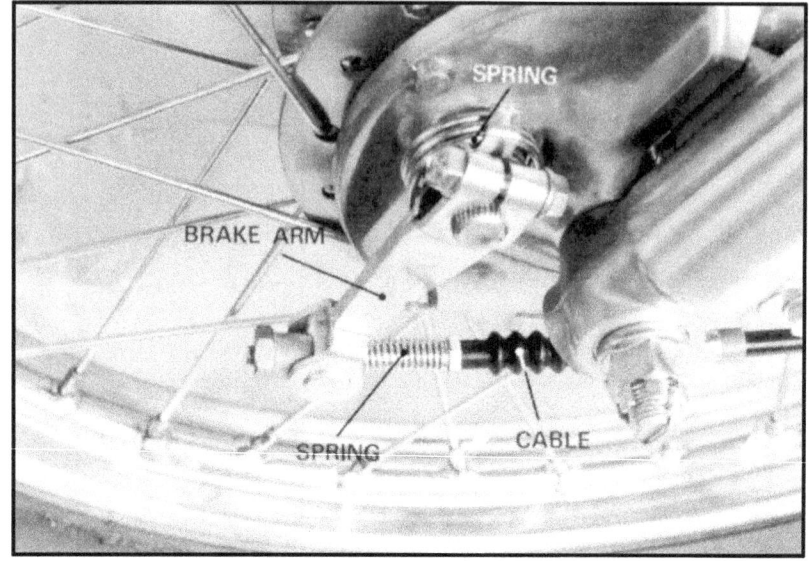

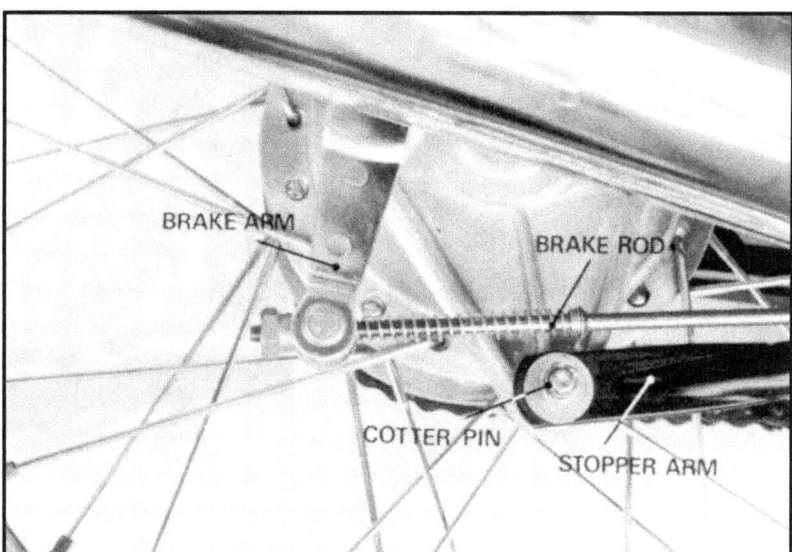

20. BRAKE LIGHT SWITCH

Adjust the brake light switch so that the stoplight will come on when the brake pedal is depressed 20 mm (3/4 in) where the brake begins engagement. Adjust by turning the switch adjusting nut.

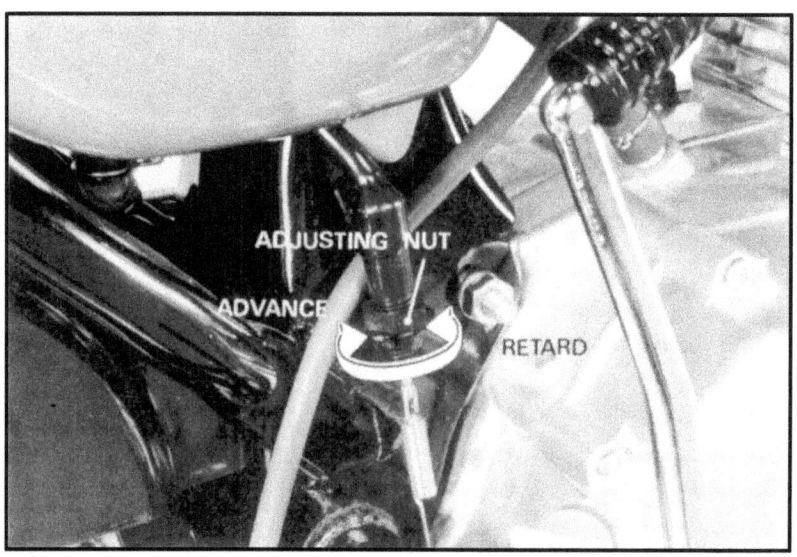

21. HEADLIGHT AIM

The headlight beam can be adjusted vertically and horizontally.

1. Adjust vertically by loosening the headlight case mounting bolts.
2. Adjust the horizontal beam with the beam adjusting screw shown.

NOTE

Adjust the headlight beam as specified by local laws and regulations.

WARNING

An improperly adjusted headlight may blind oncoming drivers, or it may fail to light the road for a safe distance.

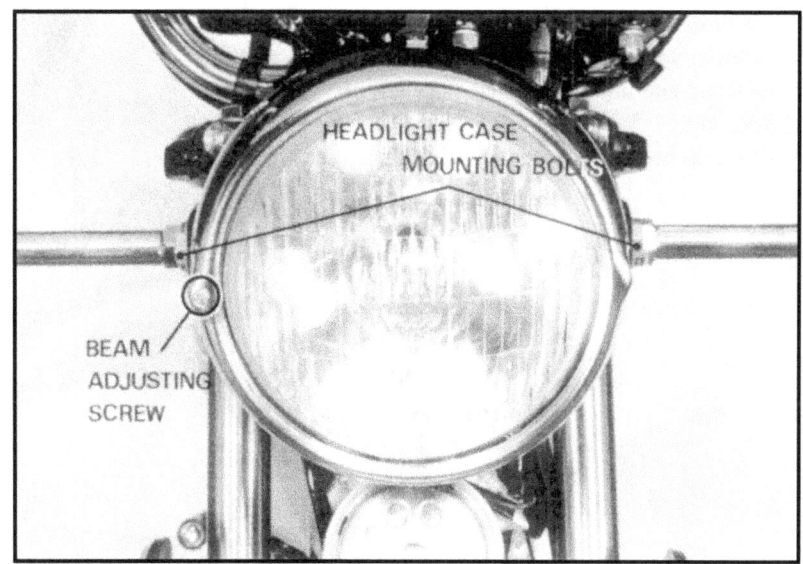

22. CLUTCH FREE PLAY

1. Measure clutch lever free play at the lever end.
   FREE PLAY: 10 – 20mm (3/8 – 3/4 in)

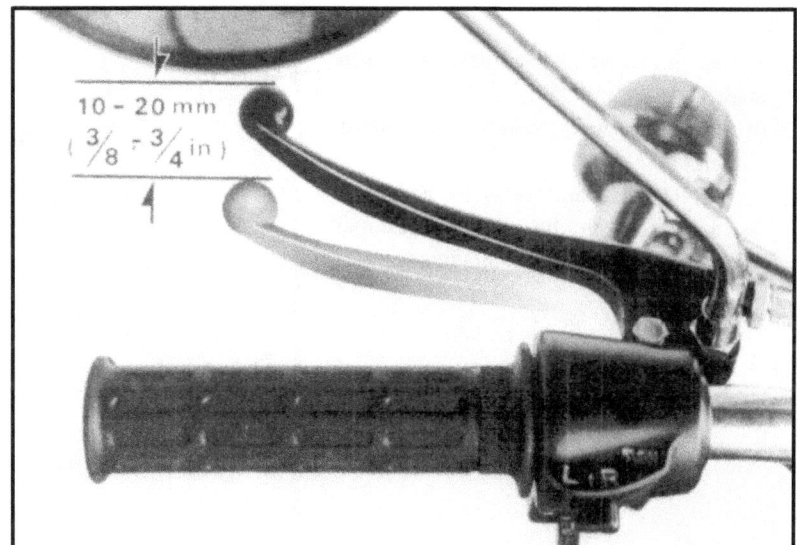

2. Perform major adjustments with the lower adjuster located at the right crankcase. Loosen the lock nut and turn the adjusting nut. Tighten the lock nut.

NOTE

Turn in the upper adjuster on the clutch lever before adjusting at the right crankcase.

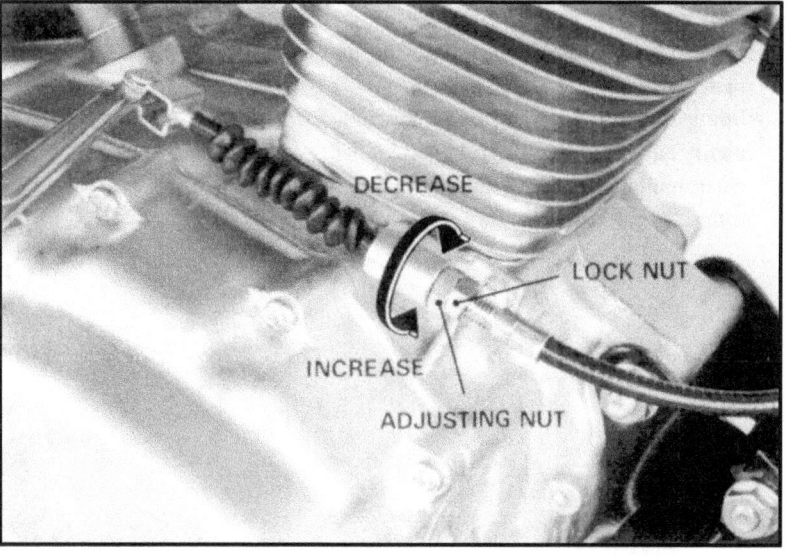

3. Perform minor adjustments with the upper adjuster on the clutch lever. Loosen the lock nut and turn the adjuster. Tighten the lock nut.
4. Recheck the clutch operation.

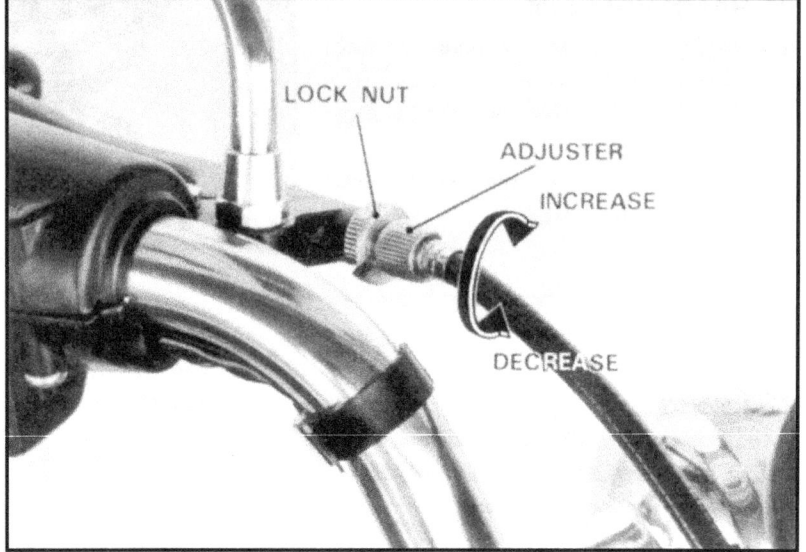

23. SIDE STAND

1. Check the rubber pad for deterioration or wear.
2. Replace if any wear extends to wear line as shown.
3. Check the side stand spring for damage or loss of tension, and the side stand assembly for freedom of movement and bend.

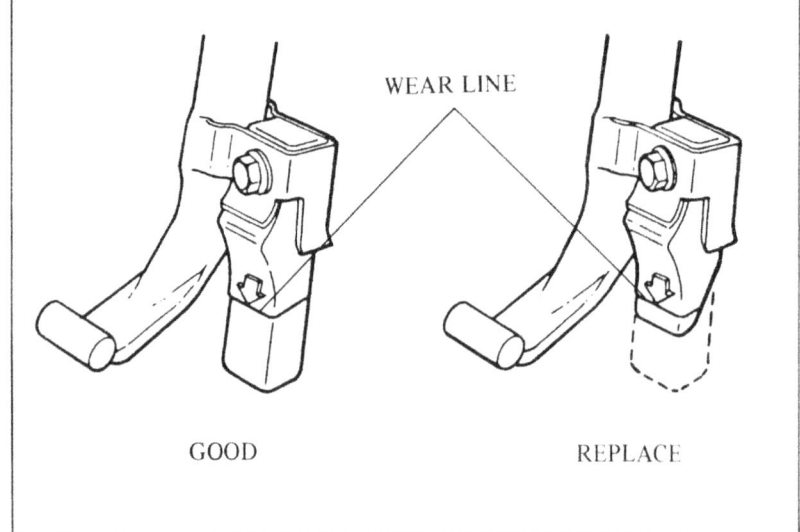

NOTE

* When replacing, use a rubber pad with the mark "BELOW 259 lbs ONLY".
* Spring tension is correct if the measurements fall within 2 – 3 kg (4.4 – 6.6 lb) when pulling the side stand lower end using a spring scale.

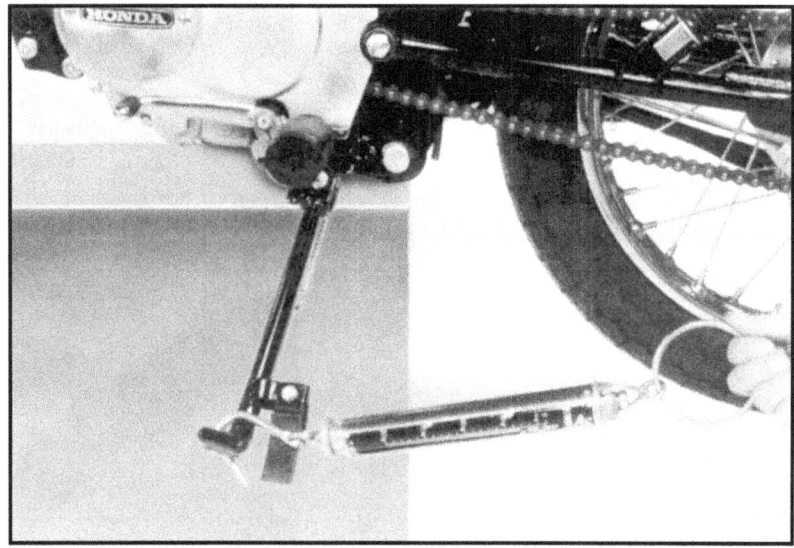

24. SUSPENSION

> **WARNING**
> *Do not ride a vehicle with faulty suspension. Loose, worn or damaged suspension components may impair vehicle stability, safety and rider control.*

FRONT

1. Check the action of the front forks by compressing them several times.
2. Check the entire fork assembly for signs of leaks, or damage. Replace damaged components they cannot be repaired.
3. Tighten all bolts and nuts to the specified torque value.

REAR

1. Place the vehicle on its side stand.
2. Move the rear wheel sideways with force to see if the swing arm bushings are worn. Replace if excessively worn.
3. Check the entire suspension assembly. Be sure it is securely mounted, and not damaged or bent.

25. NUTS, BOLTS, FASTENERS

Check that all chassis nuts, bolts and fasteners are tightened to their correct torque values.

26. WHEELS/SPOKES

TIRE PRESSURE

Check the tires for cuts, imbedded nails, or other objects.

NOTE

Tire pressure should be checked when the tires are COLD.

Cold tire pressures kg/cm² (psi)	Up to 90 kg (200 lbs) load	Front: 1.75 (24) Rear: 2.0 (28)
	Up to vehicle capacity load	Front: 1.75 (24) Rear: 2.25 (32)
Vehicle capacity load limit	135 kg (300 lbs)	
Tire size	Front: 2.75 – 18 (4 PR) Rear: 3.00 – 17 (4 PR)	

WARNING

Replace tires when tread depth becomes less than:
Front: 1.5 mm (1/16 in)
Rear: 2.0 mm (3/32 in)

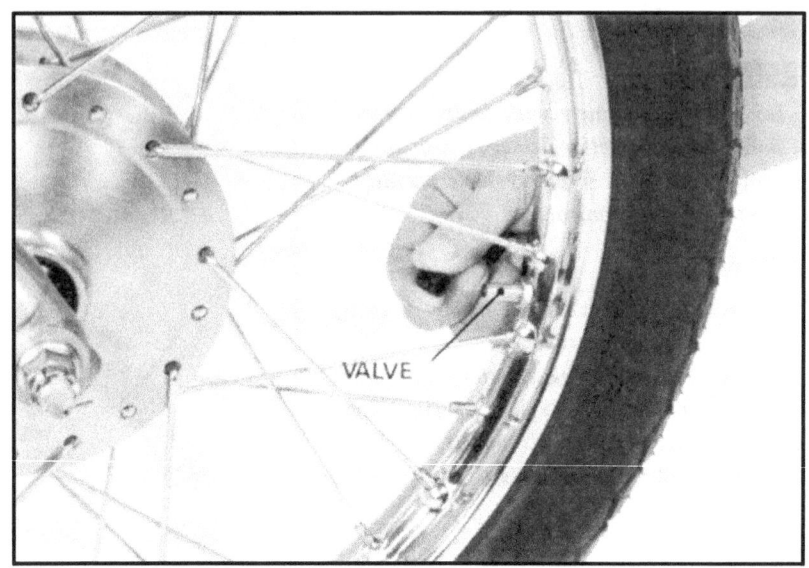

SPOKES

1. Tighten the wheel spokes periodically.
   TORQUE:
   Front: 0.15 – 0.35 kg-m
   (1.1 – 2.5 ft-lb)
   Rear: 0.15 – 0.30 kg-m
   (1.1 – 2.2 ft-lb)
2. Check front and rear wheel trueness.

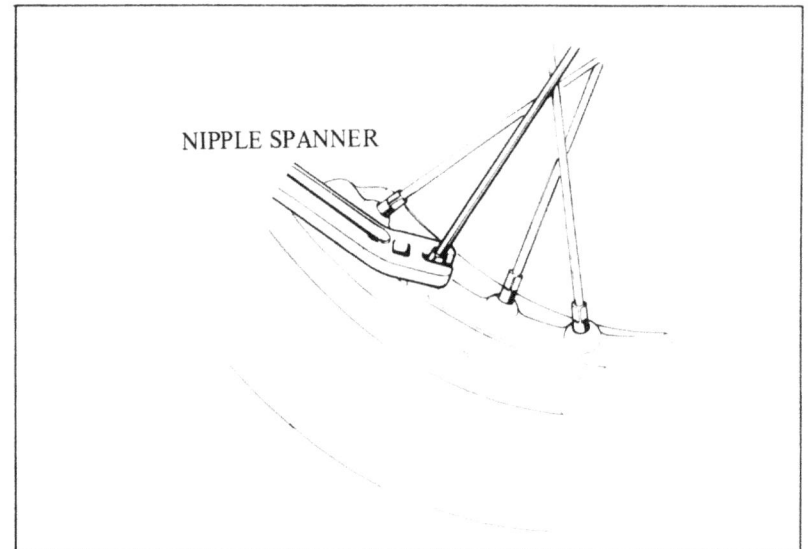

27. STEERING HEAD BEARING

NOTE

Check that the control cables do not interfere with the rotation of the handlebars.

Raise the front wheel off the ground. Check that the handlebar rotates freely.
If the handlebar moves unevenly, binds or has vertical movement, adjust the steering head bearing by turning the steering head adjusting nut with a pin spanner.

V. CARBURETOR

1. CARBURETOR SPECIFICATIONS

WARNING

Gasoline is extremely flammable and is explosive under certain conditions. Do not smoke or allow flames or sparks in your working area.

Item	Standard spec. (2,000m, 6,500 ft max.)	High altitude spec. (1,500m, 5,000 ft min.)
Identification number	PD68B	←
Main jet	#110	#100
Jet needle mark	20C	←
Float level	18.5mm (0.73 in)	←
Idle speed	1,300 ± 100 rpm	←

2. DISASSEMBLY AND ASSEMBLY

Refer to the base 100/125 Shop Manual for disassembly and assembly procedures.

NOTE

When disassembling fuel system parts, note the locations of the O-rings. Replace them with new ones on reassembly. The float bowl has a drain plug that can be loosened to drain residual gasoline.

3. PILOT SCREW ADJUSTMENT

NOTE

The pilot screw is factory pre-set. Adjustment is not necessary unless the carburetor is overhauled or a high altitude main jet installed.

1. Turn the pilot screw clockwise until it seats lightly and back it out 1 turn. This is a preliminary setting prior to the final Pilot Screw Adjustment.

CAUTION

Damage to the pilot screw seat will occur if the pilot screw is tightened against the seat.

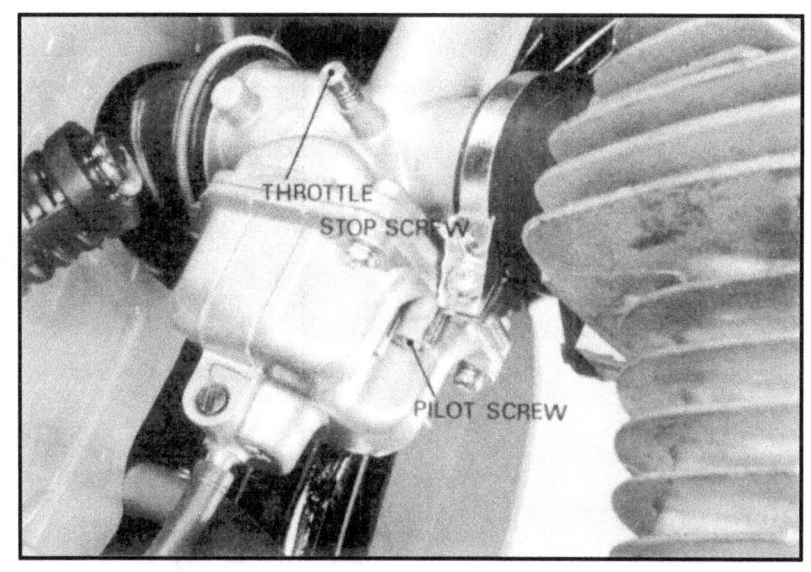

2. Warm up the engine to operating temperature. Stop-and-go driving for ten minutes is sufficient.
3. Attach a tachometer.
4. Adjust the idle speed with the throttle stop screw.
   IDLE SPEED: 1,300 rpm
5. Screw the pilot screw in gradually until the engine stops.
6. Turn the pilot screw 3/4 turn out from this position.
7. Restart the engine and readjust the throttle stop screw, if necessary.

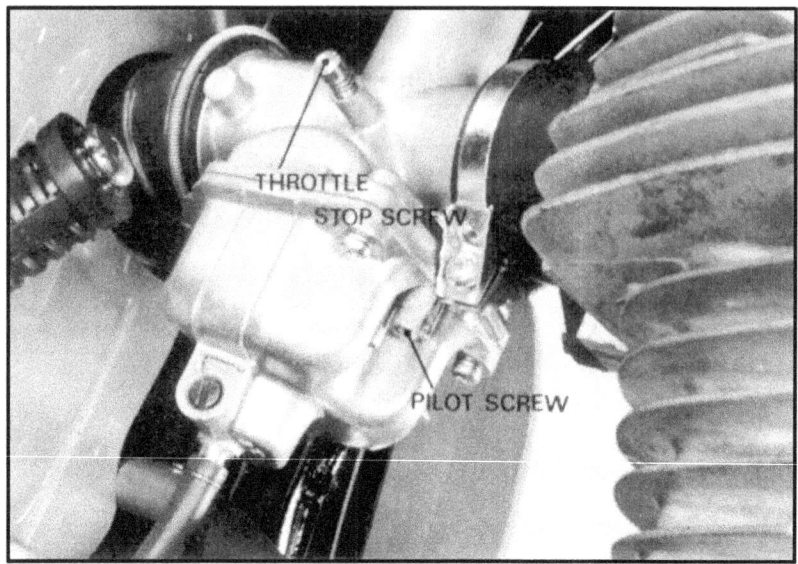

4. HIGH ALTITUDE ADJUSTMENT

The carburetor must be adjusted for high altitude riding above 2,000m (6,500 ft).
   STANDARD SETTING:
      2,000m (6,500 ft) max.
   HIGH ALTITUDE SETTING:
      1,500m (5,000 ft) min.
High altitude carburetor adjustment is as follows:
1. Loosen the drain screw to remove the fuel from the carburetor.

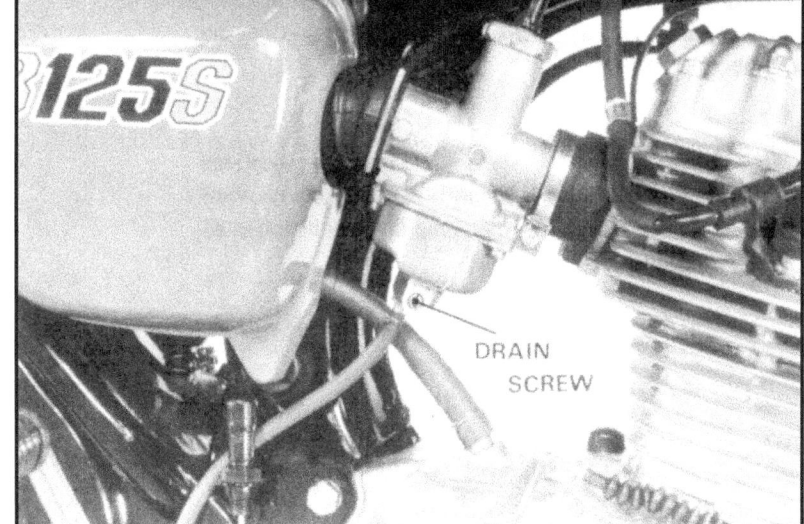

2. Remove the carburetor cap.
3. Remove the throttle valve.
4. Loosen the carburetor band and tilt the carburetor.

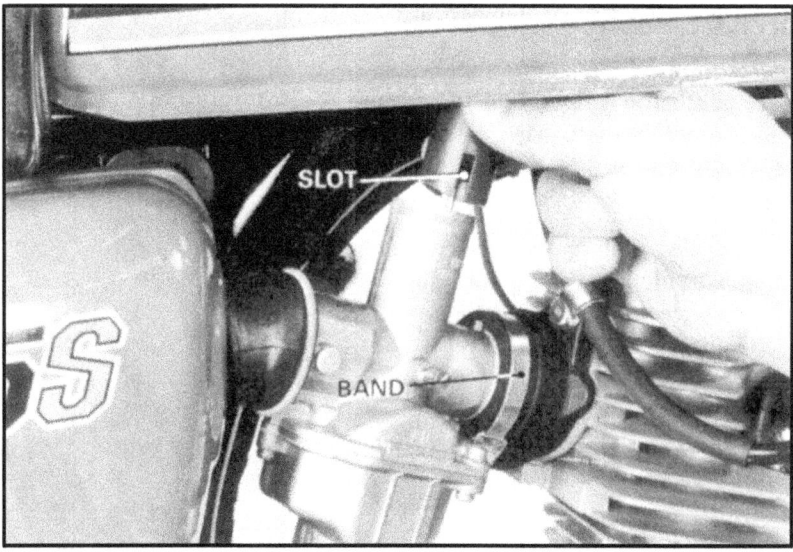

5. Remove the float bowl.
6. Replace the main jet with the high altitude type (See page 164).

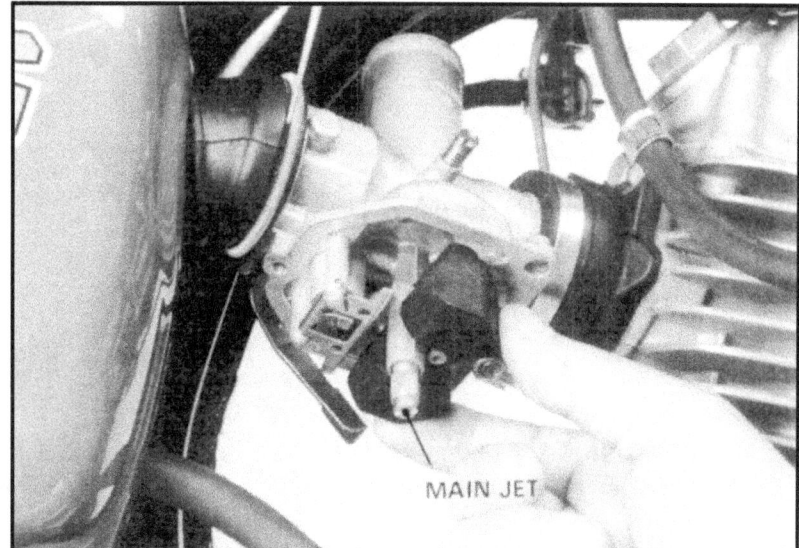

7. Install the float bowl.
8. Install the throttle valve, aligning the slot on the throttle valve with the throttle stop screw.

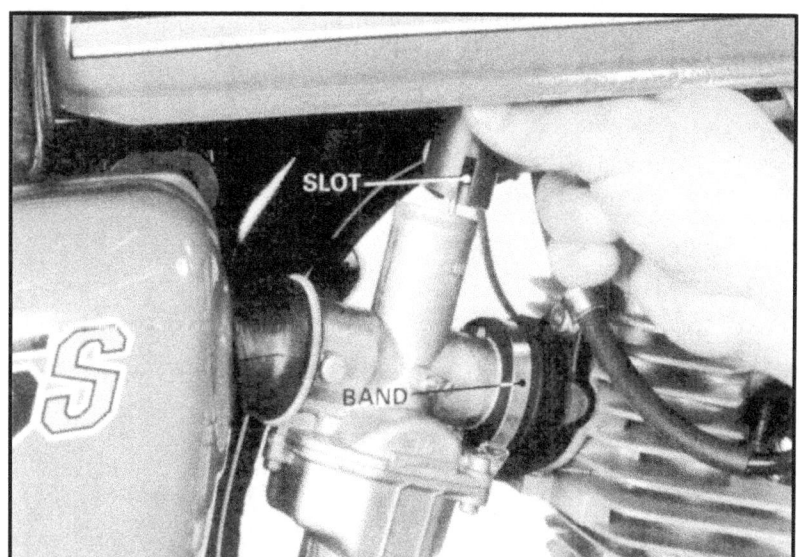

9. Install the careburetor cap.
10. Install the carburetor. Align the carburetor and insulator tangs.

11. Screw in the pilot screw 3/8 of a turn.
12. Start the engine and adjust the idle speed with the throttle stop screw.

NOTE
* Adjust the idle speed at high altitude to ensure proper high altitude operation.
* Readjust the pilot screw if the engine idles rough, misses, or stalls, according to the instructions on page 164.

CAUTION

Sustained operation at altitudes lower than 1,500m (5,000 ft) with the high altitude specifications may cause engine overheating and damage.

Reinstall the standard main jet and turn the pilot screw 3/8 turn out when operating the vehicle below 1,500 m (5,000 ft).

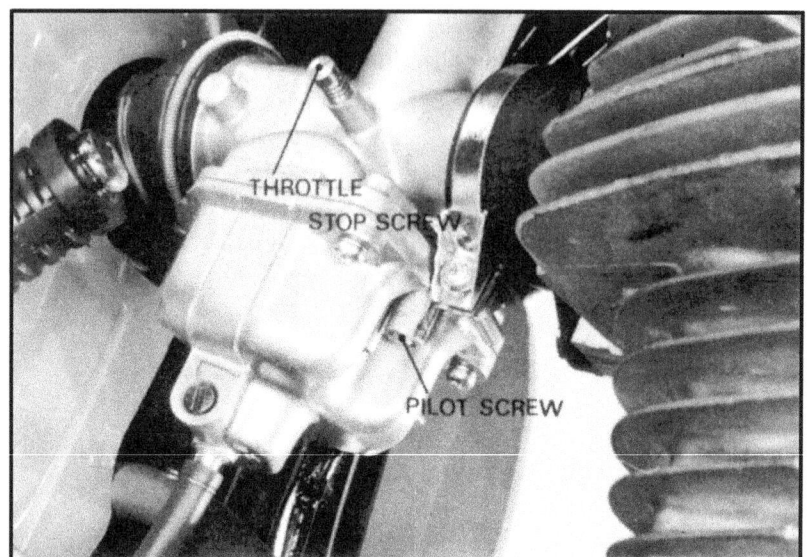

VI. WHEEL/SUSPENSION

1. FRONT WHEEL REMOVAL

1. Raise the front wheel off the ground by placing a support block under the engine.
2. Loosen the speedometer cable set screw and disconnect the speedometer cable.
3. Disconnect the front brake cable from the brake arm.
4. Pull out the cotter pin and remove the axle nut.
5. Remove the axle and wheel.

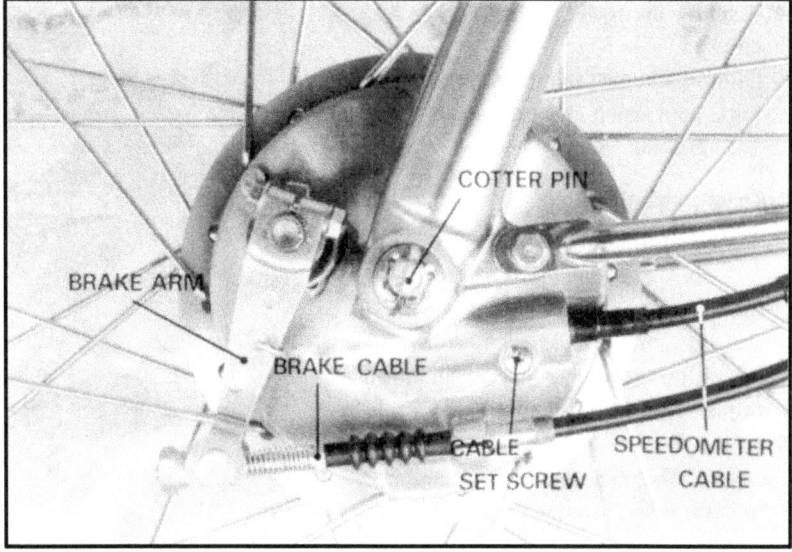

INSTALLATION NOTE

* Intall the front wheel between the fork legs. Make sure that the tang on the left fork leg is located in the slot in the brake panel.
* Axle nut torque:
  3.5 – 5.0 kg-m (25 – 36 ft-lb)
* Install the cotter pin and spread the pin ends.
* Adjust brake free play. See pages 156–157.
* Apply the brake several times and check for free wheel rotation.

CAUTION

Always replace used cotter pins with new ones.

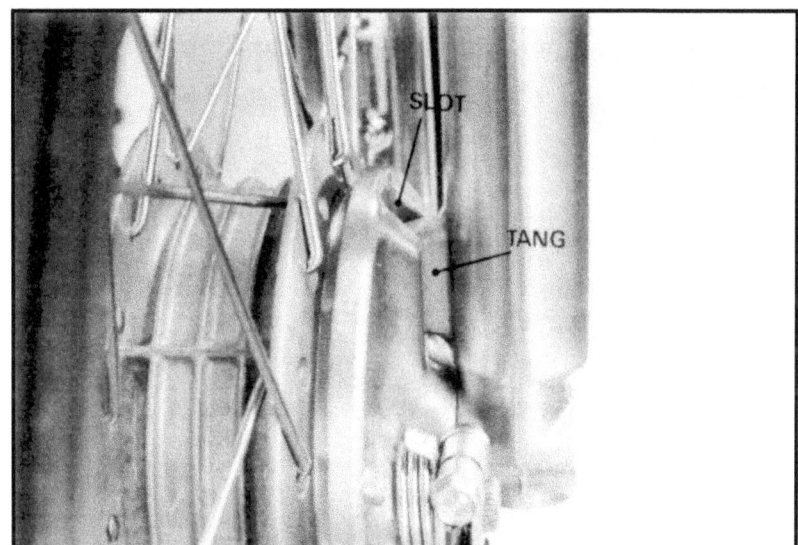

2. REAR WHEEL REMOVAL

1. Raise the rear wheel off the ground by placing a support block under the engine.
2. Remove the rear brake adjusting nut, disconnect the brake rod from the brake arm.
3. Disconnect the stopper arm from the brake panel by removing the cotter pin, nut, washer and rubber spacer.

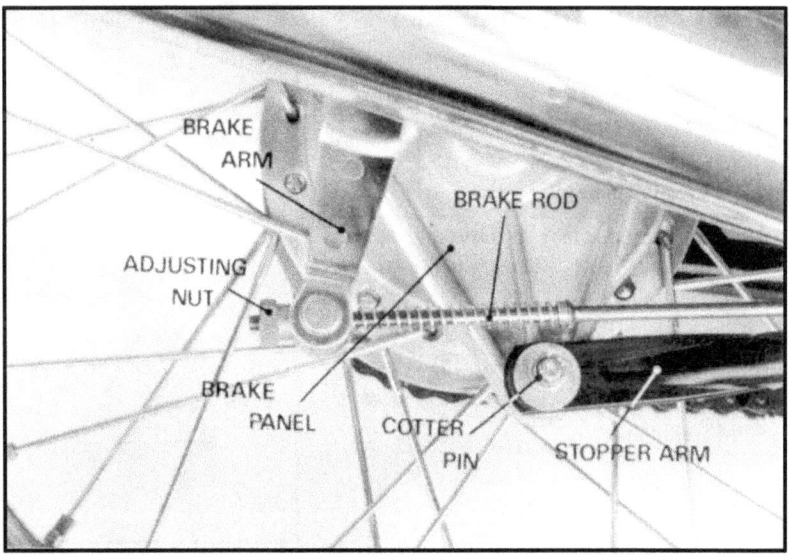

4. Remove the cotter pin and loosen the axle nut.
5. Pull out the rear axle. Push the wheel forward and derail the drive chain from the rear sprocket. Remove the rear wheel.

INSTALLATION NOTE

* Stopper arm torque:
    1.8 – 2.5 kg-m (13 – 18 ft-lb)
* Axle nut torque:
    4.0 – 5.5 kg-m (29 – 40 ft-lb)
* Install the cotter pins and spread pin ends.
* Adjust brake free play and drive chain slack.
* Apply the brake several times and check for free wheel rotation.

CAUTION

Always replace used cotter pins with new ones.

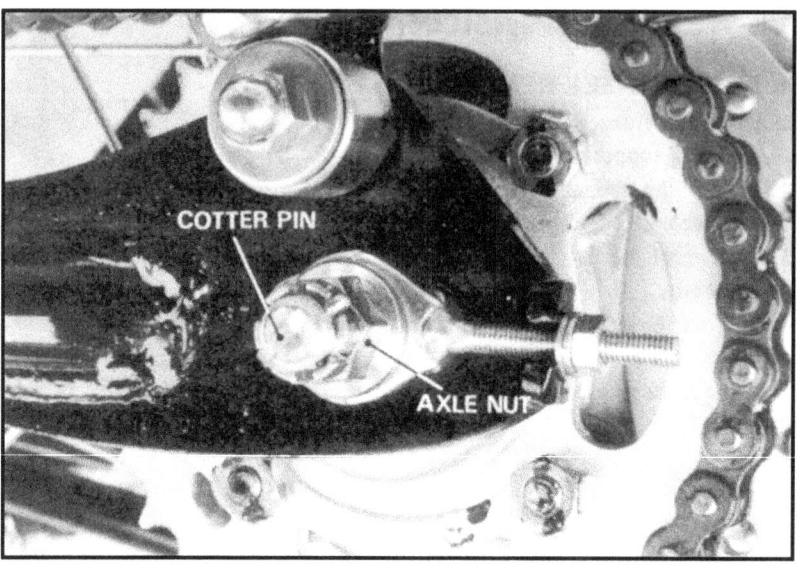

3. REAR SHOCK ABSORBERS

Each rear shock absorber has a five position spring tension adjuster.
Position I is the standard position.

INSTALLATION NOTE

* When the upper eye is replaced, apply locking agent on the threads before tightening the lock nut.
    Torque:
        2.0 – 3.5 kg-m (14 – 25 ft-lb)
* Install the spring with the tightly wound end facing up.

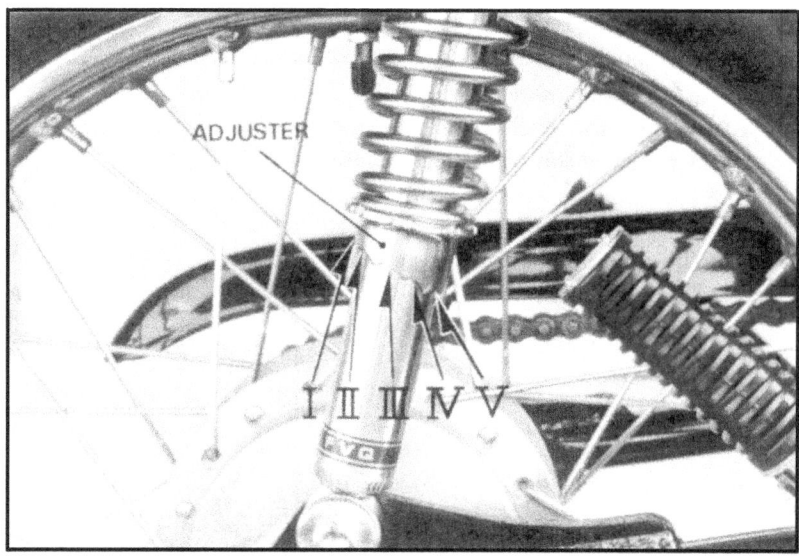

4. FRONT FORK

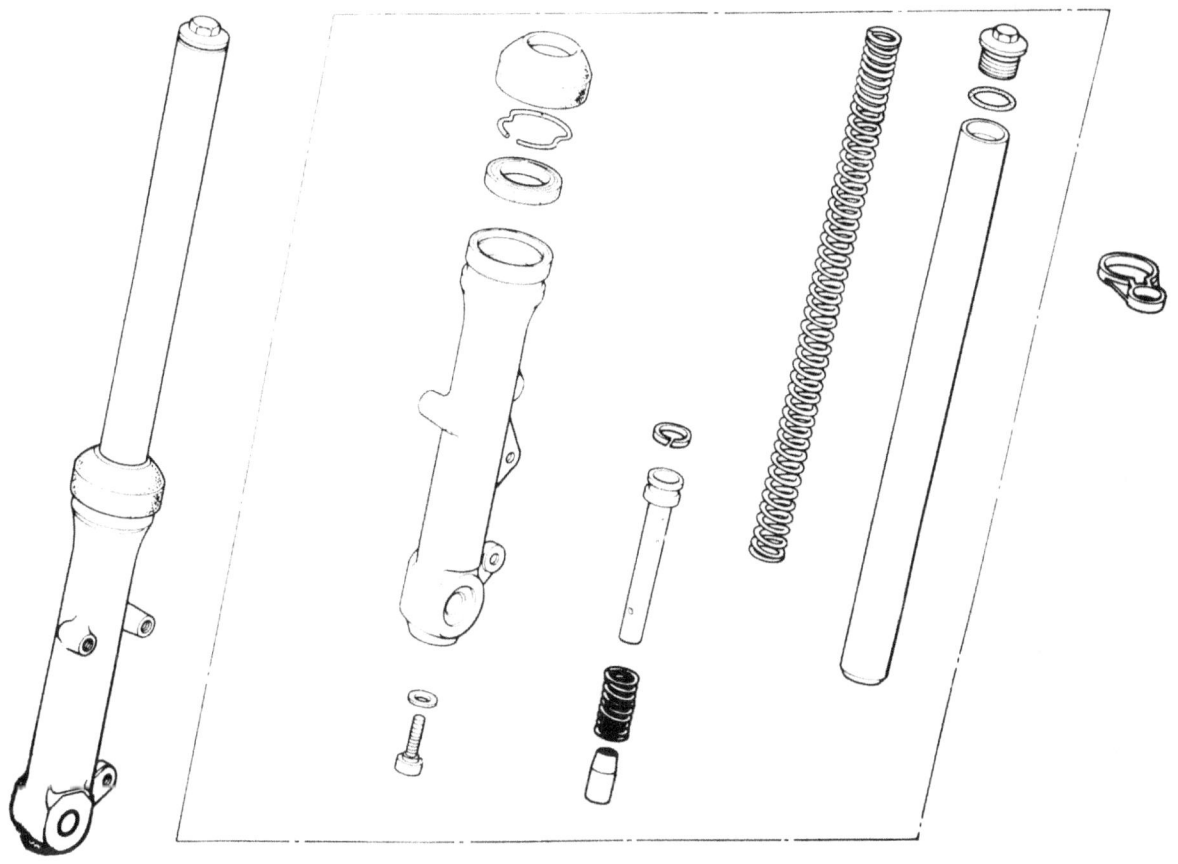

Remove the hex. bolt to disassemble the front fork.

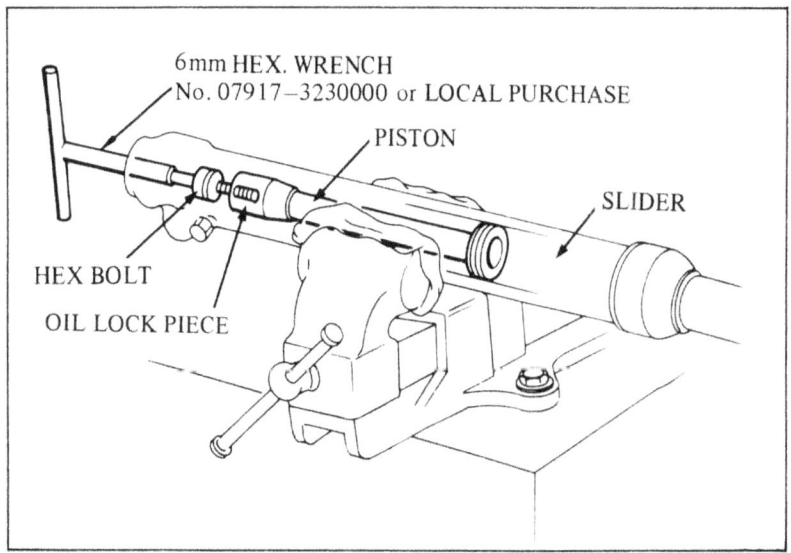

SERVICE DATA

Fork spring free length:
   Standard   : 457 mm (18.0 in)
   Service limit : 448 mm (17.6 in)
Fork tube O.D.
   Standard   : 26.939 – 26.960 mm
                  (1.0606 – 1.0614 in)
   Service limit : 26.90 mm (1.059 in)
Fork tube bend
   Service limit : 0.2 mm (0.01 in)

INSTALLATION NOTE

* Apply locking agent to the hex. bolt before installation.
* Hex. bolt torque:
   1.5 – 2.5 kg-m (11 – 18 ft-lb)
* Fork oil capacity: 80 – 85 cc (2.7 – 2.9 ozs)
* Install the fork spring with the tightly wound coils facing up.
* Fork bolt torque:
   1.5 – 3.0 kg-m (11 – 22 ft-lb)
* Install the fork tubes so that they are even with the top of the fork top bridge.
* Fork top bridge bolt torque:
   1.2 – 1.6 kg-m (9 – 12 ft-lb)
* Fork bottom bridge bolt torque:
   2.0 – 2.5 kg-m (15 – 18 ft-lb)

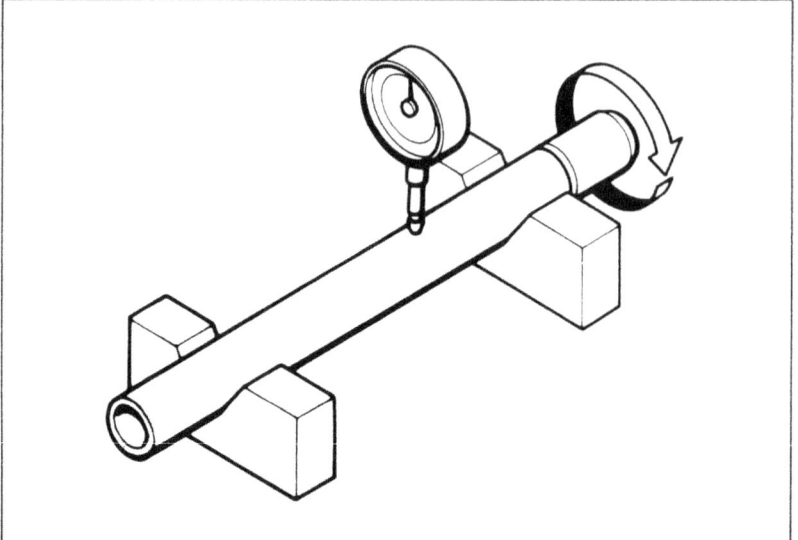

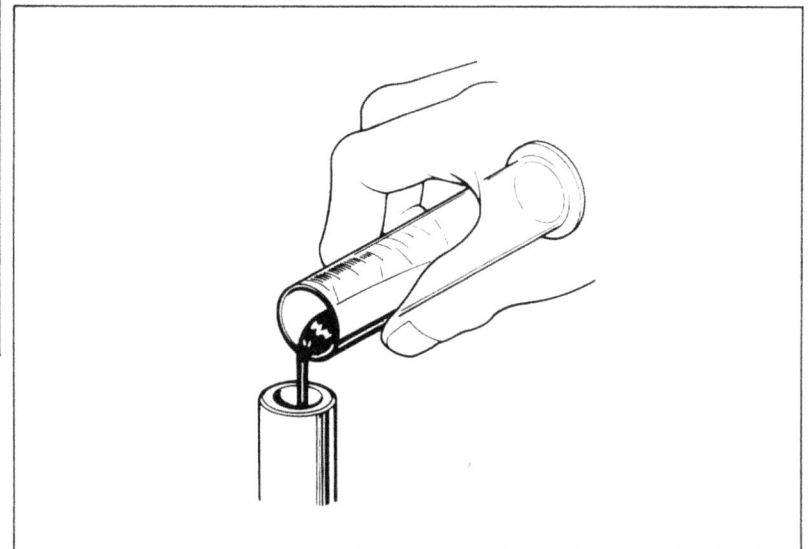

5. BRAKE DRUM AND BRAKE SHOE

SERVICE DATA

Brake drum I.D.
   Standard   : 110.0 – 110.2 mm
                  (4.33 – 4.34 in)
   Service limit : 111 mm (4.4 in)
Brake shoe lining thickness
   Standard   : 4.0 – 4.3 mm
                  (0.16 – 0.17 in)
   Service limit : 2.0 mm (0.1 in)

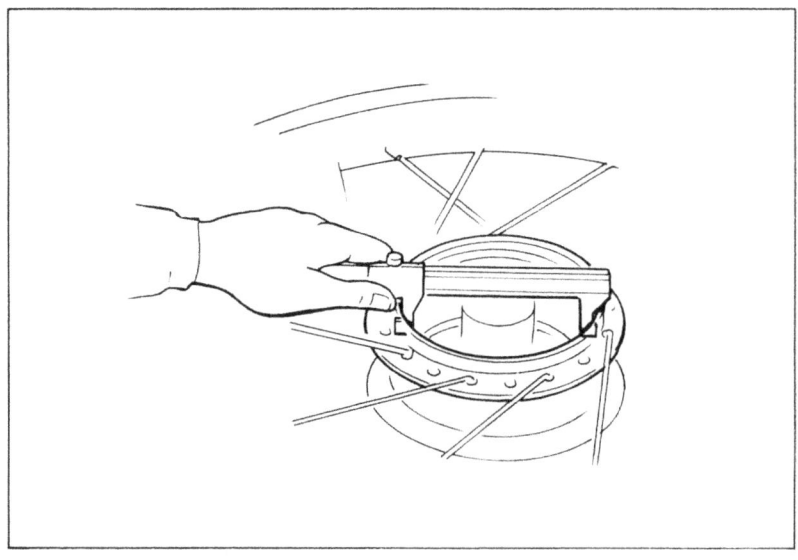

1979 CB125S ADDENDUM

VII. TROUBLESHOOTING

1. Engine Cranks but won't start
* No spark at plug — Ref. 2
* Ignition malfunction
* No fuel in tank
* No fuel to carburetor
* Engine flooded with fuel
* Air cleaner clogged
* Intake air leak
* Improper choke operation
* Improper throttle operation
* Low oil level — Ref. 6
* No or low oil pressure — Ref. 8, 10

2. Hard starting or stalling after starting
* Worn spark plug and / or breaker points
* Ignition timing incorrect — Ref. 1
* Ignition malfunction
* Idle speed incorrect
* Incorrect idle air/fuel mixture — Ref. 4, 5
* Carburetor malfunction
* Fuel contaminated
* Improper choke operation
* Low compression — Ref. 3
* Oil level low — Ref. 6
* No or low oil pressure — Ref. 8, 10

3. Rough idle
* Worn spark plug and/or breaker points
* Ignition timing incorrect — Ref. 1.
* Ignition malfunction
* Idle speed incorrect
* Incorrect carburetor air/fuel mixture — Ref. 4, 5
* Carburetor malfunction
* Fuel contaminated
* Low compression — Ref. 3

4. Misfiring during acceleration
* Worn spark plug, breaker points and/or ignition wires
* Incorrect ignition timing — Ref. 1
* Ignition malfunction
* Incorrect carburetor air/fuel mixture — Ref. 4, 5

5. Backfiring
* Ignition timing incorrect — Ref. 1
* Ignition malfunction
* Incorrect carburetor air/fuel mixture — Ref. 4, 5
* Carburetor malfunction

6. Poor performance (Driveability) and poor fuel economy
* Ignition timing incorrect — Ref. 1
* Ignition malfunction
* Incorrect carburetor air/fuel mixture — Ref. 4, 5
* Fuel system clogged
* Low compression — Ref. 3
* Oil level too low — Ref. 6
* Oil contamination — Ref. 7
* Low oil pressure — Ref. 8
* High oil pressure — Ref. 9

* Ref. 1 ~ 10 are described on page 172.

Ref. 1: Ignition timing incorrect
- * Incorrect breaker point gap
- * Faulty spark advancer

Ref. 2: No spark at plug
- * Poorly connected, broken or shorted wires
- * Faulty ignition switch and engine stop switch
- * Faulty ignition coil
- * Faulty high tension cord
- * Battery charge low
- * Faulty AC generator
- * Burned or pitted contact breaker points
- * Faulty spark plug
- * Ignition timing incorrect

Ref. 3: Low compression
- * Incorrect valve adjustment
- * Burned or bent valves
- * Incorrect valve timing
- * Weak valve spring
- * Leaking or damaged head gasket
- * Warped or cracked cylinder head
- * Improper valve seating
- * Worn piston rings and/or cylinder

Ref. 4: Lean mixture
- * Clogged fuel jets
- * Faulty float valve
- * Float level low
- * Fuel cap vent blocked
- * Fuel strainer screen clogged
- * Restricted fuel line
- * Intake air leak
- * Pilot screw misadjusted

Ref. 5: Rich mixture
- * Clogged air jets
- * Faulty float valve
- * Float valve too high
- * Choke stuck closed
- * Pilot screw misadjusted
- * Clogged air cleaner

Ref. 6: Oil level low
- * External oil leaks
- * Worn piston rings
- * Worn valve guide and/or stem seal

Ref. 7: Oil contamination
- * Oil not changed regularly
- * Oil filter rotor and screen needs cleaning
- * Worn piston rings

Ref. 8: Low oil pressure
- * Plugged oil filter screen
- * Worn oil pump
- * Oil level low

Ref. 9: High oil pressure; Broken oil ring or gasket
- * Incorrect oil being used

Ref. 10: No oil pressure
- * No oil in crankcase
- * Faulty oil pump
- * Leaks from oil circuit

VIII. CABLE AND HARNESS ROUTING

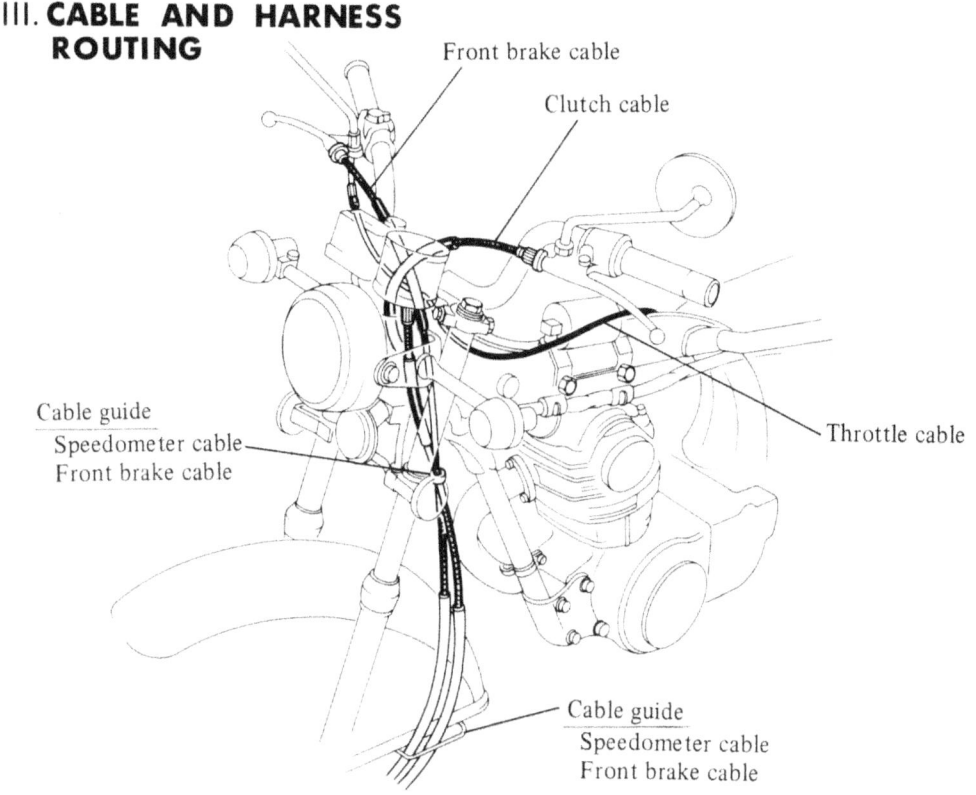

NOTE
Install the handlebar switch, aligning the switch slot with the handlebar punch mark.

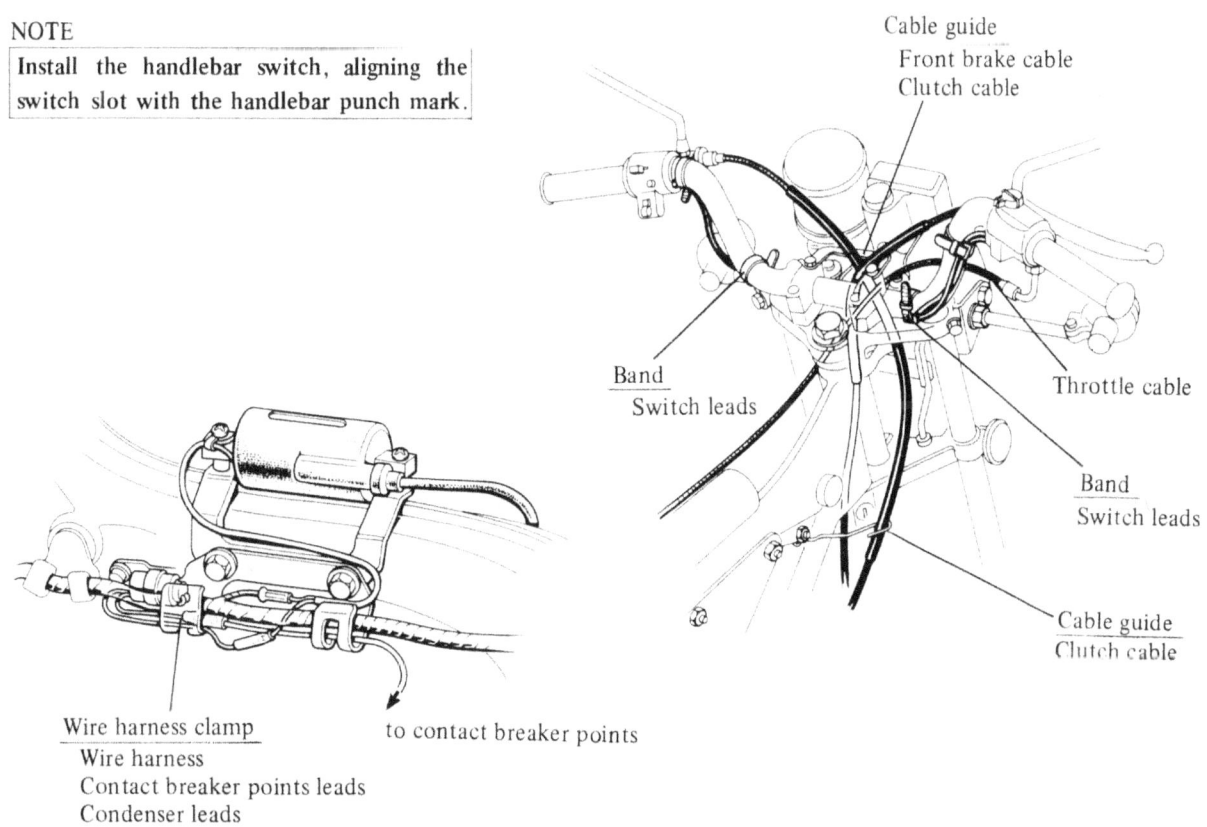

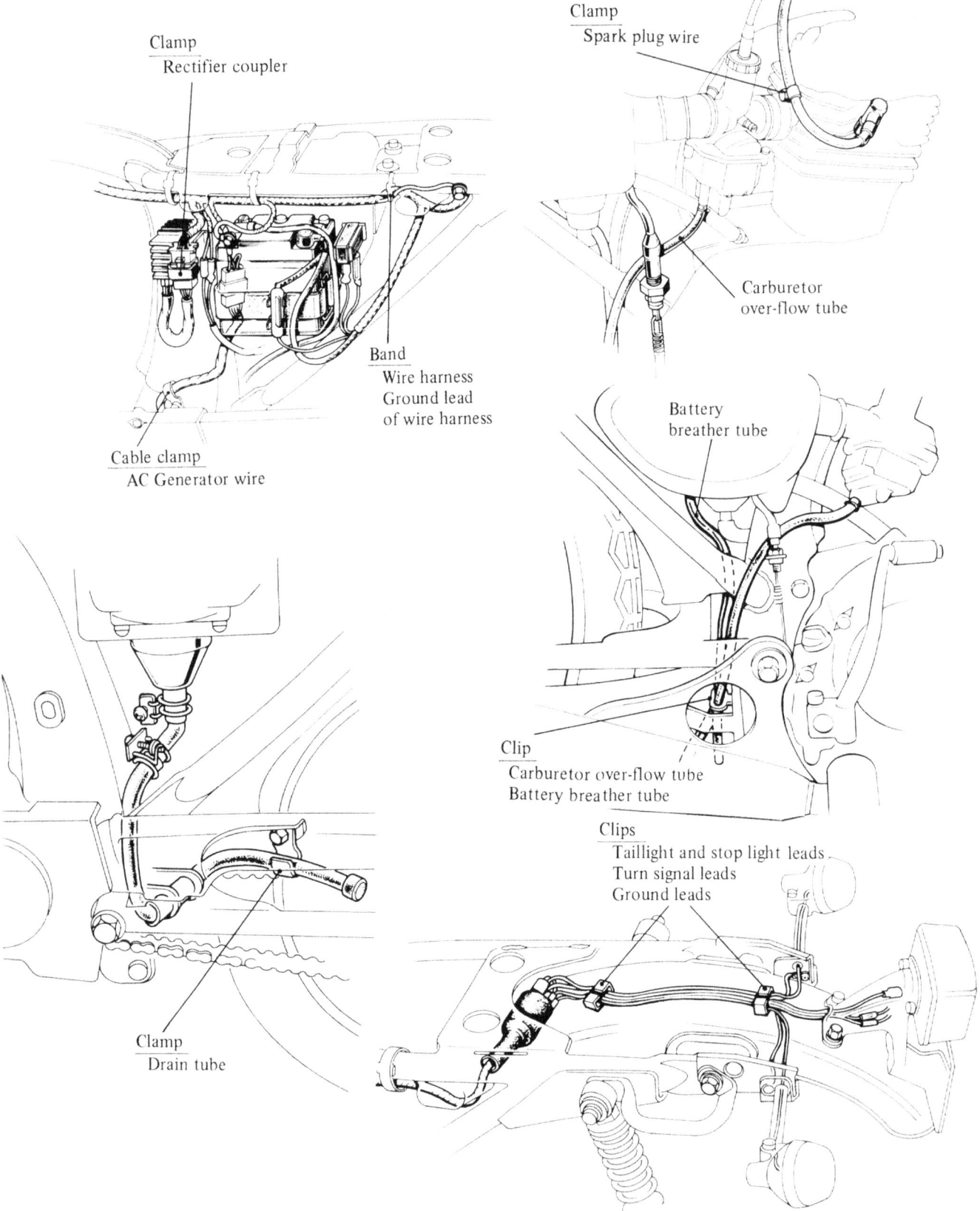

IX. SPECIAL TOOLS

Part number	Description	Application
07401 – 0010000	Float level gauge	Carburetor
07746 – 0010100	32 x 35mm bearing driver	Crankcase, rear wheel (Bearing No. 6202)
07746 – 0010400	52 x 55mm bearing driver	Crankcase (Mainshaft bearing No. 6006)
07746 – 0030100	Driver inner handle	Crankshaft bearing
07746 – 0030300	30mm inner driver	Crankshaft bearing
07746 – 0040300	15mm driver pilot	Crankcase (Bearing No. 6202)
07746 – 0040700	30mm driver pilot	Crankcase (Mainshaft bearing No. 6006)
07749 – 0010000	Driver outer handle	
07902 – 2000000	Pin wrench	Steering head
07908 – 3290100	Tappet adjusting wrench	Tappet
07908 – 3640100	Tappet adjusting wrench	Tappet
07916 – 6390001	Lock nut wrench	Oil filter rotor
07917 – 3230000	6 mm hex. wrench or local purchase	Front fork
07923 – 1070001	Clutch holder	Clutch
07933 – 2000000	Rotor puller	A.C. Generator rotor
07942 – 3290100	Valve guide remover	Valve guide
07942 – 3290200	Valve guide driver	Valve guide
07944 – 1150001	Ball race driver	Steering head
07945 – 2160000	Bearing driver	Crankshaft timing sprocket
07945 – 3330100	Bearing driver attachment	Crankcase, rear wheel (Bearing No. 6204 and 6302)
07946 – 3640000	Bearing driver attachment	Front wheel
07947 – 1180001	Fork oil seal driver	Front fork
07957 – 3290001	Valve spring compressor	Valve spring
07959 – 3290001	Rear shock absorber disassembling tool	Rear shock absorber
07967 – 1150100	Shock absorber spring holder	Rear shock absorber spring
07984 – 0980000	Valve guide reamer	Valve guide

Valve Seat Grinding

	Valve seat grinder		Valve seat cutter	
Intake	37.5° (32 mm)	07783 – 0030600	120° (35 mm)	07780 – 0012300
	63.5° (29 mm)	07783 – 0050300	60° (30 mm)	07780 – 0014000
	45° (29 mm)	07783 – 0040400	90° (29 mm)	07770 – 0010300
Exhaust	37.5° (26 mm)	07783 – 0030400	120° (28 mm)	07780 – 0012100
	63.5° (23 mm)	07783 – 0050100	60° (30 mm)	07780 – 0014000
	45° (24 mm)	07783 – 0040200	90° (24.5 mm)	07780 – 0010100
	Pilot bar	07783 – 0010100	Cutter holder	07781 – 0010100

X. WIRING DIAGRAM

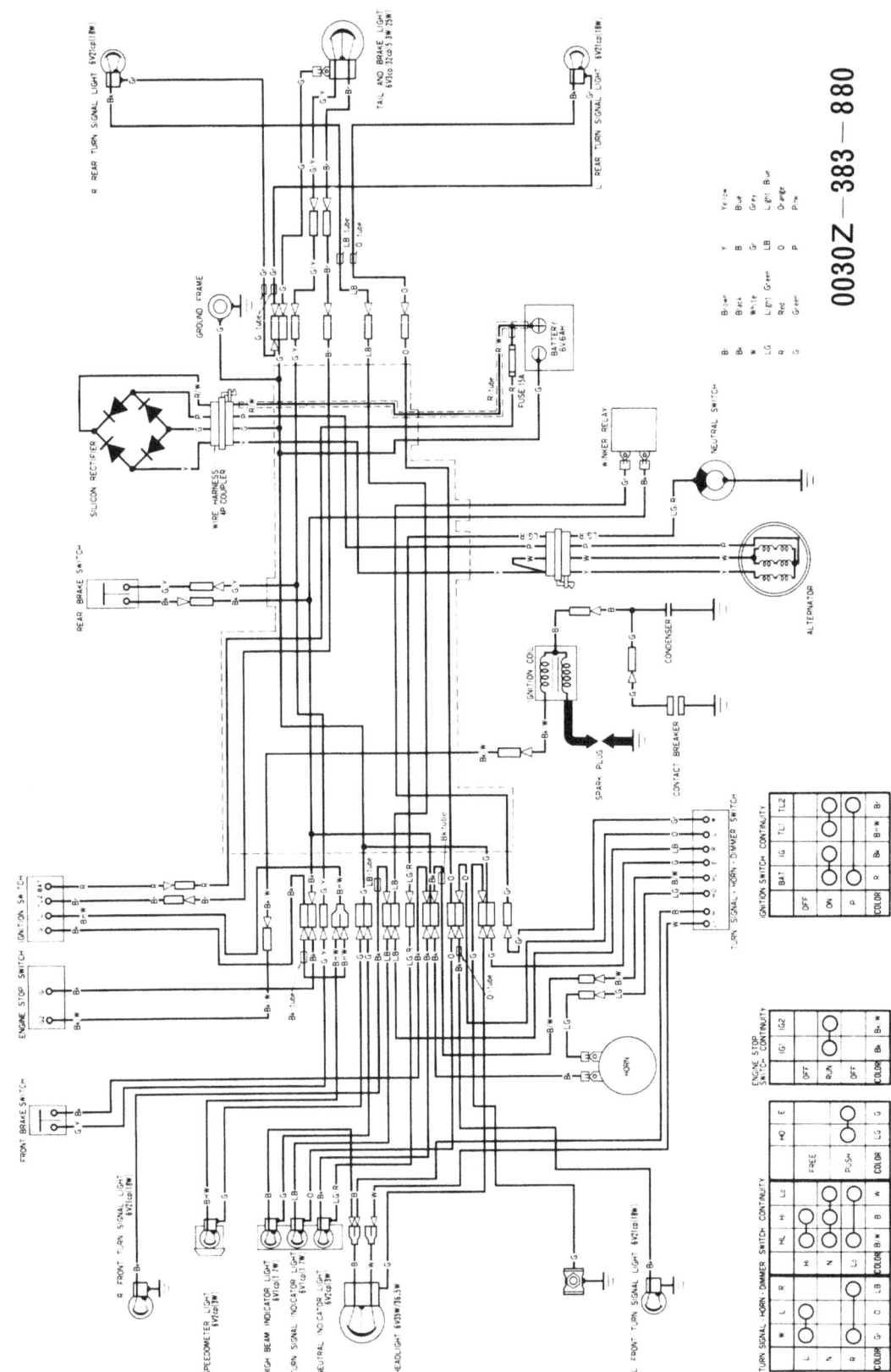

1980 CB125S ADDENDUM

INTRODUCTION

This addendum contains mandatory emissions maintenance for the 1980 CB125S. Follow the Maintenance Schedule recommendations (p. 180) to ensure that the vehicle is always in peak operating condition and the emissions levels are within the standards set by the U.S. E.P.A.

Performing the first scheduled maintenance is very important. It compensates for the initial wear that occurs during the break-in period.

Refer to the base CB125S Shop Manual for service data and procedures not included in this addendum.

CONTENTS

I. SPECIFICATIONS 178
II. MAINTENANCE SCHEDULE 180
III. INSPECTION AND ADJUSTMENT 181
   1. CARBURETOR CHOKE 181
   2. SPARK PLUG 181
   3. ENGINE OIL 182
   4. CONTROL CABLE LUBRICATION 182
IV. CARBURETOR 183
   1. SPECIFICATION 183
   2. PILOT SCREW REMOVAL/INSTALLATION 183
   3. PILOT SCREW LIMITER CAP INSTALLATION 184
   4. HIGH ALTITUDE ADJUSTMENT 185
V. CABLE AND HARNESS ROUTING 186

Date of Issue: Aug., 1979

1. SPECIFICATIONS

Item	Metric	English
DIMENSIONS		
Overall length	1,855 mm	73.0 in
Overall width	745 mm	29.3 in
Overall height	1,045 mm	41.1 in
Wheel base	1,205 mm	47.4 in
Seat height	760 mm	29.9 in
Ground clearance	140 mm	5.5 in
Dry weight	92 kg	203.0 lb
FRAME		
Type	Diamond	
Front suspension, travel	Telescopic fork, 115 mm (4.5 in)	
Rear suspension, travel	Swing arm, 65mm (2.6 in)	
Front tire size, type	2.75–18–4PR Block, (Tire air pressure: 1.75 kg/cm, 24 psi)	
Rear tire size, type	3.00–17–4PR Block, (Tire air pressure: 2.25 kg/cm, 32 psi)	
Front brake	Internal expanding shoes	
Rear brake	Internal expanding shoes	
Fuel capacity	9.5 lit	2.5 US gal
Fuel reserve capacity	2.2 lit	0.6 US gal
Caster angle	62°40′	
Trail length	98 mm	3.9 in
Front fork oil capacity	80–85 cc	2.7–2.9 US oz.
ENGINE		
Type	Air cooled 4-stroke OHC engine	
Cylinder arrangement	Single cylinder 15° inclined from vertical	
Bore and stroke	56.5 x 49.5 mm	2.224 x 1.949 in
Displacement	124 cc	7.57 cu in
Compression ratio	9.4 : 1	
Compression pressure	13 kg/cm² (1,000 rpm)	185 psi (1,000 rpm)
Carburetor, venturi dia.	Piston valve type, 22mm (0.87 in)	
Valve train	Chain driven overhead camshaft	
Oil capacity	1.0 lit	1.1 US qt
Lubrication system	Forced pressure and wet sump	
Fuel required	Any automotive gasoline with a pump octane number ($\frac{R + M}{2}$) of 86 or higher, or research octane number of 91 or higher may be used.	
Air filtration	Oiled polyurethane foam filter	
Valve timing IN Opens	10° BTDC (at 1 mm lift), 53° BTDC (at 0 lift)	
Closes	40° ABDC (at 1 mm lift), 102° ABDC (at 0 lift)	
EX Opens	40° BBDC (at 1 mm lift), 85° BBDC (at 0 lift)	
Closes	10° ATDC (at 1 mm lift), 72° ATDC (at 0 lift)	

1980 CB125S ADDENDUM

Item	Metric	English
Valve clearance IN/EX	0.05 mm	0.002 in
Engine dry weight	26 kg	57.3 lb
Idle speed	1300 ± 100 rpm	
DRIVE TRAIN		
Clutch	Wet multi-plate	
Transmission	5-speed constant mesh	
Primary reduction	4.055	
Gear ratio I	2.769	
II	1.882	
III	1.450	
IV	1.173	
V	1.000	
Final reduction	2.333 (35/15)	
Gear shift pattern	Left foot operated return system	
Drive chain size	428D 100 Links	
ELECTRICAL		
Ignition	Battery and coil	
Ignition advance "F" mark	10° BTDC, at idle (static)	
Full advance mark/rpm	36°–40° BTDC/3,700–4,000 rpm	
Starting system	Kickstarter	
Alternator	AC generator, 76 W/5,000 rpm	
Battery capacity	6 V - 6 AH	
Fuse capacity	15 A	
Spark plug	(see table below)	
Spark plug gap	0.6–0.7 mm	0.024–0.028 in
Condenser capacity	0.22–0.26 μF	
Contact breaker point gap	0.3–0.4 mm	0.012–0.016 in

USA model:

Usage / Brand	For cold climate (below 5° C, 41°F)	Standard	For extended high speed driving
NGK	D7EA	D8EA	D9EA
ND	X22ES-U	X24ES-U	X27ES-U

Canada model: NGK DR8ES-L or ND X24ESR-U

CARBURETOR SPECIFICATIONS

	Standard 2,000m (6,500 ft) max.	High altitude 1,500m (5,000 ft) min.
Identification number	PD24A	←
Main jet	#88	#85
Jet needle mark	56B	←
Float height	12.5 mm (0.49 in)	←
Pilot screw	See pages 183 ~ 184	←
Idle speed	1,300 ± 100 rpm	←

II. MAINTENANCE SCHEDULE

Perform the PRE-RIDE INSPECTION in the Owner's Manual at each scheduled maintenance period.

I: Inspect and Clean, Adjust, Lubricate or Replace if necessary.
C: Clean
R: Replace
A: Adjust
L: Lubricate

	ITEM	FREQUENCY WHICHEVER COMES FIRST ⇨ ⇩ EVERY	600mi (1000km)	2500mi (4000km)	5000mi (8000km)	7500mi (12000km)	Refer to
EMISSION RELATED ITEMS	*FUEL LINE			I	I	I	Page 148
	*THROTTLE OPERATION		I	I	I	I	Page 152
	*CARBURETOR-CHOKE			I	I	I	Page 182
	AIR CLEANER	NOTE 1		C	C	C	Page 147
	CRANKCASE BREATHER	NOTE 2		C	C	C	Page 147
	SPARK PLUG			R	R	R	Page 181
	*VALVE CLEARANCE		I	I	I	I	Page 149
	*CONTACT BREAKER POINTS		I	I	R	I	Page 150
	*IGNITION TIMING		I	I	I	I	Page 150
	ENGINE OIL	YEAR	R	R, EVERY 1250mi (2000km)			Page 145 - 182
	*ENGINE OIL FILTER SCREEN				C		Page 146
	*ENGINE OIL FILTER ROTOR				C		Page 146
	*CAM CHAIN TENSION		A	A	A	A	Page 152
	*CARBURETOR-IDLE SPEED		I	I	I	I	Page 153
NON EMISSION RELATED ITEMS	DRIVE CHAIN		I, L, EVERY 300mi (500km)				Page 153
	BATTERY	MONTH	I	I	I	I	Page 155
	BRAKE SHOE WEAR			I	I	I	Page 156
	BRAKE SYSTEM		I	I	I	I	Pages 156 - 158
	*BRAKE LIGHT SWITCH		I	I	I	I	Page 158
	*HEADLIGHT AIM		I	I	I	I	Page 159
	CLUTCH		I	I	I	I	Page 159
	SIDE STAND			I	I	I	Page 160
	*SUSPENSION		I	I	I	I	Page 161
	*NUTS, BOLTS, FASTENERS		I	I	I	I	Page 161
	**WHEELS/SPOKES		I	I	I	I	Page 162
	**STEERING HEAD BEARING		I			I	Page 162

* Should be serviced by an authorized HONDA dealer, unless the owner has proper tools and service data and is mechanically qualified.
** In the interest of safety, we recommend these items be serviced ONLY by an authorized HONDA dealer.

NOTE:
1. Service more frequently when riding in dusty areas.
2. Service more frequently when riding in rain or at full throttle (USA only).
3. For higher odometer readings, repeat at the frequency interval established here.

III. INSPECTION AND ADJUSTMENT

1. CARBURETOR CHOKE

Operate the choke lever and check for smooth operation.

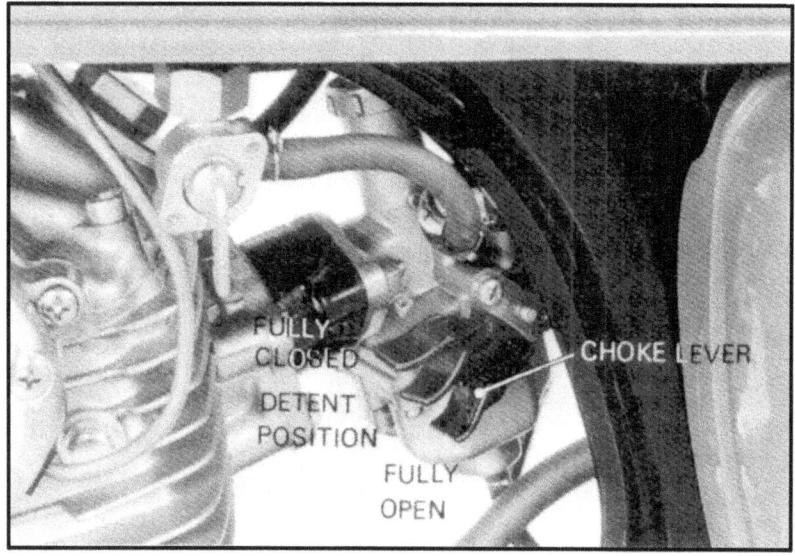

2. SPARK PLUG

Recommended spark plugs:

USA model:

Usage Brand	Spark Plugs VS Operating Conditions		
	For cold climate (below 5°C, 41°F)	Standard	For extended high speed driving
NGK	D7EA	D8EA	D9EA
ND	X22ES-U	X24ES-U	X27ES-U

Canada model:

NGK DR8ES-L or ND X24ESR-U

Clean any dirt from around the base of the spark plug.

Disconnect the spark plug cap. Remove and discard the used spark plug.

Check the electrode gap of the new spark plug, using a wire-type feeler gauge. Adjust by carefully bending the side electrode.

SPARK PLUG GAP: 0.6–0.7mm
(0.024–0.028 in.)

With the washer attached, thread the new spark plug in by hand to prevent crossthreading. After hand tightening, tighten an additional ½ turn with a spark plug wrench to compress the washer. Install the spark plug cap.

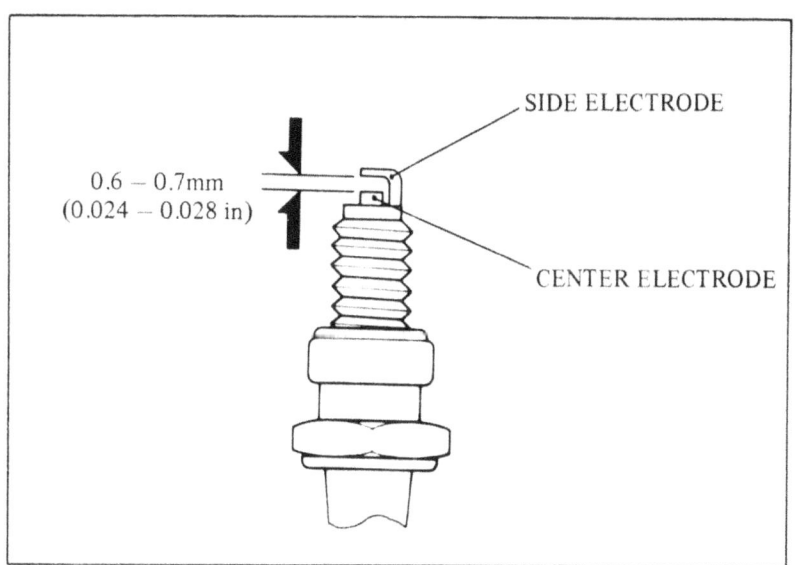

3. ENGINE OIL RECOMMENDATION

Use HONDA 4-STROKE OIL or equivalent.
API SERVICE CLASSIFICATION: SE
VISCOSITY: SAE10W–40

Other viscosities may be used when the average temperature in your riding area is within the chart's indicated range.

OIL CAPACITY: 1.0ℓ (1.1 US qt.) approx.

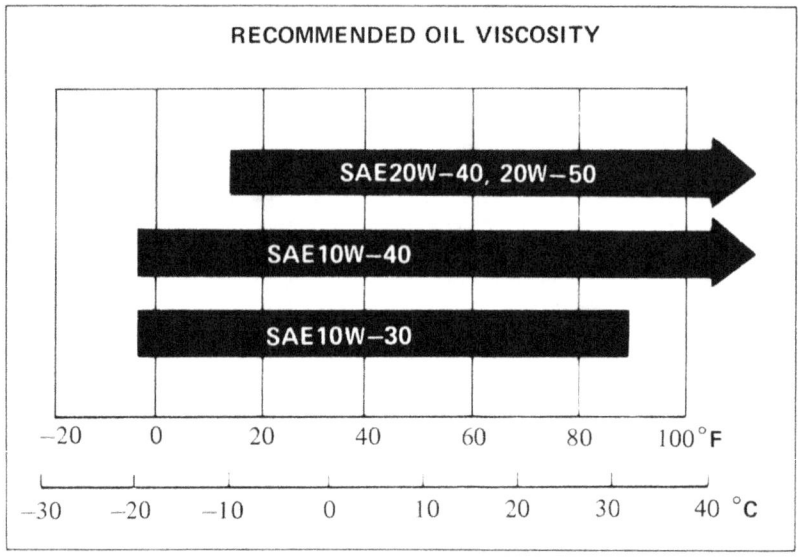

4. CONTROL CABLE LUBRICATION

Periodically disconnect the throttle, clutch and brake control cables at their upper ends. Thoroughly lubricate the cables and their pivot points with a commercially available cable lubricant.

IV. CARBURETOR

WARNING

Gasoline is extremely flammable and is explosive under certain conditions. Do not smoke or allow flames or sparks in your working area.

1. SPECIFICATIONS

Identification number	PD24A
Main jet	#88 (standard)
	#85 (high altitude)
Jet needle mark	56B
Float level	12.5mm (0.49 in)
Idle speed	1,300 ± 100rpm

2. PILOT SCREW/INSTALLATION

Remove the carburetor.

Remove the float chamber.

Turn the pilot screw in and count the exact number of turns before it seats lightly. Make a note of this to use as a reference when reinstalling the pilot screw.

CAUTION

Damage to the pilot screw and seat will occur if the screw is tightened against the seat.

Inspect the pilot screw and replace if worn or damaged.

CAUTION

Any forcible attempt to remove the pilot screw limiter cap will break the screw.

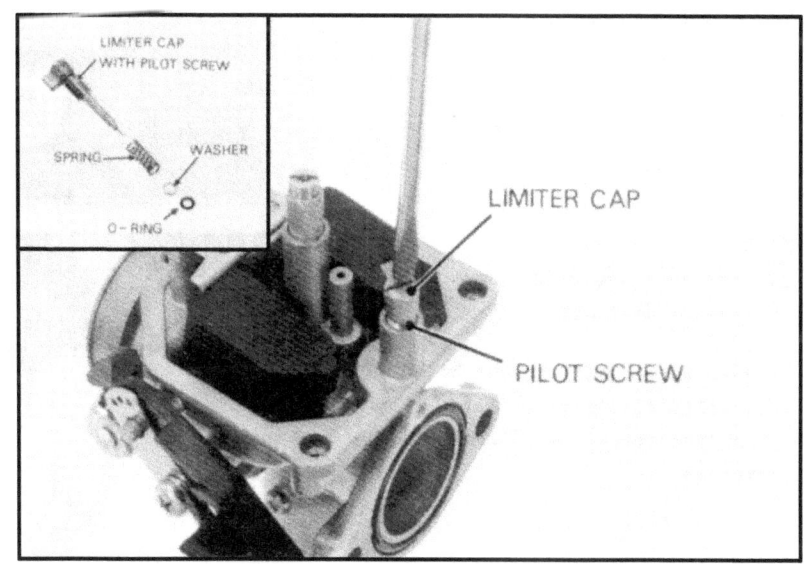

Reinstall the pilot screw and turn it to the original position, as noted during removal. If a new pilot screw is installed, turn the screw 2 turns out initially from a lightly seated position, install the float chamber, then follow the adjustment procedure described on pages 163–164 before installing the limiter cap.

Install the float chamber.

Install the carburetor.

3. LIMITER CAP INSTALLATION

If the pilot screw is replaced, a new limiter cap must be installed after pilot screw adjustment is completed.

After final adjustment, cement the limiter cap over the pilot screw, using LOCTITE® #601 or equivalent. The limiter cap should be placed against its stop, preventing further adjustment that would enrich the fuel mixture (limiter cap position permits clockwise rotation and prevents counter-clockwise rotation).

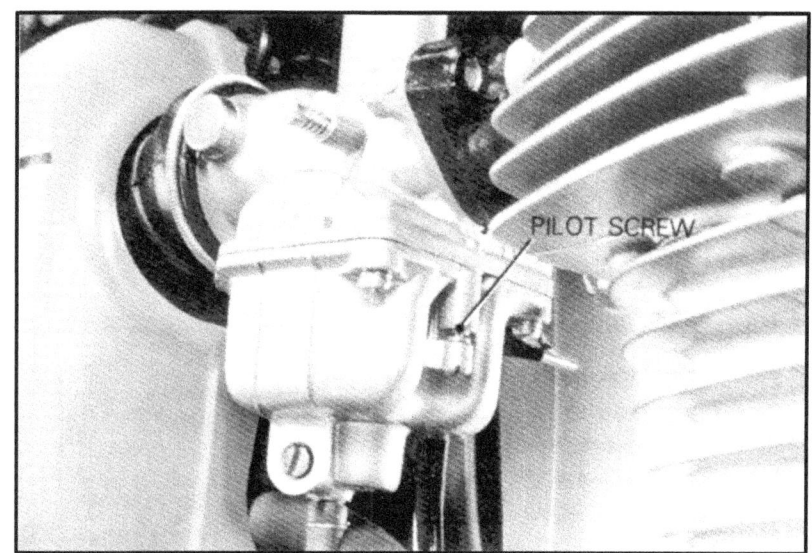

NOTE

Do not turn the pilot screw when installing the limiter cap.

A pilot screw limiter cap must be installed. It prevents misadjustment that could cause poor performance and increase exhaust emissions.

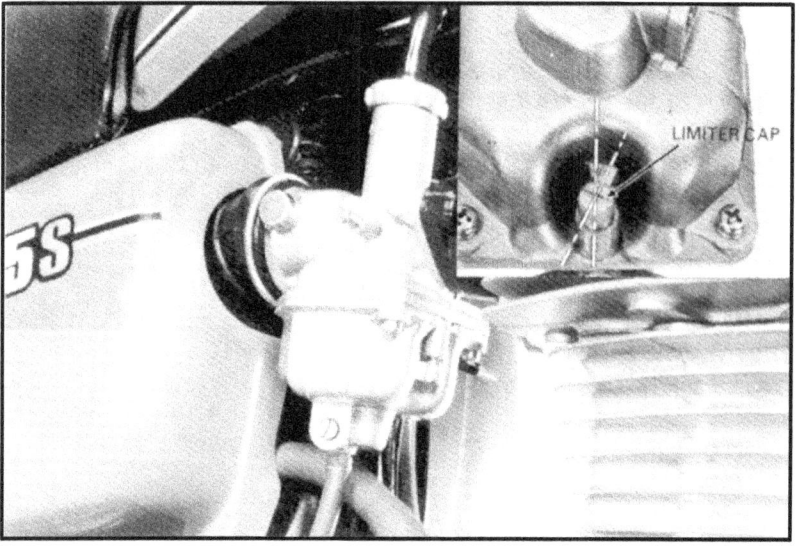

4. HIGH ALTITUDE ADJUSTMENT

The carburetor must be adjusted for high altitude riding above 2,000M (6,500 ft).

STANDARD SETTING:
　　2,000m (6,500 ft) max.

HIGH ALTITUDE SETTING:
　　1,500m (5,000 ft) min.

Carburetor adjustment is as follows:

1. Drain the carburetor and remove it.
2. Remove the float chamber.
3. Replace the main jet with the high altitude type.
4. Assemble and install the carburetor.
5. Start the engine and adjust the idle speed with the throttle stop screw.

　　IDLE SPEED: 1300 ± 100 rpm

Altitude	Main jet	Pilot screw
Below 5,000 feet (1,500m)	#88	Factory Preset Counterclockwise against stop
Above 6,500 feet (2,000m)	#85	Factory Preset Counterclockwise against stop

CAUTION

Sustained operation at altitudes lower than 1,500 meters (5,000 ft.) with the high altitude specifications may cause engine overheating and damage. Reinstall the standard main jet when operating the vehicle below 1,500 meters (5,000 ft.).

V. CABLE AND HARNESS ROUTING

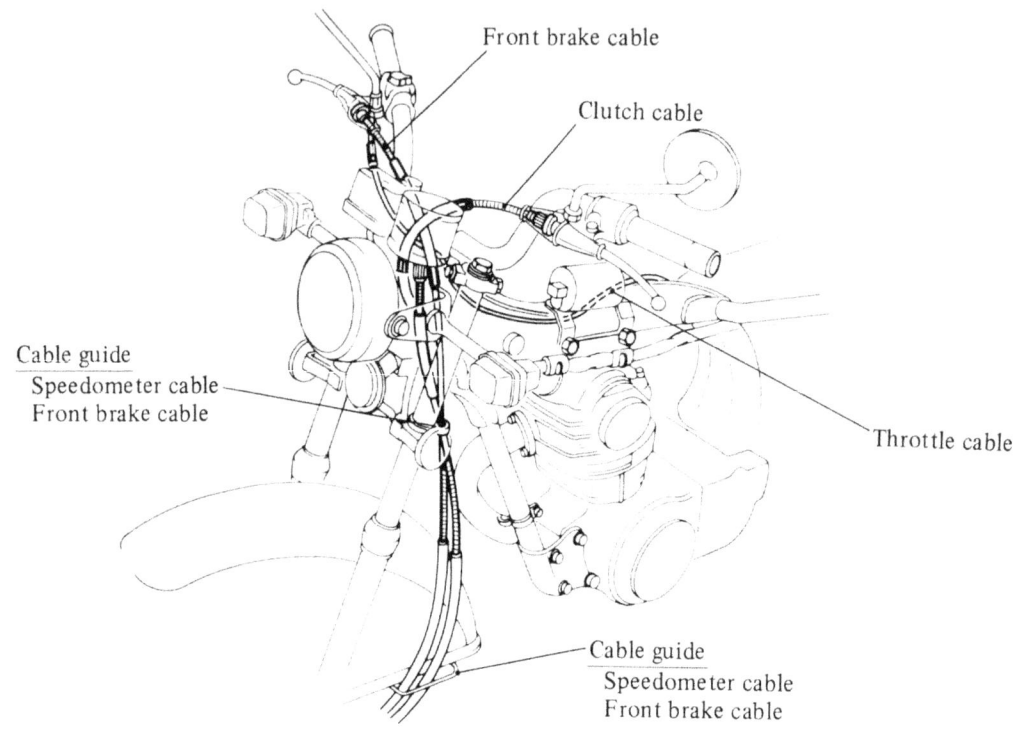

NOTE

Install the handlebar switch, aligning the switch slot with the handlebar punch mark.

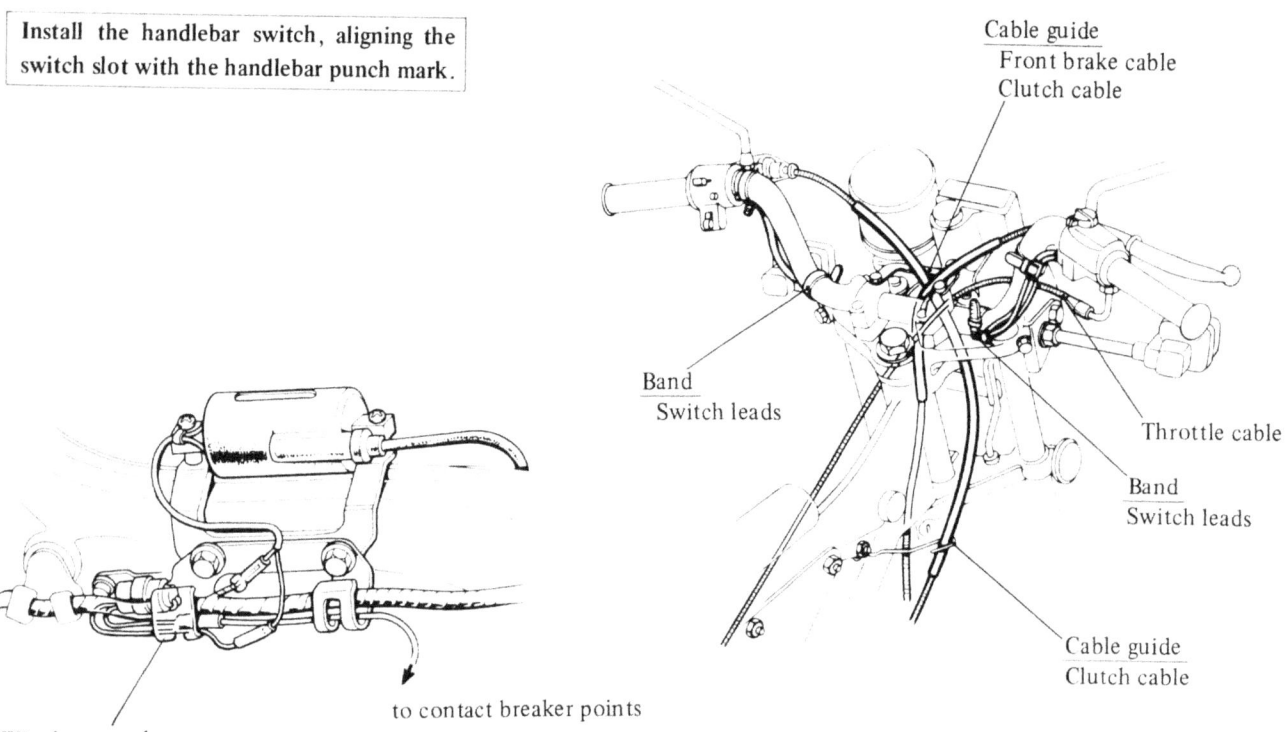

1980 CB125S ADDENDUM

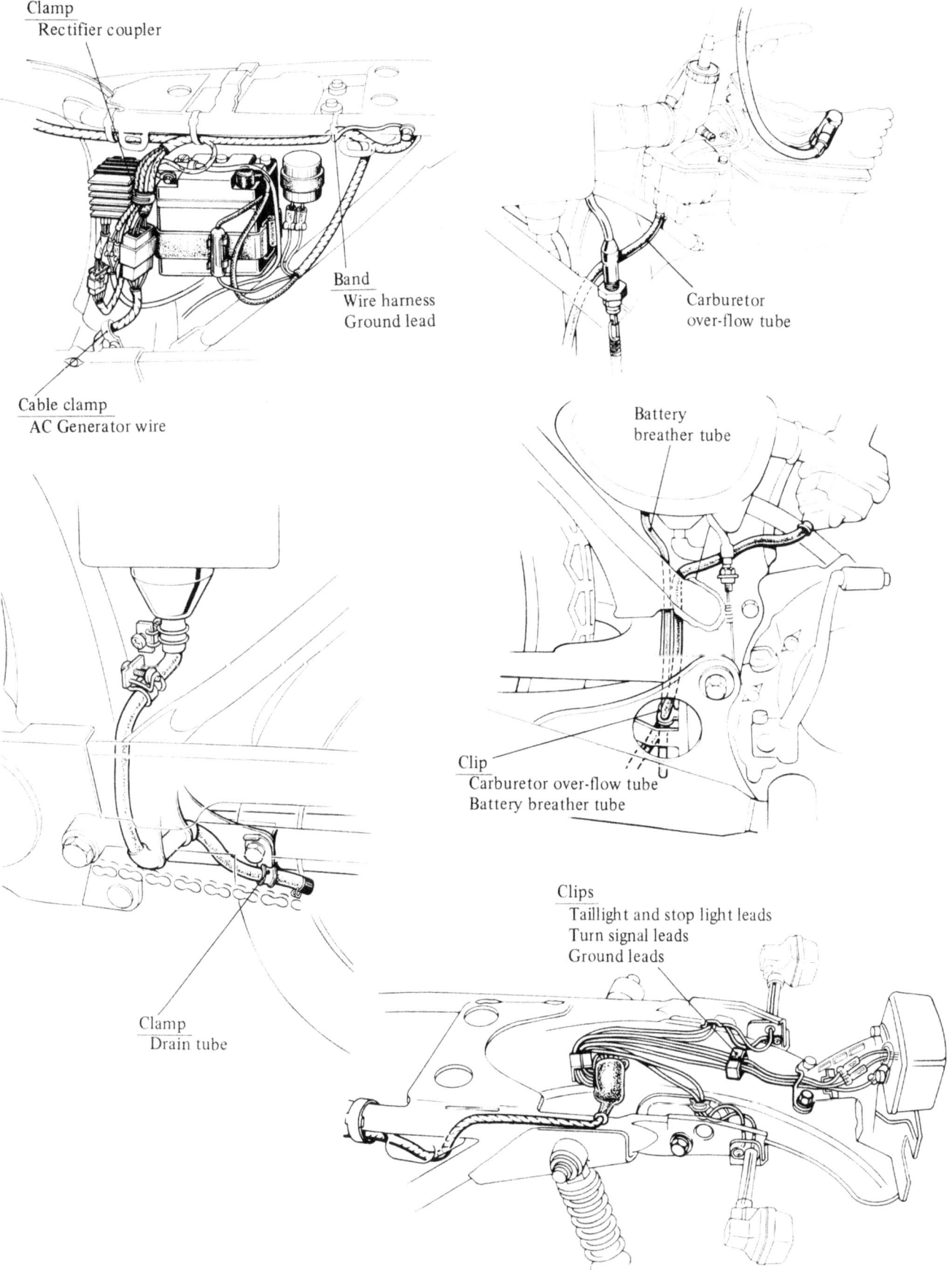

MEMO

1981 CB125S ADDENDUM

INTRODUCTION

This Addendum contains information for the 1981 CB125S. Refer to the base Shop Manual for service procedures and data not included in this addendum.

CONTENTS

I. SPECIFICATIONS 190
II. MAINTENANCE SCHEDULE 192
III. INSPECTION AND ADJUSTMENT 193
    1. Valve Clearance 193
    2. Engine Oil Change and Oil Filter Screen Cleaning 193
    3. Ignition Timing 194
    4. Battery 194
IV. ENGINE 195
    1. Kickstarter 195
    2. Valve Timing Adjustment 197
V. IGNITION SYSTEM 198
    1. Ignition Coil 199
    2. Pulser Generator 199
    3. C.D.I. Unit 203
    4. Stator Coil Inspection 204
    5. Ignition Timing 204
VI. A.C. GENERATOR/CARGING SYSTEM 205
    1. A.C. Generator 205
    2. Carging System 209
    3. Voltage Regulator/Rectifire 211
VII. SWITCHES 212
    1. Ignition Switch 212
    2. Engine Stop Switch 212
VIII. TROUBLESHOOTING 213
IX. CABLE AND HARNESS ROUTING 214
X. WIRING DIAGRAM 215

Date of Issue: Sep., 1980

1981 CB125S ADDENDUM

I. SPECIFICATIONS

Item	Metric	English
DIMENSIONS		
Overall length	1,855 mm	73.0 in
Overall width	745 mm	29.3 in
Overall height	1,045 mm	41.1 in
Wheel base	1,205 mm	47.4 in
Seat height	750 mm	29.5 in
Ground clearance	140 mm	5.5 in
Dry weight	93 kg	205.3 lb
FRAME		
Type	Diamond	
Front suspension, travel	Telescopic fork, 115 mm (4.5 in)	
Rear suspension, travel	Swing arm, 65mm (2.6 in)	
Front tire size, type	2.75–18–4PR Block, (Tire air pressure: 1.75 kg/cm, 24 psi)	
Rear tire size, type	3.00–17–6PR Block, (Tire air pressure: 2.8 kg/cm, 40 psi)	
Front brake	Internal expanding shoes	
Rear brake	Internal expanding shoes	
Fuel capacity	9.5 lit	2.5 US gal
Fuel reserve capacity	2.2 lit	0.6 US gal
Caster angle	27°20′	
Trail length	98 mm	3.9 in
Front fork oil capacity	80–85 cc	2.7–2.9 US oz.
ENGINE		
Type	Air cooled 4-stroke OHC engine	
Cylinder arrangement	Single cylinder 15° inclined from vertical	
Bore and stroke	56.5 x 49.5 mm	2.224 x 1.949 in
Displacement	124 cc	7.57 cu in
Compression ratio	9.4 : 1	
Compression pressure	13 kg/cm^2 (1,000 rpm)	185 psi (1,000 rpm)
Carburetor, venturi dia.	Piston valve type, 22mm (0.87 in)	
Valve train	Chain driven overhead camshaft	
Oil capacity	1.1 lit (1.2 US qt) at disassembly	
Lubrication system	Forced pressure and wet sump	
Fuel required	Any automotive gasoline with a pump octane number ($\frac{R + M}{2}$) of 86 or higher, or research octane number of 91 or higher may be used.	
Air filtration	Oiled polyurethane foam filter	
Valve timing IN Opens	10° BTDC (at 1 mm lift), 53° BTDC (at 0 lift)	
Closes	40° ABDC (at 1 mm lift), 102° ABDC (at 0 lift)	
EX Opens	40° BBDC (at 1 mm lift), 85° BBDC (at 0 lift)	
Closes	10° ATDC (at 1 mm lift), 72° ATDC (at 0 lift)	

1981 CB125S ADDENDUM

Item	Metric	English
Valve clearance IN/EX (cold)	0.05 mm	0.002 in
Engine dry weight	26 kg	57.3 lb
Idle speed	1300 ± 100 rpm	

DRIVE TRAIN

Clutch	Wet multi-plate
Transmission	5-speed constant mesh
Primary reduction	4.055
Gear ratio I	2.769
II	1.882
III	1.450
IV	1.173
V	1.000
Final reduction	2.333 (35/15)
Gear shift pattern	Left foot operated return system
Drive chain size	428D 100 Links

ELECTRICAL

Ignition	C.D.I
Ignition advance "F" mark	10° BTDC, at idle (static)
Full advance mark/rpm	32°–36° BTDC/3,200–3,500 rpm
Starting system	Kickstarter
Alternator	AC generator, 0.113 kW/5,000 rpm
Battery capacity	6 V - 6 AH
Fuse capacity	10 A

Spark plug — USA model:

Usage / Brand	For cold climate (below 5°C, 41°F)	Standard	For extended high speed speed riding
NGK	D7EA	D8EA	D9EA
ND	X22ES-U	X24ES-U	X27ES-U

Canada model: NGK DR8ES-L or ND X24ESR-U

	Metric	English
Spark plug gap	0.6–0.7 mm	0.024–0.028 in

CARBURETOR SPECIFICATIONS

	Standard 2,000m (6,500 ft) max.	High altitude 1,500m (5,000 ft) min.
Identification number	PD24A	←
Main jet	#88	#85
Jet needle mark	56B	←
Float height	12.5 mm (0.49 in)	←
Pilot screw	See pages 183 ~ 184	←
Idle speed	1,300 ± 100 rpm	←

1981 CB125S ADDENDUM

II. MAINTENANCE SCHEDULE

Perform the PRE-RIDE INSPECTION in the Owner's Manual at each scheduled maintenance period.

I: Inspect and Clean, Adjust, Lubricate or Replace if necessary.
C: Clean
R: Replace
A: Adjust
L: Lubricate

	ITEM	FREQUENCY WHICHEVER COMES FIRST EVERY	600mi (1000km)	2500mi (4000km)	5000mi (8000km)	7500mi (12000km)	Refer to
EMISSION RELATED ITEMS	*FUEL LINE			I	I	I	Page 148
	*THROTTLE OPERATION		I	I	I	I	Page 152
	*CARBURETOR-CHOKE			I	I	I	Page 182
	AIR CLEANER	NOTE 1		C	C	C	Page 147
	CRANKCASE BREATHER	NOTE 2		C	C	C	Page 147
	SPARK PLUG			R	R	R	Page 182
	*VALVE CLEARANCE		I	I	I	I	Page 193
	ENGINE OIL	YEAR	R	R, EVERY 1250mi (2000km)			Page 145, 193
	ENGINE OIL FILTER SCREEN		C	C, EVERY 1250mi (2000km)			Page 193
	*ENGINE OIL FILTER ROTOR				C		Page 146
	*CAM CHAIN TENSION		A	A	A	A	Page 152
	*CARBURETOR-IDLE SPEED		I	I	I	I	Page 184
NON EMISSION RELATED ITEMS	DRIVE CHAIN		I, L, EVERY 300 mi (500km)				Page 153
	BATTERY	MONTH	I	I	I	I	Page 155, 194
	BRAKE SHOE WEAR			I	I	I	Page 156
	BRAKE SYSTEM		I	I	I	I	Pages 156 - 158
	*BRAKE LIGHT SWITCH		I	I	I	I	Page 158
	*HEADLIGHT AIM		I	I	I	I	Page 159
	CLUTCH		I	I	I	I	Page 159
	SIDE STAND			I	I	I	Page 160
	*SUSPENSION		I	I	I	I	Page 161
	*NUTS, BOLTS, FASTENERS		I	I	I	I	Page 161
	**WHEELS/SPOKES		I	I	I	I	Page 162
	**STEERING HEAD BEARING		I			I	Page 162

* Should be serviced by an authorized HONDA dealer, unless the owner has proper tools and service data and is mechanically qualified.
** In the interest of safety, we recommend these items be serviced ONLY by an authorized HONDA dealer.

NOTE:
1. Service more frequently when riding in dusty areas.
2. Service more frequently when riding in rain or at full throttle (USA only).
3. For higher odometer readings, repeat at the frequency interval established here.

III. INSPECTION AND ADJUSTMENT

1. VALVE CLEARANCE

NOTE

Inspect and adjust valve clearance while the engine is cold (below 35°C/95°F).

Remove the crankshaft hole cap and timing hole cap.

Remove the valve adjuster covers.

Rotate the crankshaft counterclockwise and align the "T" mark on the generator rotor with the index mark on the left crankcase cover. The piston must be at T.D.C. (Top Dead Center) of the compression stroke.

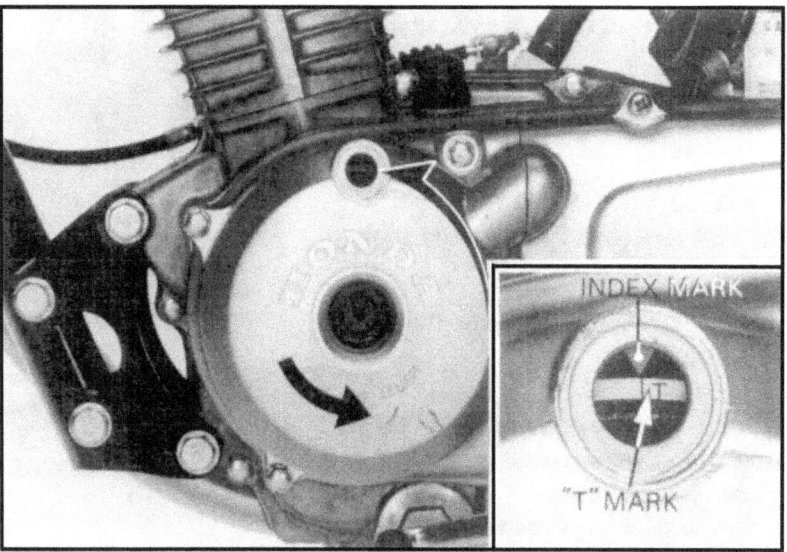

Inspect the intake and exhaust valve clearances by inserting feeler gauge between the adjusting screw and valve stem.

VALVE CLEARANCES (COLD):
INTAKE: 0.05 mm (0.002 in)
EXHAUST: 0.05 mm (0.002 in)

Adjust by loosening the lock nut and turning the adjusting screw until there is a slight drag on the feeler gauge.

Hold the adjusting screw and tighten the lock nut.

Recheck the valve clearance.

Install the valve adjuster covers.

Install the timing hole cap and crankshaft hole cap.

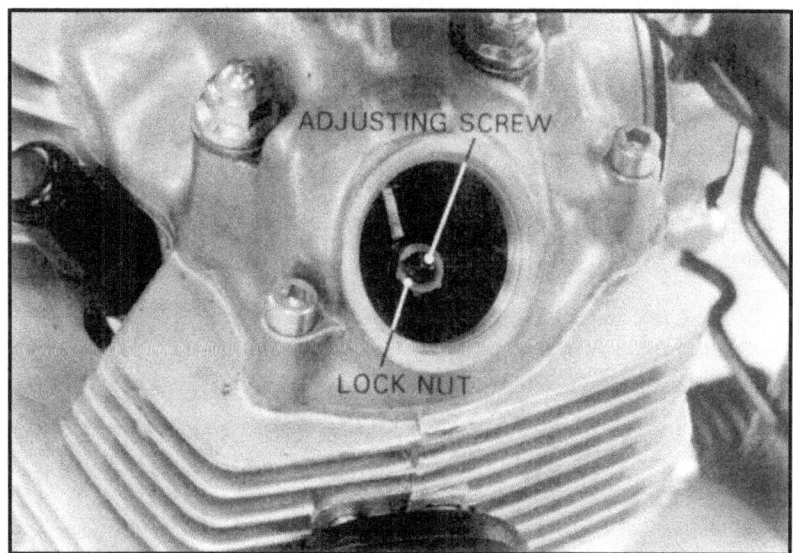

2. ENGINE OIL CHANGE AND OIL FILTER SCREEN CLEANING

NOTE

Drain the oil with the engine warm and the motorcycle on its side stand.

Remove the oil filler cap and oil filter screen cap.

NOTE

The oil filter screen and spring will come out when the oil filter screen cap is removed.

Operate the kick starter pedal several times to completely drain any residual oil.

Clean the oil filter screen.

Make sure that the oil filter screen, sealing rubber, screen cap and O-ring are in good condition.

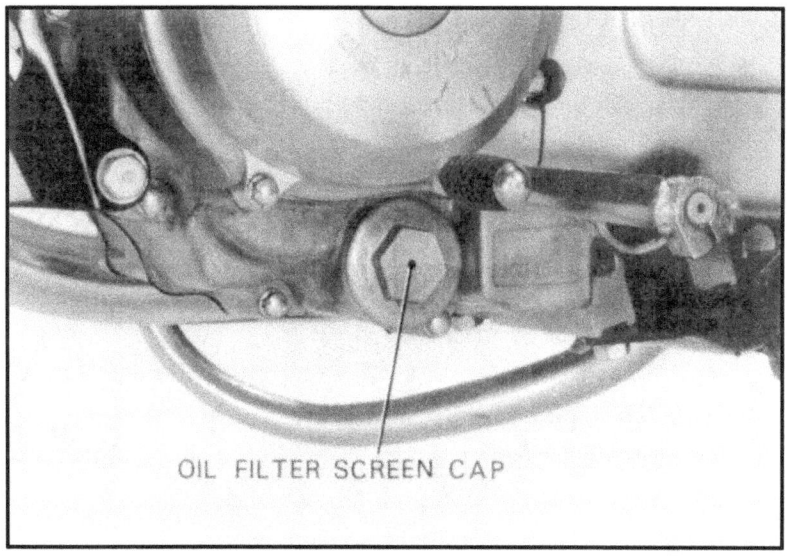

Install the oil filter screen, spring and screen cap.

Fill the crankcase with the recommended grade oil.

ENGINE OIL CAPACITY:
0.9 liters (0.95 US qt, 0.8 Imp qt)

Install the oil filler cap.
Start the engine and let it idle for 2-3 minutes.
Stop the engine.
With the motorcycle upright on level ground, make sure that the oil level is at the upper level mark.
Be sure there are no leaks.

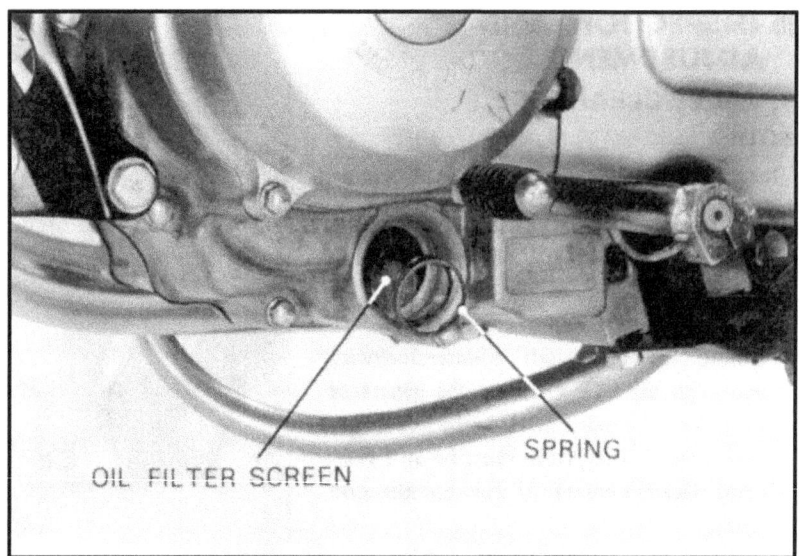

3. IGNITION TIMING

NOTE

The Capacitive Discharge Ignition (C.D.I.) system is factory pre-set and does not require adjustment. To inspect the function of the C.D.I. components, ignition timing inspection procedures are given here.

Remove the timing hole cap.
Connect the tachometer and timing light.
Start the engine and allow to idle.

IDLE SPEED: 1,300 ± 100 rpm

Inspect the ignition timing.
Timing is correct, if the "F" mark on the generator rotor is aligned with the index mark on the left crankcase cover at idle.

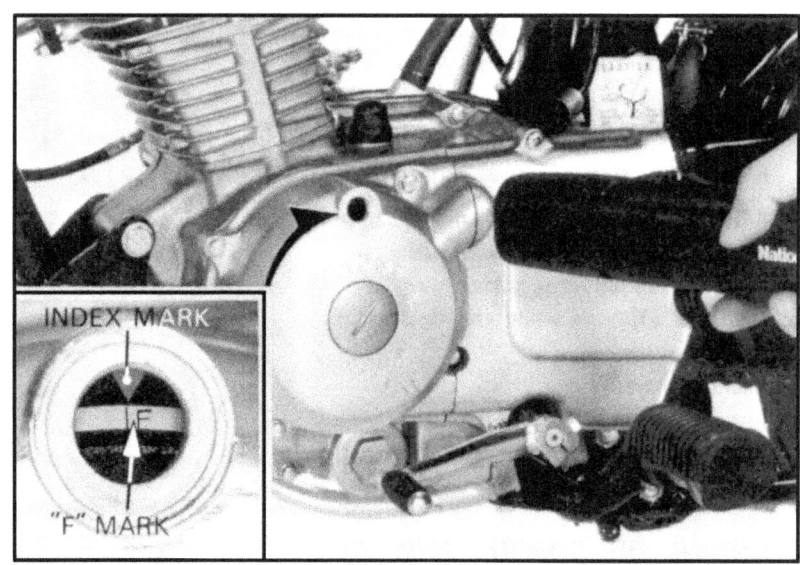

If the ignition timing is incorrect, check the C.D.I. unit and pulser generator and replace faulty parts.

4. BATTERY

Service the battery, after removing the battery from the frame body leaving the battery breather tube on the frame body.

CAUTION

Make sure the breather tube is connected to the battery breather outlet.

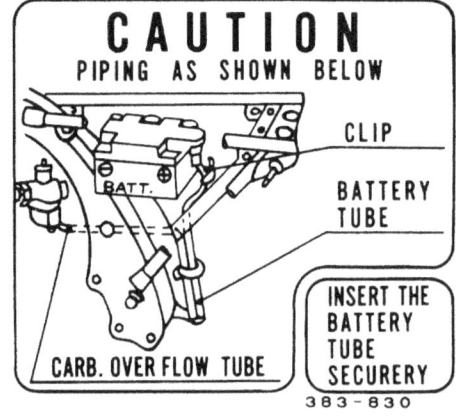

IV. ENGINE

1. KICKSTARTER

Remove the thrust washer.
Back off the stopper bolt and remove the kick starter.

Remove the 18 mm circlip, spring seat, ratchet spring and drive ratchet.
Remove the 20 mm circlip, thrust washer and pinion gear.
Remove the collar, return spring and guide plate.

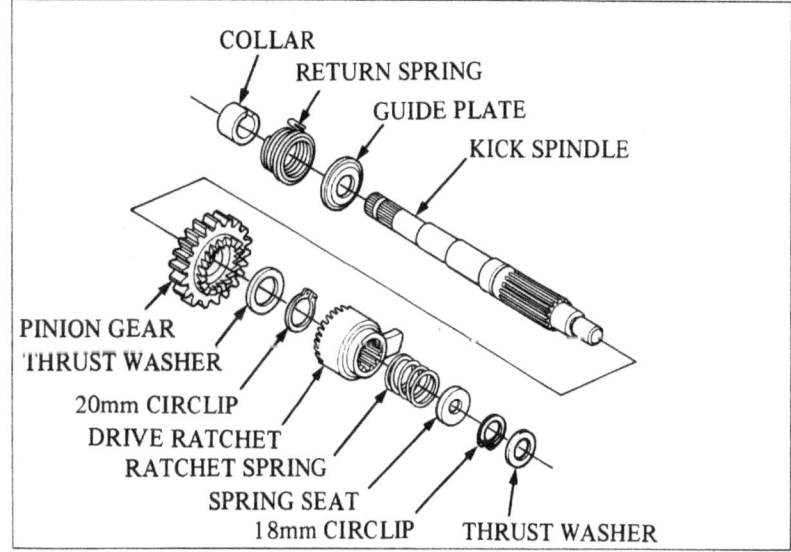

Measure the pinion I.D.

STANDARD:
 20.000–20.021mm (0.7874–0.7882 in)
SERVICE LIMIT: 20.05mm (0.789 in)

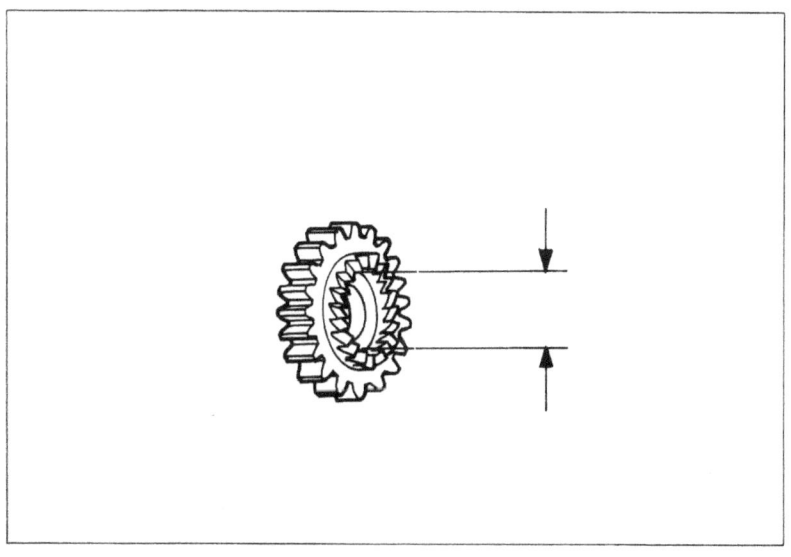

Measure the O.D. of the pinion gear sliding surface.

STANDARD:
19.957–19.980mm (0.7858–0.7866 in)
SERVICE LIMIT: 19.90mm (0.783 in)

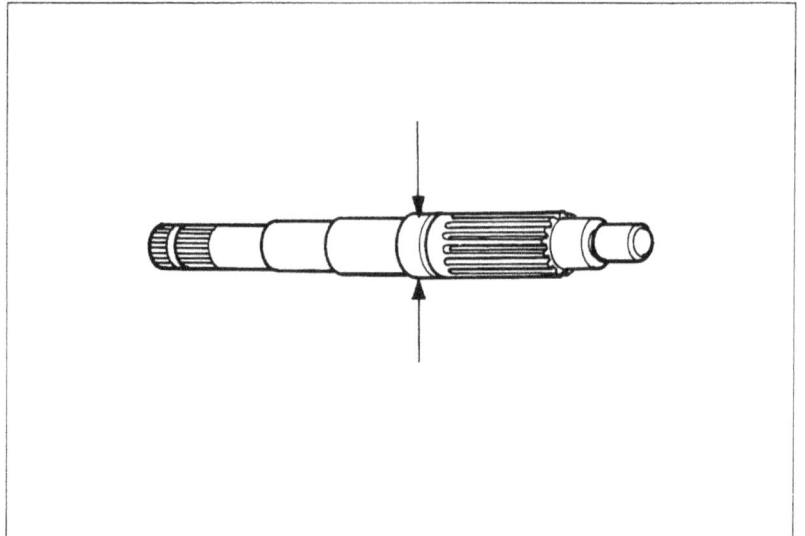

Install the guide plate, spring and collar.

NOTE

Align the collar grove with the spring.

Install the starter pinion, thrust washer and 20mm circlip on the spindle.

Install the drive ratchet.

NOTE

Align the spindle punch mark with the drive ratchet punch mark.

Install the kick starter to the right crankcase.

NOTE

Hook the end of the return spring over the right crankcase abutment.

Install the kick starter lever on the spindle and rotate the spindle.
Position the drive ratchet by installing the stopper bolt.

NOTE

> Do not forget to install the O-ring behind the stopper bolt head.

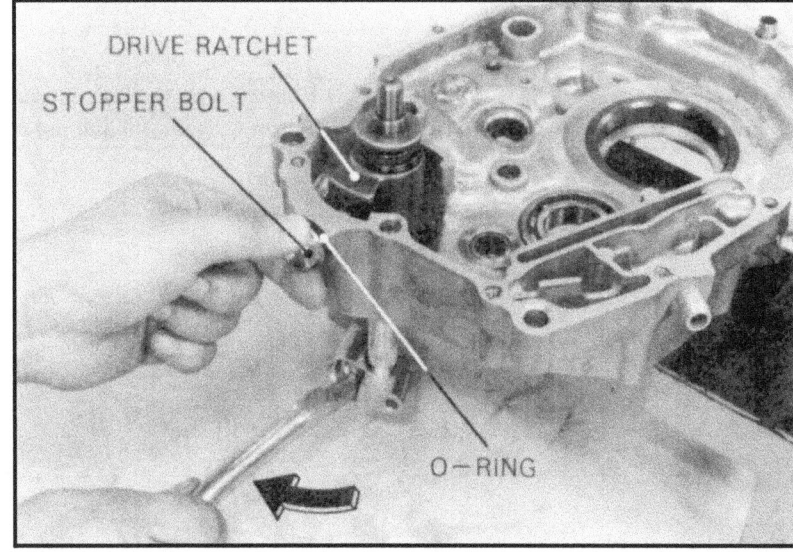

Tighten the bolt securely.
Install the thrust washer on the kick spindle and assemble the crankcase.

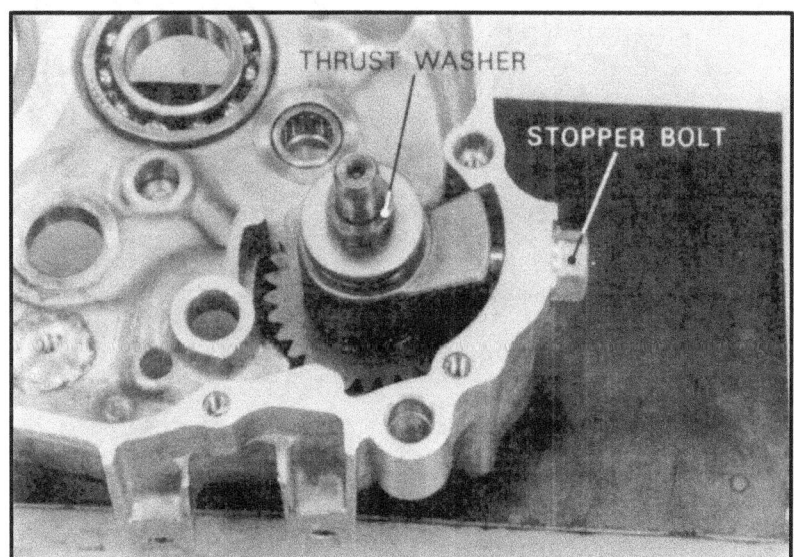

2. VALVE TIMING ADJUSTMENT

Remove the pulse generator and its base (Page 200).
Remove the cam sprocket
Turn the crankshaft counterclockwise and align the "T" mark with the index mark on the cylinder head cover.
Install the cam sprocket.

Align the "O" mark on the sprocket with the index mark on the cylinder head.
Tighten the cam sprocket bolts.
Torque: 0.8–1.2 kg-m (6–9 ft-lb)

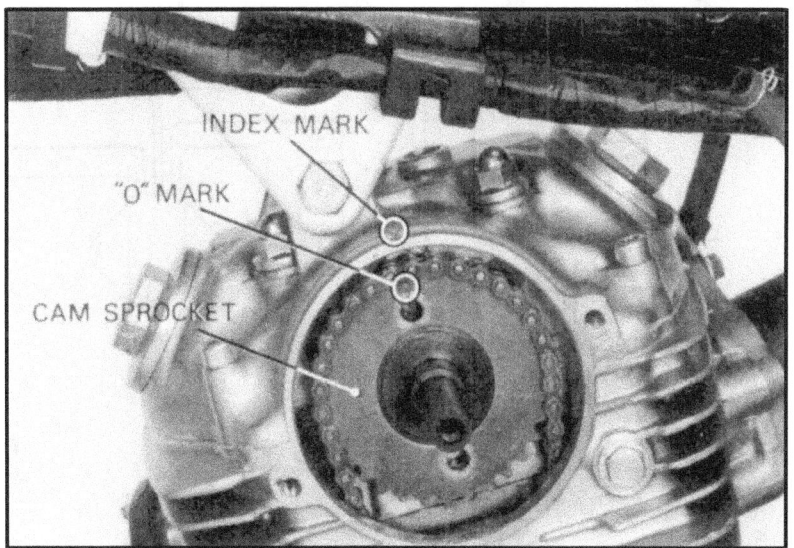

V. IGNITION SYSTEM

NOTE

Ignition timing dose not normally need to be adjusted since the C.D.I. (Capacitive Discharge Ignition) unit is factory pre-set. If ignition timing is incorrect, check the C.D.I. unit, A.C. generator and pulse generator and replace any faulty parts.

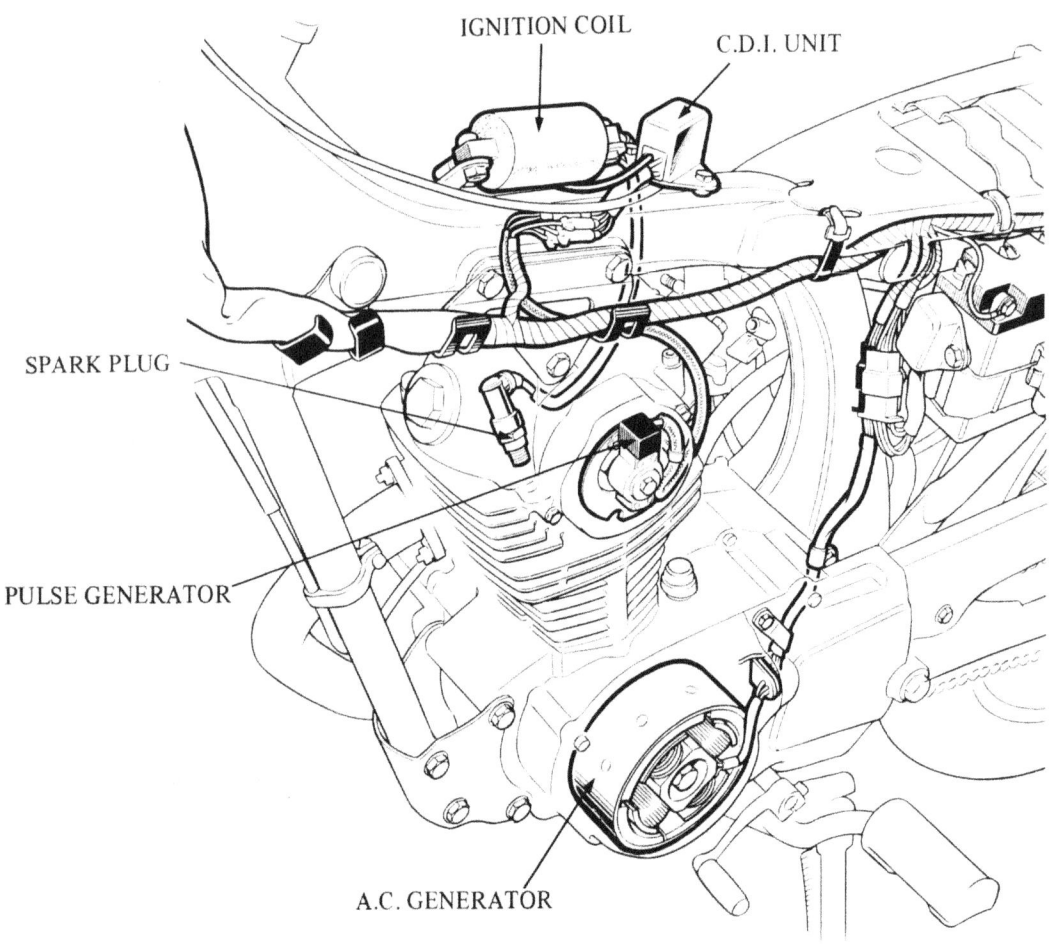

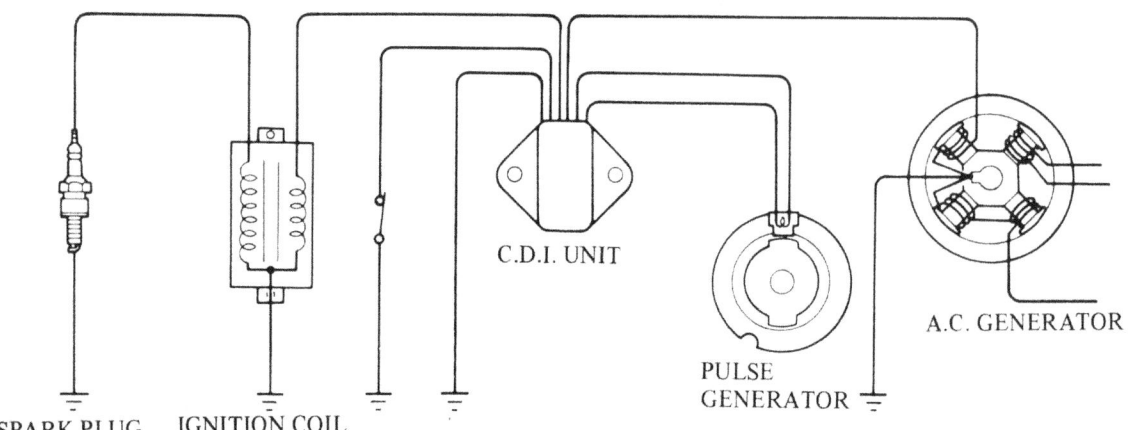

1981 CB125S ADDENDUM

1. IGNITION COIL

Remove the seat and fuel tank.
Remove the spark plug cap from the spark plug.

Disconnect the wire and remove the retaining screws.
Remove the ignition coil.

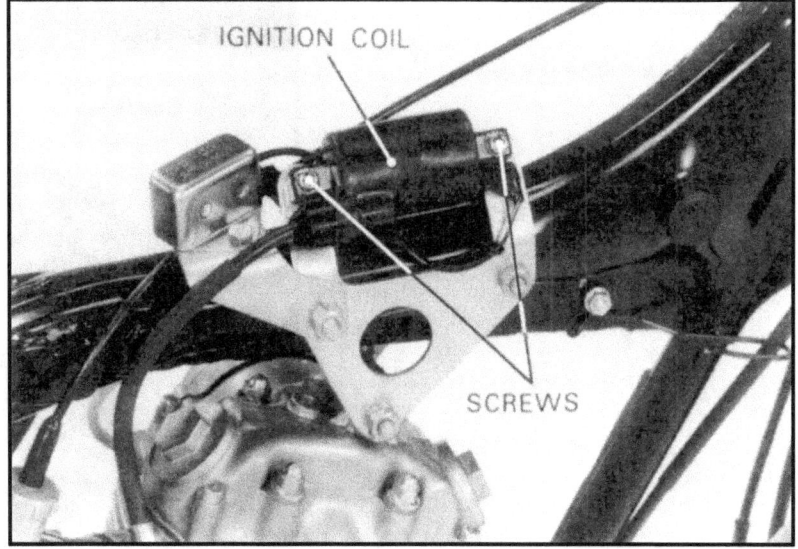

Check the resistance between the leads of the primary and secondary coils:

Primary coil: $0.2 - 0.8\ \Omega$
Secondary coil: $8 - 15\ k\Omega$

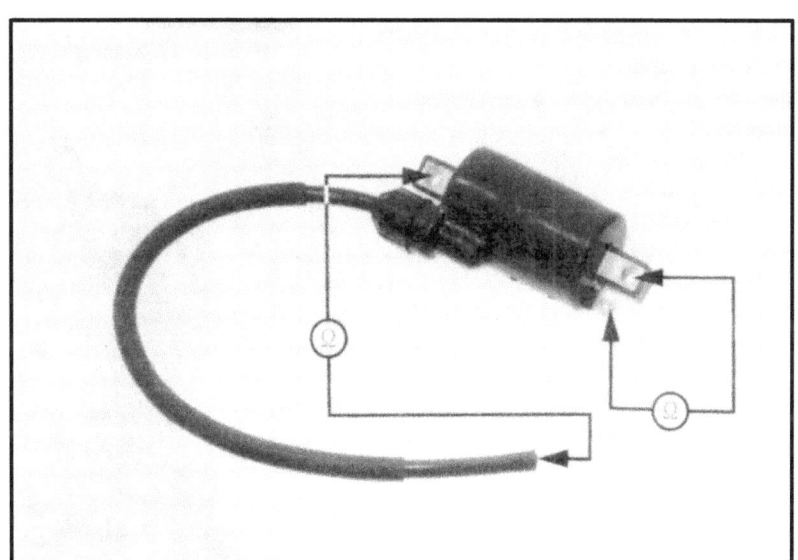

2. PULSE GENERATOR

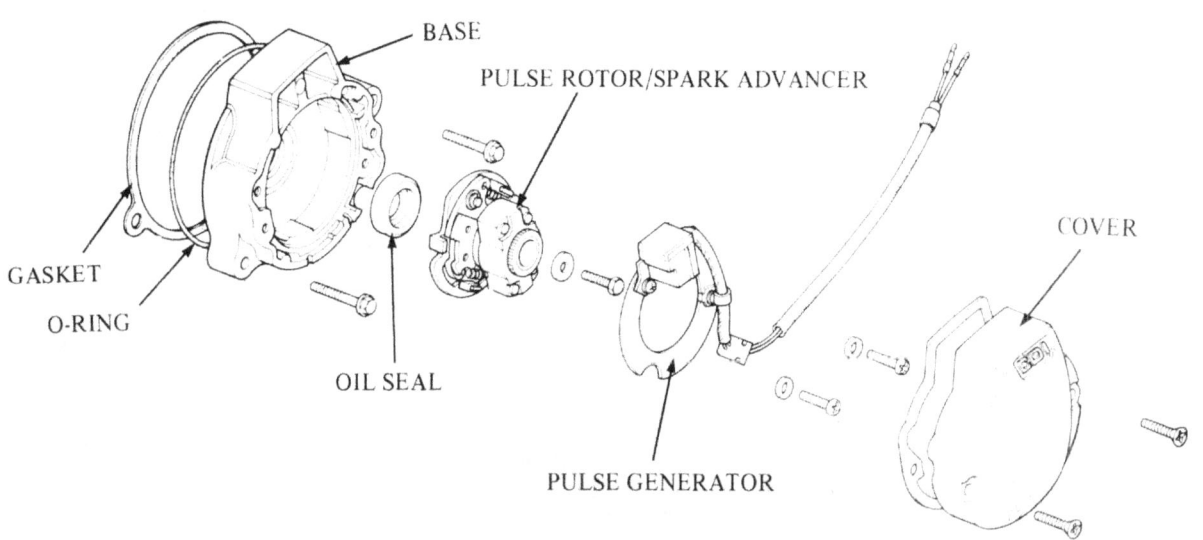

Pulse Generator Removal

Remove the pulse generator cover.

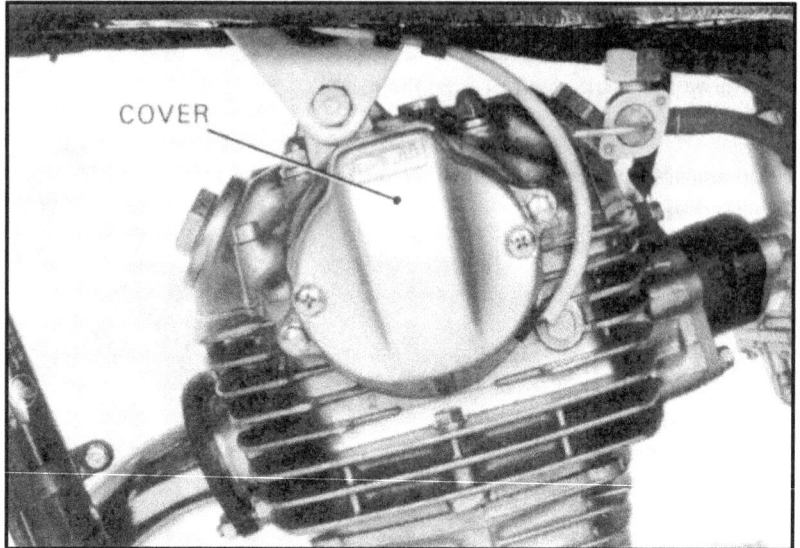

Remove the base plate screws, and remove the pulse generator.
Remove the pulse rotor by removing the 6mm bolt.

Remove the dowel pin.
Remove the base.

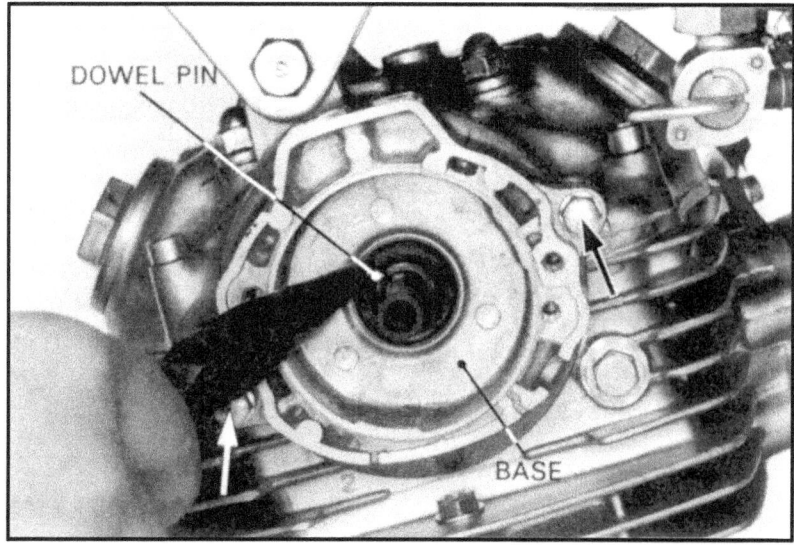

1981 CB125S ADDENDUM

Pulse Generator Inspection

Remove the seat and fuel tank.
Disconnect the pulse generator wires.

Measure the resistance between the Blue/Yellow and Blue wires.

Resistance: 20-60 Ω

NOTE

The pulse generator can be inspected while installed on the engine.

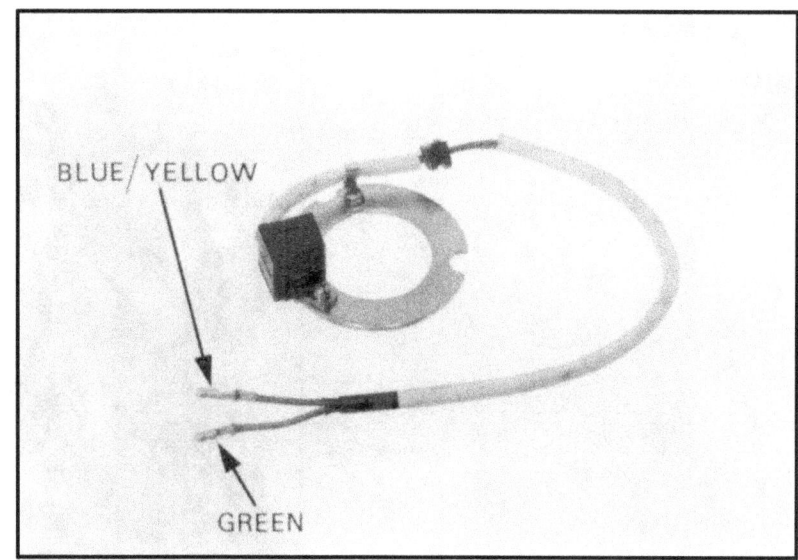

Spark Advancer Inspection

Check the mechanical advancer cam for sticking. Lubricate the sliding surfaces.

Check the spring for loss of tension and the advancer pin for excessive wear.

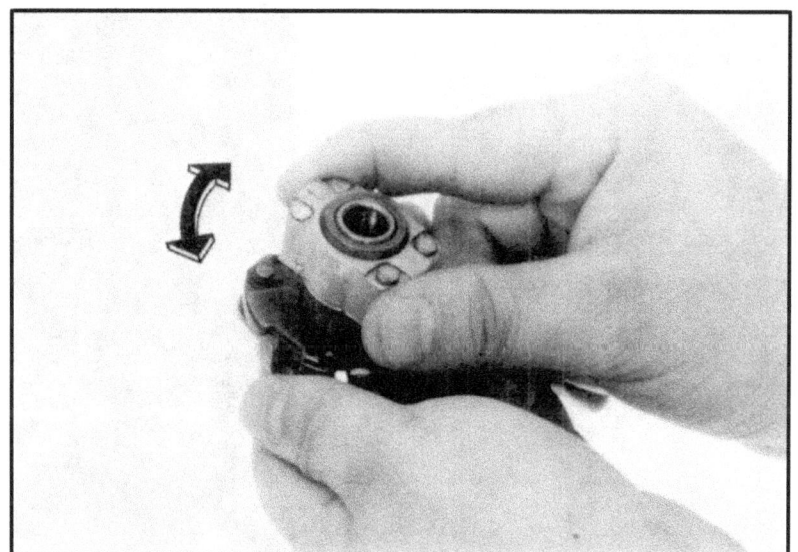

Pulse Generator Assembly

Align the punch mark on the rotor with the index mark on the spark advancer.

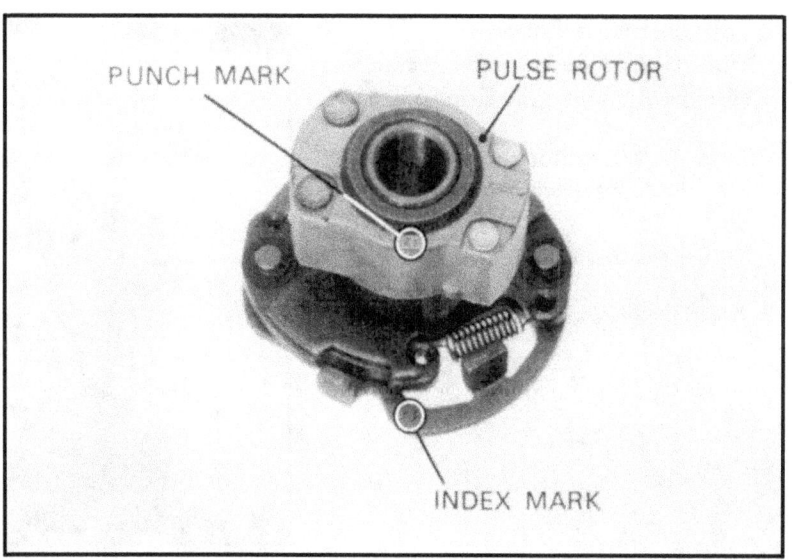

Install the base.

NOTE

Do not turn the oil seal lip inside out.

Install the dowel pins.
Install the pulse rotor.

NOTE

Align the camshaft pin with the advancer groove.

Tighten the pulse rotor bolts.

TORQUE: 0.8–1.2 kg-m (6–9 ft-lb)

Install the pulse generator.
Turn the crankshaft counterclockwise and align the "F" mark with the index mark.

Align the timing mark on the pulse rotor with the timing mark on the pulse generator.
Tighten the base plate screws.

Install the pulse generator cover.

3. C.D.I. UNIT

C.D.I. Unit Removal

Remove the seat and fuel tank.
Disconnect the stator wire leads.
Remove the C.D.I. unit.

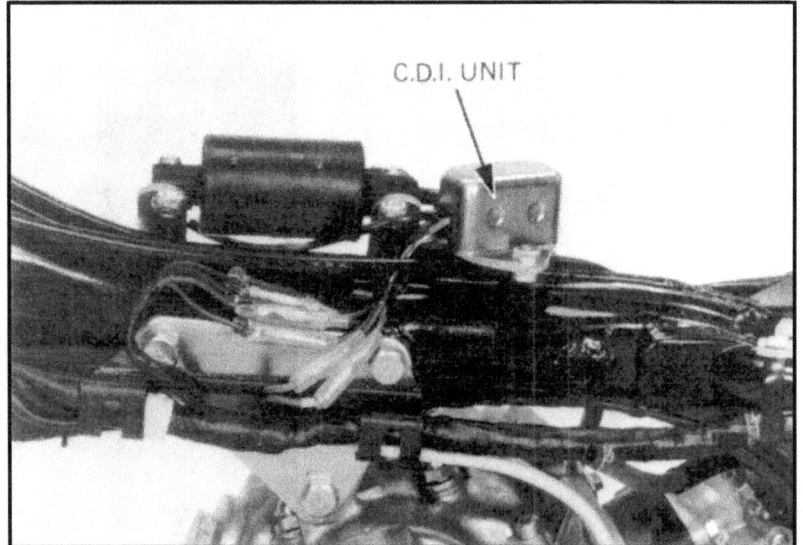

Replace the C.D.I. unit if the readings do not fall within the limits shown in the table.

NOTE

- The C.D.I. unit is fully transistorized.
- Use of an improper tester or measurements may produce inaccurate readings.
- Use SANWA ELECTRIC TESTER (P/N 07308-0020000) or KOWA ELECTRIC TESTER (TH-5H) only.

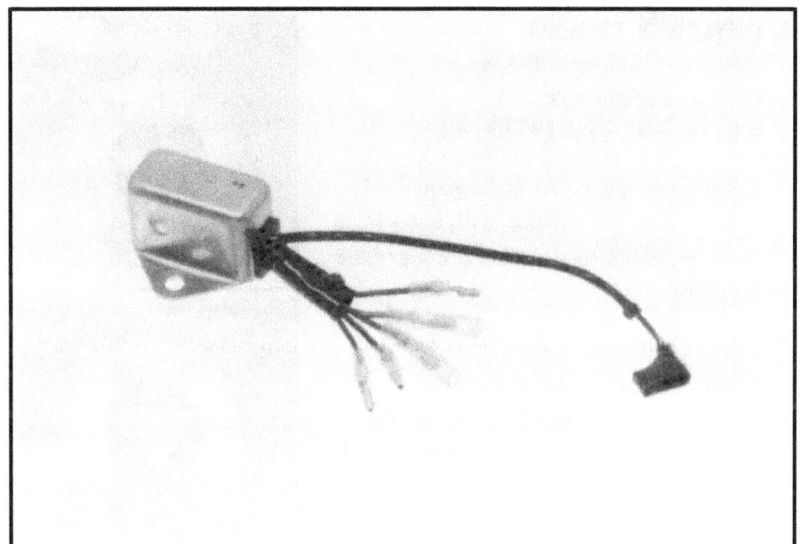

Unit: KΩ

(−) \ (+)	BLACK/WHITE	GREEN	BLACK/RED	GREEN	BLUE/YELLOW	BLACK/WHITE
BLACK/WHITE		∞	∞	∞	∞	∞
GREEN	2–50		0.5–10	—	∞	∞
BLACK/RED	0.5–10	∞		∞	∞	∞
GREEN	2–50	—	0.5–10		∞	∞
BLUE/YELLOW	2–50	0.5–10	2–50	0.5–10		∞
BLACK/WHITE	∞	∞	∞	∞	∞	

4. STATOR COIL INSPECTION

Disconnect the A.C. generator coupler. Measure the resistance between the Black/Red lead and body ground.

Resistance: 245.1 Ω

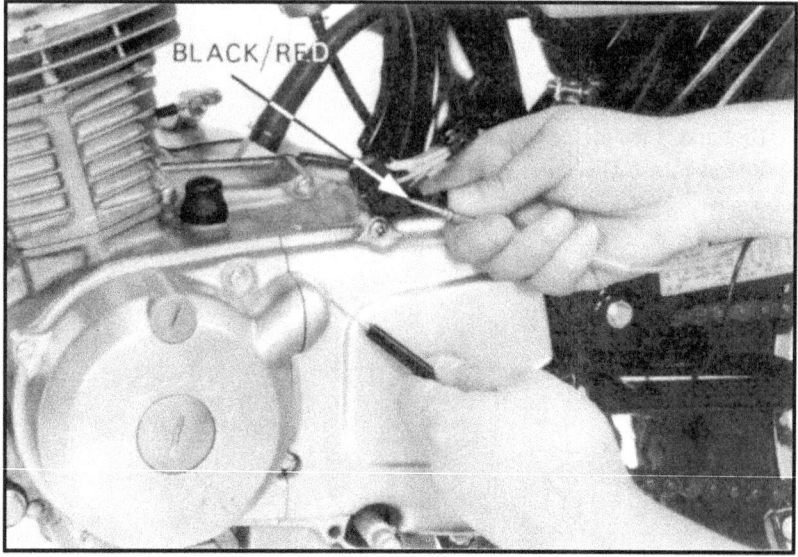

5. IGNITION TIMING

Remove the timing hole cap.
Connect a timing light.
Start the engine and allow to idle.

1,300 ± 100 rpm: "F" mark should be aligned with index mark
Increase engine speed and check the following items;

1,950 ± 150 rpm: Advances starts
3,350 ± 150 rpm: Advance stops
Index mark should be between advance marks

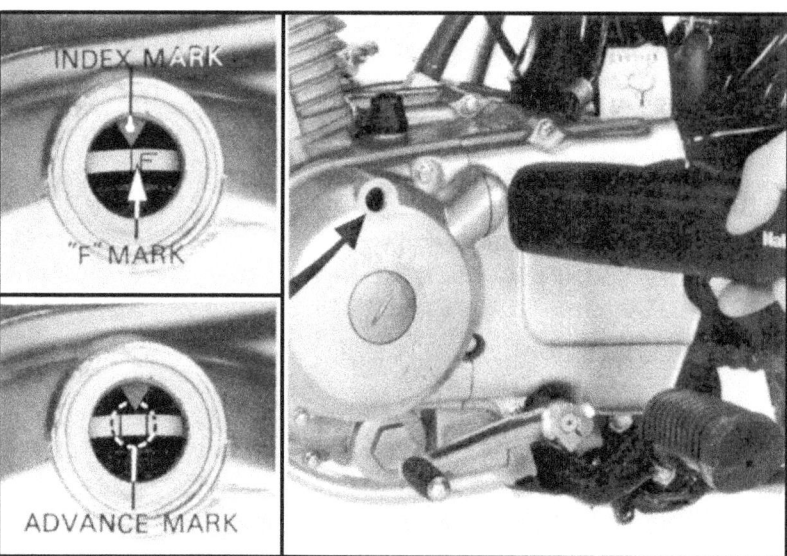

To adjust, remove the pulse generator cover, loosen the base plate attaching screws and turn the plate left or right as required.

After adjustment, check the air gap between the rotor and the coil with a feeler gauge.

Gap: 0.3–0.4 mm (0.12–0.16 in)

To adjust, loosen the coil mounting screws and move the coil up or down as required.

VI. A.C. GENERATOR/CHARGING SYSTEM

1. A.C. GENERATOR

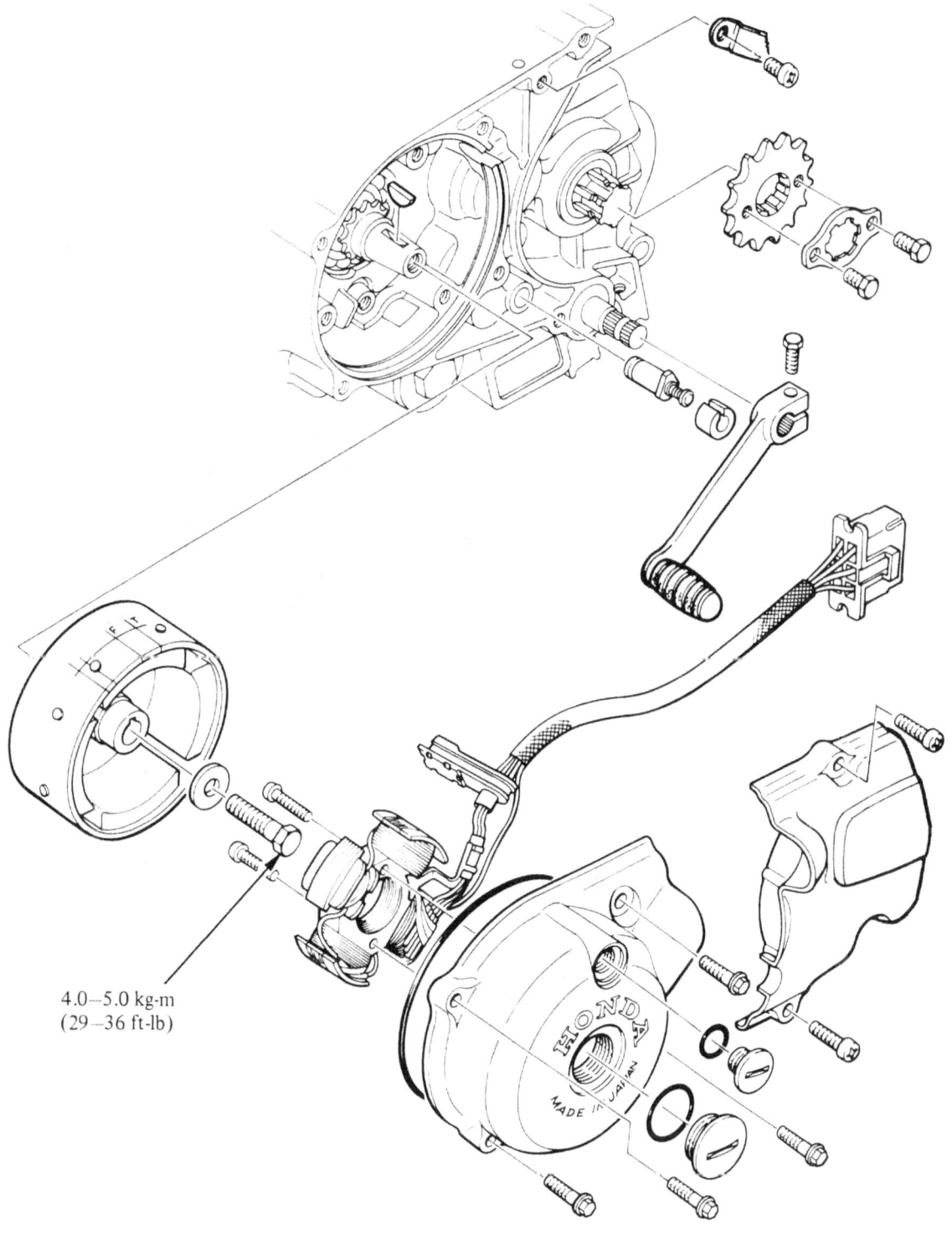

4.0–5.0 kg-m
(29–36 ft-lb)

Left Crankcase Cover Removal

Drain oil from the engine.
Remove the gearshift pedal.
Remove the drive sprocket cover.

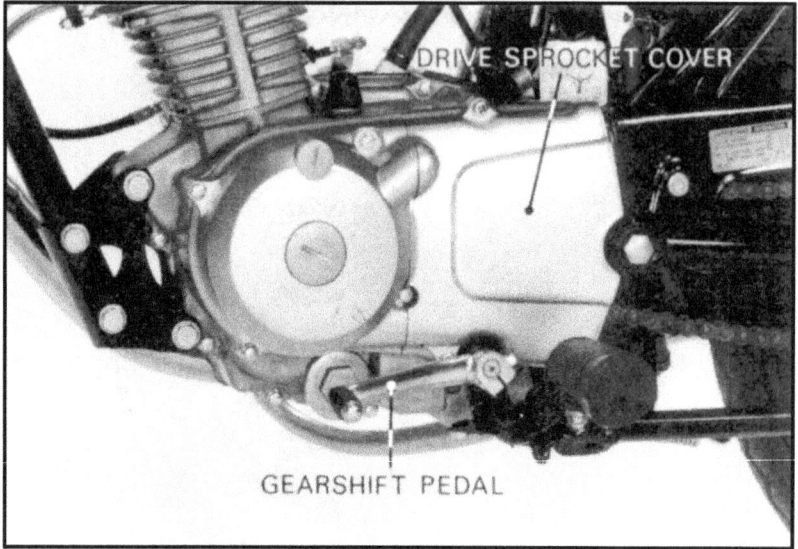

Disconnect the A.C. generagor wire coupler.
Remove the A.C. generator wire clamps.
Remove the neutral switch collar.
Disconnect the neutral switch wires.
Remove the left crankcase cover.

A.C. Generator Removal

Remove the drive chain.
Shift the transmission into top gear.

Hold the drive sprocket with a "UNIVERSAL HOLDER".
Remove the rotor bolt.

1981 CB125S ADDENDUM

Remove the rotor with a rotor puller.

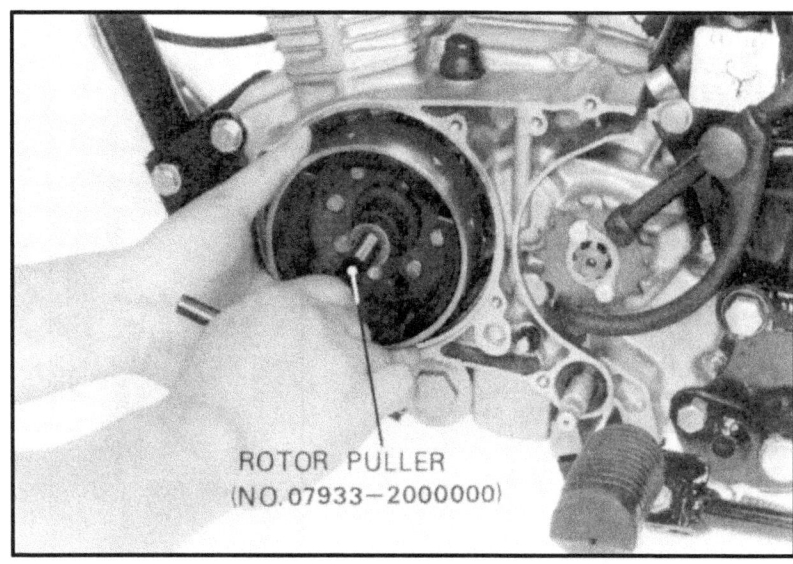

ROTOR PULLER
(NO. 07933—2000000)

A.C. Generator Installation

Install the rotor.

NOTE

> Align the woodruff key with the keyway in the crankshaft.

Tighten the rotor bolt to the specified torque.

TORQUE: 4.0–5.0 kg-m (29–36 ft-lb)

Install the drive chain.

Left Crankcase Cover Installation

Install the O-rings in the left crankcase cover.

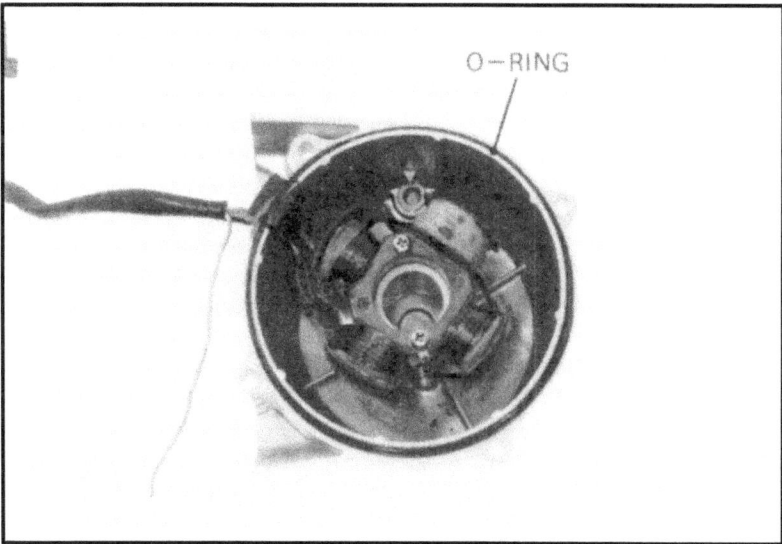

O-RING

Install the left crankcase cover.

NOTE

> Make sure that there is no foreign matter on the generator rotor.

Connect the A.C. generator wire coupler.
Install the generator wire clamp.
Connect the neutral switch wires.
Install the neutral switch collar.

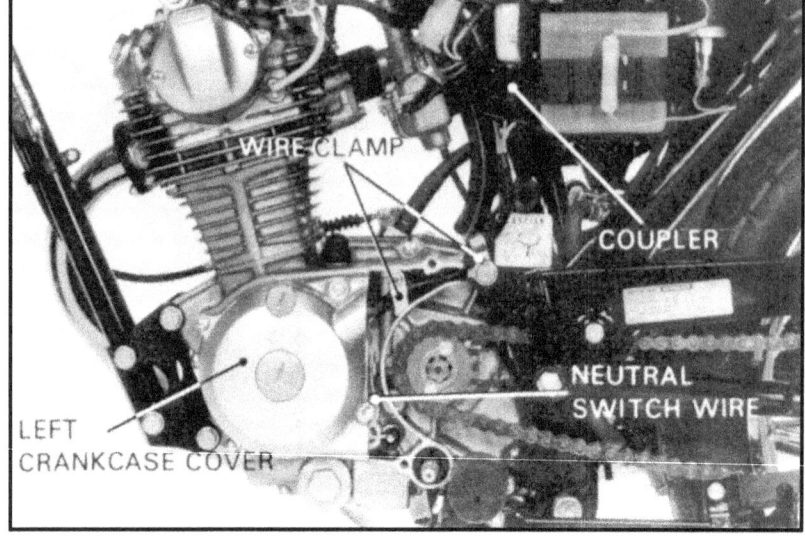

Install the drive sprocket cover.
Install the gearshift pedal.
Refill the engine with the recommended grade oil up to the upper level mark.

1981 CB125S ADDENDUM

2. CHARGING SYSTEM

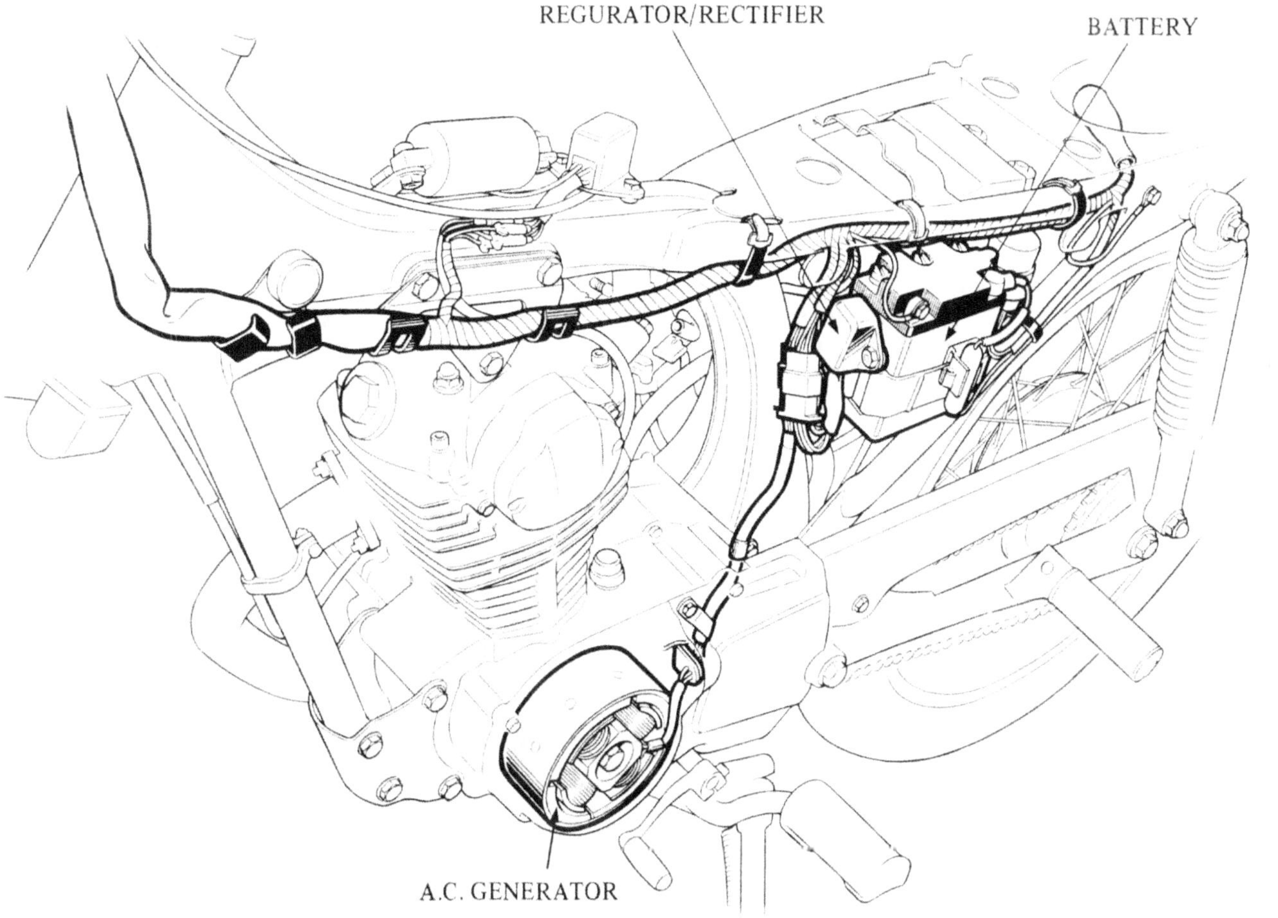

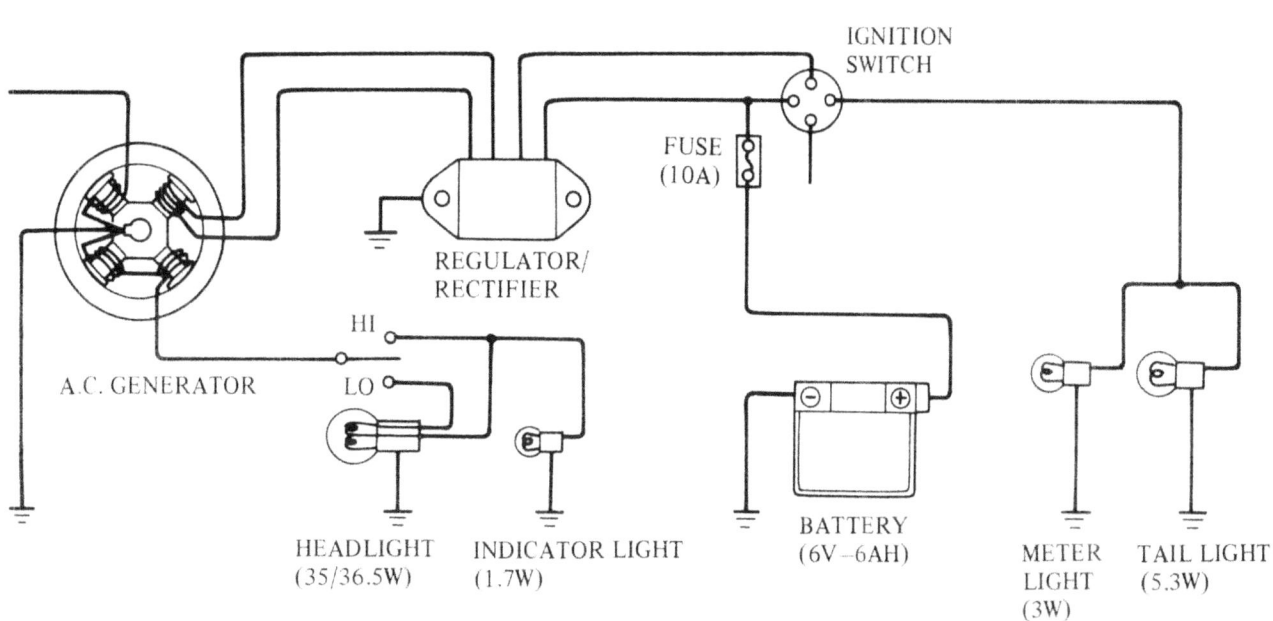

Charging Test

Perform the test after warming up the engine.

Connect a voltmeter and an ammeter to check the charging system as shown.

NOTE

Use a fully charged battery to check the charging system output.

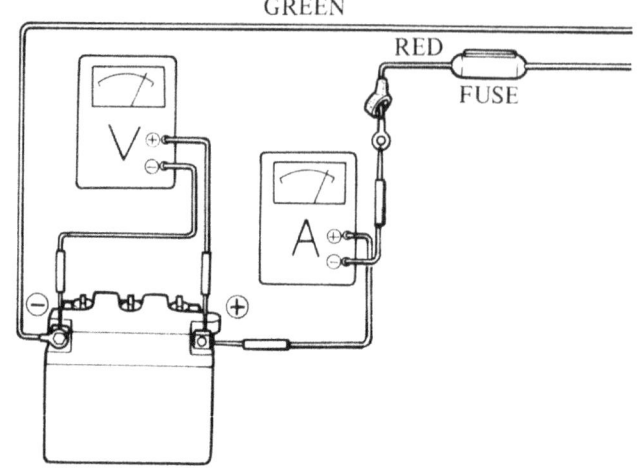

Technical Data

LIGHTING SWITCH	CHARGING START	4,000 rpm	8,000 rpm
ON (HIGHT BEAM)	1,800 rpm max.	1.2A min./8.0V	3.4A max./9.0V

Charging Coil and Lamp Coil Inspection

NOTE

It is not necessary to remove the stator to make this test.

Disconnect the A.C. generator coupler.

Check the resistance between the leads with an ohmmeter as follows:

Charging Coil (Yellow and pink): $0.58\,\Omega$
Lamp Coil (White/yellow and
　　　　　body ground): $0.47\,\Omega$

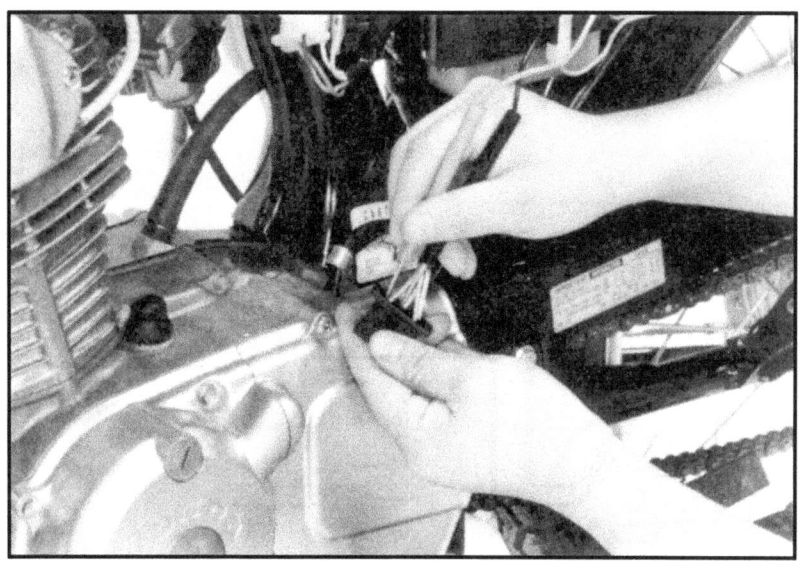

1981 CB125S ADDENDUM

3. VOLTAGE REGULATOR/RECTIFIER

Remove the left side cover.
Disconnect the coupler and connectors.
Remove the voltage regulator/rectifier.

Voltage Regulator/Rectifier Inspection

Check the resistance between the leads with an ohmmeter.

WARNING

Do not use high voltage source such as insulation resistance tester since it may damage the rectifier and give you a shock.

NOTE

- Use SANWA ELECTRICAL TESTER P/N 07308-0020000 or KOWA ELECTRICAL TESTER (TH-5H).
- SANWA and KOWA TESTERS have different measurements as shown.
- Make sure the tester contains new batteries, perform the zero adjustment in the measuring range for accurate reading.

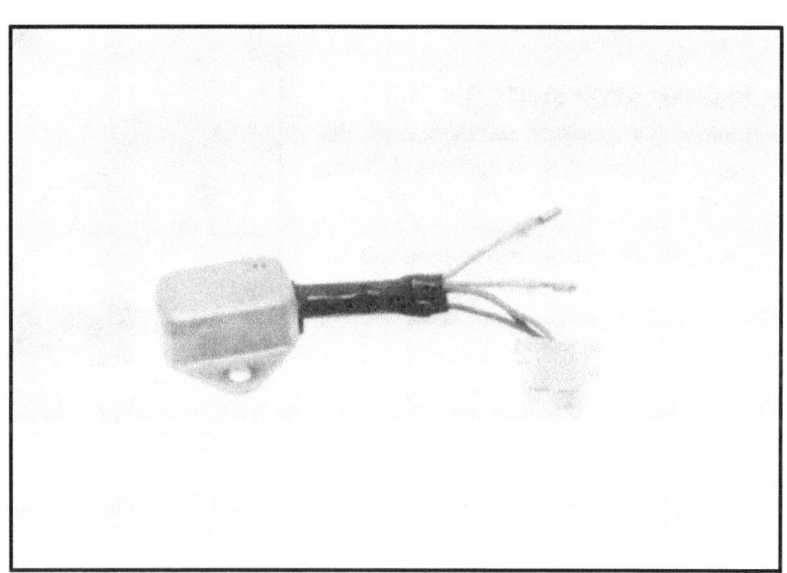

SANWA: [kΩ]

+ Probe / − Probe	Yellow	Pink	Red	Black	Green
Yellow		∞	1−25	∞	∞
Pink	10−250		1−25	1.5−35	6−150
Red	∞	∞		∞	∞
Black	5−120	5−120	10−250		5−45
Green	1−25	1−25	3−80	1.5−40	

KOWA: [× 100]

+ Probe / − Probe	Yellow	Pink	Red	Black	Green
Yellow		∞	2−50	∞	∞
Pink	100−∞		2−50	6−150	50−∞
Red	∞	∞		∞	∞
Black	50−∞	50−∞	100−∞		50−500
Green	2−50	2−50	8−200	8−200	

VII. SWITCHES

1. IGNITION SWITCH

Remove the headlight and disconnect the ignition switch connectors.

Check for continuity between terminals.

Continuity should exist between color coded wires indicated by interconnected circles.

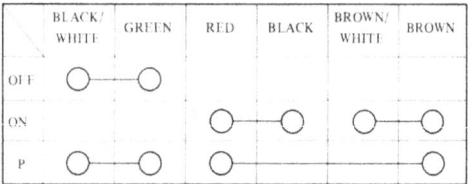

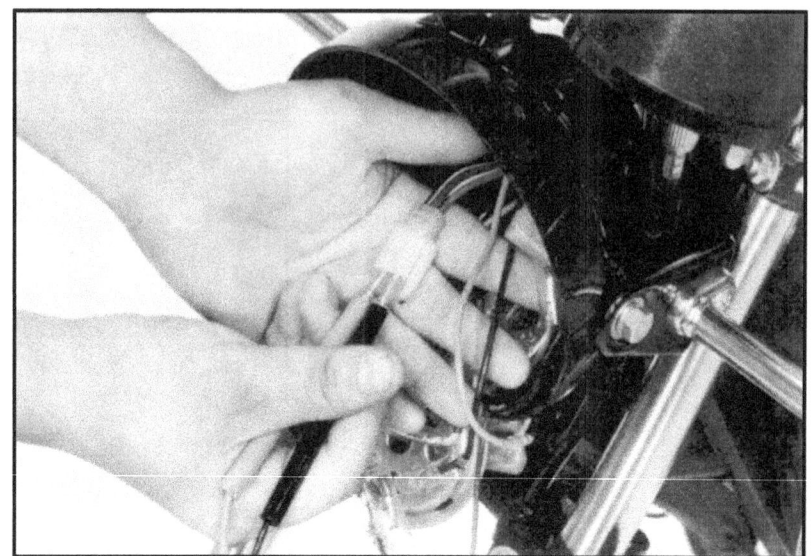

2. ENGINE STOP SWITCH

Remove the headlight and disconnect the engine stop switch wires (green and black/white).

Check for continuity between terminals.

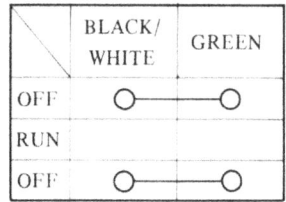

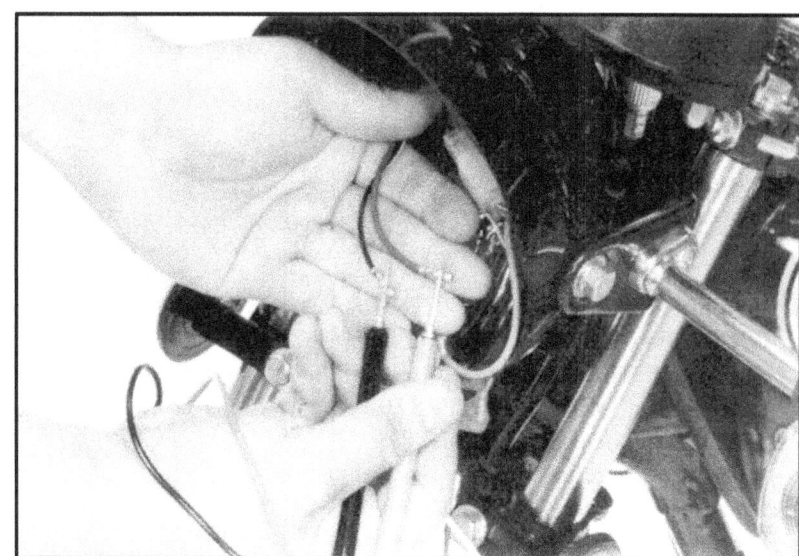

VIII. TROUBLESHOOTING

IGNITION SYSTEM

Engine starts but stops
1. No sparks at plug
2. Improper ignition timing
3. Faulty spark plug

Engine starts but runs poorly
1. Ignition primary circuit
   - Faulty ignition coil
   - Loose or bare wire
   - Faulty A.C. generator
2. Ignition secondary circuit
   - Faulty plug
   - Faulty C.D.I. unit
   - Faulty pulse generator
   - Faulty high tension cord
3. Improper ignition timing
   - Faulty advancer rotor
   - Faulty pulse generator
   - Faulty C.D.I. unit

Hard starting
1. Improper pulse generator coil air gap

No spark at plug
1. Engine stop switch "OFF"
2. Poorly connected, broken or shorted wires
   - Between A.C. generator and ignition coil
   - Between C.D.I. unit and engine stop switch
   - Between C.D.I. unit and ignition coil
   - Between C.D.I. unit and main switch
   - Between ignition coil and plug
   - Between pulse generator and C.D.I. unit
3. Faulty main switch
4. Faulty ignition coil
5. Faulty C.D.I. unit
6. Improper pulse generator coil air gap
7. Faulty pulse generator
8. Faulty A.C. generator

IX. CABLE AND HARNESS ROUTING

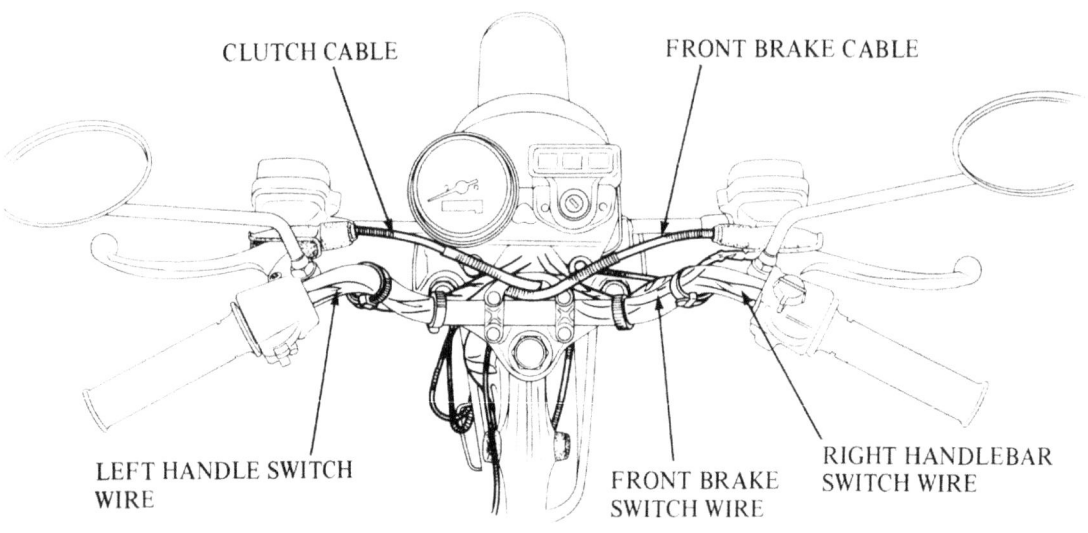

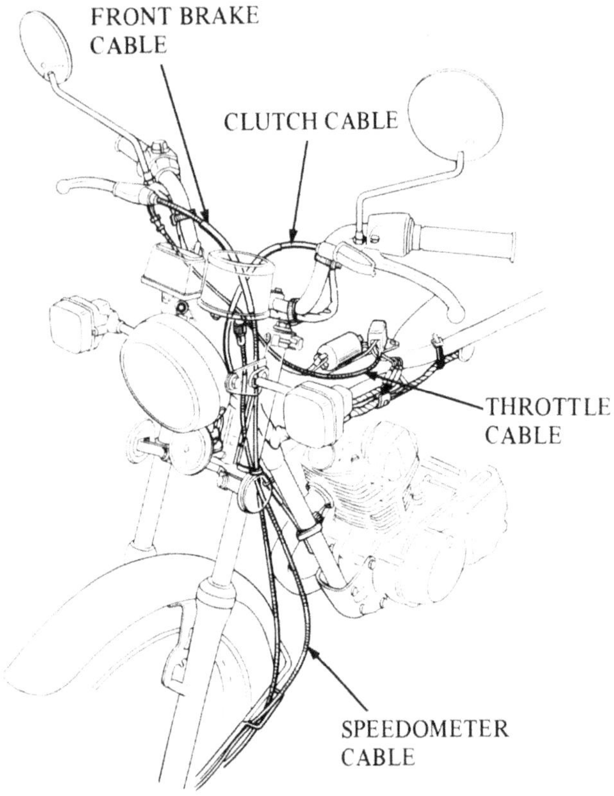

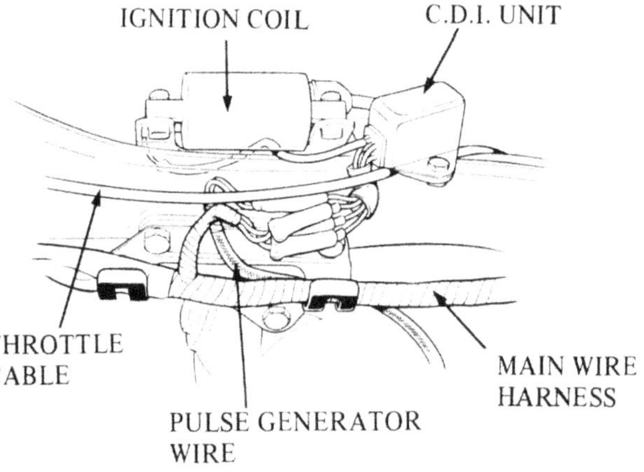

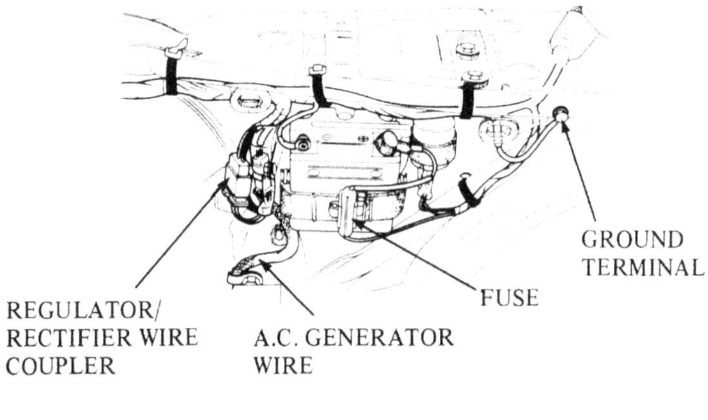

1981 CB125S ADDENDUM

X. WIRING DIAGRAM

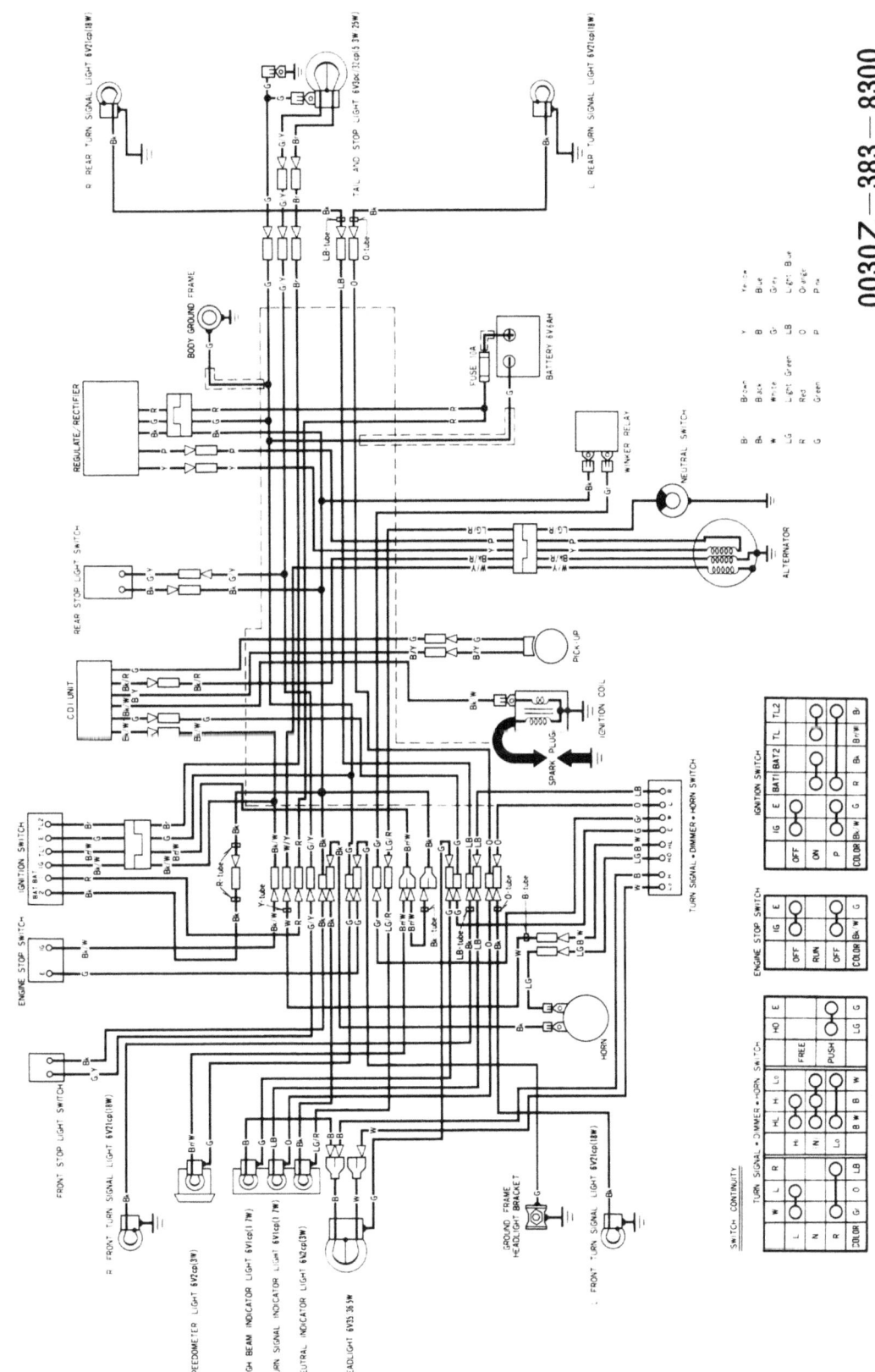

MEMO

'82 CB125S ADDENDUM

INTRODUCTION

This addendum is for the 1982 CB125S. Refer to the base Shop Manual and previous addendums for service procedures and data not included in this addendum.

CONTENTS

I. SPECIFICATIONS 218
II. MAINTENANCE SCHEDULE 219
III. LUBRICATION 220
IV. INSPECTION AND ADJUSTMENT 220
      FUEL STRAINER CLEANING 220
      SPARK PLUGS 221
V. CARBURETOR 221
      SLOW JET 221
      HIGH ALTITUDE ADJUSTMENT 222
VI. ENGINE 223
      CYLINDER HEAD 223

Date of Issue: September 1981

I. SPECIFICATIONS

This addendum lists only specifications which are new for 1982. Refer to the base manual and to the 1976-1981 addendums for information not covered here.

Item	

ELECTRICAL
  Spark plug
    Standard
    For cold climate
    For extended high-speed riding
	
	DR8ES-L (NGK) or X24ESR-U (ND)
	DR7ES (NGK) or X22ESR-U (ND)
	DR8ES (NGK) or X27ESR-U (ND)

LIGHTS
  Headlight
  Tail/stoplight
  Turn signal light (front/rear)
  Speedometer
  Neutral indicator
  Turn signal indicator
  High beam indicator
	
	35/36.5 W
	6V - 3/32 cp 5.3/25 Watt
	6V - 21/21 cp 17/17 Watt SAE No. 1129
	6V - 2 cp 3 Watt
	6V - 2 cp 3 Watt
	6V - 1 cp 1.7 Watt
	6V - 1 cp 1.7 Watt

CARBURETOR Pilot screw initial opening	 1-1/2 turns out, see pages 183-184

TORQUE VALUES

ENGINE

Item	Qty	Thread Dia	Torque, Kg-m (ft-lb)
Cylinder head cap nuts	4	8	2.8-3.0 (20-22)

II. MAINTENANCE SCHEDULE

Perform the PRE-RIDE INSPECTION in the Owner's Manual at each scheduled maintenance period.

I: Inspect and Clean, Adjust, Lubricate or Replace if necessary.

C: Clean

R: Replace

A: Adjust

L: Lubricate

	ITEM / FREQUENCY	WHICHEVER COMES FIRST EVERY	600mi (1000km)	2500mi (4000km)	5000mi (8000km)	750mi (12000km)	Refer to page
EMISSION RELATED ITEMS	*FUEL LINE			I	I	I	148
	*FUEL STRAINER		C	C	C	C	221
	*THROTTLE OPERATION		I	I	I	I	152
	*CARBURETOR-CHOKE			I	I	I	181
	AIR CLEANER	NOTE 1		C	C	C	147
	CRANKCASE BREATHER	NOTE 2		C	C	C	147
	SPARK PLUG			R	R	R	222
	*VALVE CLEARANCE		I	I	I	I	193
	ENGINE OIL	YEAR	R	R, EVERY 1250 mi (2000km)			193-221
	ENGINE OIL FILTER SCREEN		C	C, EVERY 1250 mi (2000km)			193
	*ENGINE OIL FILTER ROTOR				C		146
	*CAM CHAIN TENSION		A	A	A	A	152
	*CARBURETOR-IDLE SPEED		I	I	I	I	184
NON-EMISSION RELATED ITEMS	DRIVE CHAIN		I, L, EVERY 300mi (500km)				153
	BATTERY	MONTH	I	I	I	I	155, 194
	BRAKE SHOE WEAR			I	I	I	156
	BRAKE SYSTEM		I	I	I	I	156-158
	*BRAKE LIGHT SWITCH		I	I	I	I	158
	*HEADLIGHT AIM		I	I	I	I	159
	CLUTCH		I	I	I	I	159
	SIDE STAND			I	I	I	160
	*SUSPENSION		I	I	I	I	161, 168
	*NUTS, BOLTS, FASTENERS		I	I	I	I	161
	**WHEELS/SPOKES		I	I	I	I	162
	**STEERING HEAD BEARING		I			I	162

*Should be serviced by an authorized HONDA dealer, unless the owner has proper tools and service data and is mechanically qualified.

**In the interest of safety, we recommend these items be serviced ONLY by an authorized HONDA dealer.

NOTE:
1. Service more frequently when riding in dusty areas.
2. Service more frequently when riding in rain or at full throttle.
3. For higher odometer readings, repeat at the frequency interval established here.

III. LUBRICATION

ENGINE OIL RECOMMENDATION

Use HONDA 4-STROKE OIL or equivalent.
API SERVICE CLASSIFICATION: SE or SF
VISCOSITY: SAE 10W-40

Other viscosities may be used when the average temperature in your riding area is within the chart's indicated range.

OIL CAPACITY:

0.9 ℓ (0.95 U.S. qt, 0.8 Imp qt) after draining
1.1 ℓ (1.2 U.S. qt, 0.97 Imp qt) at disassembly

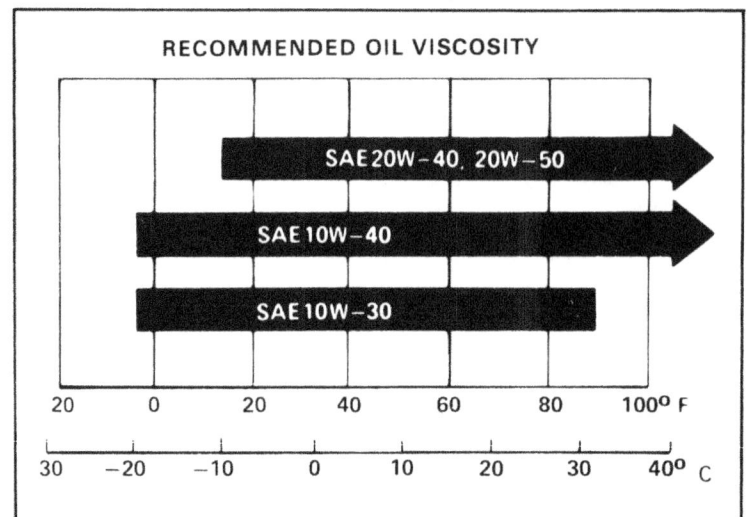

IV. INSPECTION AND ADJUSTMENT

FUEL STRAINER CLEANING

WARNING

Gasoline is flammable and is explosive under certain conditions. Do not smoke or allow flames or sparks near the equipment while draining fuel.

Turn the fuel valve OFF.

Remove the fuel cup, O-ring and filter screen and drain the gasoline into a suitable container.

Wash the cup and filter screen in clean non-flammable or high flash point solvent.

Reinstall the screen, align the index marks on the fuel valve body and filter screen. Install a new O-ring into the fuel valve body.

Reinstall the fuel cup, making sure the new O-ring is in place. Hand tighten the fuel cup and torque to specification.

TORQUE: 3-5 N·m (0.3-0.5 kg-m, 2-4 ft-lb)

After installing, turn the fuel valve ON and check that there are no fuel leaks.

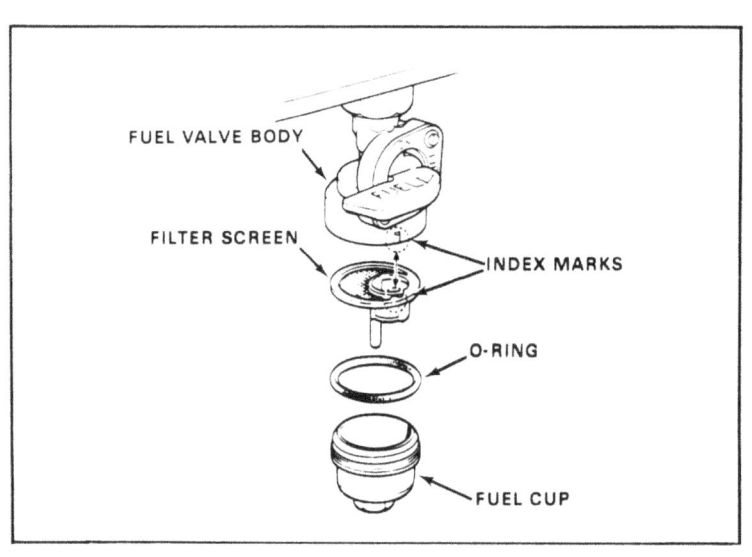

SPARK PLUGS

Recommended spark plugs:

Usage Brand	Standard	For Cold Climate (Below 5°, 41°F)	For Extended High Speed Riding
NGK	DR8ES-L	DR7ES	DR8ES
ND	X24ESR-U	X22ESR-U	X27ESR-U

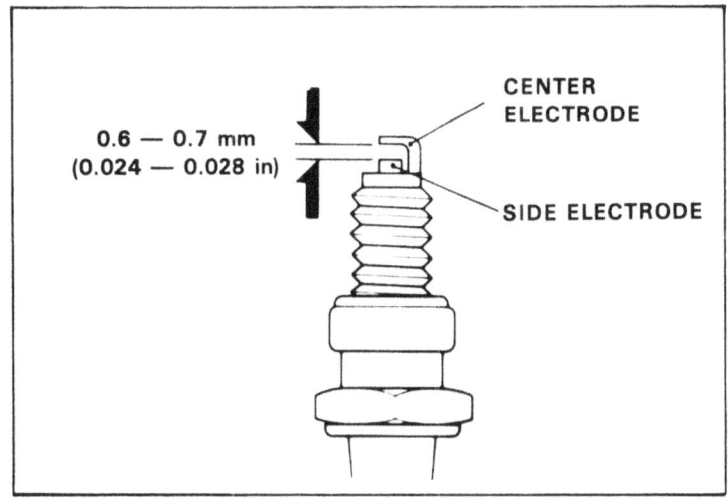

Disconnect the spark plug cap.

Clean any dirt from around the base of the spark plug.

Remove and discard the used spark plug. Check the electrode gap of the new spark plug, using a wire-type feeler gauge. Adjust by carefully bending the side electrode.

SPARK PLUG GAP: 0.6-0.7 mm (0.024-0.028 in.)

With the washer attached, thread the new spark plug in by hand to prevent crossthreading. After hand tightening, tighten an additional ½ turn with a spark plug wrench to compress the washer. Install the spark plug cap.

V. CARBURETOR

SLOW JET

Remove the carburetor.

Remove the float chamber body.

Remove the slow jet.

Blow out the slow jet with compressed air.

Inspect the slow jet for scratches or damage.

Screw in the slow jet until resistance is felt, then tighten it an additional ¾ turn.

Install the float chamber body.

Install the carburetor.

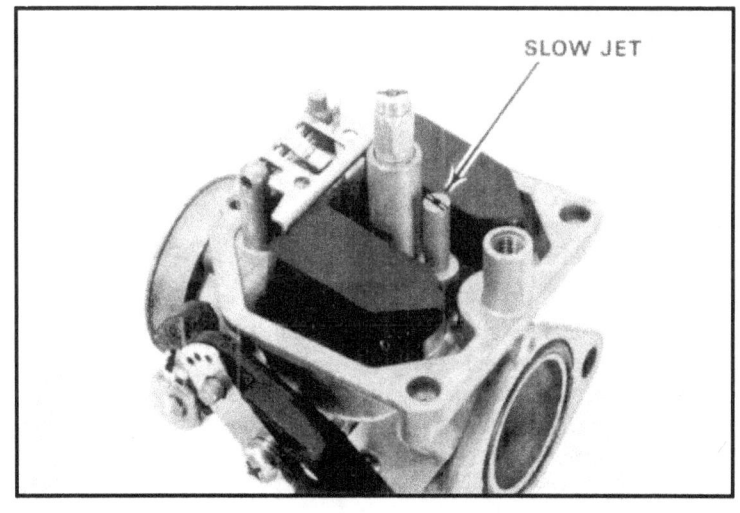

HIGH ALTITUDE ADJUSTMENT (USA only)

When the vehicle is to be operated continuously above 6,500 feet (2,000 m), the carburetor must be readjusted as described below to improve driveability and decrease exhaust emissions.

Remove the carburetor.

Remove the carburetor float chamber.

Remove the #88 main jet and install the #85 main jet.

MAIN JET SPECIFICATIONS

Altitude	Main Jet
Above 6,500 feet (2,000 m)	#85
Below 5,000 feet (1,500 m)	#88

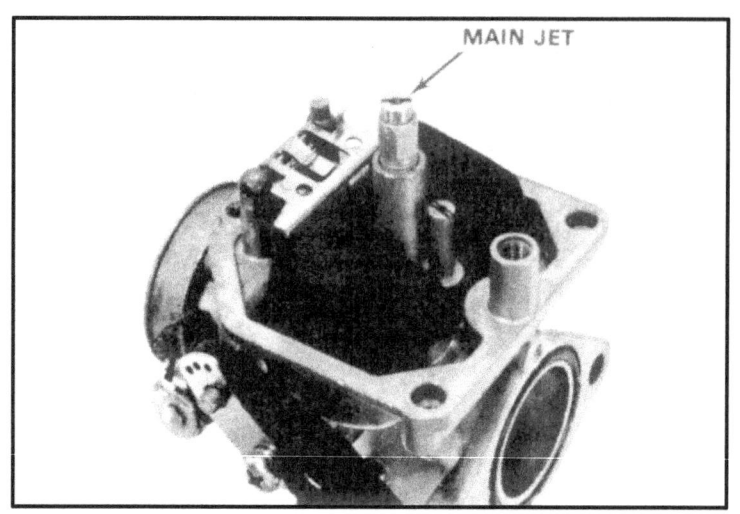

Reassemble and install the carburetor.

Warm up the engine to operating temperature.

Stop and go driving for 10 minutes is sufficient. Adjust the idle speed to 1,300 ± 100 rpm with the throttle stop screw.

NOTE

This adjustment must be made at high altitude to ensure proper high altitude operation.

Attach the Vehicle Emission Control Information Update label as shown.

NOTE

- Instructions for obtaining Vehicle Emission Control Update labels are given in Service Newsletter No. 132.
- Do not attach the label to any part that can be easily removed from the vehicle.

CAUTION

Continuous operation at an altitude lower than 5,000 feet (1,500 m) with the carburetor adjusted for high altitudes may cause the engine to idle roughly and stall and could cause engine damage from overheating.

When the vehicle is to be operated continuously below 5,000 feet (1,500 m), reinstall the #88 main jet and adjust the idle speed to 1,300 ± 100 rpm. Be sure to do these adjustments at low altitude.

VEHICLE EMISSION CONTROL INFORMATION UPDATE LABEL

VI. ENGINE CYLINDER HEAD

Tighten the four cylinder head cap nuts in a criss-cross pattern.

NOTE

> Apply engine oil to the threads of the four cap nuts before installing and tightening.

TORQUE: 2.8-3.0 kg-m (20-22 ft-lb)

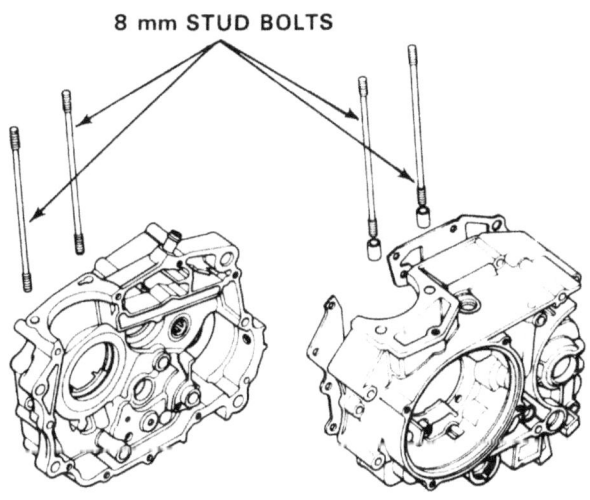

8 mm STUD BOLTS

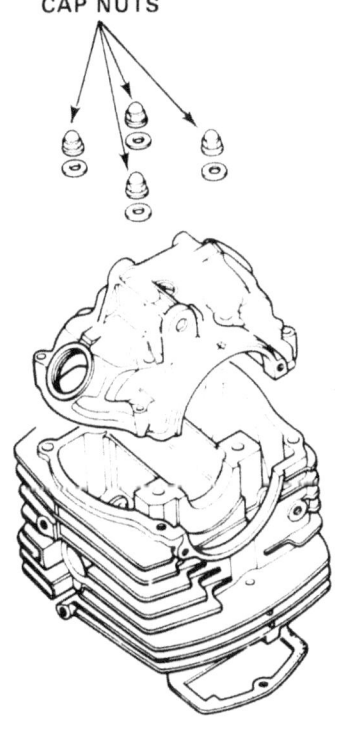

CAP NUTS

MEMO

1984 CB125S ADDENDUM

INTRODUCTION

This addendum contains information for the 1984 CB125S. Refer to the base Shop Manual and previous addenda for service procedures and data not included in this addendum.

CONTENTS

GENERAL INFORMATION	226
Model Identification	226
Specifications	227
Standards/Service Limits	229
Torque Values	231
Tools	232
Cable & Harness Routing	233
Emission Control Systems	236
LUBRICATION	238
MAINTENANCE SCHEDULE	239
INSPECTION & ADJUSTMENT	240
Evaporative Emission Control System (California Only)	240
Valve Clearance	240
Air Cleaner	241
Carburetor Idle Speed	242
Wheels/Spokes	242
FUEL SYSTEM	243
Service Information	243
Carburetor Removal/Installation	243
Float Level	244
Accelerator Pump Disassembly/Inspection	244
Accelerator Pump Linkage Adjustment	246
Accelerator Pump Cable Adjustment	246
Pilot Screw Adjustment	246
High Altitude Adjustment	247
Vacuum Hose Routing (California Only)	248
CHARGING SYSTEM	249
Service Information	250
Troubleshooting	250
Battery	251
Charging System Check	252
Alternator	252
Regulator/Rectifier	253
IGNITION SYSTEM	254
CDI Unit	255
Pulse Generator	256
Ignition Timing	256
WIRING DIAGRAM	257

Date of Issue: March, 1984

GENERAL INFORMATION

MODEL IDENTIFICATION

The engine serial number is stamped on the lower left side of the crankcase.

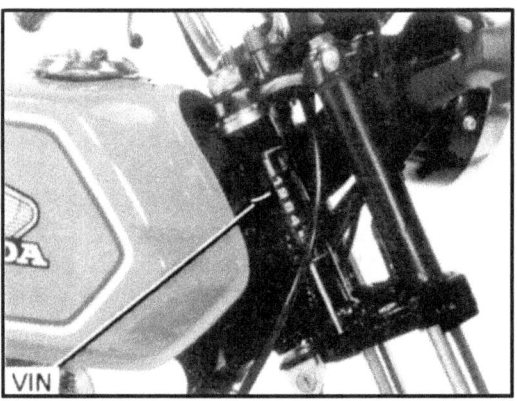

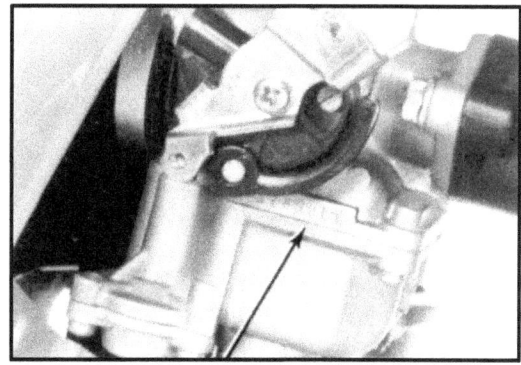

CARBURETOR IDENTIFICATION NUMBER

The vehicle identification number (VIN) is on the right side of the steering head.

The carburetor identification number is on the right side of the carburetor.

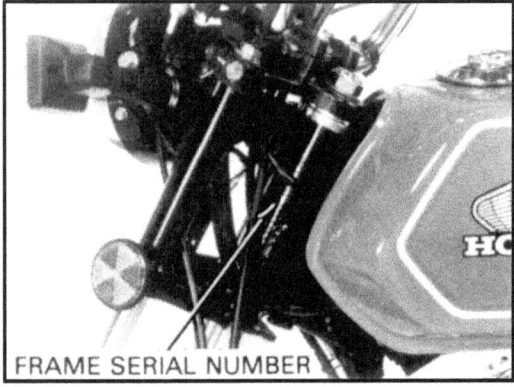

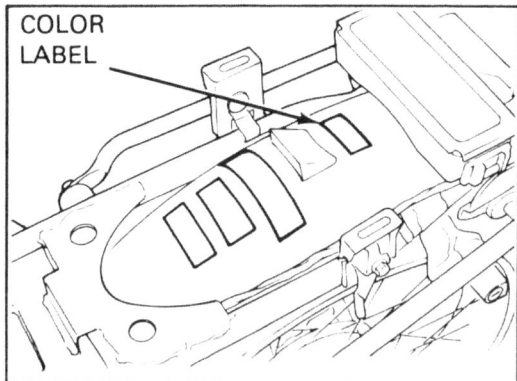

The frame serial number is stamped on the left side of the steering head.

The color label is attached to the rear fender, below the seat. When ordering a color coded part, always specify its designated color code.

1984 CB125S ADDENDUM

SPECIFICATIONS

DIMENSIONS		
	Overall length	1,935 mm (76.2 in)
	Overall width	745 mm (29.3 in)
	Overall height	1,050 mm (41.3 in)
	Wheel base	1,270 mm (50.0 in)
	Seat height	760 mm (29.9 in)
	Foot peg height	280 mm (11.0 in)
	Ground clearance	150 mm (5.9 in)
	Dry weight	99 kg (218.3 lb)
FRAME		
	Type	Diamond frame
	Front suspension, travel	Telescopic 115 mm (4.5 in)
	Rear suspension, travel	Swing arm 75 mm (2.9 in)
	Front tire size, pressure	2.75-18-42P, 1.75 kg/cm² (24 psi)
	Rear tire size, pressure	90/90-18-51P, 2.0 kg/cm² (28 psi)
	Front brake	Internal expanding shoes
	Rear brake	Internal expanding shoes
	Fuel capacity	12.5 liters (3.3 US gal, 2.75 Imp gal)
	Fuel reserve capacity	2.6 liters (0.69 US gal, 0.57 Imp gal)
	Caster	62°
	Trail	100 mm (3.9 in)
	Front fork oil capacity	85 cc (2.9 oz)
ENGINE		
	Type	Air cooled 4-stroke OHC
	Cylinder arrangement	Single cylinder inclined 15°
	Bore x stroke	56. x 49.5 mm (2.22 x 1.95 in)
	Displacement	124 cc (7.57 cu in)
	Compression ratio	9.2 : 1
	Valve train	Overhead camshaft, chain driven
	Maximum horsepower	14.5 BHP / 10,000 rpm
	Maximum torque	1.1 kg-m / 9,000 rpm
	Oil capacity	1.0 liter (1.1 US qt, 0.9 Imp qt)
	Lubrication system	Forced pressure and wet sump
	Air filtration system	Oiled polyurethane foam
	Cylinder compression	12.5 ± 1.5 kg/cm² (178 ± 21 psi)
	Intake valve OPEN	10° BTDC
	CLOSES	40° ABDC — at 1 mm lift
	Exhaust valve OPEN	40° BBDC
	CLOSES	10° ATDC
	Valve clearance (cold) Intake:	0.05 mm (0.002 in)
	Exhaust:	0.05 mm (0.002 in)
CARBURETOR		
	Type	Piston valve
	Main jet	# 105
	Pilot screw opening	Factory preset
	Float level	14 mm (0.55 in)
	Idle speed	1,400 ± 100 rpm

DRIVE TRAIN	Clutch	Wet multi-plate type	
	Transmission	5-speed constant mesh	
	Primary reduction	3.333: 1	
	Gear ratio I	2.769	
	Gear ratio II	1.882	
	Gear ratio III	1.400	
	Gear ratio IV	1.130	
	Gear ratio V	0.960	
	Final reduction	3.071	
	Gear shift pattern	Left foot operated return system	
ELECTRICAL	Ignition	C.D.I.	
	Ignition timing initial	$15° \pm 2°$ BTDC at $2{,}140 \pm 200$ rpm	
	Full advance	$35° \pm 2°$ BTDC at $3{,}740 \pm 200$ rpm	
	Alternator	110 W / 5,000 rpm	
	Battery capacity	12V 2.5 AH	
	Spark plug	For cold climate (Below 5°C, 41°F)	X22ESR-U ND DR7ES NGK
		Standard	X24ESR-U ND DR8ES NGK
		For extended high speed driving	X27ESR-U ND DR8ES NGK
	Spark plug gap	0.6—0.7 mm (0.024—0.028 in)	
	Headlight	12V 31.5/30 W	
	Tail/brake light	3 cp/32 cp (8W/27W)	
	Turn signal light	32 cp (23W)	
	Speedometer light	2 cp (3.4W)	
	Neutral indicator	2 cp (3.4W)	
	Turn signal indicator	2 cp (3.4W)	
	High beam indicator	2 cp (3.4W)	

STANDARDS / SERVICE LIMITS

	ITEM			STANDARD	SERVICE LIMIT
ENGINE	Camshaft	Cam lift	IN	31.783 mm (1.251 in)	30.8 mm (1.21 in)
			EX	31.386 mm (1.236 in)	30.4 mm (1.19 in)
		Runout		—	0.02 mm (0.0008 in)
		Bushing I.D.		20.005—20.026 mm (0.7876—0.7884 in)	20.05 mm (0.789 in)
		Journal O.D.		19.967—19.980 mm (0.7861—0.7866 in)	19.90 mm (0.783 in)
	Rocker arm		I.D.	12.000—12.018 mm (0.4724—0.4731 in)	12.05 mm (0.474 in)
	Rocker arm shaft		O.D.	11.977—11.995 mm (0.4715—0.4722 in)	11.93 mm (0.470 in)
	Valve spring	Free length	Outer	45.5 mm (1.79 in)	41.0 mm (1.61 in)
			Inner	39.4 mm (1.55 in)	35.5 mm (1.40 in)
	Valve clearance			0.05 ± 0.02 mm (0.002 ± 0.0008 in)	—
	Valve Guide	Stem O.D.	IN	5.450—5.465 mm (0.2146—0.2151 in)	5.42 mm (0.213 in)
			EX	5.430—5.445 mm (0.2138—0.2144 in)	5.40 mm (0.212 in)
		Guide I.D.	IN	5.475—5.485 mm (0.2155—0.2159 in)	5.50 mm (0.216 in)
			EX	5.475—5.485 mm (0.2155—0.2159 in)	5.50 mm (0.216 in)
		Stem-to-guide clearance	IN	0.010—0.035 mm (0.0004—0.0013 in)	0.08 mm (0.003 in)
			EX	0.030—0.055 mm (0.0011—0.0021 in)	0.10 mm (0.004 in)
		Valve seat width		1.2 mm (0.05 in)	1.5 mm (0.06 in)
	Cylinder	Cylinder I.D.		56.50—56.51 mm (2.224—2.225 in)	56.60 (2.228 in)
		Taper		—	0.1 mm (0.004 in)
		Out of round		—	0.1 mm (0.004 in)
		Warpage across top		—	0.1 mm (0.004 in)
	Piston, piston rings and piston pin	Piston O.D. at skirt		56.45—56.48 mm (2.222—2.223 in)	56.35 mm (2.218 in)
		Piston pin bore		15.002—15.008 mm (0.5906—0.5908 in)	15.04 mm (0.592 in)
		Piston ring end gap	Top/second	0.1—0.25 mm (0.004—0.010 in)	0.5 mm (0.02 in)
			Oil (Side rail)	0.2—0.5 mm (0.008—0.020 in)	—
		Piston ring-to-ring groove clearance	Top	0.010—0.040 mm (0.0004—0.0015 in)	0.13 mm (0.005 in)
			Second	0.015—0.045 mm (0.0006—0.0018 in)	0.12 mm (0.0047 in)
		Cylinder-to-piston clearance		0.029—0.060 mm (0.0011—0.0023 in)	0.1 mm (0.004 in)
		Piston pin O.D.		14.994—15.000 mm (0.5903—0.5905 in)	14.96 mm (0.589 in)

		ITEM	STANDARD	SERVICE LIMIT
ENGINE (cont'd)	Clutch	Lever free play	10—20 mm (0.4—0.8 in)	—
		Spring free length	35.50 mm (1.40 in)	34.20 mm (1.35 in)
		Disc thickness	2.40—3.00 mm (0.094—0.118 in)	2.00 mm (0.08 in)
		Plate warpage	—	0.20 mm (0.008 in)
	Oil pump	Tip clearance	0.15 mm (0.006 in)	0.20 mm (0.008 in)
		Rotor-to-body clearance	0.30—0.36 mm (0.012—0.014 in)	0.40 mm (0.016 in)
		End clearance	0.15—0.20 mm (0.006—0.008 in)	0.25 mm (0.010 in)
	Gearshift fork	I.D.	12.000—12.018 mm (0.4724—0.4731 in)	12.05 mm (0.474 in)
		Pawl thickness	4.93—5.00 mm (0.194—0.197 in)	4.50 mm (0.177 in)
	Shift fork shaft	O.D.	11.976—11.994 mm (0.4715—0.4722 in)	11.96 mm (0.471 in)
		Runout	—	0.1 mm (0.004 in)
	Crankshaft	Connecting rod small end I.D.	15.010—15.028 mm (0.5909—0.5916 in)	15.08 mm (0.594 in)
		Connecting rod big end side clearance — Axial	0.05—0.30 mm (0.002—0.012 in)	0.6 mm (0.024 in)
		Connecting rod big end side clearance — Radial	0—0.008 mm (0—0.0003 in)	0.05 mm (0.002 in)
	Kick starter	Spindle O.D.	19.959—19.980 mm (0.7858—0.7866 in)	19.90 mm (0.783 in)
		Pinion I.D.	20.000—20.021 mm (0.7874—0.7882 in)	20.05 mm (0.789 in)
FRAME	Axle shaft runout		—	0.2 mm (0.008 in)
	Wheel rim runout	Radial	—	2.0 mm (0.08 in)
		Axial	—	2.0 mm (0.08 in)
	Brake lining thickness		3.9—4.0 mm (0.153—0.157 in)	2.0 mm (0.08 in)
	Front brake drum I.D.		130.0 mm (5.12 in)	131.0 mm (5.16 in)
	Rear brake drum I.D.		110.0 mm (4.33 in)	111.0 mm (4.37 in)
	Front fork	Spring free length	457.0 mm (17.99 in)	447.8 mm (17.63 in)
		Tube O.D.	26.937—26.960 mm (1.0605—1.0614 in)	26.90 mm (1.059 in)
		Tube runout	—	0.2 mm (0.008 in)
	Rear shock absorber spring free length		197.7 mm (7.78 in)	192.0 mm (7.56 in)

TORQUE VALUES

ENGINE

Tightening Point	Quantity	Thread dia. (mm)	Tightening Torque	
			kg-m	ft-lb
Cylinder head	4	8	2.8—3.0	20—22
Cam chain tensioner pivot bolt	1	8	0.8—1.2	6—9
Flywheel	1	8	4.0—4.6	29—33
Clutch outer	1	16	4.0—5.0	29—36
Oil filter rotor	1	16	4.0—5.0	29—36
Oil filter rotor screen cap	1	36	1.0—2.0	7—14

FRAME

Tightening Point	Quantity	Thread dia. (mm)	Tightening Torque	
			kg-m	ft-lb
Steering stem nut	1	22	6.0—9.0	43—65
Front fork top bridge	2	7	1.2—1.3	9—10
Handlebar holder	4	6	0.9—1.1	7—8
Front fork bottom bridge	2	8	2.0—2.5	14—18
Front axle nut	1	12	4.0—5.0	29—36
Engine mount bolt	10	8	2.0—2.5	14—18
Rear axle nut	1	14	4.0—5.0	29—36
Final driven sprocket	4	10	5.5—6.5	40—47
Rear brake torque link	2	8	1.0—2.0	7—14
Rear shock absorber	4	10	3.0—4.0	22—29
Foot peg	4	8	1.5—2.0	11—14
Gearshift pedal	1	6	0.8—1.2	6—9
Kickstarter pedal	1	6	0.8—1.2	6—9
Seat band	2	6	0.8—1.2	6—9

Torque specifications listed above are for the most important tightening points. If a torque specification is not listed, follow the standards given below.

STANDARD TORQUE VALUES

Type	Torque kg-m (ft-lb)	Type	Torque kg-m (ft-lb)
5 mm bolt, nut	0.45—0.6 (3.3—4.3)	5 mm screw	0.35—0.5 (2.5—3.6)
6 mm bolt, nut	0.8—1.2 (6—9)	6 mm screw	0.7—1.1 (5—8)
8 mm bolt, nut	1.8—2.5 (13—18)	6 mm flange bolt, nut	1.0—1.4 (7—10)
10 mm bolt, nut	3.0—4.0 (22—29)	8 mm flange bolt, nut	2.4—3.0 (17—22)
12 mm bolt, nut	5.0—6.0 (36—43)	10 mm flange bolt, nut	3.0—4.0 (22—29)

1984 CB125S ADDENDUM

TOOLS

SPECIAL

DESCRIPTION	TOOL NUMBER	ALTERNATE TOOL	TOOL NUMBER
Universal bearing puller	07631—0010000	Equivalent tool commercially available in U.S.A.	
Hex head wrench, 6 mm	07917—3230000	Equivalent tool commercially available in U.S.A.	
Clutch center holder	07923—9580000	Clutch outer holder	07923—1070001
Flywheel puller	07933—KG20000	Rotor puller	07933—2000000
Bearing remover set, 15 mm	07936—KC10000	Bearing remover, 15 mm	07936—KC10500 (USA only)
Remover weight	07936—3710200	Remover weight	07741—0010201
Remover handle	07936—3710100		
Ball race remover	07944—1150001	Bearing remover	M9360—277—91774
Bearing driver	07946—GC40000	Not available in U.S.A.	
Valve guide reamer, 5.47 mm	07984—0980000		
Shock absorber compressor	07959—3290001		
Shock absorber spring compressor attachment	07967—1150100		
Kowa digital multimeter (U.S.A. only)	KS-AHM-32-003	Sanwa electrical tester	07308—0020000

COMMON

DESCRIPTION	TOOL NUMBER	ALTERNATE TOOL	TOOL NUMBER
Float level gauge	07401—0010000		
Spoke wrench 5.8 x 6.1 mm	07701—0020300	Equivalent tool commercially available in U.S.A.	
Pin spanner	07702—0020000	Pin spanner	M9361—412—099788
Valve adjustment wrench	07708—0030200	Equivalent tool commercially available in U.S.A.	
Adjustment wrench B	07708—0030400	Valve adjuster	89201—200—000
Lock nut wrench	07716—0020100		
Extension bar	07716—0020500	Equivalent tool commercially available in U.S.A.	
Universal holder	07725—0040000		
Universal holder	07725—0030000		
Valve guide driver, 5.5 mm	07742—0010100		
Attachment, 32 x 35 mm	07746—0010100		
Pilot, 15 mm	07746—0040300		
Attachment, 42 x 47 mm	07746—0010300		
Pilot, 20 mm	07746—0040500		
Attachment, 37 x 40 mm	07746—0010200		
Pilot, 12 mm	07746—0040200		
Attachment, 52 x 55 mm	07746—0010400		
Pilot, 30 mm	07746—0040700		
Driver	07749—0010000		
Driver	07746—0020100		
Driver	07746—0020300		
Driver, 40 mm I.D.	07746—0030100		
Attachment, 30 mm I.D.	07746—0030300		
Fork seal driver body	07747—0010100	Fork seal driver	07947—1180001
Fork seal driver attachment	07747—0010300		
Valve spring compressor	07757—0010000		
Bearing remover shaft	07746—0050100		
Remover head, 12 mm	07746—0050300	Equivalent tools commercially available in U.S.A.	
Remover head, 15 mm	07746—0050400		
Valve guide driver	07742—0020200		

CABLE & HARNESS ROUTING

Note the following when routing cables and wire harnesses:

- A loose wire, harness or cable can be a safety hazard. After clamping, check each wire to be sure it is secure.
- Do not squeeze wires against the weld or end of its clamp when a weld-on clamp is used.
- Secure wires and wire harnesses to the frame with their respective wire bands at the designated locations. Tighten the bands so that only the insulated surfaces contact the wires or wire harnesses.
- Route harnesses so they are not pulled taut or have excessive slack.
- Route wire harnesses to avoid sharp edges or corners and the projected ends of bolts and screws.
- Protect wires and harnesses with electrical tape or tubes if they contact a sharp edge or corner. Clean the attaching surface thoroughly before applying tape.
- Do not use a wire or harness with a broken insulator. Repair by wrapping them with protective tape or replace them.
- Keep wire harnesses away from the exhaust pipes and other parts that get hot.
- Be sure grommets are seated in their grooves properly.
- After clamping, check each harness to be certain that it is not interferring with any moving or sliding parts.
- Wire harnesses routed along the handlebars should not be pulled taut, have excessive slack, be pinched, or interfere with adjacent or surrounding parts in all steering positions.
- After routing, check that the wire harnesses are not twisted or kinked.

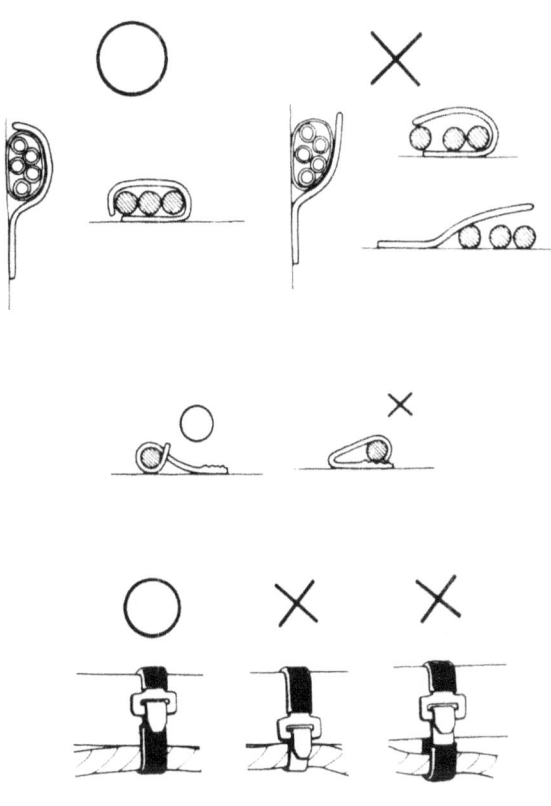

O: CORRECT
X: INCORRECT

1984 CB125S ADDENDUM

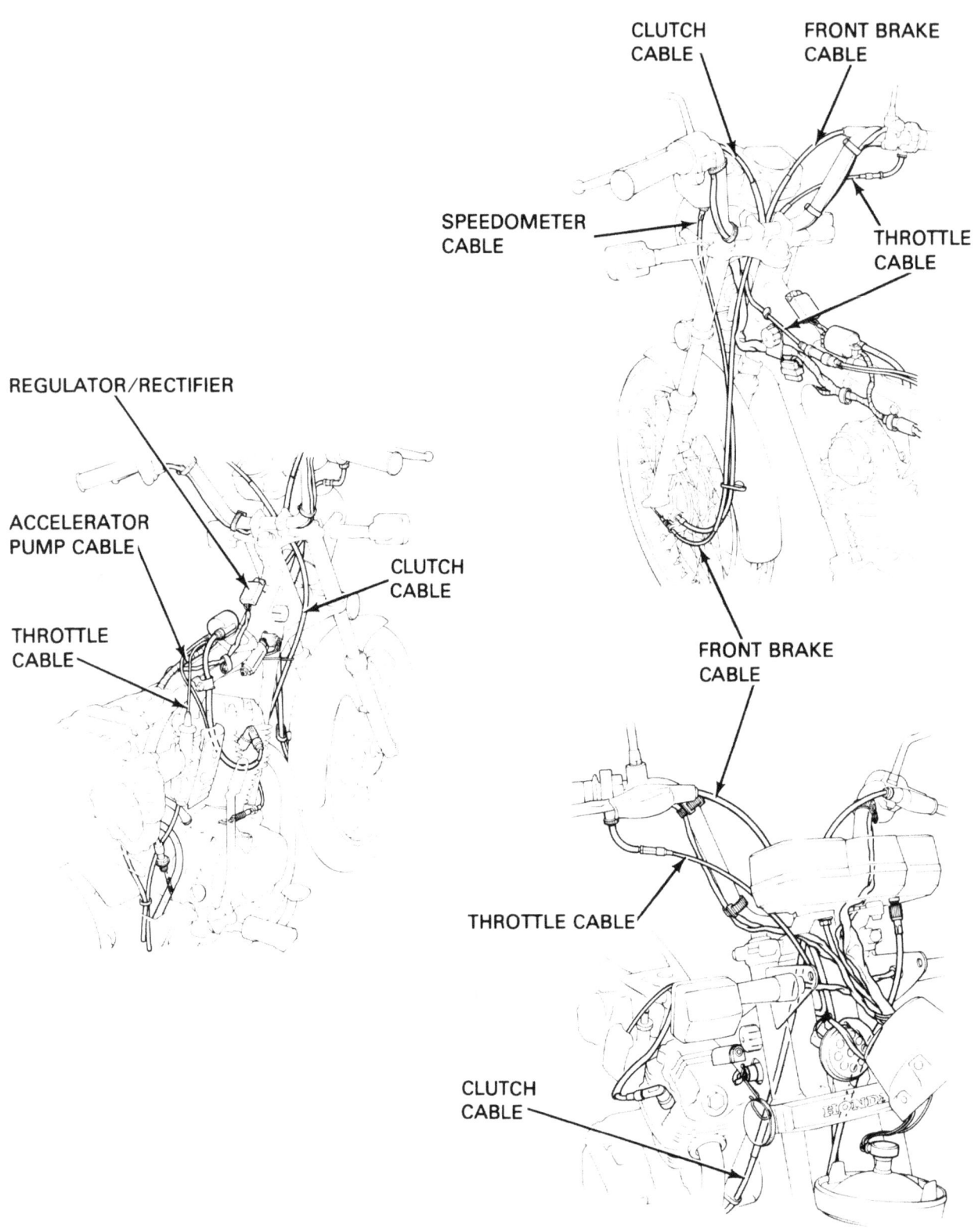

1984 CB125S ADDENDUM

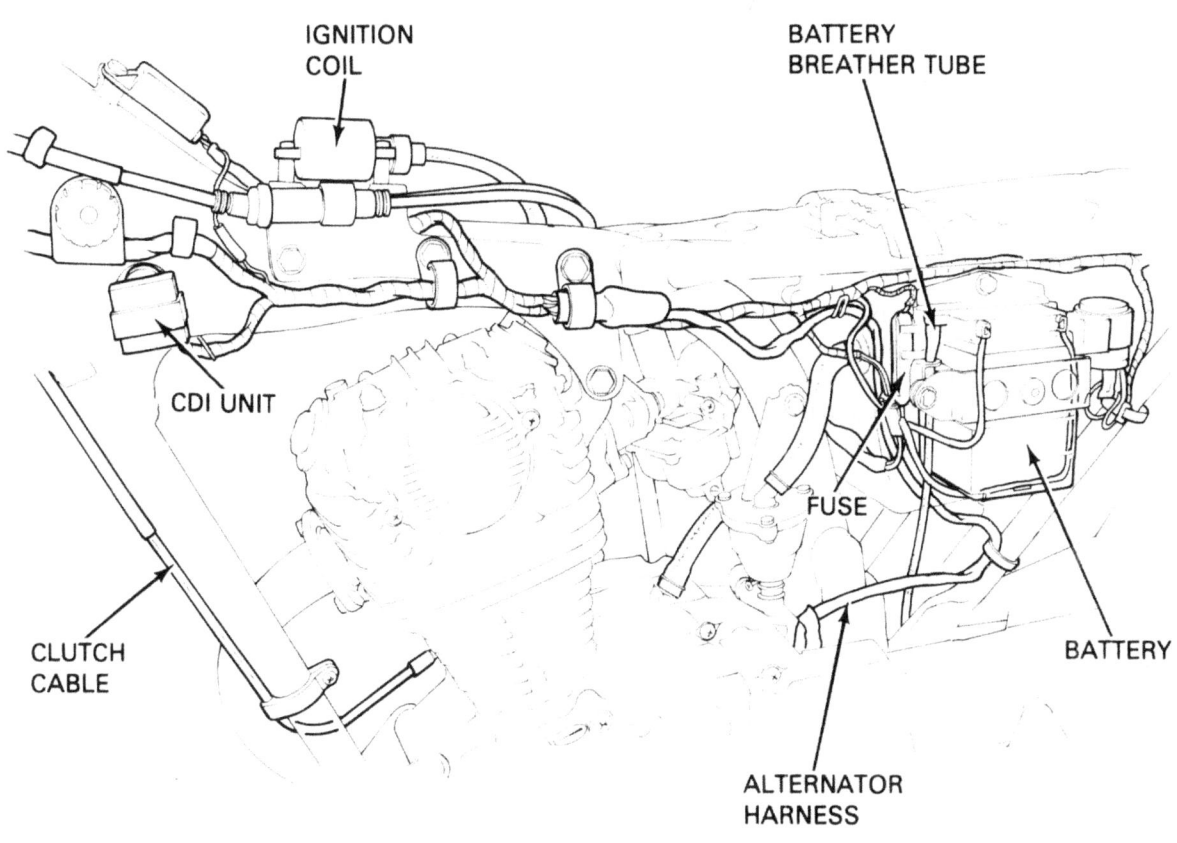

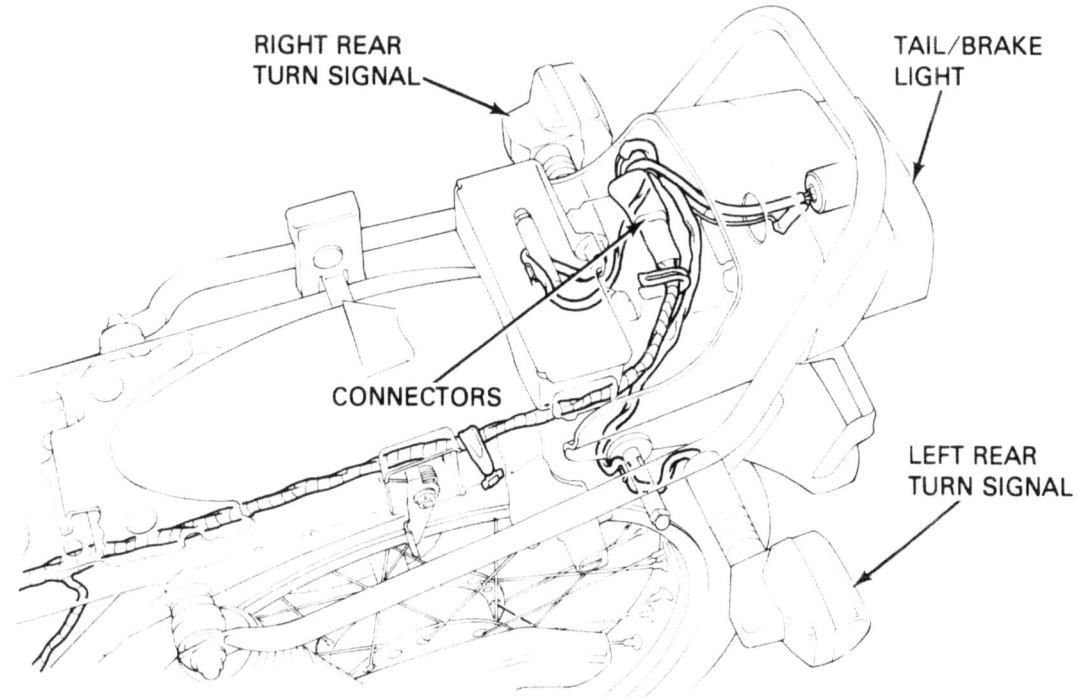

1984 CB125S ADDENDUM

EMISSION CONTROL SYSTEMS

The U.S. Environmental Protection Agency and California Air Resources Board (CARB) require manufacturers to certify that their motorcycles comply with applicable exhaust emissions standards during their useful life, when operated and maintained according to the instructions provided, and that motorcycles built after January 1, 1983 comply with applicable noise emission standards for one year or 2,000 km (3,730 miles) after the time of sale to the ultimate purchaser, when operated and maintained according to the instructions provided. Compliance with the terms of the Distributor's Warranties for Honda Motorcycle Emission Control Systems is necessary in order to keep the emission warranty in effect.

SOURCE OF EMISSIONS

The combustion process produces carbon monoxide and hydrocarbons. Control of hydrocarbons is very important because, under certain conditions, they react to form photochemical smog when subjected to sunlight. Carbon monoxide does not react the same way, but it is toxic.

Honda Motor Co., Ltd. utilizes lean carburetor settings as well as other systems to reduce carbon monoxide and hydrocarbons.

EVAPORATIVE EMISSION SYSTEM (California model only)

The CB125S complies with the California Air Resources Board (CARB) requirements for evaporative emissions regulations.

Fuel vapor from the fuel tank is directed into the charcoal canister where it is adsorbed and stored while the engine is stopped. When the engine is running, fuel vapor in the charcoal canister is drawn into the engine through the air cleaner and carburetor.

NOISE EMISSION CONTROL SYSTEM

TAMPERING WITH THE NOISE CONTROL SYSTEM IS PROHIBITED: Federal law prohibits the following acts or the causing thereof: (1) The removal or rendering inoperative by any person, other than for purposes of maintenance, repair or replacement, of any device or element of design incorporated into any new vehicle for the purpose of noise control prior to its sale or delivery to the ultimate purchaser or while it is in use; or (2) the use of the vehicle after such device or element of design has been removed or rendered inoperative by any person.

AMONG THOSE ACTS PRESUMED TO CONSTITUTE TAMPERING ARE THE ACTS LISTED BELOW:

1. Removal of, or puncturing the muffler, baffles, header pipes or any other component which conducts exhaust gases.

2. Removal of, or puncturing of any part of the intake system.

3. Lack of proper maintenance.

4. Replacing any moving parts of the vehicle, or parts of the exhaust or intake system, with parts other than those specified by the manufacturer.

1984 CB125S ADDENDUM

VEHICLE EMISSION CONTROL INFORMATION LABEL

The Vehicle Emission Control Information label is on the rear fender underneath the seat.

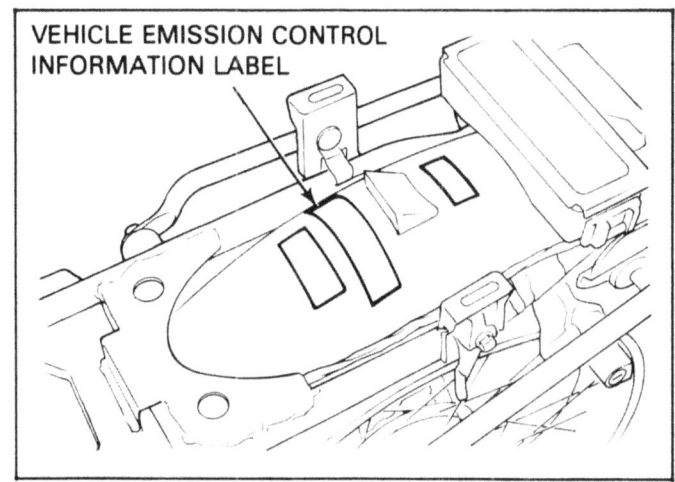

VACUUM HOSE ROUTING DIAGRAM LABEL (California model only)

A Vacuum Hose Routing Diagram label is on the rear fender underneath the seat.

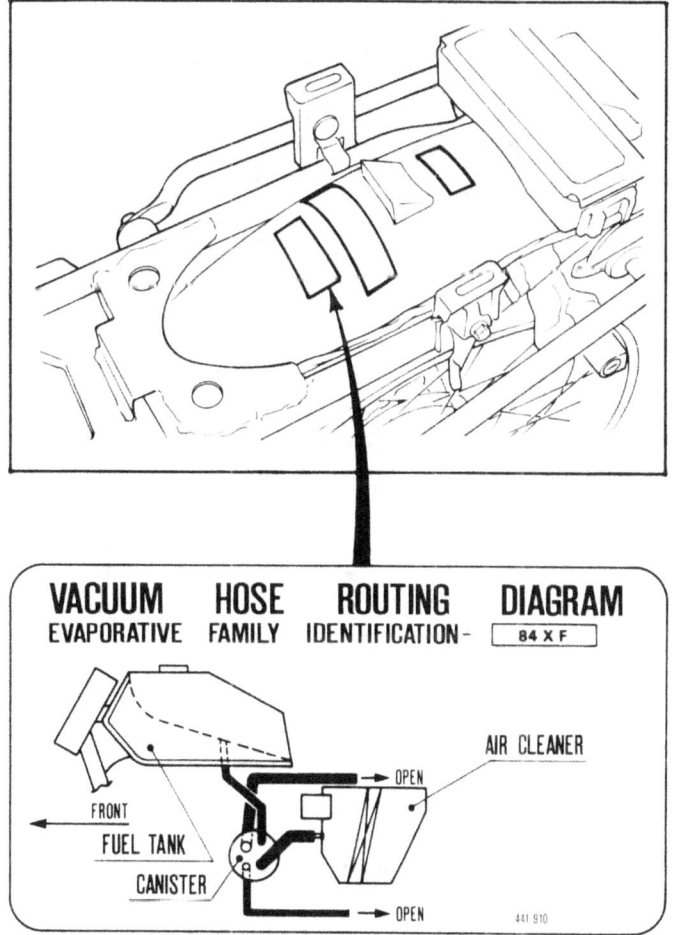

LUBRICATION

LUBRICATION POINTS

Use general purpose grease when not otherwise specified here. Apply oil or grease to sliding surfaces not shown here.

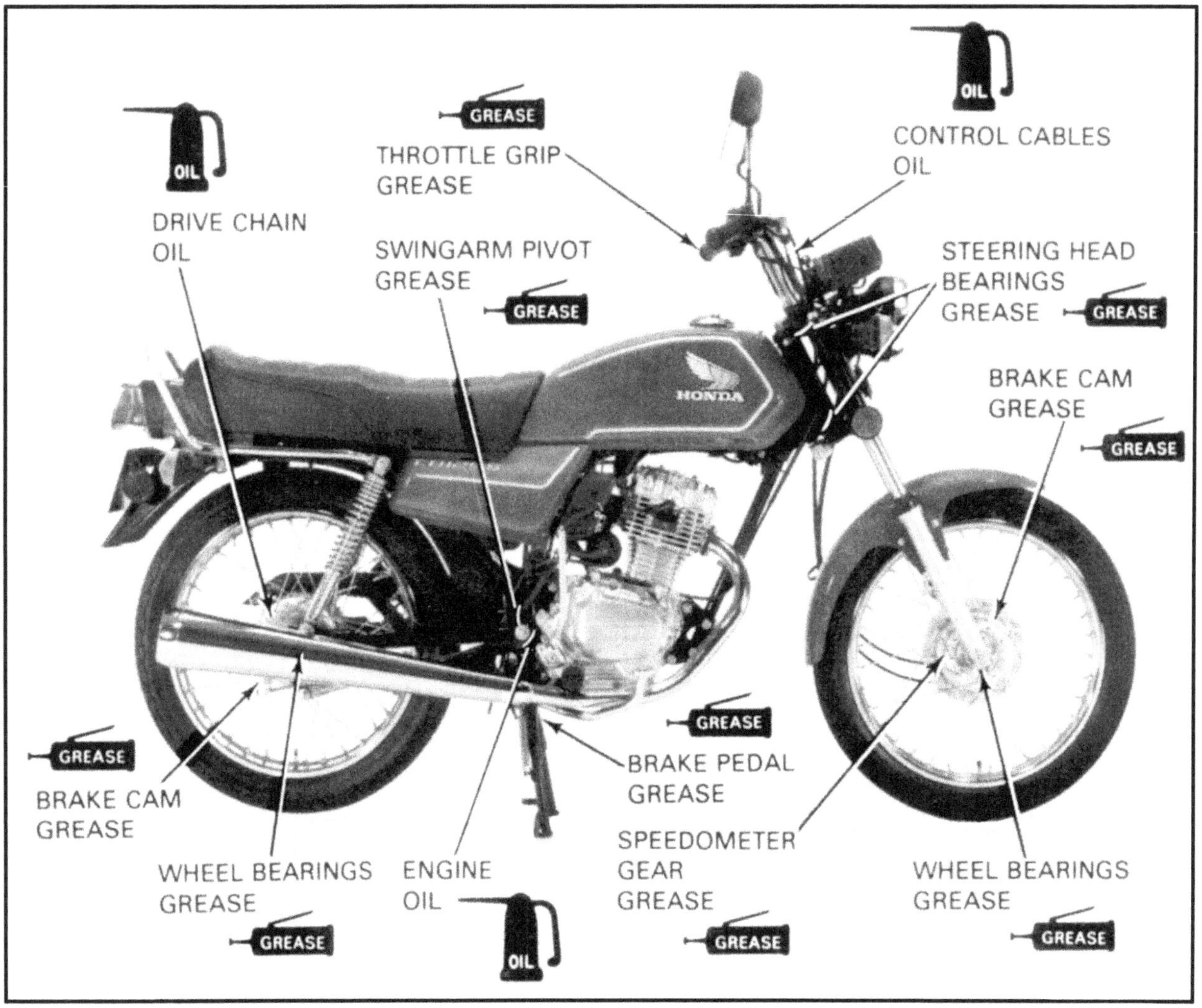

ENGINE OIL RECOMMENDATION

Use Honda 4-Stroke Oil or equivalent API Service Classification: SE or SF VISCOSITY: SAE 10W-40.
Other viscosities shown in the chart may be used when the average temperature in your riding area is within the indicated range.

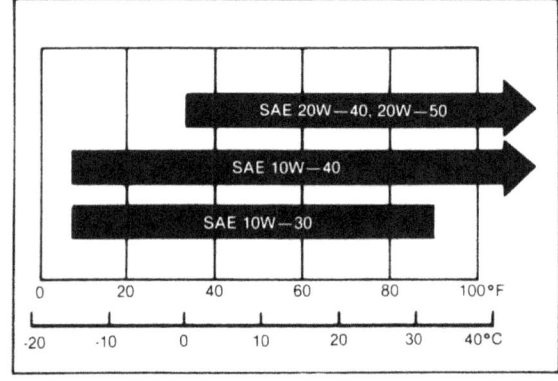

OIL CAPACITY
1.0 liters (1.1 U.S. qt, 0.9 Imp. qt)

1984 CB125S ADDENDUM

MAINTENANCE SCHEDULE

Perform the PRE-RIDE INSPECTION in the Owner's Manual at each scheduled maintenance period.
I: INSPECT AND CLEAN, ADJUST, LUBRICATE, OR REPLACE IF NECESSARY
C: CLEAN   A: ADJUST   R: REPLACE   L: LUBRICATE

	ITEM	FREQUENCY — WHICHEVER COMES FIRST / EVERY	600 mi (1,000 km)	2,500 mi (4,000 km)	5,000 mi (8,000 km)	7,500 mi (12,000 km)	Refer to page
EMISSION RELATED ITEMS	* FUEL LINES			I	I	I	148
	* FUEL STRAINER		C	C	C	C	220
	* THROTTLE OPERATION		I	I	I	I	152
	* CARBURETOR-CHOKE			I	I	I	181
	AIR CLEANER	NOTE 1		C	C	C	241
	CRANKCASE BREATHER	NOTE 2		C	C	C	147
	SPARK PLUG			R	R	R	221
	* VALVE CLEARANCE		I	I	I	I	240
	ENGINE OIL	YEAR R	R	REPLACE EVERY 1,250 mi (2,000 km)			193, 238
	ENGINE OIL FILTER SCREEN		CLEAN EVERY 1,250 mi (2,000 km)				193
	* ENGINE OIL FILTER ROTOR				C		146
	* CAM CHAIN TENSION		A	A	A	A	152
	* CARBURETOR-IDLE SPEED		I	I	I	I	242
	* EVAPORATIVE EMISSION CONTROL SYSTEM	NOTE 3				I	240, 248
NON-EMISSION RELATED ITEMS	DRIVE CHAIN		I, L EVERY 300 mi (500 km)				153
	BATTERY	MONTH I	I	I	I	I	155, 251
	BRAKE SHOE WEAR			I	I	I	156
	BRAKE SYSTEM		I	I	I	I	156, 158
	* BRAKE LIGHT SWITCH		I	I	I	I	158
	* HEADLIGHT AIM		I	I	I	I	159
	CLUTCH		I	I	I	I	159
	SIDE STAND			I	I	I	160
	* SUSPENSION		I	I	I	I	161, 168
	* NUTS, BOLTS, FASTENERS		I	I	I	I	161
	** WHEELS / SPOKES		I	I	I	I	242
	** STEERING HEAD BEARINGS		I			I	162

* SHOULD BE SERVICED BY AN AUTHORIZED HONDA DEALER, UNLESS THE OWNER HAS PROPER TOOLS AND SERVICE DATA AND IS MECHANICALLY QUALIFIED.
** IN THE INTEREST OF SAFETY, WE RECOMMEND THESE ITEMS BE SERVICED ONLY BY AN AUTHORIZED HONDA DEALER.

NOTES:
1. SERVICE MORE FREQUENTLY WHEN RIDING IN DUSTY AREAS.
2. SERVICE MORE FREQUENTLY WHEN RIDING IN RAIN, OR AT FULL THROTTLE.
3. CALIFORNIA TYPE ONLY.
4. FOR HIGHER ODOMETER READINGS, REPEAT AT THE FREQUENCY INTERVAL ESTABLISHED HERE.

INSPECTION & ADJUSTMENT

EVAPORATIVE EMISSION CONTROL SYSTEM (CALIFORNIA ONLY)

Check the vacuum hoses for clogging, deterioration or damage and replace if necessary.

VALVE CLEARANCE

NOTE:

> Inspect and adjust valve clearance while the engine is cold (below 35°C / 95°F).

Remove the crankshaft hole cap and timing hole cap.

Remove the valve adjuster covers.

Rotate the crankshaft counterclockwise and align the "T" mark on the alternator rotor with the index mark on the left crankcase cover. The piston must be a T.D.C. (Top Dead Center) of the compression stroke.

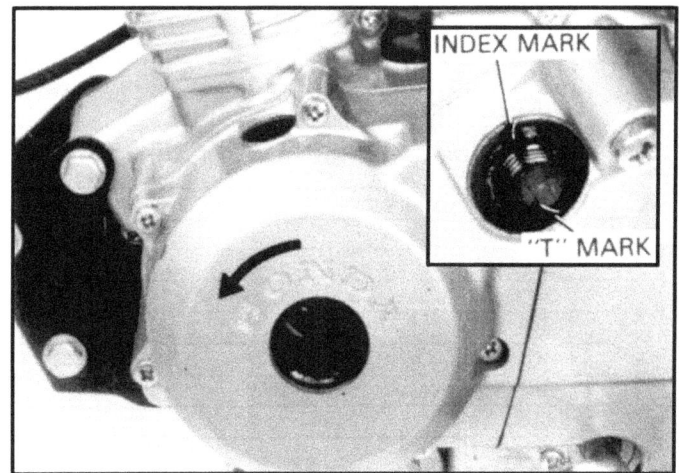

Inspect the intake and exhaust valve clearances by inserting a feeler gauge between the adjusting screw and valve stem.

VALVE CLEARANCES (COLD)
INTAKE: 0.05 mm (0.002 in)
EXHAUST: 0.05 mm (0.002 in)

Adjust by loosening the lock nut and turning the adjusting screw until there is a slight drag on the feeler gauge.

Hold the adjusting screw and tighten the lock nut.

Recheck the valve clearance.

Install the valve adjuster covers.

Install the timing hole cap and crankshaft hole cap.

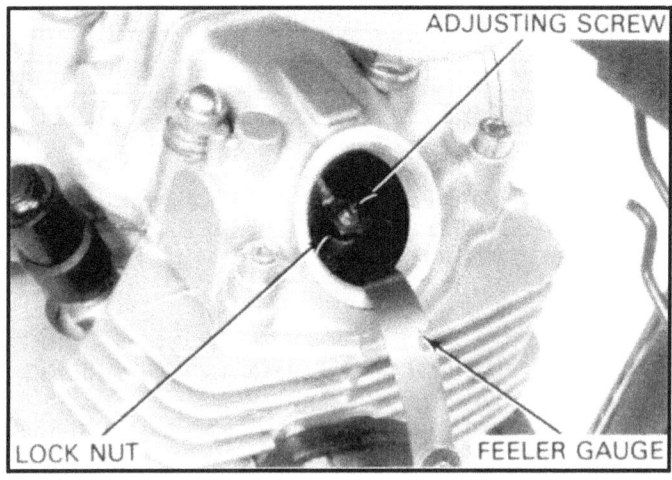

AIR CLEANER

Remove the right side cover using the ignition key to unlock it.

Remove the six air cleaner cover screws and the cover.

Slide the air cleaner element out of the air cleaner case.

Remove the air cleaner holder.

Wash the air cleaner element in non-flammable or high flash point solvent and let it dry.

WARNING

Never use gasoline or low flash point solvents for washing the air cleaner element. A fire or explosion could result.

Soak the element in clean gear oil (SAE 80-90) and squeeze out the excess.

Install the air cleaner in the reverse order of removal.

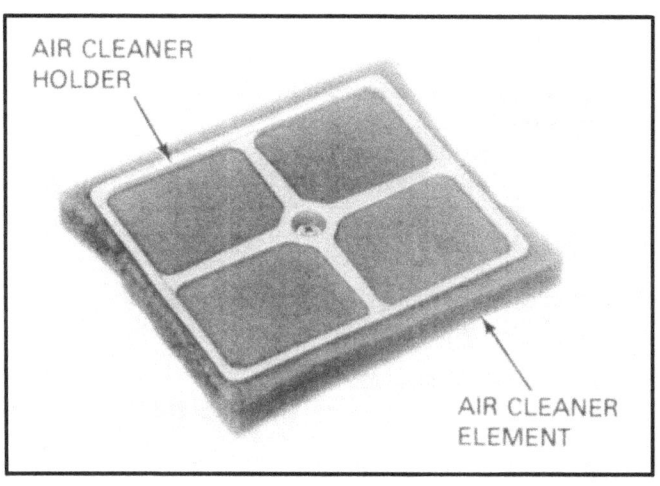

CARBURETOR IDLE SPEED

NOTES:
- Inspect and adjust idle speed after all other engine adjustments are within specifications.
- The engine must be warm for accurate adjustment. Ten minutes of stop-and-go riding is sufficient.

Warm up the engine, shift to NEUTRAL, and place the motorcycle on its center stand. Turn the throttle stop screw as required to obtain the specified idle speed.

IDLE SPEED: 1,400 ± 100 rpm

WHEELS/SPOKES

TIRE PRESSURE

NOTE:
Tire pressure should be checked when the tires are COLD.

Cold tire pressures kg/cm² (psi)	Up to 90 kg (200 lbs) load	Front: 1.75 (24) Rear: 2.0 (28)
	Up to vehicle capacity load	Front: 1.75 (24) Rear: 2.25 (32)
Vehicle capacity load limit	150 kg (330 lbs)	
Tire size	Front: 2.75—18—42P Rear: 90/90—18—51P	

WARNING

Replace tires when tread depth becomes less than:
Front: 1.5 mm (1/6 in)
Rear: 2.0 mm (3/32 in)

SPOKES

Periodically tighten the wheel spokes and check front and rear wheel trueness.

SPOKE NIPPLE TORQUE
Front: 0.15—0.35 kg-m (1.1—2.5 ft-lb)

Rear: 0.15—0.30 kg-m (1.1—2.2 ft-lb)

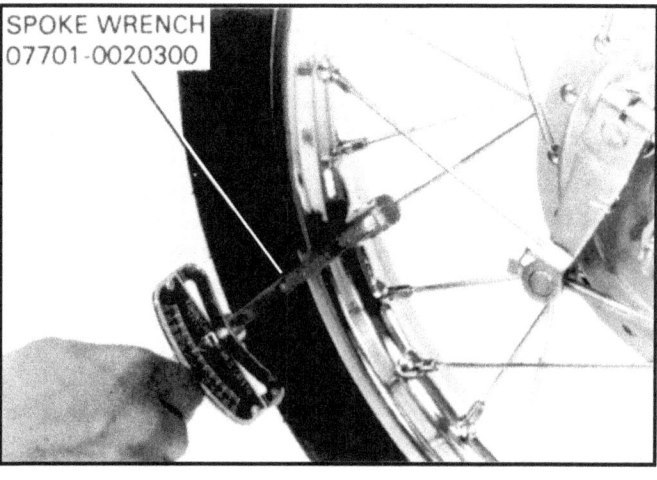

FUEL SYSTEM

SERVICE INFORMATION

WARNING

Gasoline is extremely flammable and is explosive under certain conditions. Do not smoke or allow flames or sparks in your working area. Always work in a well ventilated area.

NOTES:
- When disassembling fuel system parts, note the location of O-rings. Replace them with new ones during reassembly.
- The carburetor has a drain plug that can be loosened to drain residual fuel in the float bowl.

Carburetor	Piston valve type
Identification number	PD17F
Venturi diameter	24 mm (0.9 in)
Main jet	#105
Float level	14 mm (0.55 in)
Pilot screw initial opening	1-3/4 turns
Idle speed	1,400 ± 100 rpm

CARBURETOR REMOVAL/INSTALLATION

Turn the fuel valve OFF and disconnect the fuel line.

Remove left and right side covers, seat and fuel tank.

Loosen the carburetor drain plug and drain the fuel into a suitable container.

WARNING

Wipe up spilled gasoline at once.

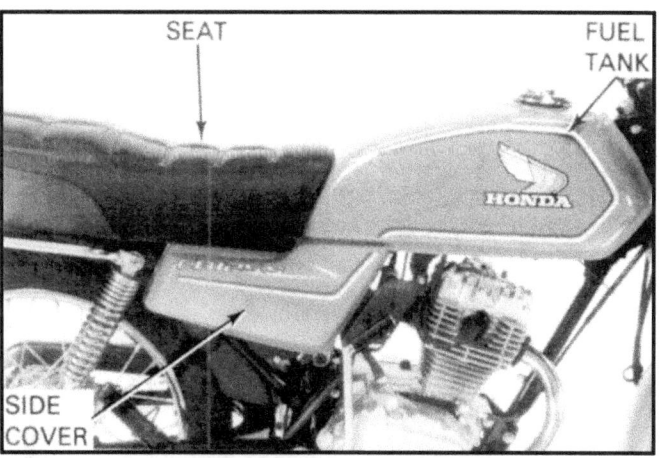

Remove the carburetor cover.

Loosen the screw securing the carburetor clamp and then remove the two carburetor mounting nuts.

Remove the accelerator pump cable.

Unscrew the carburetor top and remove the throttle valve.

Remove the carburetor.

Install the carburetor in the reverse order of removal.

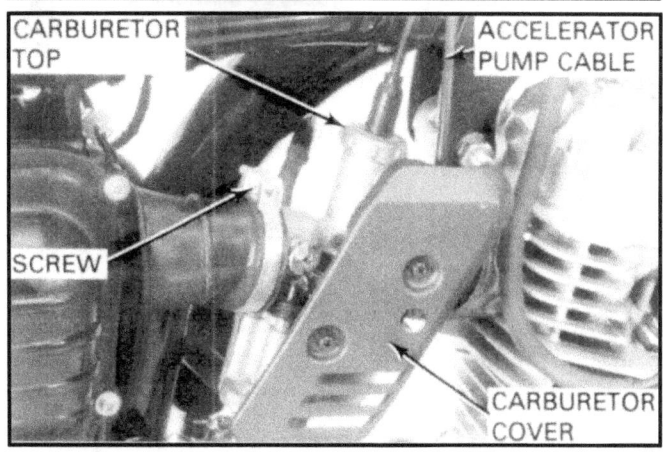

FLOAT LEVEL

Measure the float level with a float level gauge.

FLOAT LEVEL:
  14.0 ± 1.0 mm (0.55 ± 0.04 in)

If the float level is not within specification, replace the float with a new one.

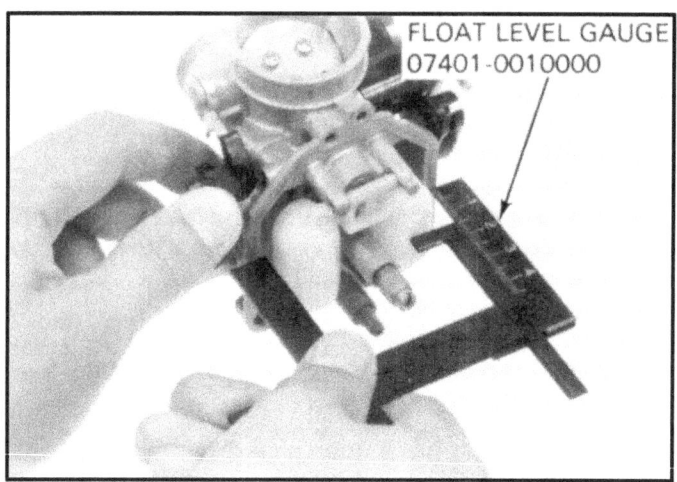

ACCELERATOR PUMP DISASSEMBLY / INSPECTION

Remove the three screws, accelerator pump cover and spring.

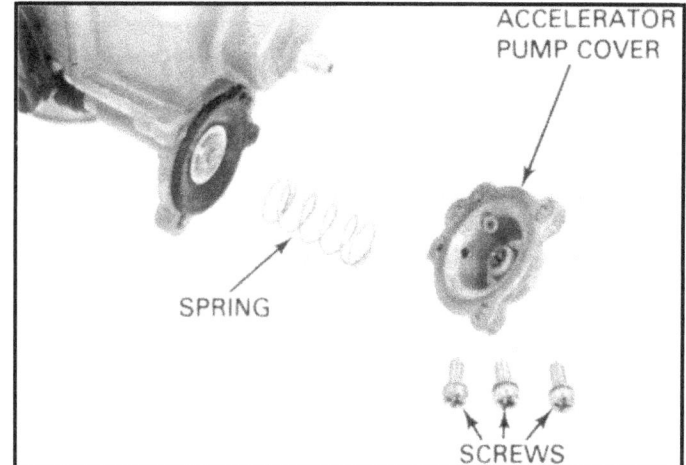

Remove the diaphragm assembly.

Inspect the diaphragm for cracks or brittleness and make sure the rod is not bent.

Replace the diaphragm assembly if necessary.

Assemble the removed parts in the reverse order of disassembly.

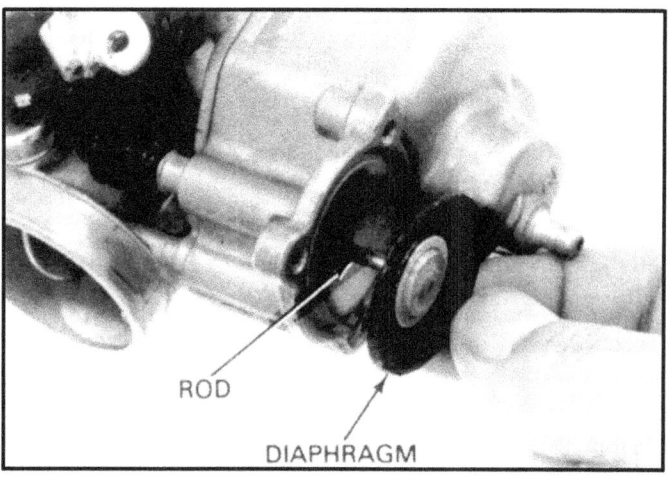

Loosen the lock nut and turn the adjuster screw counterclockwise until there is clearance between the adjuster and the cam on the pump arm.

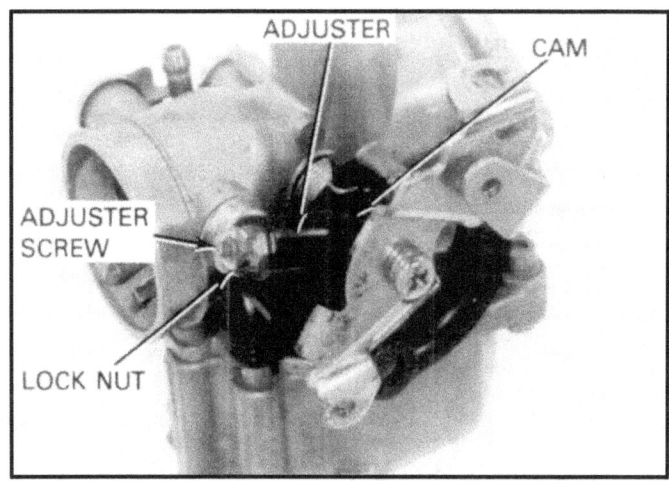

Disassemble the accelerator pump linkage by removing the screw, set plate, pump arm, spring, collar, adjuster and dust seals.

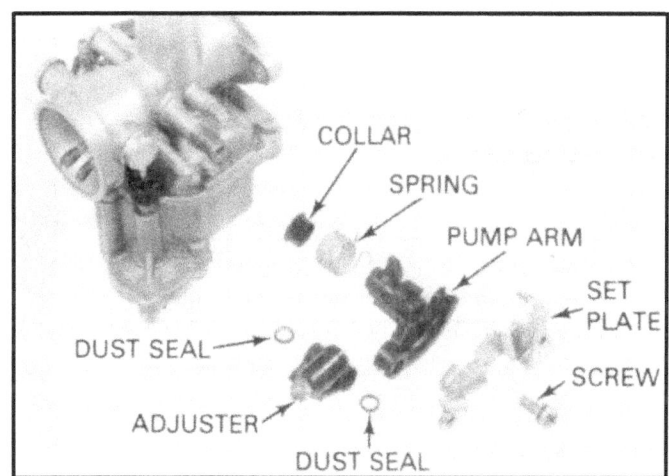

Inspect the cam on the pump arm for wear.

If it is worn excessively, replace the pump arm with a new one.

Assemble the removed parts in the reverse order of disassembly.

NOTE:

Coat the sliding surfaces of the pump arm and adjuster with molybdenum grease.

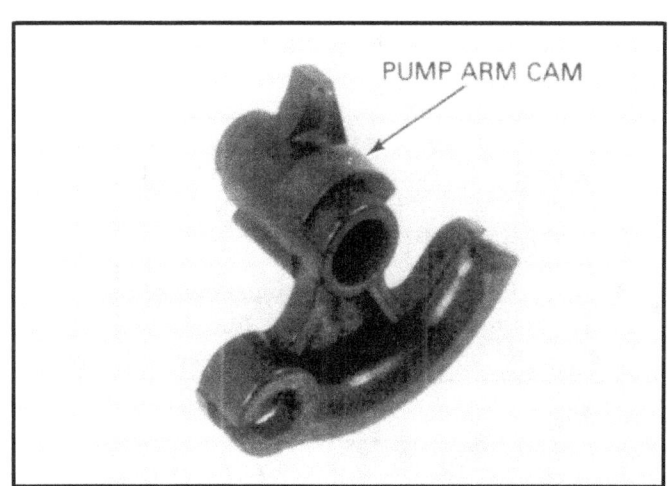

ACCELERATOR PUMP LINKAGE ADJUSTMENT

NOTE:

> The accelerator pump is factory pre-set and no adjustment is necessary unless the linkage has been disassembled.

Loosen the adjuster lock nut.

Make sure there is a small amount of clearance between the adjuster and the pump arm cam (A) and a small amount of clearance between the adjuster tab and the pump rod (B).

Turn the adjuster screw counterclockwise to provide clearance if necessary.

Turn the adjuster screw clockwise until the adjuster just contacts the pump arm cam (A) and the pump rod (B). From this position turn the adjuster screw clockwise 1-1/2 turns and then tighten the lock nut.

ACCELERATOR PUMP CABLE ADJUSTMENT

NOTE:

> Adjust throttle grip free play (page 152) before adjusting accelerator pump cable.

Turn the throttle grip to the fully open position and check that the index marks on the pump arm and set plate align. If the index marks do not align, adjust the cable by loosening the lock nut and turning the adjuster. Tighten the lock nut.

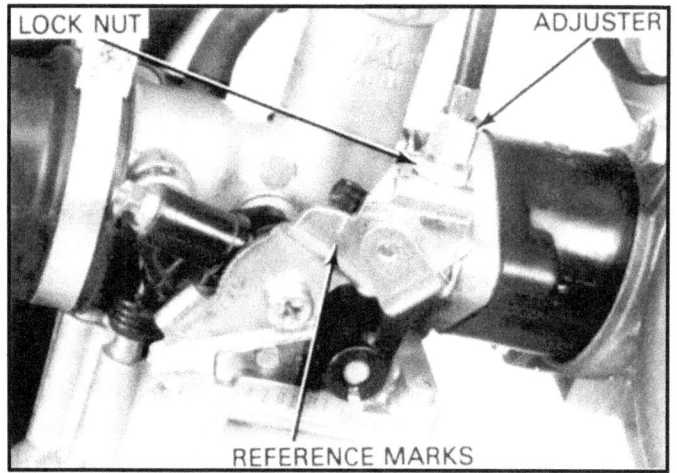

PILOT SCREW ADJUSTMENT

IDLE DROP PROCEDURE (U.S.A. ONLY)

NOTES:

- The pilot screw is factory preset and no adjustment is necessary unless the pilot screw is replaced (see removal, page 183).
- A limiter cap restricts adjustment to 7/8 of a turn.
- Use a tachometer with graduations of 100 rpm or smaller and that will accurately indicate a 100 rpm change.

CAUTION:

> *Any forcible attempt to remove the pilot screw limiter cap will cause screw breakage.*

1. Turn the pilot screw clockwise until it seats lightly and back it out to the specification given. This is an initial setting prior to the final pilot screw adjustment.
   INITIAL OPENING: 1-3/4 turns out
2. Warm up the engine to operating temperature. Stop and go driving for 10 minutes is sufficient.
3. Attach a tachometer.
4. Adjust the idle speed with the throttle stop screw.
   IDLE SPEED: 1,400 ± 100 rpm
5. Turn the pilot screw in or out slowly to obtain the highest engine speed.
6. Readjust the idle speed with the throttle stop screw.
7. Turn the pilot screw in gradually until the engine speed drops 100 rpm.

NOTE:

If the pilot screw seats before lowering the engine speed 100 rpm, continue to step 8.

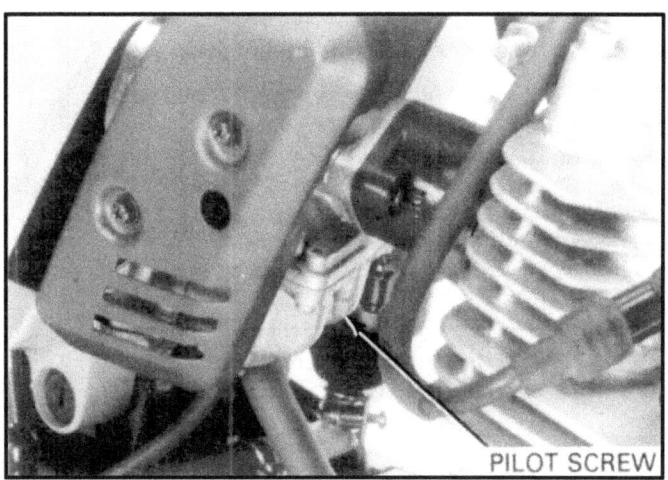

8. Turn the pilot screw 1 turn open from the position obtained in step 7.
9. Readjust the idle speed with the throttle stop screw.
10. Apply Loctite ® 601 or equivalent to the inside of the limiter cap. Place the cap over the pilot screw so that its tab rests against the float chamber stop so it can be turned clockwise only. This will prevent adjustment in the counterclockwise direction which richens the fuel mixture.

NOTE:

Be careful not to turn the pilot screw when installing the limiter cap.

HIGH ALTITUDE ADJUSTMENT (U.S.A. ONLY)

When the vehicle is to be operated continuously above 6,500 feet (2,000 meters), the carburetor must be readjusted as described below to improve driveability and decrease exhaust emissions.

Remove the carburetor (page 243) and remove the carburetor float chamber.

Remove the #105 main jet and install the #98 main jet.

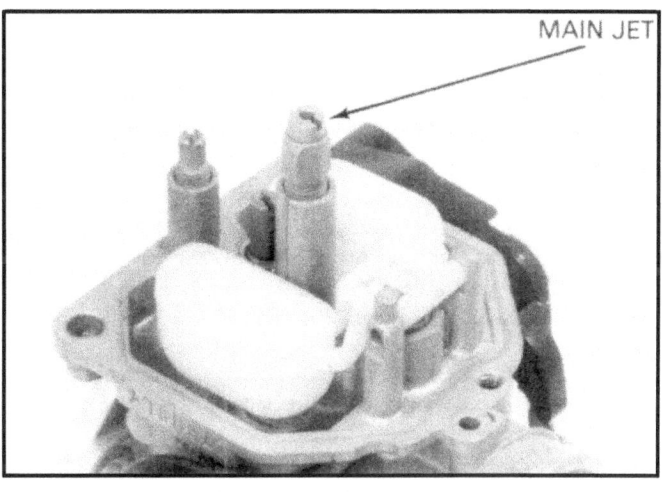

MAIN JET SPECIFICATION

Altitude	Main jet
Above 6,500 feet (2,000 meters)	#98
Below 5,000 feet (1,500 meters)	#105

Reassemble and install the carburetor.

Warm up the engine to operating temperature.

Stop and go driving for 10 minutes is sufficient.

Adjust the idle speed to 1,400 ± 100 rpm with the throttle stop screw.

NOTE:

> This adjustment must be made at high altitude to ensure proper high altitude operation.

Attach the Vehicle Emission Control Information Update label as shown.

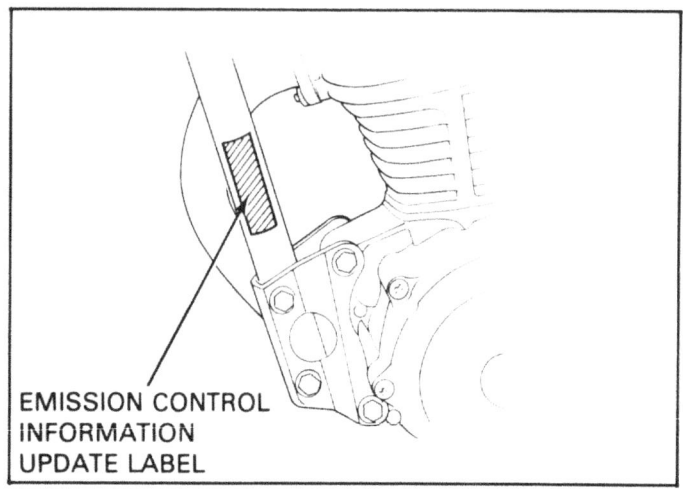

NOTES:

> - Instructions for obtaining Vehicle Emission Control Update labels are given in Service Letter No. 132.
> - Do not attach the label to any part that can be easily removed from the vehicle.

CAUTION:

> *Continuous operation at any altitude lower than 5,000 feet (1,500 meters) with the carburetor adjusted for high altitudes may cause the engine to idle roughly, stall and could cause engine damage from overheating.*
>
> *When the vehicle is to be operated continuously below 5,000 feet (1,500 meters); reinstall the #105 main jet and adjust the idle speed to 1400 ± 100 rpm. Be sure to do these adjustments at low altitude.*

VACUUM HOSE ROUTING (CALIFORNIA ONLY)

Route the Evaporative Emission Control System vacuum hoses as shown on the Vacuum Hose Routing Diagram Label. This label is located on the rear fender underneath the seat.

NOTES:

> - Be careful not to bend, twist or kink the hoses when installing them.
> - Slide the end of each hose onto its fitting completely and then secure it with a clamp.
> - Replace any hose with a new one if it shows signs of deterioration or damage.
> - Check that the hoses are not contacting sharp edges.

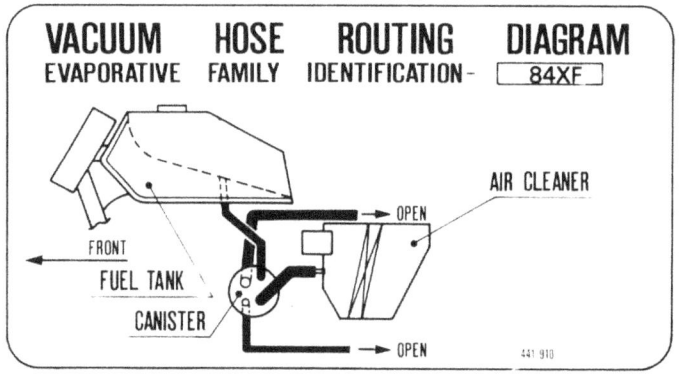

1984 CB125S ADDENDUM

CHARGING SYSTEM

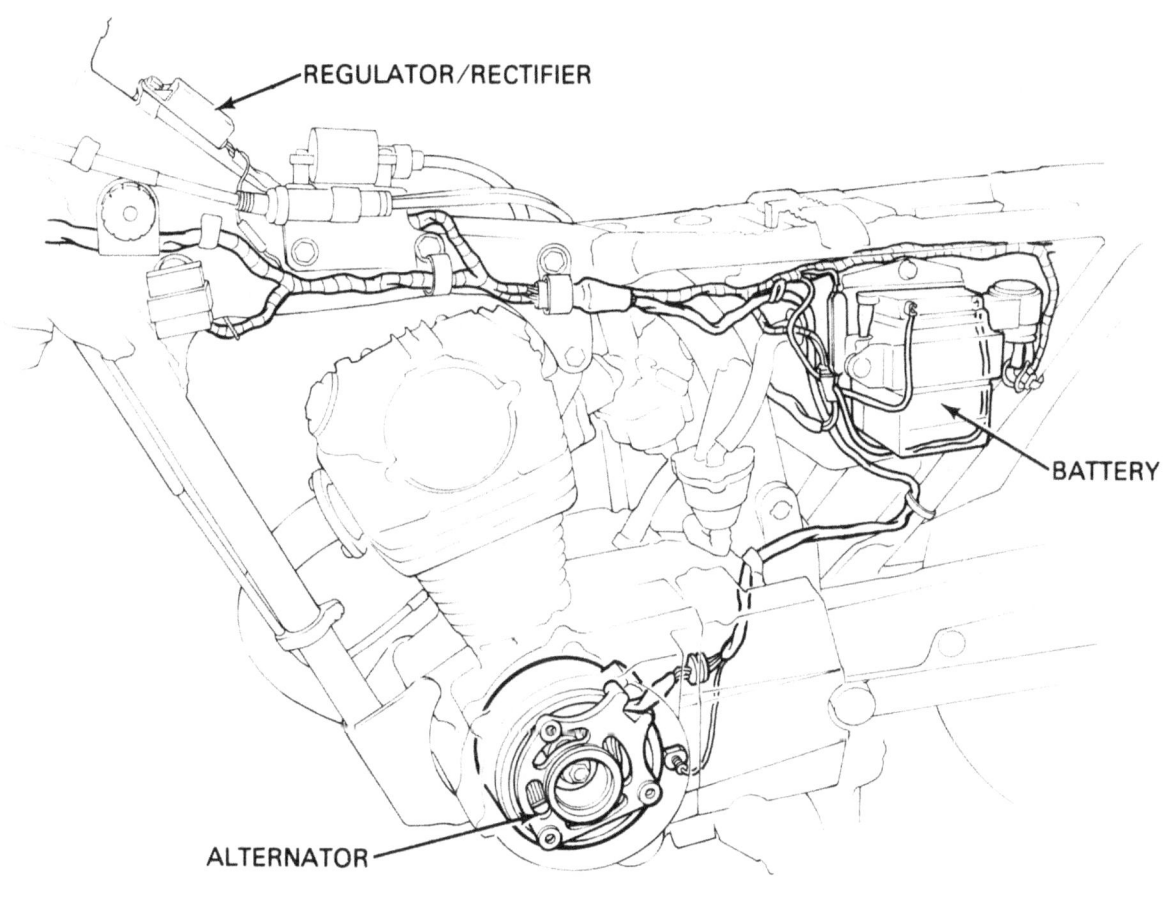

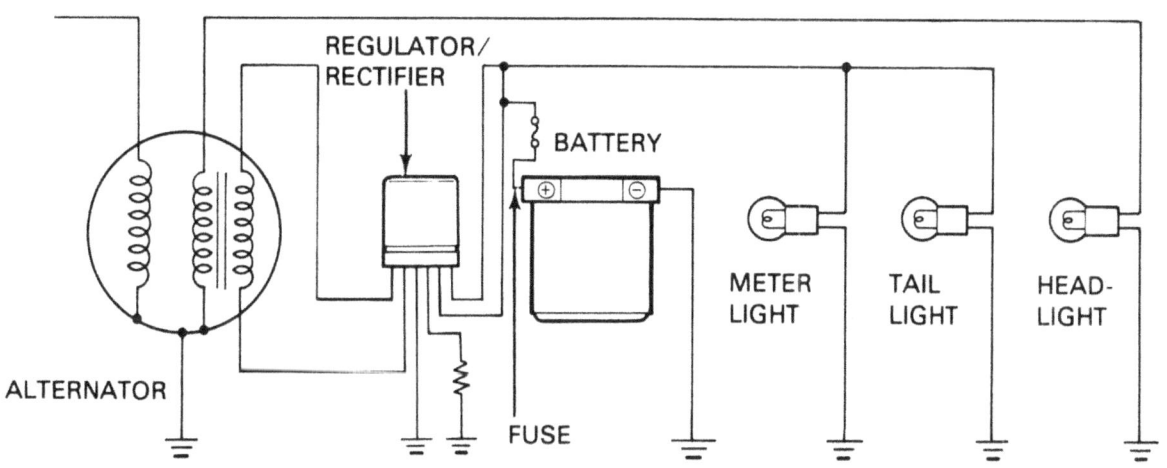

1984 CB125S ADDENDUM

SERVICE INFORMATION

NOTES:

When testing the voltage regulator / rectifier or alternator use one of the following electrical testers:
- Kowa Digital Multimeter KS-AHM-32-003, (U.S.A. ONLY)
- Kowa Electrical Tester (TH-5H)
- Sanwa (07308-0020000)

Charging starts	Approximately 2,200 rpm
Charging coil output	17.9V / 1.8A minimum at 4,000 rpm
	18.2V / 4.5A minimum at 8,000 rpm
Lighting coil output (Regulator disconnected)	12V minimum at 3,000 rpm (low beam on)
	16V maximum at 10,000 rpm (low beam on)
Battery capacity	12V / 2.5AH
Fuse	10A
Voltage regulator / rectifier	Transistorized non-adjustable
Battery charging rate	0.25A maximum

TROUBLESHOOTING

No Power — Key Turned ON:

1. Dead battery
   - Battery not charged
   - Battery electrolyte evaporated
   - Charging system failure
2. Disconnected battery cable
3. Main fuse burned out
4. Faulty ignition switch

Low Power — Key Turned On:

1. Weak battery
   - Low battery electrolyte level
   - Battery run down
   - Charging system failure
2. Loose battery connection

Low Power — Engine Running:

1. Battery undercharged
   - Low battery electrolyte level
   - One or more dead cells
2. Charging system failure

Intermittent Power:

1. Loose battery connection
2. Loose charging system connection
3. Loose connection or short circuit in ignition system
4. Loose connection or short circuit in lighting system

Charging System Failure:

1. Loose, broken, or shorted wire or connection
2. Faulty voltage regulator / rectifier
3. Faulty alternator

1984 CB125S ADDENDUM

BATTERY

⚠️ **WARNING**

The battery electrolyte contains sulfuric acid. Protect your eyes, skin and clothing. In case of contact, flush thoroughly with water and call a doctor if your eyes were exposed.

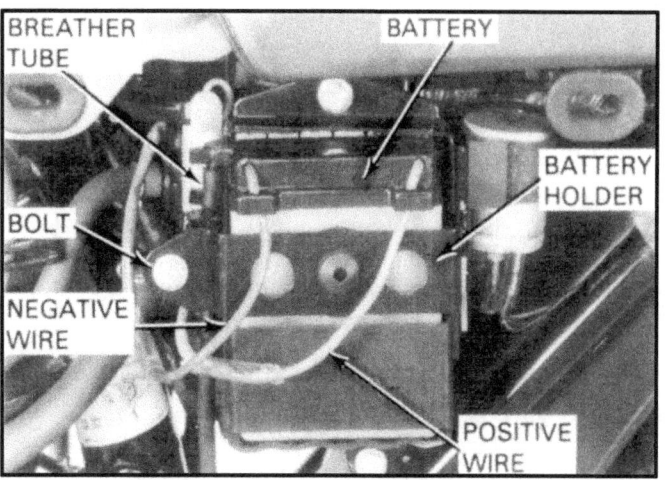

Remove the left side cover and disconnect the battery wires.

NOTE:

Disconnect the negative wire first, then disconnect the positive wire.

Disconnect the breather tube from the battery.

Remove the bolt and open the battery holder.

Remove the battery.

Use a hydrometer to test the specific gravity of the electrolyte in each cell.

SPECIFIC GRAVITY (20°C, 68°F):
- 1.26 – 1.28   Full charge
- 1.22 or less   Low charge

Charge the battery if it is in a state of low charge.

MAXIMUM CHARGING CURRENT:
0.25 amperes

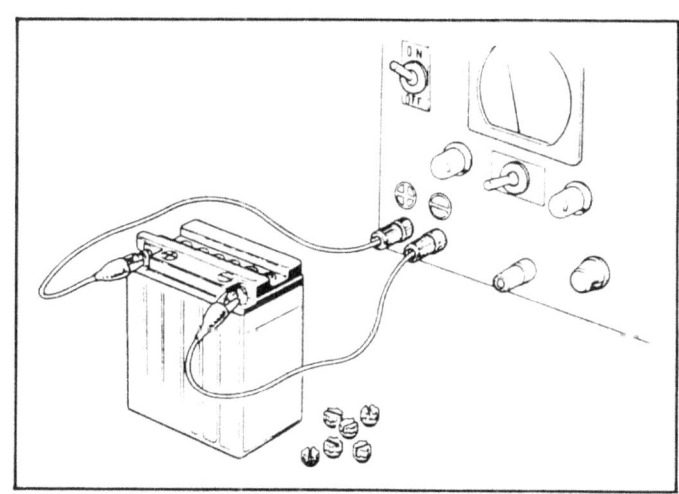

NOTE:

Be sure to use the charger's 12V range.

Install the battery in the reverse order of removal.

CAUTION:

Be sure the breather tube is routed as shown on the caution label.

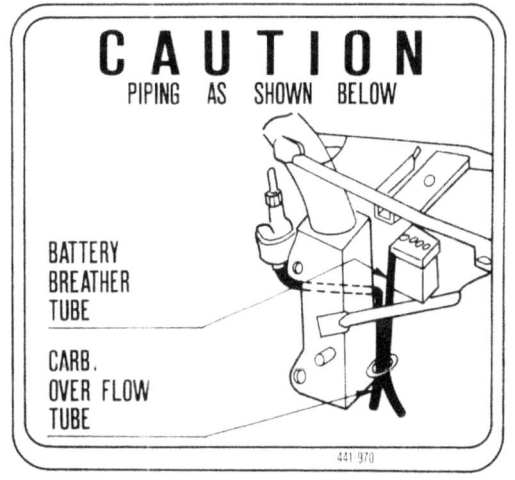

CHARGING SYSTEM CHECK

NOTE:

> Use a fully charged battery to check the charging system output.

Warm up the engine before taking a reading.

Disconnect the black wire from the regulator/rectifier coupler.

Connect a voltmeter and an ammeter to check charging system output.

Start the engine and check the meter readings while increasing engine speed slowly.

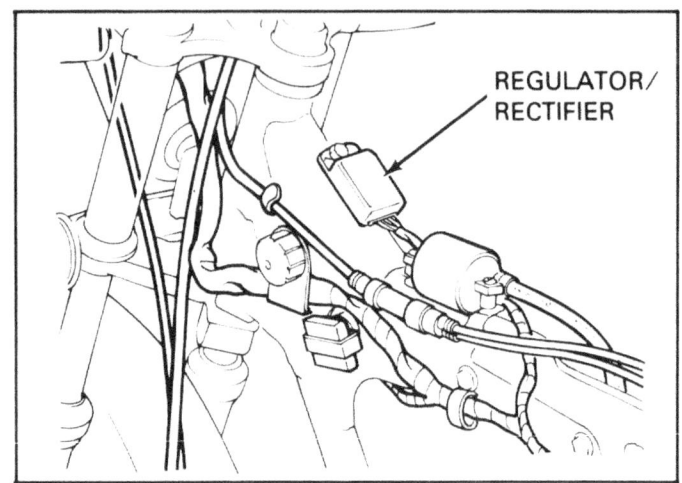

CHARGING SPECIFICATIONS

Charging	Begins by 2,200 rpm
4,000 rpm	17.9 V/1.8 A min.
8,000 rpm	18.2 V/4.5 A max.

If there is no charging current, check each charging circuit connection for looseness or corrosion. If the connections are good, check the alternator charging coil for continuity.

ALTERNATOR

NOTE:

> It is not necessary to remove the stator to make this test. Check the coils at the alternator wire connectors under the fuel tank.

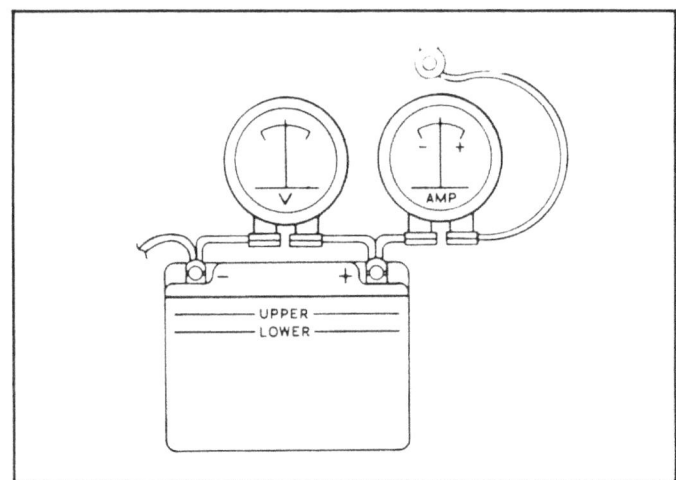

CHARGING COIL:

The charging coil is good if there is continuity between the pink and white/yellow wires.

**RESISTANCE IN NORMAL DIRECTION:
0.2—1 OHMS**

LAMP COIL:

The lamp coil is good if there is continuity between the green wire and yellow wire.

**RESISTANCE IN NORMAL DIRECTION:
0.2—1 OHMS**

If there is no continuity in either coil replace the stator assembly.

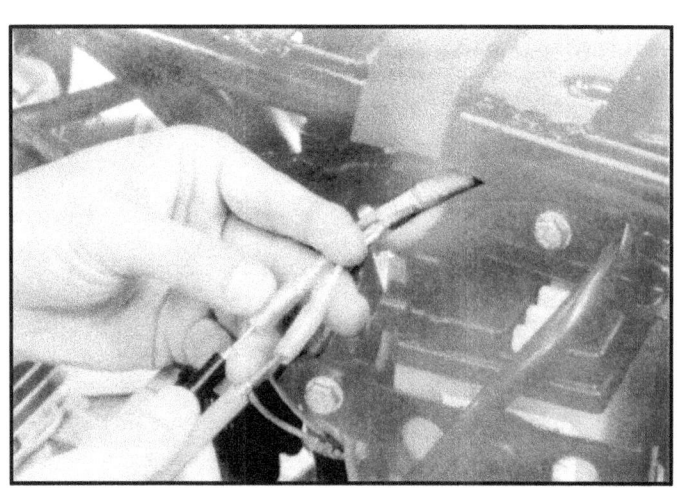

REGULATOR / RECTIFIER

Check the resistances between the leads with an ohmmeter.

NOTES:

- Use Sanwa Electrical Tester P/N 07308-0020000, or Kowa Electrical Tester TH-5H, or Kowa Digital Multimeter (U.S.A. only) KS-AHM-32-003.
- Sanwa and Kowa testers have different measurements as shown.
- Make sure the tester contains new batteries and perform zero adjustments in the measuring range for accurate readings.

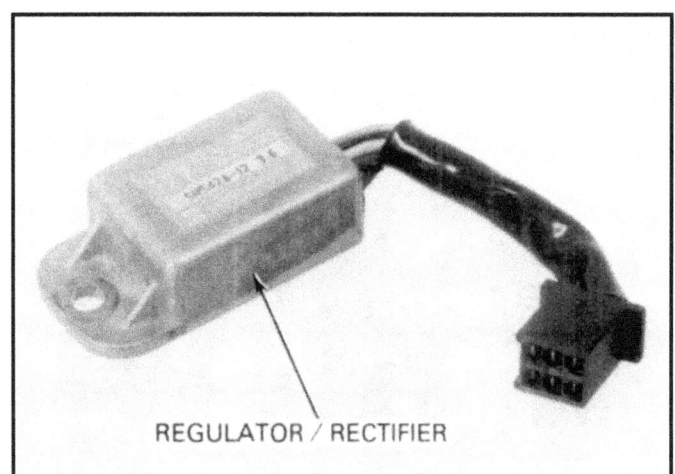

REGULATOR / RECTIFIER

Range: Sanwa: kΩ
Kowa: x 100 Ω

+Probe / −Probe	Yellow	Pink	Green	Red	Black
Yellow		∞	∞	1—20	∞
Pink	∞		∞	1—20	∞
Green	1—20	1—20		3—100	0.2—20
Red	∞	∞	∞		∞
Black	1—50	1—50	0.2—10	3—100	

IGNITION SYSTEM

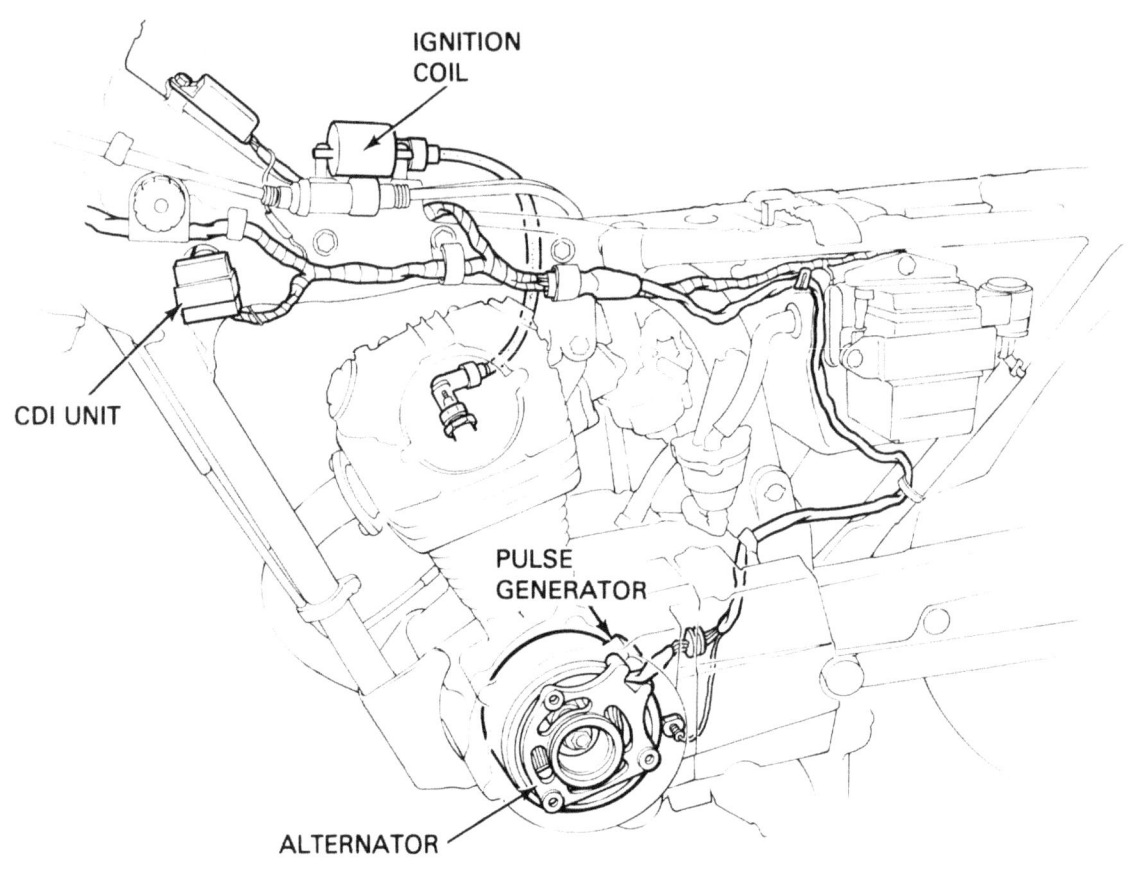

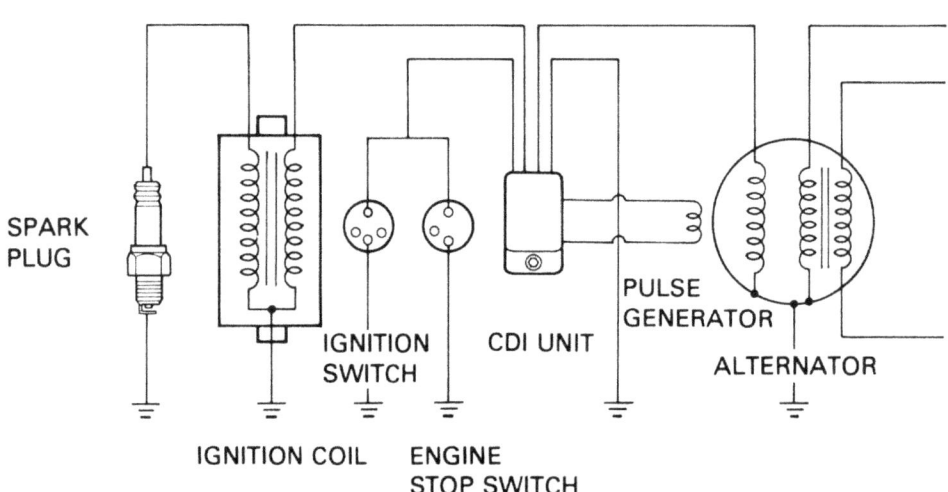

CDI UNIT

Disconnect the CDI Unit coupler and remove the unit.

Check continuity of the CDI terminals. Replace the CDI unit if the readings do not fall within the limits shown in the table.

NOTES:

- The CDI unit is fully transistorized.
- For accurate testing, it is necessary to use a specified electric tester. Use of an improper tester or measurements in improper range may give false readings.
- Use a Sanwa Electrical Tester P/N 07308-0020000, or Kowa Electric Tester TH-5H, or Kowa Digital Multimeter (U.S.A. only) KS-AHM-32-003.

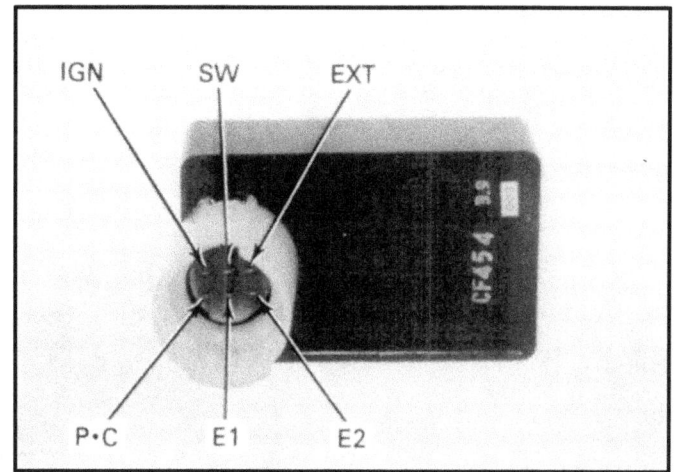

Test Range: Sanwa: xkΩ
Kowa: x100 Ω

+Probe / −Probe	SW	EXT	P•C	E1•E2	IGN
SW		∞	∞	∞	∞
EXT	0.1—20		∞	∞	∞
P•C	20—300	1—100		1—100	∞
E1•E2	0.5—50	0.1—20	1—100		∞
IGN	∞	∞	∞	∞	

PULSE GENERATOR

Unplug the pulse generator wire connectors and measure the resistance between the Blue/White and Green/White wires.

SPECIFICATION: 50-170 ohms

IGNITION TIMING

Remove the timing hole cap.

Connect a timing light and tachometer.

Start the engine and check the ignition timing.

At idle (1,400 ± 100 rpm): The index mark should be aligned with the "F" mark.

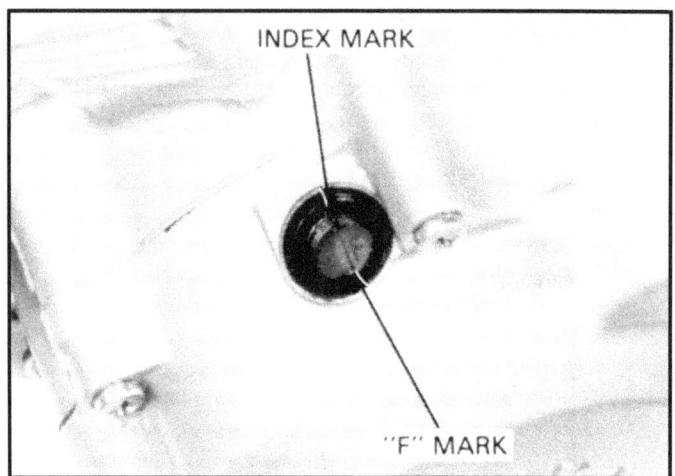

At 1,800-2,500 rpm: Timing advance should begin.

At 3,400-4,100 rpm: The index mark should be between the full advance marks.

If ignition timing is incorrect, check the CDI unit and replace if necessary.

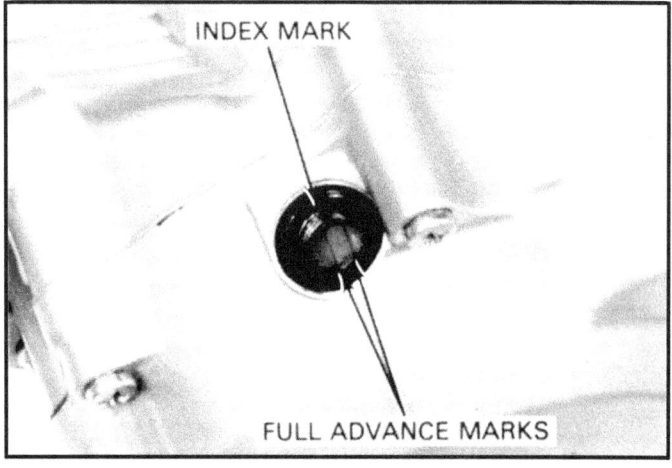

1984 CB125S ADDENDUM

WIRING DIAGRAM

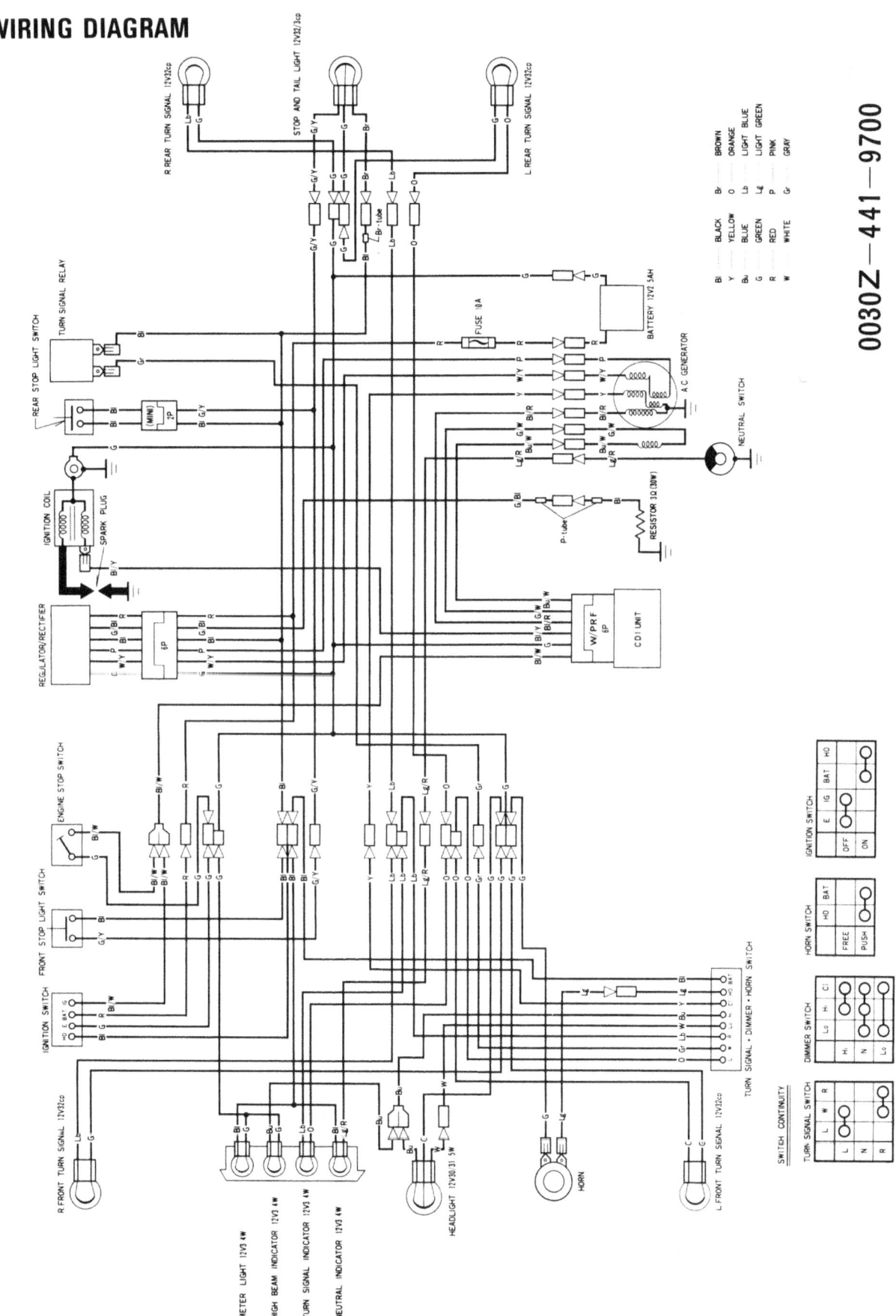

VELOCEPRESS MANUALS – MOTORCYCLE BY MAKE

AJS 1932-1948 SINGLES & TWINS 250cc THRU 1000cc (BOOK OF)
AJS 1945-1960 SINGLES 350cc & 500cc MODELS 16 & 18 (BOOK OF)
AJS 1955-1965 SINGLES 350cc & 500cc (BOOK OF)
AJS 1957-1966 FACTORY WSM - ALL SINGLES & TWINS
ARIEL UP TO 1932 (BOOK OF)
ARIEL 1932-1939 PREWAR MODELS (BOOK OF)
ARIEL 1933-1951 (WORKSHOP MANUAL)
ARIEL 1939-1960 4 STROKE SINGLES (BOOK OF)
ARIEL 1958-1964 LEADER & ARROW (BOOK OF)
BMW R26 R27 (1956-1967) FACTORY WORKSHOP MANUAL
BMW R50 R50S R60 R69S (1955-1969) FACTORY WORKSHOP MANUAL
BRIDGESTONE 90 SERIES FACTORY WSM & PARTS CATALOGUE
BRIDGESTONE 175 SERIES FACTORY WSM & PARTS CATALOGUE
BRIDGESTONE 350 SERIES FACTORY WSM & PARTS CATALOGUES
BSA SERVICE SHEETS MASTER CATALOGUE ALL MODELS 1945-1967
BSA BANTAM D1 TO D7 1948-1966 FACTORY SERVICE SHEETS MANUAL
BSA BANTAM ALL MODELS FROM 1948 ONWARDS (BOOK OF)
BSA BANTAM D14 FACTORY WORKSHOP & INSTRUCTION MANUAL
BSA DANDY FACTORY WORKSHOP MANUAL (COMPILATION)
BSA SINGLES & V-TWINS UP TO 1927 (BOOK OF)
BSA SINGLES & V-TWINS UP TO 1930 (BOOK OF)
BSA SINGLES & V-TWINS UP TO 1935 (BOOK OF)
BSA SINGLES & V-TWINS 1936-1939 (BOOK OF)
BSA C10, C11 & C12 1945-1958 FACTORY SERVICE SHEETS MANUAL
BSA OHV & SV SINGLES 250-600cc 1945-1959 (BOOK OF)
BSA C15 & B40 1958-1967 FACTORY SERVICE SHEETS MANUAL
BSA OHV & SV SINGLES 250cc (ONLY) 1954-1970 (BOOK OF)
BSA B31, B32, B33 & B34 1945-60 FACTORY SERVICE SHEETS MANUAL
BSA OHV SINGLES 350 & 500cc 1955-1967 (BOOK OF)
BSA M20, M21 & M33 1945-1963 FACTORY SERVICE SHEETS MANUAL
BSA TWINS A7 & A10 1948-1962 FACTORY SERVICE SHEETS MANUAL
BSA TWINS A7 & A10 1948-1962 (BOOK OF)
BSA TWINS A50 & A65 1962-1965 FACTORY WORKSHOP MANUAL
BSA TWINS A50 & A65 1962-1969 (SECOND BOOK OF)
DOUGLAS 1929-1939 PREWAR ALL MODELS (BOOK OF)
DOUGLAS 1948-1957 POSTWAR ALL MODELS FACTORY SHOP MANUAL
DUCATI 160cc, 250cc & 350cc OHC MODELS FACTORY SHOP MANUAL
HONDA 50 ALL MODELS UP TO 1970 INC MONKEY & TRAIL (BOOK OF)
HONDA 90 ALL MODELS UP TO 1966 (BOOK OF)
HONDA 50-65-70-90cc OHC SINGLES 1959-1983 FACTORY WSM
HONDA 100-125cc SINGLES 1970-1984 CB-CD-CL-SL-TL (All Variants)
HONDA 125-150cc TWINS C/CS/CB/CA FACTORY WORKSHOP MANUAL
HONDA 125-160-175-200cc TWINS 1964-1980 WORKSHOP MANUAL
HONDA 250-305 TWINS C/CS/CB 1959-1967 FACTORY WSM
HOHDA 250-350 TWINS CB/CL/SL 1968-1973 FACTORY WSM
HONDA 450 CB/CL 1965-1974 K0 TO K7 WORKSHOP MANUAL
HONDA C100 SUPER CUB FACTORY WORKSHOP MANUAL
HONDA C110 SPORT CUB 1962-1969 FACTORY WORKSHOP MANUAL
HONDA TWINS & SINGLES 50cc THRU 305cc 1960-1966 (BOOK OF)
HONDA TWINS ALL MODELS 125cc THRU 450cc UP TO 1968 (BOOK OF)
INDIAN PONYBIKE, BOY RACER & PAPOOSE ILL PARTS LIST & SALES LIT
J.A.P. ENGINES 1927-1952 & MOTORCYCLES 1934-1952 (BOOK OF)
MATCHLESS 1931-1939 ALL MODELS 250cc THRU 990cc (BOOK OF)
MATCHLESS 1945-1956 350 & 500cc SINGLES (BOOK OF)
MATCHLESS 1955-1966 350 & 500cc SINGLES (BOOK OF)
MATCHLESS 1957-1966 FACTORY WSM - ALL SINGLES & TWINS
NEW IMPERIAL ALL SV & OHV FROM 1935 ONWARDS (BOOK OF)
NORTON 1932-1939 PREWAR MODELS (BOOK OF)
NORTON 1932-1947 (BOOK OF)
NORTON 1938-1956 (BOOK OF)
NORTON 1955-1963 MODELS 19, 50 & ES2 (BOOK OF)
NORTON 1955-1965 DOMINATOR TWINS (BOOK OF)
NORTON 1960-1970 TWIN CYLINDER FACTORY WORKSHOP MANUAL
NORTON 1970-1975 COMMANDO FACTORY WORKSHOP MANUAL
NORTON 1975-1978 MK 3 COMMANDO FACTORY WORKSHOP MANUAL
PANTHER 1932-1958 LIGHTWEIGHT MODELS 250 & 350cc (BOOK OF)
PANTHER 1938-1966 HEAVYWEIGHT MODELS 600 & 650cc (BOOK OF)
RALEIGH MOTORCYCLES 1919-1933 (BOOK OF)
ROYAL ENFIELD 1934-1946 SINGLES & V TWINS (BOOK OF)
ROYAL ENFIELD 1937-1953 SINGLES & V TWINS (BOOK OF)
ROYAL ENFIELD 1946-1962 SINGLES (BOOK OF)
ROYAL ENFIELD 1958-1966 250cc & 350cc SINGLES (SECOND BOOK OF)
ROYAL ENFIELD 736cc INTERCEPTOR FACTORY WORKSHOP MANUAL
RUDGE 1933-1939 (BOOK OF)
SUNBEAM 1928-1939 (BOOK OF)
SUNBEAM 1946-1957 S7 & S8 (BOOK OF)
SUZUKI 50cc & 80cc UP TO 1966 (BOOK OF)
SUZUKI T10 1963-1967 FACTORY WORKSHOP MANUAL
SUZUKI T20 & T200 1965-1969 FACTORY WORKSHOP MANUAL
SUZUKI TWINS 1962 ONWARDS 125-500cc WORKSHOP MANUAL
TRIUMPH 1935-1939 PREWAR MODELS (BOOK OF)
TRIUMPH 1935-1949 (BOOK OF)
TRIUMPH 1937-1951 (WORKSHOP MANUAL)
TRIUMPH 1945-1955 FACTORY WORKSHOP MANUAL
TRIUMPH 1945-1958 TWINS (BOOK OF)
TRIUMPH 1956-1969 TWINS (BOOK OF)
VELOCETTE 1925-1970 ALL SINGLES & TWINS (BOOK OF)
VILLIERS ENGINE UP TO 1959 INC. 3 WHEELERS (BOOK OF)
VILLIERS ENGINE UP TO 1969 (BOOK OF)
VINCENT 1935-1955 (WORKSHOP MANUAL)
YAMAHA 1961-1967 YA5 & YA6 (WORKSHOP MANUAL & ILL PARTS LIST)
YAMAHA 1971-1972 JT1 & JT2 (WORKSHOP MANUAL & ILL PARTS LIST)

VELOCEPRESS TECHNICAL BOOKS – MOTORCYCLE

1930'S BRITISH MOTORCYCLE CARBS & ELEC COMPONENTS (BOOK OF)
1930'S BRITISH MOTORCYCLE ENGINES (OVERHAUL & MAINTENANCE)
1930'S BRITISH MOTORCYCLE GEARBOXES & CLUTCHES (BOOK OF)
CATALOG OF BRITISH MOTORCYCLES (1951 MODELS)
LUCAS ELECTRONICS BRITISH M/CYCLES REPAIR & PARTS (1950-1977)
MOTORCYCLE ENGINEERING (P.E. Irving)
MOTORCYCLE ROAD TESTS 1949-1953 (Motor Cycle Magazine UK)
SPEED AND HOW TO OBTAIN IT (Motor Cycle Magazine UK)
TUNING FOR SPEED (P.E. Irving)
WIPAC (COMBO) MANUAL NUMBER 3 + M/CYCLE & SCOOTER MANUAL

VELOCEPRESS MANUALS – SCOOTERS BY MAKE

BSA SUNBEAM SCOOTER WORKSHOP MANUAL 1959-1965
BSA SUNBEAM SCOOTER 1959-1965 (BOOK OF)
LAMBRETTA 1947-1957 ALL 125 & 150cc MODELS (BOOK OF)
LAMBRETTA 1957-1970 LI & TV MODELS (SECOND BOOK OF)
NSU PRIMA 1956-1964 ALL MODELS (BOOK OF)
TRIUMPH TIGRESS SCOOTER WORKSHOP MANUAL 1959-1965
TRIUMPH TIGRESS SCOOTER (BOOK OF)
VESPA 1951-1961 (BOOK OF)
VESPA 1955-1963 125 & 150cc & GS MODELS (SECOND BOOK OF)
VESPA 1955-1968 GS & SS (BOOK OF)
VESPA 1963-1972 90, 125 & 150cc (THIRD BOOK OF)

VELOCEPRESS MANUALS – MOPEDS & MOTORIZED BICYCLES

CYCLEMOTOR (BOOK OF)
NSU QUICKLY 1953-1963 ALL MODELS (BOOK OF)
PUCH MAXI N & S MAINTENANCE & REPAIR (3 MANUAL COMPILATION)
RALEIGH MOPEDS 1960-1969 (BOOK OF)

VELOCEPRESS MANUALS - THREE WHEELER'S

BOND MINICAR THREE WHEELER 1948-1967 (BOOK OF)
BMW ISETTA FACTORY WORKSHOP MANUAL
BSA THREE WHEELER (BOOK OF)
RELIANT REGAL THREE WHEELER 1952-1973 (BOOK OF)
VINTAGE MORGAN THREE WHEELER (BOOK OF)

VELOCEPRESS MANUALS – AUTOMOBILE BY MAKE

ALFA ROMEO GIULIA WORKSHOP MANUAL 1300 TO 2000cc 1962-1975
ALFA ROMEO GIULIA TECH MANUAL CARBURETED CARS FROM 1962
ALFA ROMEO GIULIA TECH MANUAL FUEL INJECTED CARS FROM 1969
ALFA ROMEO GIULIETTA & GIULIA 750 & 101 SERIES 1955-1965 WSM
AUSTIN-HEALEY SPRITE & MG MIDGET WORKSHOP MANUAL 1958-1971
BMW 600 LIMOUSINE FACTORY WORKSHOP MANUAL
BMW 600 LIMOUSINE OWNERS HAND BOOK & SERVICE MANUAL
BMW 2000 & 2002 1966-1976 WORKSHOP MANUAL
CORVAIR 1960-1969 WORKSHOP MANUAL
CORVETTE V8 1955-1962 WORKSHOP MANUAL
FIAT 500 FACTORY WORKSHOP MANUAL 1957-1973
FIAT 600, 600D & MULTIPLA FACTORY WORKSHOP MANUAL 1955-1969
JAGUAR E-TYPE 3.8 & 4.2 SERIES 1 & 2 WORKSHOP MANUAL
JAGUAR MK 7, 8, 9 & XK120, 140, 150 WORKSHOP MANUAL 1948-1961
METROPOLITAN FACTORY WORKSHOP MANUAL
MGA & MGB OWNERS HANDBOOK & WORKSHOP MANUAL
MG MIDGET TC, TD, TF & TF1500 WORKSHOP MANUAL
PORSCHE 356 1948-1965 WORKSHOP MANUAL
PORSCHE 911 2.0, 2.2, 2.4 LITRE 1964-1973 WORKSHOP MANUAL
PORSCHE 911 2.7, 3.0, 3.2 LITRE 1973-1989 WORKSHOP MANUAL
PORSCHE 912 WORKSHOP MANUAL
TRIUMPH TR2, TR3, TR4 1953-1965 WORKSHOP MANUAL
VOLKSWAGEN TRANSPORTER, TRUCKS & WAGONS 1950-1979 WSM
VOLVO 1944-1968 ALL MODELS WORKSHOP MANUAL

VELOCEPRESS TECHNICAL BOOKS - AUTOMOBILE

FERRARI 250/GT SERVICE AND MAINTENANCE
FERRARI GUIDE TO PERFORMANCE
FERRARI OWNER'S HANDBOOK
FERRARI TUNING TIPS & MAINTENANCE TECHNIQUES
HOW TO BUILD A FIBERGLASS CAR
HOW TO BUILD A RACING CAR
HOW TO RESTORE THE MODEL 'A' FORD
MASERATI OWNER'S HANDBOOK
OBERT'S FIAT GUIDE
PERFORMANCE TUNING THE SUNBEAM TIGER
SOUPING THE VOLKSWAGEN
SOLEX CARBURETORS (EMPHASIS ON UK & EU AUTOMOBILES)
SU CARBURETORS (EMPHASIS ON UK AUTOMOBILES)
WEBER CARBURETORS (EMPHASIS ON ALFA & FIAT)

VELOCEPRESS BOOKS & GUIDES - AUTOMOBILE

ABARTH BUYERS GUIDE
COMPLETE CATALOG OF JAPANESE MOTOR VEHICLES
FERRARI 308 SERIES BUYER'S AND OWNER'S GUIDE
FERRARI BERLINETTA LUSSO
FERRARI BROCHURES AND SALES LITERATURE 1946-1967
FERRARI BROCHURES AND SALES LITERATURE 1968-1989
FERRARI SERIAL NUMBERS PART I - ODD NUMBERS TO 21399
FERRARI SERIAL NUMBERS PART II - EVEN NUMBERS TO 1050
FERRARI SPYDER CALIFORNIA
HENRY'S FABULOUS MODEL "A" FORD
MASERATI BROCHURES AND SALES LITERATURE

VELOCEPRESS BOOKS – RACING

CARRERA PANAMERICANA - MEXICAN ROAD RACE (BOOK OF)
DIALED IN - THE JAN OPPERMAN STORY
IF HEMINGWAY HAD WRITTEN A RACING NOVEL
VEDA ORR'S NEW REVISED HOT ROD PICTORIAL

AUTOBOOKS WORKSHOP MANUALS & BROOKLANDS ROAD TEST PORTFOLIOS

FOR A COMPLETE LISTING OF THE AUTOBOOKS & BROOKLANDS TITLES THAT WE CURRENTLY HAVE AVAILABLE, PLEASE VISIT OUR WEBSITE.

www.VelocePress.com

www.ingramcontent.com/pod-product-compliance
Lightning Source LLC
Chambersburg PA
CBHW080428230426
43662CB00015B/2222